I0796810

Revolts Against Rome

Revolts Against Rome

Rebellions and Mutinies in the First Century AD

John S. McHugh

Pen & Sword
MILITARY

First published in Great Britain in 2025 by
Pen & Sword Military
An imprint of Pen & Sword Books Limited
Yorkshire – Philadelphia

ISBN 978 1 39903 196 7

A CIP catalogue record for this book is
available from the British Library.

Typeset by Mac Style
Printed in the UK by CPI Group (UK) Ltd, Croydon, CR0 4YY.

The Publisher's authorised representative in the EU for product safety is Authorised Rep Compliance Ltd., Ground Floor, 71 Lower Baggot Street, Dublin D02 P593, Ireland.
www.arccompliance.com

For a complete list of Pen & Sword titles please contact

PEN & SWORD BOOKS LIMITED
47 Church Street, Barnsley, South Yorkshire, S70 2AS, England
E-mail: enquiries@pen-and-sword.co.uk
Website: www.pen-and-sword.co.uk
or
PEN AND SWORD BOOKS
1950 Lawrence Road, Havertown, PA 19083, USA
E-mail: uspen-and-sword@casematepublishers.com
Website: www.penandswordbooks.com

I am grateful to my family for their unerring support and Megan Woolsgrove for her work on the book's cover. Tony Walton has also been invaluable in proofreading the work and making suggestions for amendments using his vast expertise as a specialist copy editor.

Contents

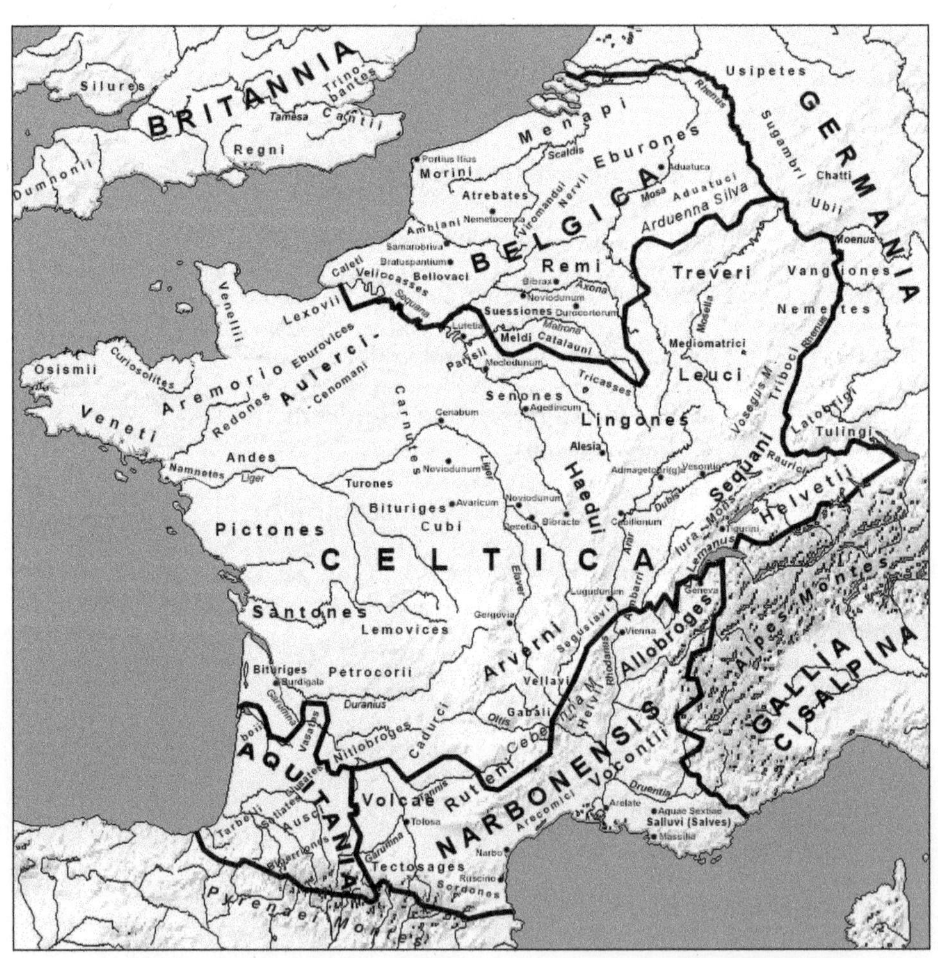

Map 1. The tribes of Roman Gaul. (*Feitscherg via Wikimedia Commons/CC BY-SA 3.0*)

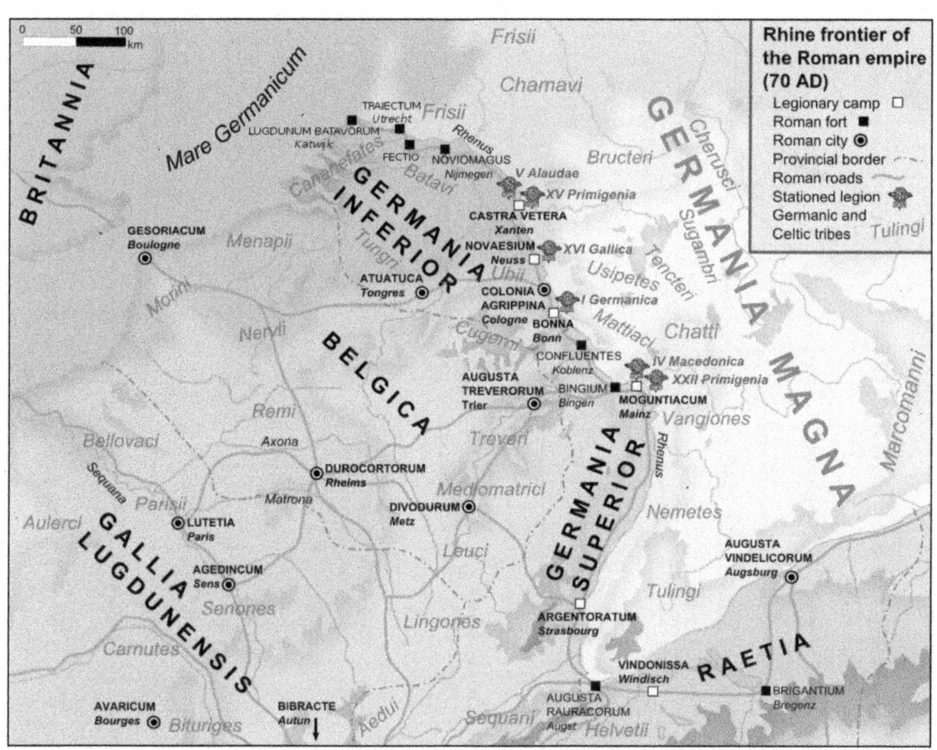

Map 2. Tribal groups and Roman fortifications along the Rhine.

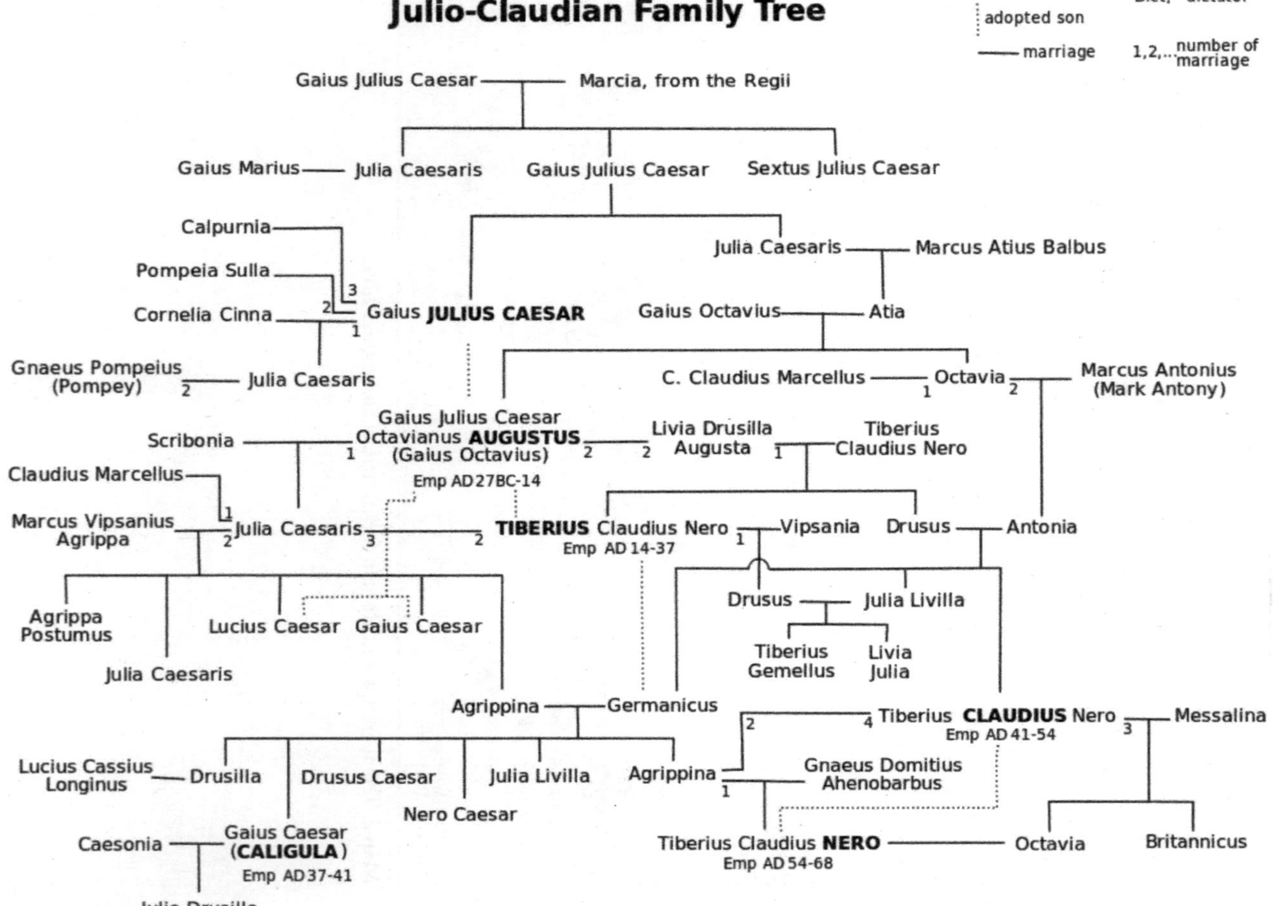

Julio-Claudian Family Tree
son/daughter
adopted son
marriage
Emp, emperor
Dict, dictator
1,2,... number of marriage
Gaius Julius Caesar
Marcia, from the Regii
Gaius Marius
Julia Caesaris
Gaius Julius Caesar
Sextus Julius Caesar
Calpurnia
Pompeia Sulla
Cornelia Cinna
Gaius JULIUS CAESAR
Julia Caesaris
Marcus Atius Balbus
Gaius Octavius
Atia
Gnaeus Pompeius (Pompey)
Julia Caesaris
C. Claudius Marcellus
Octavia
Marcus Antonius (Mark Antony)
Scribonia
Gaius Julius Caesar Octavianus AUGUSTUS (Gaius Octavius)
Emp AD 27BC-14
Livia Drusilla Augusta
Tiberius Claudius Nero
Claudius Marcellus
Marcus Vipsanius Agrippa
Julia Caesaris
TIBERIUS Claudius Nero
Emp AD 14-37
Vipsania
Drusus
Antonia
Agrippa Postumus
Julia Caesaris
Lucius Caesar
Gaius Caesar
Drusus
Julia Livilla
Tiberius Gemellus
Livia Julia
Agrippina
Germanicus
Tiberius CLAUDIUS Nero
Emp AD 41-54
Messalina
Lucius Cassius Longinus
Drusilla
Drusus Caesar
Nero Caesar
Julia Livilla
Agrippina
Gnaeus Domitius Ahenobarbus
Caesonia
Gaius Caesar (CALIGULA)
Emp AD 37-41
Julia Drusilla
Tiberius Claudius NERO
Emp AD 54-68
Octavia
Britannicus

Flavian Family Tree

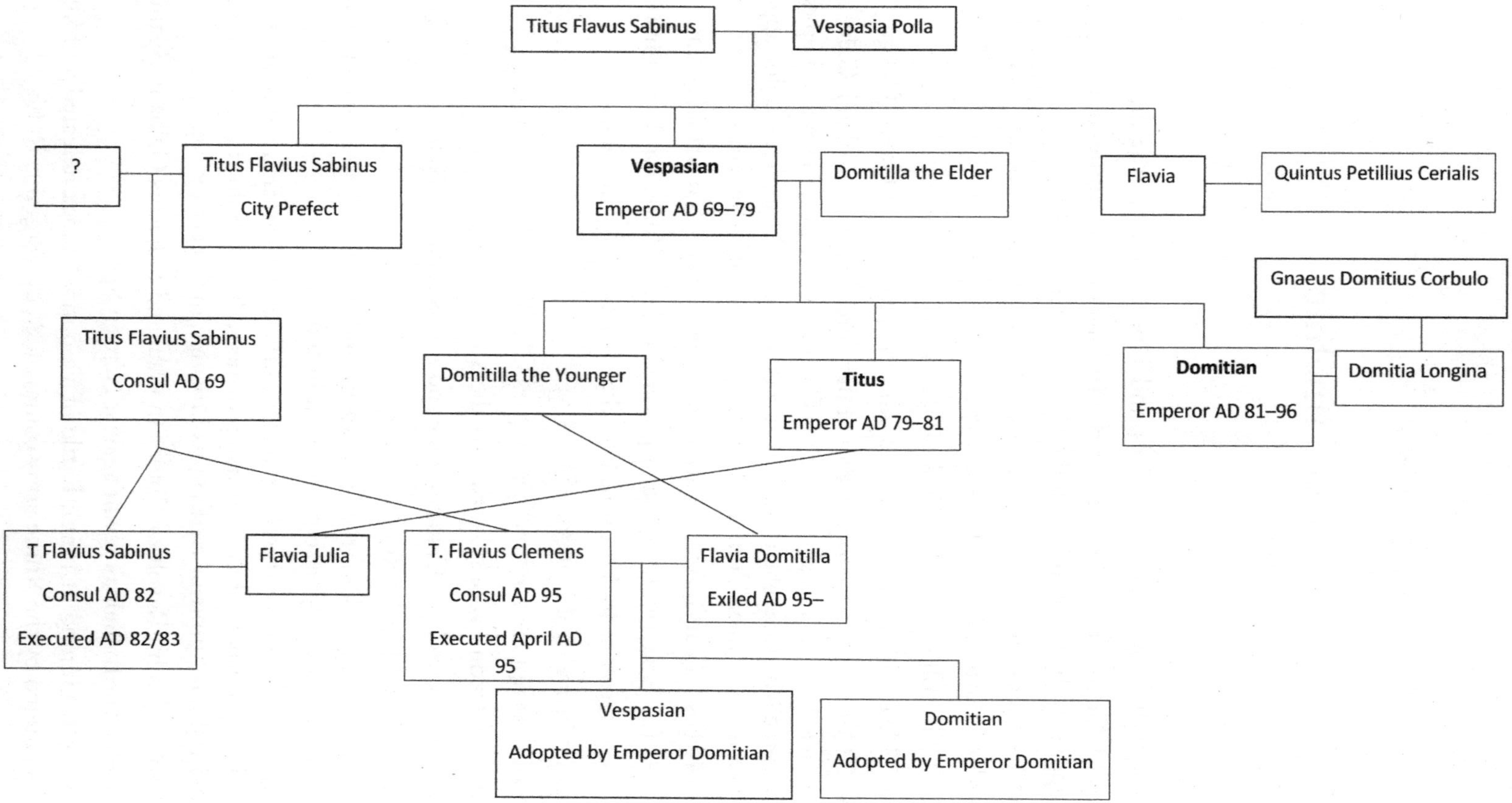

Titus Flavus Sabinus

Vespasia Polla

?

Titus Flavius Sabinus
City Prefect

Vespasian
Emperor AD 69–79

Domitilla the Elder

Flavia

Quintus Petillius Cerialis

Gnaeus Domitius Corbulo

Titus Flavius Sabinus
Consul AD 69

Domitilla the Younger

Titus
Emperor AD 79–81

Domitian
Emperor AD 81–96

Domitia Longina

T Flavius Sabinus
Consul AD 82
Executed AD 82/83

Flavia Julia

T. Flavius Clemens
Consul AD 95
Executed April AD 95

Flavia Domitilla
Exiled AD 95–

Vespasian
Adopted by Emperor Domitian

Domitian
Adopted by Emperor Domitian

Timeline

AD 14 (19 August): Augustus dies, and Tiberius ascends the throne.

AD 14 (September): Mutiny of the legions on the Rhine and in Pannonia suppressed by Germanicus and Tiberius' son, Drusus.

AD 14–16: Germanicus leads a series of campaigns against the German tribes.

AD 19: Death of Germanicus in Syria.

AD 21: Revolt of Sacrovir and Florus in Gaul.

AD 37 (March): Death of Tiberius and the accession of Gaius (Caligula)

AD 39 (September–October): Plot of the Three Daggers involving Gaius' sisters, M. Aemilius Lepidus and Cornelius Gaetulicus in Upper Germany. Lepidus was executed with Gaetulicus, and his sisters were exiled. Sulpicius Galba appointed governor of Upper Germany to restore discipline in the army.

AD 41 (24 January): Assassination of Gaius and accession of Claudius.

AD 41 (25 January): Date Gaius planned to leave Rome for Alexandria.

AD 42: Revolt of L. Arruntius Camillus Scribonianus in Dalmatia.

AD 43: Invasion of Britain.

AD 49: Agrippina the Younger marries Claudius.

AD 50: Claudius adopts Agrippina the Younger's son, Nero.

AD 54 (13 October): Claudius dies and is succeeded by Nero.

AD 64: Great Fire of Rome.

AD 66 (autumn): Nero travels to Greece and appoints Vespasian commander of Roman forces suppressing the revolt in Judaea.

AD 67: Execution of the commander of the eastern armies, Domitius Corbulo, and the governors of the German provinces, Publius Sulpicius Scribonius Rufus and Publius Sulpicius Scribonius Proculus, in Greece by Nero.

AD 68 (March): Revolt of Vindex in Gaul and Sulpicius Galba in Spain.

AD 68 (April): Galba's revolt against Nero in Spain.

AD 68 (beginning of June): Battle of Vesontio. Vindex defeated and his army slaughtered by the Rhine army commanded by Verginius Rufus.

AD 68 (8 June): Nymphidius Sabinus falsely reports to the Praetorian Guard that Nero has fled to Egypt. Nero commits suicide the following day.

AD 68 (December): Vitellius arrives in his province of Lower Germany.

AD 69 (1 January): Two legions refuse to take the oath of allegiance to Galba. Vitellius was acclaimed emperor the following day.

AD 69 (15 January): Galba murdered and Otho acclaimed emperor by the Praetorian Guard.

AD 69 (14 April): First Battle of Cremona (also called the Battle of Bedriacum). Otho's forces were defeated by Vitellian troops led by Aulus Caecina Alienus and Fabius Valens. Otho commits suicide the following day.

AD 69 (April): Batavian revolt starts with an attack on forts on 'the island' by the Canninefates and Frisians.

AD 69 (1 July): Vespasian is declared emperor by legions in Alexandria, Egypt.

AD 69 (24 October): The second Battle of Cremona. Vitellian forces were defeated by Flavian legions commanded by Antonius Primus.

AD 69 (20 December): Vitellius murdered in Rome.

AD 79 (June): Death of Vespasian and accession of Titus.

AD 81 (September): Death of Titus and accession of Domitian.

AD 82: Conspiracy against Domitian led by T. Flavius Sabinus and leading senators including Dio of Prusa.

AD 87: Plot against Domitian is indicated from the inscription by the Arval Brethren.

AD 89: Revolt of Saturninus on the Rhine.

AD 96: Murder of Domitian and accession of Nerva.

AD 97 (summer): Praetorians mutiny and murder Parthenius and Petronius Secundus who had been leaders of the plot against Domitian.

AD 97 (September): Nerva adopts Trajan as his son and names him his heir.

AD 98 (January): Death of Nerva and Trajan becomes sole emperor.

AD 117 (August): Death of Trajan and accession of Hadrian.

Dates of the Emperors

JULIUS CAESAR *dictator* 49–44 BC

JULIO-CLAUDIAN DYNASTY

AUGUSTUS (assumed name in 27 BC) 31 BC–AD 14
TIBERIUS AD 14–37
GAIUS (CALIGULA) AD 37–41
CLAUDIUS AD 41–54
NERO AD 54–68

CIVIL WAR

GALBA AD 68–69
OTHO AD 69
VITELLIUS AD 69

FLAVIAN DYNASTY

VESPASIAN AD 69–79
TITUS AD 79–81
DOMITIAN AD 81–96

ADOPTIVE EMPERORS of the ANTONINE DYNASTY

NERVA AD 96–98
TRAJAN AD 98–117
HADRIAN AD 117–138
ANTONINUS PIUS AD 138–161
MARCUS AURELIUS and LUCIUS VERUS AD 161–169
MARCUS AURELIUS (sole rule) AD 169–180
COMMODUS (son of Marcus Aurelius) AD 180–192

Chapter 1

The Pannonian Mutiny (August–September AD 14)

'But whip-cut and sword cut, stern winter and harassed summer, red war or barren peace – these, God knew, were always with them.'
(Tacitus, *Annals*, 1.17)

This was the daily existence of the legionaries stationed in the summer camp near the colony of Emona, modern Ljubljana. Many had fought in the 'major and bloody' conquest of Pannonia[1] from 14–10 BC. Then, even more of their number had waged red war in the gruelling Illyrian revolt from AD 6–9, fighting a guerilla-style struggle across the impenetrable forests of Bosnia and the mountain fastnesses and barren karst of Dalmatia.[2] Losses had been so great, and the magnitude of the threat so daunting, that the emperor Augustus had even conscripted former slaves into the ranks of the Roman Army when not enough volunteers had come forward. Veterans who had recently retired with their discharge bounties were recalled.[3] They had glimpsed the joys and freedoms of civilian life but now faced an uncertain future.

The commander in both these conflicts had been Augustus' adopted son, Tiberius. He was a talented and skilful general but a strict disciplinarian. Despite numerous but costly victories, the imperial army had suffered from poor morale. In the last season of the war, Tiberius had been so afraid of mutiny that he was forced to divide his army into three as the men were weary of a conflict devoid of plunder, with their misery intensified by huge casualties.[4]

All legionaries looked forward to their gratuity when they had completed their years of service, if they lived that long. More than half would die before then, however; the three legions at Emona had lost more than most. Like all legions, they took immense pride in their history and battle honours. The *IX Hispana* and *XV Apollinaris* had been stationed in Illyria for many years and had conquered Pannonia. The Ninth Legion had been awarded its title by Augustus for its service during the Cantabrian wars in Spain (25–19 BC). The Fifteenth was named after Apollo, Augustus' favourite god. It possibly received its name after making a crucial contribution to the defeat of Mark Antony at the Battle of Actium. The Eighth Legion was honoured with the name of Augustus himself. It too had campaigned in the Cantabrian wars and was subsequently transferred to either Moesia or the East, from where it was dispatched to crush the Illyrian revolt.[5]

Most of these legionaries had been recruited on the definite terms set by Augustus in 13 BC, so they 'should find no excuse for revolt on this score'. The emperor looked to precedents established during the Republic and set the period of service in the legions to sixteen years, and twelve for the Praetorian Guard, with an unspecified monetary bonus on discharge as opposed to a grant of land. However, 'these measures caused the soldiers neither pleasure nor anger for the time being because they neither obtained all they desired nor yet failed of all'.[6] There was an expectation that many of these retired soldiers would volunteer to remain with the army as *evocati*, who would serve in separate units of veterans without the burdens of fatigues or other onerous duties.[7] They were also entitled to carry rods like those carried by centurions to denote their status. However, there was a shortage of volunteers and money.

Augustus recognized that the 'soldiers were sorely displeased at the paltry character of the rewards given them for the wars which had been waged at this time and none of them consented to bear arms for longer than the regular period of service'. In AD 5, Augustus was forced to act. To increase recruitment, the discharge bonus was set at 12,000 sesterces for legionaries, which was equivalent to fourteen years' pay, but, much to the anger of the common soldiers, 16,000 sesterces was granted for Praetorians. To reduce the financial burden on the state, the period of service was extended to twenty years for legionaries, with a further five in the reserve, and sixteen years for the Guard. Those veterans who volunteered to continue in the army were organized in separate units under their own colours, or *vexillum*, rather than the legionary standards. The increase in years of service would also mean many more soldiers would die before reaching retirement age, reducing the total amount paid in retirement bonuses. Many legionaries, though, were retained long after serving either sixteen or twenty years. A group of inscriptions dedicated by veterans settled from around Narona on the Illyrian coast offering prayers to Augustus and Tiberius proudly boast that they served from twenty-five to thirty-three years.[8]

In AD 9, just as the final embers of the Illyrian revolt were being extinguished, a huge Roman army campaigning beyond the Rhine was destroyed in an ambush in the dense forests and swamps of Germania. Its commander, Publius Quinctilius Varus, chose suicide, fearing capture and being sacrificed to the German gods. Three legions were massacred, a total of around 12,000–15,000 men, as well as six auxiliary infantry cohorts and three *alae* of cavalry. Upon hearing the news, Augustus tore off his clothes and, in an act of mourning, refused to cut his hair for months. For the remaining years of his life, the emperor was often heard to cry out as he beat his head against a door: 'Quinctilius Varus, give me back my legions.'[9] It would take years to replace these experienced soldiers. It being expected that the Germans would cross the Rhine and invade Gaul, an emergency levy was held at Rome, with freeborn men, slaves and freedmen conscripted, raising at least thirty-two cohorts of dubious quality and no military experience. The Rhine frontier held, but the shortage of recruits and battle-hardened soldiers remained.

In these circumstances, time-served veterans were retained in the ranks.[10] Furthermore, there was little money available to pay their discharge bonuses. In AD 6, Augustus had created a new treasury, the *aerarium militare*, to cover military expenditure. This was funded by a payment of 170 million sesterces from the personal fortune of the emperor, a new 5 per cent tax on inheritances and a 1 per cent sales tax. This caused uproar amongst the elite, who objected to contributing towards the defence of the Empire.[11] It is estimated that the total cost to the state of the maintenance of military forces was between 350 and 380 million sesterces a year, which included 48 million for discharge bonuses. This consumed over half of all state revenue and would continue to be a financial problem for all emperors. The need for further revenue led to the introduction of a 2 per cent tax on the sale of slaves in the following year. The resentment of the wealthy grew until, in AD 13, tensions erupted into political confrontation. Augustus asked the Senate to devise another way to raise the necessary funds, only to be met with impotence. Instead, the emperor suggested a tax on land and buildings, without stating the amount he had in mind. Panic set in and the Senate settled for the existing arrangements, under the threat of contributing more for the protection of the Empire.[12]

Faced with the entrenched opposition of the elite to further taxes, Augustus was forced to make savings. Soldiers who had completed twenty years' service were entitled to serve in the reserve, without camp duties and only being called upon in emergencies. However, they were retained on active service. Few were ever granted their honourable discharge. The rules, regulations and edicts were ignored, twisted and exploited by officers eager for the approval of the governor or legate. Legionaries enfeebled by age or wounds were a common sight in the forts and camps. Probably over 500 in each legion had served their time but were denied retirement.[13] These men burned with anger and resentment, especially those in the Pannonian legions. Younger soldiers saw in them their fate as these 'white-haired men, many of whom had lost a limb by wounds, were making their thirtieth or fortieth campaign. Even after discharge, their warfare was not accomplished: still under canvas by the colours they endured the old drudgeries under an altered name.'[14]

Even the benefits of retirement had been undermined by Augustus' need to save money. Instead of a cash gratuity, those Pannonian veterans allowed to retire were given land. These men were mainly recruited from northern Italy, and inscriptions of veterans from the *VIII Augusta* and *XV Apollinaris* demonstrate that previously, land had been allotted to them around Aquileia and Verona. However, the *XV Apollinaris* was being moved from its winter fort at Emona to Carnuntum on the Danube. Emona was given colonial status and discharged veterans were allocated land in the surrounding area. The money would be saved in buying cheap land in a remote and barren expanse rather than giving them the promised cash gratuity or buying expensive farmland.[15]

The legionaries may have accepted land in the fertile plains of northern Italy surrounded by well-established towns and cities instead of money, but Emona was located on a limestone plateau in the foothills of the eastern Alps, in present-day Slovenia, devoid of water and covered by only thin soil and scrub. There is some fertile land on the edges of this plain, but the southern part around the modern town of Ljubljansko Barje is a vast swamp which even today defies the best efforts of farmers to drain it and make it suitable for agriculture.[16] The area had also been devastated by these same legionaries during the Illyrian revolt. After giving their blood and youth fighting for Rome, they were being abandoned to a future of hunger surrounded by their former enemies. The historian Tacitus puts their anger into the mouth of one mutineer, who denounces the treatment of the Pannonian legionary who 'survived this multitude of hazards: he was dragged once more to the ends of the earth to receive under the name of a "farm" some swampy morass or barren mountain side'.[17] They had fought and many of their comrades had died for this barren peace.

These legions had spent the hot, harassed summer of AD 14 building the infrastructure to match Emona's elevated status as a *colonia*. All three legions were based in a temporary camp between the Save and Drave rivers in south-west Pannonia. A large detachment was also engaged in repairing a road and bridges near Nauportus (modern Vrhnika), improving communications between Emona and Aquileia over the Julian Alps. These were under the command of the camp prefect, Aufidienus Rufus, a strict authoritarian who had risen from the ranks to lead centurion and was now effectively third in command of his legion and chief logistics officer. He used the gruelling work to re-establish the iron discipline of old. A partially preserved inscription records the construction of a monumental structure in Emona, probably stone walls and towers reflecting the new status of the *colonia*.[18]

Construction was hard, pitiless work, especially during the heat of the summer months. However, quarrying the stone blocks was even worse. A pair of letters preserved in Egypt dating to AD 107 from a legionary to his parents record his relief at avoiding the quarry. As a recruit, he would have been given the worst jobs, but unlike most he was able to read and write. He boasts to his father that he approached the governor and was allocated the job of clerk (*librarius*) in his legion. In a separate letter to his mother, he writes: 'I give thanks to Serapis [a Graeco-Egyptian goddess] that while the others are working hard all day cutting stones, I am now a *principalis* and stand around doing nothing.'[19]

The *principalis*, like the *immunis*, were a privileged group of soldiers who avoided the daily drudge of fatigues, training or manual labour through promotion to specialized posts and duties. These posts might include farriers, medical sergeants, pilots, orderlies, wagon makers, coppersmiths, bow makers, clerks and junior officers below the post of centurion. An Egyptian papyrus records that eight legionaries from a century of eighty held this status. Jobs completed by the remainder included guard duty and the watch, cleaning the baths and toilets, transporting provisions, cutting stone or patrols. Then, for those who remained in the camp, there was the brutal training, marches in full armour and parades in the oppressive heat or rain.

Discipline was enforced by the centurions, who carried a vine rod about 3ft in length which was used to indicate direction in drills and manoeuvres when commands might not be heard in the din of battle or on the march. Many also used it to beat soldiers who attracted their ire. The knotted and sinuous wood would easily break the skin on a soldier's back, opening deep wounds. Most centurions had risen from the ranks after ten to fifteen years of promotion through the lower officer grades. There was a hierarchy within the centurionate in each legion. The highest status belonged to the *primus pilus* of the First Cohort, then the remaining four centurions of the First Cohort. The centurions of the remaining nine cohorts were of equal rank but not seniority, and were distinguished from those of the First Cohort, who had greater status. Promotion within the cohorts was from the *hastus posterior* to *princeps posterior*, and then through the top three ranks of *hastatus*, *princeps* and finally *primus pilus*. The *primus pilus* attained equestrian rank upon discharge. Some equestrians used the power and influence of their patrons to gain direct appointment to these posts. Other centurions were appointed after serving in the Praetorian Guard. All centurions received five times the pay of a Praetorian, and a *primus pilus* twenty times. There were probably only around ninety vacancies for a centurion post available per year, so access to them was extremely limited for the legionaries. Some might progress to a tribunate in the *Vigiles*, Urban cohorts or the Praetorians in Rome.[20]

The centurions, with their privileged status and hopes of further advancement, were allied mostly with the equestrian officer corps and senatorial commanders rather than the ordinary soldiers. They were a closely knit elite group of officers central to the discipline, organization and function of the Roman Army.[21]

The legionaries accepted men who had shared their hardships, but former guardsmen from Rome or a young equestrian with no military experience would find it difficult to gain the respect of the common soldier. Their ability and character were doubted, as they had acquired their rank through favour, not bravery.[22] A man who had shown his mettle in the heat of battle would be more accepted. Many centurions used beatings to instil fear, having failed to earn deference. These produced resentment and anger, as in civilian life the law prohibited the beating of a Roman citizen. The use of corporal punishment on slaves was seen as entirely acceptable, so legionaries as citizens not only carried the physical scars but also the resentment from the assault on their status, honour and pride. The marks of the lash and the rod were a permanent reminder of their harsh treatment.[23]

This treatment was widespread and accepted, as there was nothing a soldier could do. Soldiers were legally denied the civil right of *provocatio*, an appeal against injustice to a magisterial authority.[24] A plea to an officer was likely to be ignored and result in further ill-treatment. If the soldier was disobedient, grabbed the vine rod or insulted a centurion, he could be demoted to a lesser branch of the military, for example the fleet. Executions were inflicted on any soldier who broke a vine rod, grabbed or hit a centurion. Roman military law served to reinforce the authority of all officers rather than to alleviate injustice. To strike an officer was an assault on his status and honour, which the law was vigilant to protect.[25]

The Pannonian legionaries suffered from the beatings of one centurion in particular, named Lucilius. They gave him the nickname *Cedo alteram*, or 'Give me another', as he regularly shouted for a new vine rod after he had smashed his own on the back of a legionary. Others were hated for their bullying behaviour, in particular their demands for bribes from soldiers to escape from the more unpleasant jobs in the camp.[26] This was a complaint amongst all soldiers and was deeply resented. Legionaries at this time were paid 900 sesterces a year which they received in three instalments. From this, a proportion was deducted to pay for clothes, weapons, tents and compulsory savings. Many soldiers also had to support their families, as although marriage was legally prohibited for legionaries, many had taken partners and had children who lived in the local town attached to their winter fort. Their pay was less than a labourer earned in Rome, being roughly equivalent to the earnings of a farm worker. This insulted their status, as the ordinary soldier saw himself as above the *humiliores*, the lowest strata of society, although many had been recruited from this class.[27]

Some soldiers were well off. As well as warm winter barracks, a secure daily income and access to baths and medical care, they had enough surplus income to save in the unit's bank. Papyrus from Alexandria records the pay of two auxiliaries. After deductions, one was able to save 28 per cent of his annual pay and the other 22 per cent. Once a new soldier had paid for his armour, weapons and clothes, he would have been able to retain a greater proportion of his pay.[28] Furthermore, if he had no family to support, he would have been relatively comfortable.

Some soldiers also had support from their parents to supplement their income. Another papyrus records the frivolous spending of one young soldier whose unrestrained spending caused his financial problems:

> 'Dear mother, I hope you are in good health. When you get this letter, please send me some money. I have absolutely nothing left since I bought a donkey cart and used up all my money on it. Please send me a riding coat, oil, and especially my monthly allowance. The last time I was home you promised not to leave me without money, but now you are treating me like a dog. My father came to visit me yesterday, but he gave me nothing. Everyone is making fun of me now and saying that although my father is a soldier, he gives me nothing. Valerius' mother sent him a pair of pants, some oil, a food parcel, and some money. Please send me some money and don't leave me in this state. Love to everyone at home. Your loving son.'[29]

However, some soldiers were destitute through no fault of their own. Interest on debts or supporting their family, bad luck or poor investments took their toll. Amongst the Pannonian legionaries were many who wore 'threadbare clothes' or were virtually naked and had sunken into 'repulsive squalor'.[30] The legion was a reflection of Roman society at large. The majority who were not members of the officer corps or promoted to the rank of *principalis* or *immunis* were at the mercy of the centurions. These men are labelled by the senatorial historian Tacitus as 'the off-scourings of the army', as opposed to 'the better elements'. Soldiers with no money were unable to escape the quarry, the road constructions, daily patrols or the toilet and bath duties. Furthermore, an amateur and wealthy senior officer corps imbued with the idea of *amicitiae*, where favours had to be paid for in kind, gave bribery free rein.[31]

The long-held resentments, grudges and anger festered in the souls of the Pannonian legionaries over the summer of AD 14. However, they remained loyal to Augustus as the emperor who had rewarded these legions with their special titles and battle honours, taking immense pride in their unit's identification with the emperor.[32] This changed suddenly towards the evening of 24 August. Their commander, Junius Blaesus, called an assembly for all troops in the summer camp.[33] The timing made the legionaries immediately aware that something unexpected was to be announced. The three legions drew up in their cohorts in their full armour, with their military cloaks, shields and weapons. The centurions ensured Bleasus was met with respectful silence from the assembled thousands as he ascended the elevated wooden tribunal with his legates, tribunes and advisors. The eagles of the legions and standards of the cohorts were gathered behind him, carrying the image of Augustus. This formal address, the *adlocutio*, was always a solemn and imposing occasion, communicating the majesty of the emperor and promoting the military excellence of his general.[34]

Junius Blaesus stepped forward and looked over the ranks of men, their armour reflecting the descending sun. The soldiers waited and watched as he pulled out the scroll. Augustus, emperor of Rome for longer than most of them had lived, was dead. His adopted son, Tiberius, was the new emperor and his adopted son, Germanicus, was the new heir. After glorifying the reign of Augustus, he would doubtless have reminded them of the many battles they had won under Tiberius in the Pannonian war and the Illyrian revolt. Their new emperor had led them to victory. Blaesus then announced three days of mourning, with all duties and activities cancelled. The soldiers were dismissed and they returned to their tents.

Immediately, a wave of unrest flowed through the camp. The break in the normal daily routines and demands allowed the soldiers time to reflect and vocalize their grievances, firstly to the eight men they knew well in their tents, then in their centuries and cohorts. Time allowed them to visit those soldiers they rarely had the opportunity to consort with in other cohorts of their legion, and possibly soldiers in the other two legions. They soon realized there was widespread discontent, their confidence rising with a growing realization that their numbers meant collective indiscipline was likely to go unpunished. The first signs of the gathering conflagration were increased insubordination and petulance among the ranks towards their officers. These sparks were not extinguished, and the fire took hold.[35]

An ordinary soldier took the lead, gathering men of a similar mind around him to add fuel to the situation by spreading the rumour that Tiberius would further undermine their terms of service. The historian Tacitus shared the prevalent derisive attitude of Rome's wealthy elite towards the common people, whom they considered were little better than slaves, freedmen and foreigners. The soldiers were recruited from this group and it was believed they were motivated by a base desire 'for luxury and ease, disdainful of discipline and work'.[36]

The leader of the growing mutiny came from the lowest rank of society. Percennius, in Tacitus' view, was a rabble-rouser and demagogue. He was 'a private soldier with an abusive tongue, whose experience of stage rivalries had taught him the art of inflaming an audience'.[37] In civilian life he had been a cheerleader in one of the theatre factions that supported an actor. The theatres were noisy, confined and often violent, with organized groups supporting different actors to the point of attacking rival followers. Cheerleaders would initiate and lead rhythmic chanting by the crowd, start applause or jeers and, when the occasion demanded, spearhead the fighting. They sought strength in their numbers and were both hated and feared for their capacity to spread violence and spark unrest.[38]

The legionary career in the Roman Army had lost its appeal. Opportunities for plunder were now limited and the new conditions of service were unpopular. Volunteers no longer filled the ranks, and instead the state increasingly resorted to conscription, especially in times of emergency. Some wealthier men went into hiding or resorted to bribery to avoid the draft. However, others welcomed the opportunity to escape from gruelling poverty or the courts. The military was also in the process of moving from being a temporary career to a permanent one. This would not have been liked or even recognized by some soldiers. Tiberius complained in AD 23 that 'there was a dearth ... of volunteers; and, even when forthcoming, they failed to show the old courage and discipline, since it was often the destitute and the vagrant who enlisted of their own accord'. These were men who had failed in civilian life and never had the opportunity to succeed.[39]

Percennius was unlikely to have left his role in the theatre faction voluntarily. However, he adapted his skills to his new military life. He knew how to organize, incite, enflame, but above all else, lead. He gathered around him men he could trust, and under the cover of darkness, they went round the tents. They found a receptive audience in each. The death of Augustus provided a brief opportunity to act on their grievances. Tiberius' position was fragile. The contemporary Velleius Paterculus recalled 'men's nervousness at the time, the alarm in the senate, the anxiety of the people, the apprehension in Rome, the fine line that we saw drawn between safety and disaster'.[40]

The aims of the mutineers were disparate, depending on their age and experiences. However, the core of the mutiny was centred on the older soldiers, especially those who were serving beyond their discharge date.[41] Their demands were entirely reasonable. They wanted military service to be based on a fixed term of sixteen years, with no further obligation to serve in the reserve. The discharge gratuity was to be paid in money, not land, and for those soldiers long entitled to it, paid immediately as promised by Augustus in 13 BC. Promises had been made then and not kept. Others demanded a pay increase to a denarius a day. As justification, they looked to the Praetorians who received two denarii a day and could retire after sixteen years, having served free from hardship or danger in Rome.[42]

To unify their aims and prevent future division, it was suggested that the three separate legions should join into one. Immediately arguments arose as individual soldiers suggested their own legionary title and standard be retained, with the others subsumed. However, the rivalry between these legions was so intense and the loyalty to their own unit's honour and prestige so powerful that none were prepared to compromise. Each man identified with their tent companions, their century, cohort and – most of all – their own legion. It was their family and their world. A simple solution was devised, where each legion's standards were taken from their separate chapels in the headquarters buildings and placed together, symbolizing unity of purpose.[43]

There was no attempt to turn mutiny into revolt, nor was there any attempt to use the unrest as an opportunity to desert. There was no effort to persuade their commander, Junius Blaesus, to try for the throne. The soldiers knew he was steadfast in his support for the new emperor. He would not have been appointed as governor if there had been any doubts as to his loyalty by either Augustus or Tiberius. The soldiers saw him as an obstacle to their designs rather than a potential asset. He was a new man (*novus homo*), the first of his family to attain the consulship, so he lacked the required status to own any imperial ambitions. Furthermore, his sister was married to L. Seius Strabo, the faithful Praetorian Prefect.[44] He knew loyalty would be rewarded if he could quell the growing unrest in his troops.

The removal of the standards was the first real indication that events were spinning beyond the governor's control. It was reported that the soldiers were constructing a new tribunal out of sods of earth. Percennius wanted to address the legions, but realized that using the camp's existing tribunal would be equivalent to open mutiny as this action would symbolize his assumption of the role of commander. However, the construction of a second tribunal was an affront to the authority of Blaesus. In desperation, he grabbed the soldiers cutting the turf and then tried to pull back the men building the platform. He told them to kill him to save him from the dishonour, crying out, 'Alive, I will keep my legions loyal, or, murdered, hasten their repentance.'[45] The soldiers continued their work and the tribunal continued to rise.

A change in strategy brought an end to this. Instead of trying to impose his authority, Blaesus sought to placate his men and suggested sending a delegation to Tiberius to present their demands. To reassert his authority, he called an *adlocutio*. The soldiers assembled on the parade ground, and he ascended the wooden platform. He told the crowd to select deputies and gave them instructions, thereby arming them with his authority. The soldiers responded with a shout. The leaders of the mutiny had already made their decision on who was to represent them and had communicated the choice to the men. Junius Blaesus' son, who was a tribune in the entourage of his father, would lead the embassy, and they had reduced their demands to just one request. They asked for the discharge of all soldiers who had served sixteen years or more. Other grievances could be addressed if this one small victory was achieved.[46]

The delegation departed and order returned. It was probably at this point that Bleasus sent a messenger ahead to Tiberius, informing him of events and the nature of the approaching embassy. Percennius had demonstrated shrewd leadership. The one main demand of the veterans had the implicit support of the governor and was to be delivered to the emperor by his son. It would otherwise have been easy to dismiss the demands of lowly soldiers. Furthermore, the leader of the mutiny hoped to survive the breakdown of military discipline. For Blaesus, the situation was recoverable as it stood, and he remained commander of three legions. His son was also safe, away from the unpredictable and impulsive mutineers.

This delicate and carefully balanced state was suddenly shattered by the arrival of the legionaries who had been building near Nauportus. These soldiers were probably not veterans, nor holders of any privileged status. They had already destroyed any hope of compromise through the depravity of their actions. When they had received news of the mutiny in the camp, they 'went as far as taking up arms, the sword was drawn, and their unchecked behaviour all but exploded into an orgy of violence'.[47] These men had torn down the images of Tiberius and, when their centurions attempted to stop them, had attacked them. This was an act of treason and insubordination far beyond anything contemplated by their comrades in the summer camp. There, Percennius had been a restraining hand. These men were now let loose. The town of Nauportus and its surrounding villages were plundered. Sated and ladened with plunder, the soldiers took their revenge on the grizzled disciplinarian, Aufidienus Rufus. He 'was dragged from his carriage, loaded with baggage, and driven at the head of the column, was plied with sarcastic inquiries whether he found it pleasant to support these huge burdens, these weary marches'.[48]

The villages along the 15-mile route from Nauportus to the camp near Emona probably suffered a similar fate. Once these soldiers arrived and stored their booty, they started to pillage again, roaming the countryside to rob, plunder and murder. Blaesus was forced to impose his authority. He gathered the centurions and 'the respectable members of the rank and file',[49] who probably included many of the *principalis* and the *immunis*, as well as promoted soldiers holding junior staff posts. These included the *optio*, who were second in command to the centurion and chosen by him. Other posts that virtually guaranteed further promotion included the *tesserarius,* who passed on the watchword, and *signifer,* who had responsibility for the unit's standard and the men's savings. They must have had some rudimentary education, but, most importantly, they were trusted by their comrades. These three grades formed a tight-knit group, their interests aligned with the officers rather than the rank and file.[50]

The commander and his escort waited for the marauders to enter the camp and targeted a small number of the soldiers who were the most heavily ladened with loot. They were seized and dragged towards the prison, where they were to be lashed. The sudden attempt to restore some discipline had caught them and the rest of the camp by surprise. They begged for help from their friends, from their century, their cohort and then soldiers of their legion. Once they were caged, their comrades rose as one to secure their release. The guard was overcome and the doors were thrown open; out poured all those who were awaiting execution for criminal offences or desertion. These had most to lose by the restoration of order and discipline, and took a lead in ensuring the chaos continued: 'Sedition found fresh leaders.'[51]

The legionaries gathered in the open space before the tribunal. A new leader arose, literally hoisted onto the shoulders of his friends so he could address the crowd around him. Vibulenus claimed that his brother had been sent as a messenger from the Rhine legions that had also mutinied, but had been murdered by the gladiators bought by Blaesus for games he planned to give. The murder of a Roman citizen, as all legionaries were, at the hands of slaves was sure to inflame his audience. The unjust execution of comrades was bound to rouse the passion of the soldiers. These same gladiators could soon be used against them. His loss was visibly illustrated for those who could not hear him by his dramatic beating of his face and chest, weeping, and finally he threw himself down and clung to the legs of all who would listen as a supplicant.[52]

This was not a spontaneous demonstration of grief but carefully planned, as the enraged mob was quickly divided into three groups. The first descended upon the gladiators, who were quickly chained and imprisoned. The second party entered the governor's residence and took his household slaves and freedmen. These were tortured to find out what happened to Vibulenus' brother. The remainder scoured the camp searching for his corpse. Blaesus himself came close to losing his life, but evidently he was more useful alive than dead. His death would have ended any chance of their demands being met.[53]

Vibulenus and his background were well known to the governor's staff, torture revealing that he never had a brother. He was probably amongst those who had been released from the prison and had been awaiting trial before Blaesus. Nevertheless, the truth no longer mattered as the mutiny grew. The change in leadership is reflected in the increased use of intimidation. They had menaced their commander, and now threatened 'to cause the whole province to revolt, and then to march upon Rome'. If Tiberius would not sanction their demands, they would replace him with someone who would. The nature and aims of mutinies commonly shift and change over time, and Vibulenus knew how to rouse the mob.[54]

The officers were now targeted. Blaesus was to remain a hostage, but his tribunes and the despised camp prefect, Aufidius Rufus, were ejected from the camp. Their tents and property were ransacked. The centurions were then hunted down. The brutal Lucilius was killed, but the mutineers fell into dispute over the fate of another. The legionaries of the Eighth wanted him dead, but those of the Fifteenth protected him. He was possibly promoted from a legionary of the latter to a centurion of the former. The argument grew increasingly heated, and swords were drawn. The legionaries of the Ninth attempted to calm the situation, and when their pleas were drowned out, they threatened violence against both sides, which diffused the situation. The fate of the unfortunate centurion is unknown.[55]

Most centurions managed to find safety beyond the confines of the camp or were hidden by sympathetic soldiers. One, Julius Clemens, was retained, as they believed his 'quick wits might be of service in presenting their claims'. He was amongst a group of officers 'whose qualities made them popular with the ranks'.[56] He was probably one of the officers who was universally respected for his bravery in battle and reluctance to enforce commands through brutality, who did not line his own pockets through bribery.

The morning of 27 September brought news that the emperor's son, Drusus, was approaching the camp with a large escort. As befitted a prince of the imperial house, the customary two cohorts of the Praetorian Guard accompanied him. They had been augmented with picked troops from the other cohorts, as well as the Praetorian horse guard and the Batavian cavalry. Yet these 3,000 men would be no protection against three legions. Instead, they were there to add imperial weight to the authority of Drusus. However, they were despised by the legionaries, who saw themselves as the true Roman Army. They still retained the scale armour and oval shields of the old Republican army, which had been replaced in the legions with segmented armour. The Guardsmen had been told to ignore the inevitable provocations to avoid any excuse for the mutineers to attack them. The Batavians would have similarly been warned, but their Latin was limited so the risk of a confrontation was minimal.[57]

The 17-year-old Drusus had little leadership experience, having only held the junior office of quaestor. Tiberius therefore surrounded him with experienced advisors. Amongst them was the 65-year-old Gnaeus Cornelius Lentulus the Augur, consul in 14 BC and renowned for his 'military fame' won against the

Getae beyond the Danube. He had served in Pannonia under Tiberius, who held him in the highest esteem. However, others were less impressed. Seneca considered his advancement the consequence of a great name and imperial recommendation, for he possessed 'a barren mind, and a spirit no less feeble. He was the greatest of misers, but freer with coins than talk, so dire was his poverty of speech. He owed all his advancement to Augustus.' Furthermore, the legionaries despised him, as he had the reputation of a brutal disciplinarian. This man's *dignitas* and *auctoritas* meant he was Drusus' principal advisor.[58]

Another important advisor was L. Aelius Sejanus, recently appointed Praetorian Prefect alongside his father, Seius Strabo. He was the nephew of the governor Blaesus, but it was his abilities and great capacity for hard work that had earned the respect of Tiberius. He had received specific instructions from the emperor 'to act as a monitor to the young prince and to keep before the eyes of the rest the prospects of peril or reward'.[59] The mutiny offered the opportunity for an ambitious noble with the requisite ancestry and experience to present himself to these legions as an alternative to Tiberius. Sejanus' role was to ensure that none of Drusus' party seized this chance. As Tiberius had not given his son any specific instructions, it probably also fell to Sejanus to guide him on what he could concede.[60]

As Drusus approached the camp, the legionaries lined each side of the road to demonstrate their continued loyalty. Custom dictated that the soldiers meet him in their full amour, wearing battle honours and decorations. However, with no officers to organize the centuries and cohorts, the imperial party was met by a rabble. No cheers and rousing shouts were raised as he passed towards the gates, only a sullen, curt silence. Once Drusus and his advisors had entered, the gates were shut behind them, preventing most of his escort from entering. The leaders of the mutiny ordered guards posted along the ramparts and around the camp. They had already strengthened the defences in anticipation of this moment. Drusus and his party were now virtual prisoners.[61]

Drusus kept his composure and ascended the tribunal. The legionaries flocked around him without order. There was a continual roar from thousands of voices. Behind him stood Lentulus, Sejanus, Blaesus and his advisors, with the standards of the guard units that had accompanied him. There was nothing more. The crowd wanted to hear Tiberius' response to their demands. Drusus held up his hand for silence, and slowly the cacophony stilled 'to vague murmurings, savage yells and sudden stillness'. This took time. At last, he started to read out Tiberius' letter. The emperor 'had personally a special regard for the heroic legions in whose company he had borne so many campaigns; that as soon as his thoughts found a rest from grief, he would state their case to the Conscript Fathers; meantime he had sent his son to grant without delay any reforms that could be conceded on the spot; the others must be reserved for the Senate, a body which they would do well to reflect, could be both generous and severe.'[62]

Tiberius attempted to appeal to the legionaries as their former commander and as a fellow soldier who had shared the same hardships as them, drawing upon his distinguished reputation as a great general. However, the men were not convinced. Just as it had been outrageous to shout and delay a commander's *adlocutio*, especially a member of the imperial house, it was expected that those in attendance would applaud its end with repeated roars of approval. There were none. Instead, the centurion Clemens was sent forward to repeat the same demands. Drusus was perfectly aware of what they were, as Blaesus and his son were standing on the tribunal with him. Drusus replied that he could not grant their request, nor could the emperor as it was the Senate's prerogative to decide.[63]

The legionaries were not politically aware, nor mindful of the complexities of the Augustan constitution. However, they were not fools. The emperor was their commander-in-chief, acclaimed regularly as *imperator*. His images on the standards were before them when they had given their oath of loyalty and when they received their pay. They gathered around these standards in battle. When they were punished, it was done in the name of the emperor. The deceit of Tiberius' letter and the duplicity of his son were transparent to all. The anger of the assembled troops was quickly apparent. Many started shouting out, asking, 'Why had he come, if he was neither to raise the pay of the troops nor to ease their burdens – if, in short, he had no leave to do a kindness? Yet death and the lash, Heaven was their witness, were within the competence of anyone.' Some may have felt their oath was no longer binding, as their emperors had failed to keep their side of the bargain. Relations in Roman society were after all reciprocal.[64]

These legionaries knew their emperor. They had made requests to him during the Illyrian revolt, but their commander had prevaricated by making the excuse that he was not empowered to grant them; instead, he had forwarded them on to Augustus in Rome. Drusus now employed the same tactic learnt from his father. As the temperature rose, the assembly was sensibly dismissed. However, as they left, the legionaries first tried to initiate a confrontation with the few Praetorians in front of the tribunal. Then all control was lost as a riot ensued, with members of Drusus' staff and his advisors being attacked and wounded.[65]

The focus of the storm was Cornelius Lentulus, as the mutinous soldiers felt he was advising Drusus to stand firm and resist their demands. His presence was adding fuel to the fire and his life was in danger. Drusus decided to try to smuggle him out, with instructions to make for the garrison fort at nearby Emona. So as not to attract attention, the Praetorians did not accompany the small group to the gate. However, they were recognized and soon surrounded by a baying mob demanding to know where they were going. Stones flew towards Lentulus and he was hit. Bleeding, the elderly senator readied himself for death. However, the Praetorians soon arrived and rescued them. They retreated to their residence, which was then surrounded by a guard to prevent any further escape attempts during the night.[66]

Drusus had relied heavily on his father's letter, which had only served to inflame the soldiers' sense of injustice. The unfortunate Lentulus became the focus of their anger, as to target the imperial prince was an act of treason, a step too far for many of them. Drusus, hesitant and impotent, seethed in his tent. It was impossible to leave without precipitating violence, nor could he contact the Praetorian and Batavians outside the camp. However, fate saved him.

Dusk had brought a pause: 'It was a night of menace and foreboded a day of blood, when chance turned peacemaker: for suddenly the moon was seen to be losing light in the clear sky.' Luna, the goddess of heaven, whose brightness and purity symbolized the righteousness of their cause, was slowly engulfed by darkness. The soldiers left their tents to witness the lunar eclipse. The huddled silence was suddenly broken with the blaring sounds of gongs, trumpets and horns as the legionaries offered their support in Luna's battle against the malignancy that devoured their goddess. As they gazed upwards, they saw the fight turn against her. She dimmed, and as the clouds slowly enveloped her, they stood in complete darkness. They believed the gods had turned their faces away from the pollution of their sacred oaths.[67]

The soldiers had a simple and rudimentary education, and their understanding of the world was framed against winning the favour of the gods, who controlled all aspects of life and nature. If the gods were offended, divine vengeance would inevitably follow. Their piety was simple, free of the nuances and complexities which the better-educated understood in their relationships with the divine.[68]

Drusus sensed an opportunity to use this to break the support for the mutiny. He appreciated that 'wisdom should reap where chance had sown'. He sent for the centurion Clemens and 'any other officer whose qualities had made him popular with the ranks'.[69] All the other centurions were either in hiding or outside the camp, whilst the legions' tribunes had been evicted, so the available officers were members of the junior grades, who remained firmly rooted in esteem of their fellow legionaries but hopeful of promotion. As well as the *optiones* and those who held the posts of *tesserarius* and *signifer*, there were promoted soldiers on the headquarters staff such as *beneficiarius tribuni* and *singularis praefecti praetorio.* These men, who had deserved promotion through bravery and competence rather than favour, held the respect of the rank and file. They were carefully chosen. The soldiers would listen to them, as their sentiments held weight. Their job was to sow the seeds of discord, ask questions and divide support for the mutiny. The confidence of the mutineers was already collapsing; now they were encouraged to turn on each other, and 'under the influence of their mutual suspicions they separated one more recruit from veteran, legion from legion'.[70]

These officers left Drusus and 'insinuated themselves everywhere, among the watches, the patrols, the sentries at the gates, suggesting hope and emphasising fear'. To the veteran, they asked whether Vibulenus or Percennius would grant their discharge gratuity or farm. Would they overthrow Tiberius to make one of these lowly born men emperor? Should they swear their oath of loyalty to these two? This raised the issue of the oath they had sworn to the emperor and his family, which included Drusus, who they now besieged in his own camp. Did they think they could keep the emperor's son hostage without retribution? To the legionary, they questioned who was to grant their pay. There was also the issue of the donative promised in Augustus' will and doubled by Tiberius to tempt the recalcitrant and tame the revolutionary. All would have known that those individuals who were first to return to the fold would escape severe punishment, unlike those who refused, for 'private favour is quickly earned and quickly paid'. It may have been suggested that some units were about to abandon the cause as legion turned against legion.[71]

The mutiny thus collapsed. The legionary standards and eagles were returned to their separate chapels, the gates left unguarded, and Drusus and his staff were allowed to move freely around the camp. As dawn broke, the imperial prince called an *adlocutio* to reassert his authority. Drusus commended the return of sanity and emphasized that he would never surrender to demands supported by threats and intimidation. If, however, they acted as supplicants and returned to duty, then he would write to his father supporting their requests. The suggestion was met with a roar of approval, so Blaesus' son was once more despatched to the emperor, accompanied by Justus Catonius, a first-rank centurion, and L. Apronius, an equestrian from Drusus' staff. The tide had turned. The choice of envoys was made purely by Drusus. All three would go on to have illustrious careers. Catonius rose rapidly to become a Praetorian Prefect under Claudius, whilst Apronius would end his career as Prefect of Baeterrae in the province of Gallia Narbonensis and Blaesus' son was consul in AD 26.[72]

Drusus, supposedly no orator, had cloaked his speech in religious connotations. They had demonstrated impiety by breaking their sacred oath to the emperor. The gods, though, were not placated. A great storm arose, whose ferocity forced the men to take shelter in their tents. None went outside to witness the divine anger. The ferocious rain quickly flooded the camp, making it impossible for the leaders of the mutiny to gather their cohorts. The wind nearly carried away the standards, which had to be rescued and secured. Instead, the legionaries huddled together in their tents, their world reduced to the seven men they shared it with. They believed the camp was cursed by their actions. Their spiritual redemption could only be earned through absolving themselves of their guilt and then returning to their permanent garrison forts. The language the senatorial historian Tacitus uses implies that their pollution of the camp was caused by a form of madness.[73]

Drusus called his advisors together in his tent for a *concilium*. The mutiny had ended but he wanted to consult their opinions on the next steps. These senators and equestrians equated the mutiny to a form of madness that infected the legions. There is no acknowledgement that the legionaries had genuine grievances. Instead, the disease needed to be treated with either mild remedies or severe purging. The former group suggested waiting for the return of the embassy to Tiberius, allowing the infection to dissipate over time. The others recommended using fear to cure temporary insanity. The aristocracy favoured severity in the imposition of military discipline. Drusus was never a man to take a step back. He had also been treated with disdain by the mutineers, so vengeance would be delivered and the contagion cut out. Percennius and Vibulenus were ordered to attend the prince in his tent. They were not fools, but bereft of all support, they obeyed the imperial command. The language used at the *adlocatio* was conciliatory, so perhaps they found some solace in that. They should have run.[74]

Once they had entered the prince's pavilion, they were immediately cut down by the Praetorians. Their bodies, according to some, were buried in the ground inside the tent. Others report they were thrown outside the camp and left on view. A massacre followed. All those who had taken a leading role in the mutiny were hunted down by centurions and Praetorians. Some managed to escape the camp but were cut down outside. Others were handed over by the men who hours before had urged them on. They thought that this treachery would save them from further punishment.[75]

Drusus was well satisfied with the morning's work. The canker had been cut out and his honour restored. He was praised by contemporary historians for applying the 'old, traditional severity'. The gods gave their judgement as the ceaseless rain and icy wind continued to lash the camp. Many men only thought of the warmth of their barracks in the winter camps. The delegation to Tiberius would take many days to return. The *VIII Augusta* was the first to break camp and march away. They were soon followed by the Fifteenth. The legionaries of the *IX Hispana* had insisted on waiting for the return of Tiberius' response. Left alone by the other legions, they too waivered, their confidence undermined by the defection of their comrades. Soon they dismantled the camp and returned to their permanent base. Drusus now felt confident enough to return with his Praetorians to Rome, leaving the dispirited legions under the command of the governor, Blaesus. His departure announced to all his complete disinterest in the complaints of the legionaries. He had been ordered to end the mutiny; that was all.[76]

Drusus had made minimal concessions. This met with the approval of his father, as forced compromises would in his mind only encourage further unrest.[77] Drusus' severity also met with the approval of the senatorial class, who rationalized military discontent as the result of either the greed of the rank and file or weak generals. He was consul in the following year and soon after governor of Illyricum. Blaesus also continued to enjoy a prestigious career until the fall of his nephew, Sejanus. The Praetorian Prefect had also proven himself and rose to become the right hand of the emperor. The young Drusus had started to develop a deep hatred of Sejanus, angered by his 'overweening behaviour' and intolerant of a rival to his father's esteem. This culminated in AD 23 with Drusus striking the Praetorian Prefect in the face. Perhaps, like the legionaries, Sejanus had not treated him with the respect he felt he deserved. Drusus possessed a fiery temper and instinctively met opposition with aggression. He had reaped the rewards of deploying uninhibited brutality and violence in crushing the Pannonian mutineers. He would apply the same approach again.[78]

The imperial prince made a leisurely return to Rome and probably visited the new colony at Emona on the way to inspect the progress on the walls and other public buildings. Many veterans were soon settled in its vicinity; however, another group is attested at Scarbantia, modern Sopron, near Lake Neusiedl. The veterans may have been given a choice of locations as a compromise. Certainly, the land in this area was more fertile. The promise to discharge time-served veterans may have been a compromise offer Drusus used to regain control.[79]

The three legions returned to their permanent forts. The *VIII Augusta* marched to Poetovio, modern Ptuj on the River Drave, whilst the *XV Apollinaris* settled into their new home at Carnuntum on the Danube facing the hostile Marcomanni. The *IX Hispana* garrisoned the city of Siscia, now known as Sisak on the confluence of the Kupa and Sava rivers. Units drawn from this legion would fight under the command of Junius Blaesus in Africa from AD 21–23 against the warlord Tacfarinus. Little changed for these legionaries. In AD 23, Tiberius would again address the Senate concerning the desperate need for recruits, as the legions were still packed with 'time-expired veterans and [there was a] need of fresh conscription to maintain the armies at strength'. Only a few continued to be discharged when they had served their time. A legionary career remained unpopular, for 'there was a dearth, he said, of volunteers'. The army continued to be a harsh and unrewarding profession for most, yet surprisingly the soldiers did not use the mutiny to desert. They sought simply to protect their interests and were frustrated by changes to their terms of service. Promises made had been broken.[80]

In battle, they fought and died together as a unit, but the mutiny was crushed by their officers exploiting their divisions. Their cohesion was undermined by a disparity in aims between the recent recruits and veterans, between those who had served beyond their time and those who hadn't, between the *principalis* with privileges to defend and the rank and file, and between junior officers with hopes of future promotion and the legionaries. The eclipse allowed Drusus to exploit these divisions. Hesitant at first, armed merely with his father's letter and protected by his insignificant escort, the prince was until then impotent. Luck saved him. Then his instinctive recourse to violence and aggression was released. The madness was all his.[81]

Chapter 2

Mutiny on the Rhine (August–October, AD 14)

'This was the bravest of all armies, peerless among the Roman troops in discipline, in action, and in battle experience. Falling victim to the apathy of its leader, the treachery of the enemy, and the unfairness of Fortune.'
(Velleius Paterculus, *The Roman History*, 2.119.2, blames Rome's defeat on a failure of leadership)

The ghosts of Publius Quinctilius Varus and his lost legions had haunted the Roman psyche since September AD 9. Over three fateful autumn days, the XVII, XVIII and XIX legions, three cavalry squadrons and six auxiliary cohorts were annihilated by a coalition of German tribes, led by the chief of the Cherusci, Arminius. More than 20,000 men were lost at the Battle of the Teutoburg Forest, as well as some 10,000 camp followers, slaves, women and children attached to the army.[1] Their bones were left to bleach on the dark forest floor at the foot of the Kalkriese Hill, just north of the modern town of Osnabrück. This was Rome's greatest military defeat since the destruction wrought upon the Romans by Hannibal at the Battle of Cannae in 216 BC. The aura of Roman invincibility had been shattered and its planned occupation of Germany was abandoned forever.[2]

Augustus feared the tribes would cross the Rhine and plunder Gaul. However, the brave resistance of the garrison at Aliso on the River Lippe bought enough time for the forts along the frontier to be reinforced and further disaster averted.[3] The emperor sent his adopted son, Tiberius, to shore up the defences and attempt to restore Rome's shattered reputation.[4] Rome's best general had only just crushed the Illyrian revolt. He would remain for the next three years. He brought the battle-hardened *XX Valaria Victrix* from Dalmatia, which had originally received its eagle from Tiberius, and *XIII Gemina* to replace the legions lost with Varus. They were united with another legion that had served in Pannonia, the *XXI Rapax*, which joined the *V Alaudae* at Vetera (Xanten) guarding the confluence of the Lippe and the Rhine. The *V Alaudae* and *I Germanica* had held the frontier in the immediate aftermath of the disaster at

Teutoburg. The *II Augusta* was soon summoned from Spain and garrisoned Mogontiacum (Mainz).

Rome could not replace the lost legionaries, so Tiberius campaigned with great caution, moving slowly to avoid ambush. He aimed to restore morale in the Rhine army and punish the German tribes by destroying their crops and villages. He could ill afford to lose more soldiers.[5] Augustus attempted to raise more men, but this was an abject failure as

> 'there were no citizens of military age left worth mentioning, and the allied forces that were of any value had suffered severely. Nevertheless, he made preparations as best he could, given the circumstances; and when no men of military age showed a willingness to be enrolled, he made them draw lots, depriving them of [their] property and disenfranchising every fifth man of those still under thirty-five and every tenth man among those who had passed that age. Finally, as a great many paid no heed to him even then, he put some to death. He chose by lot as many as he could of those who had completed their term of service and from the freedmen, and after enrolling them sent them in haste with Tiberius into the province of Germany.'

Many of those who enlisted were *Vigiles*, freemen who received citizenship after serving six years in the capital's fire service and night watch. Their immediate grant of citizenship to serve in the legions on the distant Rhine frontier would hardly compensate for the loss of a secure and comfortable future in Rome. More men were drawn from the three Urban cohorts, who, although classed as legionaries, received higher pay.[6]

The Rhine legions were filled with conscripts from the unruly urban populace of Rome or time-served veterans forced to return to the standards. In the circumstances, no soldiers would be discharged after they had served their twenty years. Morale was thus low. This 'swarm of city-bred recruits swept from the capital by the recent levy, familiar with licence and chafing at hardship'[7] resented their enforced enlistment. To the senatorial historian Tacitus, the urban populace was characterized by greed, ignorance and emotional instability, and was morally bankrupt.[8] Tiberius had to meld and train these men into a fighting machine to match the victorious Germans. Hard discipline and traditional *severitas* (the inflicting of exemplary punishment) were used to forge them into soldiers. Tiberius 'imposed the severest discipline on his men: reviving obsolete methods of punishment or branding men with ignominy for misbehaviour'.[9] Such strictness was considered so unusual to be deserving of comment. The soldiers believed there existed a thin line between necessary military discipline and illegitimate cruelty. Although the legionaries came from the lower social strata or *humiliores*, they took pride in their citizenship, which raised them above most provincials.[10] Tiberius' use of fear of punishment and shame only served to build resentment. He did, however, attempt to lead by example, eating while sitting on the ground like his men and sleeping in the open rather than under cover.[11]

A huge number of experienced officers had also been lost, leading to the appointment of men in whom Tiberius had little confidence. They required constant instruction, to the extent that he 'even degraded a legionary commander because he had sent a few soldiers across the river as escort for one of his freedmen who was hunting there'. Such was the state of the Rhine legions that Tiberius 'did not see fit to cross the Rhine' in AD 10. The following year, he was joined by his adopted son, Germanicus, who had earned a distinguished reputation serving under Tiberius in Dalmatia and Illyricum. After a year of training and drills, he finally felt confident enough to cross the Rhine, but 'they did not win any battle there, however, since no one came to close quarters with them, nor did they reduce any tribe; for in their fear of falling victims to a fresh disaster they did not advance very far beyond the Rhine'. The Germans simply melted away into the dense forests and endless swamps. There the Romans remained, frustrated, until the late autumn when they returned to the frontier.[12]

This was no more than a training exercise in enemy territory. Tiberius knew a lack of discipline or failure to follow orders would cost them their lives. Many officers were invited to his *concilium* to learn, and he inspected the baggage train and the marching line. He always committed his orders to writing, demanding that 'any officer who was in doubt about any matter was required to consult him personally at any hour of the day or night'.[13] Little was achieved, and Tiberius was forced to return to Rome to be at the side of the ailing Augustus.

This was the untested army that Germanicus inherited in AD 13. He also campaigned beyond the Rhine with the Upper German legions on what were optimistically called 'mopping up operations'. He had overall control of all eight legions along the river. The *V Alaudae*, *XXI Rapax*, *I Germanica* and *XX Valeria Victrix* in Lower Germany were commanded by Aulus Caecina Severus, whilst another four in Upper Germany were led by Gaius Silius. There were also difficulties in Gaul, centred on the town of Vienne. In addition, Germanicus was instructed to carry out a financial reorganization of the province. The legions of Lower Germany had not crossed the Rhine in AD 13. All four were stationed together in a summer camp on the bank of the Rhine in the territory of the Ubii at Novaesium (Neuss), 24 miles from Cologne. They likely spent the summer carrying out drills in preparation for another invasion of Germany the following year. The relentless hard labour involved in building parapets, entrenching, cutting timber and construction fuelled their anger.[14]

Novaesium had been used as a base by Nero Drusus, Germanicus' natural father and brother of Tiberius. He had launched the conquest of Germany, leading Roman legions beyond the Elbe in a series of brilliant campaigns. In 9 BC, however, he fell from his horse whilst returning to the Rhine and died a month later from gangrene. After his death, he was awarded the honorary title *Germanicus*, which his son inherited along with the adoration of his legionaries, who built a huge monument in his honour at Mogontiacum. The *V Alaudae* had crossed the Wesser and Elbe with Nero Drusus, and he had led the *XXI Rapax* in the conquest of Raetia in 15 BC. The *I Germanica* had won their title with him at their head. The glory that Germanicus' father brought to these legions would have been passed on to recruits by the men who had served under him. The *XIII Gemina*, *XIV Gemina* and *XVI Gallica* in Upper Germany had also been commanded by him.[15]

The death of Augustus was seen as an opportunity to demand change. Germanicus was absent in Belgica, with the two Praetorian cohorts accompanying him to mark his status as heir to the throne. Caecina, like Blaesus in Pannonia, ordered the suspension of normal duties during the period of official mourning. This allowed the mutiny's leaders to assess backing for their actions and coordinate their plans. The core of support was drawn from time-served veterans, especially those who 'belonged to the city troops that Augustus had enrolled as an extra force after the disaster of Varus'. The leaders were not limited to a Percennius or solitary Vibulenus; this 'was the sedition of many tongues and voices'. However, their demands were the same as those of their comrades in Pannonia. They demanded the discharge of all legionaries who had served twenty years and wanted those who had served sixteen to be allotted to the reserve without fatigues. Other legionaries called for a pay increase, but more wanted an end to the bribery and brutality of the centurions.[16]

The leaders of the mutiny are unnamed by the ancient sources, as traditionally befitted *humiliores*. Yet Tacitus expresses a certain respect for their ability to command and retain the unqualified esteem of the rank and file. The mutiny was indeed carefully planned and organized. Thought was given to controlling events after they had seized the camp, for 'there were no spasmodic outbreaks instigated by a few firebrands, but everywhere one white heat of anger, one silence, and withal a steadiness and uniformity which might well have been accredited to discipline'.[17]

The revolt began with the *V Alaudae* and *XXI Rapax*. Most of the leaders probably came from these two legions. The normal command structure was to be removed. There was no plan to send a delegation to Tiberius with their demands; instead, they were to be presented to Germanicus when he returned to the camp. It was hoped that the imperial heir would be persuaded to take the throne with the support of all eight German legions. If so, he was to grant all their demands in return for their support. Their 'hopes ran high that Germanicus Caesar unable to brook the sovereignty of another, would throw himself into the arms of his legions', as the 'German legions were unanimously opposed to Tiberius' succession and would have acclaimed Germanicus emperor'.[18]

Germanicus had done little to encourage such hopes. However, their fondness for him and his family blinded them to reality. He was married to Agrippina, the granddaughter of Augustus. Tiberius was not directly related to Augustus, only through adoption. Just as Germanicus inherited the lustre of his father, so he bathed in the reflected glory of the imperial claims of his wife and their son, Gaius, known to history as Caligula. The toddler, born just two years previously, was dressed by his parents in a miniature uniform and military boots, earning the affectionate nickname Caligula, or 'little boots'. Both Germanicus and his father were fellow soldiers. The men regarded all three of the family with the greatest affection and saw Germanicus as 'far superior to Tiberius'.[19]

The mutiny broke with a sudden and planned attack on all the centurions. The hatred many soldiers felt for them was given full vent. Each officer was apprehended by armed soldiers and then stripped and given sixty lashes, one for each centurion in a legion. This was as much a physical assault as an attack on their status and honour. They too were degraded and humiliated, as the soldiers had been. The lifeless bodies of the officers were then either thrown over the rampart into the ditch with the refuse or dumped into the Rhine. One centurion escaped the clutches of his captors and fled to the tribunal where the legate sat, impotent as the storm raged around him. The centurion ran up the steps onto the platform claiming sanctuary and, falling as a supplicant at the feet of his commander, implored him for help. The soldiers did not dare ascend the stage, but insisted the man be handed over. Caecina surrendered him to his fate.[20]

One man showed remarkable bravery and determination. Cassius Chaerea is described as 'an old-fashioned sort of man', probably a proponent of traditional discipline.[21] He drew his sword and challenged the multitude that crowded around him, ultimately avoiding the fate of many of his fellow officers. Many years later, he carved his name in history as the Praetorian tribune who cut down the emperor Caligula, who as a child he had seen running around the camp.[22]

Caecina, like Blaesus, is partly blamed by Tacitus for the mutiny by allowing his soldiers free time during the mourning period, as this was when the 'mischief began'.[23] Both, however, continued to pursue illustrious careers after the mutiny. Little blame was attached to their actions by Tiberius. Caecina was an experienced and brave general, having spent four years suppressing the Illyrian revolt under

Tiberius. In AD 7, he won a victory near Sirmium, then he threw back an invasion into his province of Moesia by Dacians and Sarmatians. He was a military man to his core, with thirty-nine years of active service behind him. From AD 15–16, he campaigned beyond the Rhine, earning accolades both for his bravery and his victory over Arminius in the Battle of the Long Causeways. He was not a man to lose his nerve when faced with mutiny, but he knew when to delay and when to fight. Now was the time to avoid battle, even if it cost the lives of many of his centurions.[24]

All four legions in the camp at Novaesium were now unified under the command of the unnamed leaders of the mutiny. Commands issued by Caecina, the legates, the Camp Prefect and the tribunes were ignored. Instead, 'watches, patrols, every duty which circumstances indicated as vital, the mutineers distributed amongst themselves'.[25] The Germans beyond the Rhine were aware of the mutiny, so the legions remained watchful. The ghost of Varus and his army was ever-present. The legionaries had lost kin and friends in the Teutoburg Forest, and any who hadn't still considered those who had fallen members of their own family. Even Caecina, when surrounded by hordes in the swamps of Germania in AD 15, dreamt that 'he saw Quintilius Varus, risen, blood-bedraggled, from the marsh, and hearing him calling, though he refused to obey and pushed him back when he extended his hand'.[26] This existential threat commanded the attention of the legions of Lower Germany as much as their demands. They were not a rabble but remained a disciplined force, making their threat even more potent. The legions of Upper Germany, meanwhile, were also in a rebellious mood. The governor, Gaius Silius, did not dare attempt to make them take the oath to Tiberius. Instead, they watched and waited.[27]

Germanicus was in Belgica when he received the news that Augustus was dead. He immediately administered the new oath of allegiance to his escort and the towns in the area. He then received a message that the legions of Lower Germany had mutinied and immediately hurried to the camp at Noveasium. As custom dictated, he was met outside the camp by the legionaries, who were silent and without their armour. However, 'as soon as he entered the lines, a jangle of complaints began to assail his ears. Some of the men seized his hand, and with a pretence of kissing it pushed the fingers between their lips, so that he should touch their toothless gums; others showed him limbs bent and bowed with age.'[28] These were the disgruntled veterans who were at the very heart of the mutiny.

Germanicus ascended the tribunal on the parade ground and the soldiers gathered around him. With no tribunes or centurions to impose order, and no standards to assemble around, they stood like a crowd at the games rather than an army. Germanicus, determined to assert his authority from the start, 'commanded them to divide into companies: they told him they could hear better as they were. At least, he insisted, bring the ensigns forward; there must be something to distinguish the cohorts: they obeyed, but slowly.'[29] This was the first of many compromises.

The soldiers stood behind their standards in silence, ready for the *adlocutio* to begin. The prince was in a perilous situation. Many of those before him hoped he would lead them to Rome and overthrow Tiberius.[30] Their support could be bought through the granting of their demands. The prince was in no real physical danger, yet politically he stood on the precipice. Tiberius was by nature distrustful and suspicious. Germanicus had to avoid giving any credence to claims made by his enemies that his loyalty was questionable, his allegiance to his adopted father uncertain. Both knew each other well. Germanicus was the heir. Time would bring him the throne, so 'the nearer Germanicus stood to supreme ambition, the more energy he threw into the cause of Tiberius'.[31] What Germanicus wanted was to lead his father's armies into Germany, to march in the footsteps of Nero Drusus and avenge Varus, whose defeat had put the conquest of Germania into doubt. The soldiers assembled before him were the weapons he hoped to wield in attaining glory.

The speech began with fulsome praise of Augustus and Tiberius, 'keeping his liveliest praise for the laurels he had won in the Germanies at the head of those very legions'.[32] Some of the time-served veterans would have campaigned under Tiberius from 8–7 BC after the death of Nero Drusus. His army reached the Elbe and destroyed the Sicambri. The survivors were settled on the banks of the Rhine, whilst Tiberius was awarded a triumph in Rome.[33] Those standing before Germanicus who had fought then would have been in the ranks for at least twenty-one years. The rest would remember Tiberius as the brutal disciplinarian, hardening the city troops or the conscripts from Rome raised after the defeat of Varus. Both groups continued to listen in respectful silence, but gradually their anger manifested in 'suppressed murmurs'.[34]

Germanicus moved on to 'the unanimity of Italy and the loyalty of the Gallic provinces, the absence everywhere of turbulence or disaffection'.[35] This they would have known to be patently untrue. The legions of Upper Germany were ready to support a revolt with Germanicus at their head, and they may have received reports of unrest in the Pannonian legions. After all, Vibulenus knew that the Lower German legions had mutinied when he claimed his brother had been sent as a messenger to them, but had been murdered by Blaesus' gladiators.[36]

Germanicus continued, disregarding the changing mood of the crowd. He now 'touched on the mutiny and asked where was their soldierly obedience? Where the discipline, once their glory? Wither had they driven their tribunes – their centurions?' This was too much. The soldiers close to the tribunal tore off their tunics and showed the prince the scars earned in battle, their badges of courage. Others turned to show him the marks of the lash, the symbols of injustice. Germanicus had ignored their justifiable grievances. Some shouted out their demands. One voice called for a pay increase, another railed at the severity of the work, and others complained of the bribes they were expected to pay centurions for release from duty. The veterans were the most voracious, demanding their immediate release after some had served more than thirty years. All insisted on the distribution of the gratuity included in Augustus' will. Germanicus was losing control. The crowd was transformed; it now resembled a mob from Rome's ampitheatres.[37]

From the back, hidden by the crowd – and no doubt pre-planned – came a chorus of abuse aimed at Tiberius. Then others saluted Germanicus as their emperor.[38] The multitude would have taken up a rhythmic chant, with more and more drawn in. They were ready if Germanicus made a bid for the throne. After much futile pleading, Germanicus attempted to frustrate their attempt to acclaim him emperor by jumping from the platform and forcing his way through the ranks. The soldiers barred his way, refusing to move, drawing their weapons to force him back onto the tribunal. Theatrically, the prince drew his sword and threatened to kill himself, shouting that he would rather die than turn traitor. Some of the soldiers grabbed his arm to prevent him from plunging it into his own body. They were convinced he would have done so. Some of the crowd then pushed forward, revelling in their power, and urged him to strike home. In the chaos, a legionary stepped forward and drew his blade, offering it to Germanicus 'with the commendation that "it was sharper"'. The act was so shocking that the soldiers drew back. There was a pause as the men realized that events had spun out of control. Germanicus seized the opportunity and, surrounded by his friends, was rushed into the comparative safety of his pavilion.[39]

The prince and the leaders of the mutiny were at an impasse. The German legions identified with Germanicus, but their offer to raise him to the purple had been emphatically rejected.[40] They realized that the insult to their commander's *dignitas* made it unlikely that their demands would be met. Germanicus called a *concilium* to take the opinions of his *amici* and Caecina. Informants within the camp reported troubling news. Messengers were being sent to the Upper German legions to persuade them to join the mutiny, with the incentive of a joint attack on Cologne, the capital of the Ubii. These were a Germanic tribe who had been settled as Roman allies on the western bank of the Rhine by M. Vipsanius Agrippa in 39 BC. However, to the legionaries they were Germans, and thus 'marked out for destruction'. Once the legions had pillaged their Germanic allies, they planned to fall upon the Gallic provinces to loot and plunder. Germanicus was also aware that the tribes beyond the Rhine knew of the mutiny and were gathering to cross the river if it was left without a garrison.[41]

Meanwhile, the auxiliary cohorts remained loyal, as did the Roman cavalry, who considered themselves superior to legionaries. Germanicus discussed using these to bring the legionaries into line. However, using provincial forces against Roman citizens would be a dangerous precedent, 'nothing less than an act of civil war'. Nor was it safe for the legions to leave the Rhine forts unmanned and ransack imperial territory. Germanicus also planned to use these soldiers in his invasion of Germany to restore his father's legacy. He understood that the mutineers had remained loyal to his name, if not Tiberius. His position was very different to that of Drusus in Pannonia. Germanicus revelled in his reputation amongst the German legions, one of which even bore his name.[42]

Once 'all the arguments had been revolved and balanced, it was decided to have letters written in the name of the emperor, directing that all men who had served twenty years should be finally discharged; that any who had served sixteen should be released from duty and kept with the colours under no obligation beyond that of assisting to repel an enemy; and that the legacies should be paid and doubled'. This was not a consequence of a flawed personality who instinctively sought compromise and conciliation, rather than conflict and division; this was a cool calculation. All were aware that the legionaries would realize this was a forgery, otherwise Germanicus would have referred to it when he had addressed the soldiers upon his arrival in the camp. The mutineers would understand that Germanicus was playing a game. The concessions had been offered in Tiberius' name as Germanicus had no authority to make them, but he also wanted to avoid accusations of treason. Implicitly, however, they carried the sanction of Germanicus, and it was understood the prince would honour this commitment.[43]

The offer divided the mutiny. The veterans were at its heart, and they had achieved their aims. Many were former *Vigiles* and soldiers in the Urban Cohorts, whose terms of service had been ignored in the aftermath of the Varian emergency. Those veterans retained in the reserve could be sent to another province under the pretence of a barbarian incursion. The doubling of Augustus' donative was, however, extraordinary, and was meant to sate any desire for plunder. The promised money also bound the men to Germanicus. He now had his army to attack the German tribes.

Another *adlocutio* was held. This time, Germanicus was met with a respectful silence that befitted his status. He read the fake letter to the ranks, who 'saw that all this was invented for the occasion'. The mutineers were concerned that Tiberius would receive reports of Germanicus' actions and veto the promises. The veterans were therefore discharged at once by the tribunes. Two of the four legions wanted the money promised to be paid immediately rather than in their permanent fort. They too knew Tiberius might rescind the promised donative. The *V Alaudae* and *XXI Rapax* legions refused to move until they were paid. Consequently, Germanicus and his *amici* used their funds stored in travelling chests to distribute the cash. This was the surest way to quell the unrest and secure Germanicus' popularity with these legions.[44]

Caecina then led the *I Germanica* and *XX Valeria Victrix* legions with the discharged veterans to Cologne, whilst the *V Alaudae* and *XXI Rapax* marched under their legates to Vetera. In the meantime, Germanicus rushed to Upper Germany to administer the oath to the legions there. The Second, Thirtieth and Sixteenth took the vow without any incident, but the Fourteenth hesitated. Once they had been offered the same terms as those accepted by the legions of Lower Germany, they also took the oath to Tiberius. The mutiny had been extinguished and the Upper German legions returned to obedience. Germanicus returned to his headquarters at Cologne.[45]

Unlike Tiberius' son, Drusus, Germanicus had not been able to use the eclipse to his advantage. No mention is made of it. Low clouds may have hidden it from view. Germanicus had dealt with a far more dangerous situation than that faced by Drusus. There were more legions involved, and Drusus was never going to be offered the throne by the soldiers as he enjoyed no connection to Augustus apart from through his father. Nor did he possess any military reputation. Both had acted with courage and worked to divide support for the mutiny, but Germanicus demonstrated more alacrity. His gesture of suicide was not a hysterical response, only being made to counter the offer of the throne.[46]

Unquestioning obedience was not restored, nor trust in the decisions made by superiors. A detachment of soldiers drawn from the Lower Rhine legions was sent to garrison a fort amongst the Chauci between the River Weser and the Elbe. The spectre of Varus' army walked the forests around them, and these men were not prepared to wait to die. Their commander, Manius Ennius, a Camp prefect, faced a renewal of the mutiny deep inside hostile territory. He quickly executed two leaders, but this earned no more than a brief respite before it erupted again. Ennius fled, but was discovered and dragged before his troops. Knowing his brutal attempt to restore order would likely result in his death, the officer invoked the name of Germanicus. 'It was no camp marshal, he cried, whom they were affronting; it was Germanicus, their general – Tiberius, their emperor.' He then grabbed a standard of one of the cohorts and declared that any man who fell out from the march would be treated as a deserter. With that, he abandoned the fort and led the men back towards the Rhine. The legionaries were angered by being sent to a fort deep in enemy territory with no chance of relief should they come under attack. The mutineers sought safety, and Ennius was probably an experienced commander whom they trusted to lead them successfully through the forests and swamps. United, they successfully fought their way to safety.[47]

The legionaries retained a deep-seated mistrust of the elite. Around 7 October, the soldiers at Cologne heard news that a senatorial delegation had arrived in the town. A rumour spread that the senators had been sent by Tiberius to cancel the promises made in the forged letter. Their real purpose was to inform Germanicus that the Senate had renewed his proconsular *imperium*. The veterans who had been allocated to the reserve were in Cologne under their new standards. Already 'nervous' at the thought of a senatorial commission reversing the concessions, they now feared an immediate return to the ranks. Munatius Plancus, a consul in the previous year, was believed to have introduced this legislation into the Senate. With every added detail, the rumour grew in believability. As night fell, the veterans gathered – probably in the inns – and fuelled by drink, they decided to rescue their new standard from Germanicus' headquarters. They thought the standard would guarantee their existence as it embodied their new status. They rushed through the streets to the house Germanicus had made his quarters, but found the doors locked. However, 'they forced the door, and dragging the prince from bed, compelled him on pain of death to hand over the ensign'. Agrippina and their children would have witnessed the threats.[48]

The senators heard the commotion in the streets and unwisely decided to seek safety with Germanicus. Led by Plancus, they made their way through the streets, only to be met by the rioting veterans. They were quickly surrounded, whereupon the insults became increasingly aggressive. All the delegates fled, apart from Plancus, 'whose dignity debarred him from flight'. He realized there was no hope of reaching Germanicus, but the gates of the fort of the First Legion were close by. Although he was admitted, his presence roused these legionnaires into equal fury. The former consul, dignity abandoned, made for the sanctuary of the legionary chapel. Veneration for the eagle meant the chapel where it was kept was revered. He lay on the floor, clasping the legionary eagle and as many of the other standards as he could. The religious sanctity of these should have protected him from the spilling of his blood. Nevertheless, the soldiers attempted to drag him out and then murder him. The *aquilifer* (eagle-bearer), Calpurnius, protected the senator and the sanctity of his standard before his fellow soldiers and the gods. The assault against Plancus would have been seen as 'a crime almost unknown even between enemies – an ambassador of the Roman people would in a Roman camp have defiled with his blood the altars of heaven'.[49]

Calpurnius shielded the senator throughout the night, holding his fellow soldiers at bay. Although ranked as a private, an *aquilifer* was one of the most important posts below the rank of a centurion but above an *optio*. His status was signified by receiving double the pay of a legionary. A legion that lost its eagle to the enemy was disgraced, all its soldiers being given a dishonourable discharge without the gratuity, land or legal privileges of a retired veteran. Consequently, the man chosen to carry the eagle was renowned for his bravery in battle and the respect he commanded. He alone was allowed to wear a lion's fur, with its head strapped to his helmet. Calpurnius stood proud defending his standard and the soldiers' quarry. His prestige was his shield and only defence.[50]

As dawn broke, Calpurnius and his charge were rescued, probably by a cohort of Praetorians, and brought to the tribunal. Germanicus had summoned the *I Germanica*. The prince had probably spent the previous hours gathering his Praetorians who had been quartered in the town and securing the integrity of the *XX Valeria Victrix* legion, which was not involved in the mayhem. He was no doubt grateful to see the senator still alive, as the murder of a former consul and representative of the Senate would have forced him to exact the severest punishment on the men assembled in front of him. The *adlocutio* allowed him to reassert his authority and gauge the mood of the men.[51]

Germanicus decided to shame the soldiers but avoided blaming them. With Plancus standing beside him on the tribunal, Germanicus addressed the crowd, rebuking the 'fatal madness, rekindled not so much by their own anger as by that of heaven'.[52] Blaming the gods shifted the responsibility away from the soldiers' actions but reminded them of their impiety in attacking a man seeking sanctuary. He then explained the reasons for the senator's visit and the rights and status of the man standing beside him. He expounded on the disgrace they had brought on the First Legion and then dismissed the delegation, announcing that they would be guarded by auxiliary cavalry rather than legionaries. This was meant as a further rebuke to their honour. He dismissed the soldiers, 'after reducing his hearers to stupor, if not to peace'.[53] Their temper remained volatile, so he decided to dishonour them further with another emotive move. The indiscipline of the veterans who had invaded his living quarters also needed addressing.

Germanicus spent the next hours planning for the departure of his family and the wives of the other officers. This would not happen in the dead of night in a clandestine operation to guard their safety, but in the full light of day. There being no real threat to them, he arranged for their withdrawal to be a performance to tear at the heartstrings. Agrippina was supposedly against it, declaring that she was the 'descendant of the deified Augustus, and danger would not find her degenerate'. She possessed a forceful personality and strong determination, which she amply demonstrated in her later political battles with Tiberius and Sejanus. Like her demonstrative husband, she possessed the ability to deliver dramatic performances. The scene they painted was based on a defeated enemy forced to leave their sacked city.[54]

The carriages began their slow progress through the town. There was no escort. This was an affront to her status as the wife of the imperial heir. There would have been Praetorians with Germanicus, but they remained idle. The soldiers were raised from their barracks and duties by the wails and cries of a host of women. At their head was Agrippina, pregnant, with the infant Gaius. The men asked where they were going. They said they were to stay at Augusta Treverorum, the capital of the Gallic Treveri. They were fleeing from the disgraceful behaviour of Roman citizens to place themselves in the unpredictable hands of foreigners; their commander had sent his family away from them. 'There followed shame and pity and memories of her father Agrippa, of Augustus, her grandfather. She was the daughter-in-law of Drusus, herself a wife of notable fruitfulness and shining chastity. There was also her little son, born in the camp and bred the playmate of the legions; whom soldier-like they had dubbed "Bootikins" – Caligula.' The greatest disgrace, though, was their destination. However, there existed a more sinister possibility for Germanicus sending his family away. A collective punishment could now be applied to innocent and guilty alike. It needed only to be implied. Panic ensued.[55]

Some men ran to obstruct their exit, but most ran to the commander's living quarters. He was waiting for them. His speech was prepared and his terms for accepting their forgiveness were ready. They implored him to instruct his wife and son to return. He played the mob, saying that whilst he was prepared to risk his own life by remaining with the soldiers, he would not risk the lives of his wife and son. Were they indeed soldiers when they had threatened the lives of the descendants of Augustus and ambassadors of the Senate? He then offered the incentive for returning to obedience. He would lead them in avenging Varus and his lost legions in an invasion of Germany, invoking the names of Augustus and Nero Drusus. Their shame and dishonour would be purged in the glory of victory and the pillaging and destruction of their enemies. That future was conditional on allowing the senatorial delegation to leave, as well as his wife and child. Most importantly, he demanded they hand over their leaders for punishment in return for their return to allegiance.[56]

As in Pannonia, the soldiers were keen to cleanse their involvement in the mutiny by abandoning the men who had led them. This was an act of self-cleansing as well as a desperate attempt to avoid collective punishment. Germanicus listened to their pleas. They begged him to punish the guilty, forgive those who had joined the mutiny and allow his family to remain in Cologne. He compromised, saying the winter on the Rhine would be too harsh for his pregnant wife, but he relented by allowing his son to remain with him. However, to absolve himself of any responsibility for the brutality that he knew his restoration of order and discipline would entail, he demanded that what was needed to be done, should be done by them. He did not want to compromise the devotion of the soldiers.[57]

The men scattered, hunting down their former leaders. Some they murdered, whilst others they threw into chains. An assembly of the two legions was then called, with the legate of the *I Germanica*, Gaius Caetronius, sat on the tribunal. His legion had taken the lead in the disturbance, and he was attempting to restore the prince's trust in his abilities. The legate of the *XX Valeria Victrix* was notable by his absence; he wanted no part in the proceedings. Germanicus also removed himself from the bloodlust to come. The soldiers 'were stationed in front with drawn swords; the accused was displayed on the platform by a tribune; if they cried "Guilty", he was thrown down and hacked to death. The troops revelled in the butchery, which they took as an act of purification; nor was Germanicus inclined to restrain them – the orders had been none of his, and the perpetrators of the cruelty would have to bear its odium.' This was a variation on the punishment of decimation, where every tenth man selected at random was beaten to death by members of his century.[58]

The veterans were treated in the same way and, as they were at the centre of the unrest, were then sent away to Raetia, which was supposedly threatened by a barbarian invasion. The terms of the agreement with them had been kept and their former leaders were all dead at their hands. They meekly marched away and disappeared from the pages of history.[59]

Both legions lacked centurions. Many had been murdered in the initial uprising, but many more had escaped. These officers were the foundations on which the legion functioned. However, Germanicus did not want to reignite the mutiny by reappointing those who had used unrestrained brutality or rapacious bribery. He recognized that they had genuine grievances. Some, however, were respected and experienced officers who would be needed for the campaign in Germany. A solution needed to be found to restore discipline and retain the loyalty of the legions to him.[60]

He decided to adapt the assembly employed to punish the leaders of the mutiny. This time he would be present. There was a precedent. A commander's assembly, or *contio*, was sometimes used, where soldiers could shout out complaints. However, it had never been used to assign centurions.[61]

One by one, the surviving centurions were brought onto the tribunal before the soldiers. Germanicus was using his status and standing with the men to select those he wished to retain, and those he was prepared to sacrifice. The tribunes had no doubt also been given his list. Each stood and 'gave his name, company, and country; the number of his campaigns, his distinctions in battle and his military decorations, if any'. Those officers renowned for their leadership and bravery would have worn their scars with pride and pointed to their awards on their armour. Some would have worn a crown for being the first over an enemy palisade or wall, while others had a golden torc around their necks or a gold band around their arm for bravery. More had discs on their breastplate for distinguished conduct in the heat of battle. When Germanicus gave a citation indicating his approval, the tribunes led a shout of approval and the man was retained. Those falling short, who had a reputation for 'cruelty or rapacity', were condemned with a lacklustre commendation and were immediately dismissed with a dishonourable discharge.[62]

Germanicus now turned his attention to the *V Alaudae* and *XXI Rapax* at Vetera, who remained mutinous. Caecina was struggling to enforce his commands and no new centurions had been appointed to restore discipline. They were aware that *I Germanica* and *XX Valeria Victrix* at Cologne had been brought into line, but they continued with their discord, unhappy with the terms in the forged letter on which Germanicus had staked his reputation. They probably wanted a pay increase. Germanicus gathered ships and auxiliary cohorts from along the Rhine and prepared to travel the 60 miles to their fort. He also had eight cavalry *alae* 'whose discipline had not been affected by the late mutiny'.[63]

Once the forces had been gathered together, Germanicus made one last attempt to avoid direct responsibility for the confrontation. He despatched a letter to Caecina, informing him that he was 'coming in strength, and, unless they forestall him by executing the culprits, would put them impartially to the sword'. He threatened decimation. Germanicus had once more placed responsibility for the restoration of order upon the shoulders of another. Caecina summoned a *concilium* devoid of legates, tribunes and centurions. He read the letter to two *aquilifers*, *signifers*, *optiones* and other men he felt he could trust. Their position in the military hierarchy made them amenable. He explained that unless they took immediate action, their lives were in danger, for 'when war threatens, the innocent and the guilty fall side by side'. They also knew that promotion to centurion was a certain reward for averting a crisis. Motivated, these well-connected junior officers sampled the extent of support for the leaders of the mutiny, finding that most of both legions remained 'dutiful'. It was these officers, not Caecina, who organized the purge of opposition. Caecina gave his assent but wanted to avoid the odium associated with the shedding of the blood of fellow citizens.[64]

The officers knew who they could approach to help them. Weapons were distributed in the middle of the night when all were asleep. The 'most objectional and active of the incendiaries' were targeted for death. At the given signal, they descended upon their unsuspecting victims. However, most of the soldiers were unaware of the plan, and all control was lost. Chaos and mayhem resulted as they gathered their weapons to defend themselves or their tent mates. Soon everyone realized what was happening and took sides. The surviving leaders of the mutiny also distributed weapons and took command of their supporters. Civil war thus broke out inside the walls of a legionary camp. Missiles flew, units formed up, charged and made to kill their comrades or were cut down instead. Many would have not known on whose side they were fighting, but merely defended a friend or companion. There were no generals, tribunes or centurions to call a halt to the slaughter. Weariness and dawn brought an end.[65]

When Germanicus arrived around 19 October, he broke down in tears. 'This is not a cure, but a calamity,' he declared. The statement is revealing. He, like Drusus and Rome's elite, believed the mutineers were infected by a madness or disease that required brutal remedy. The contagion had been cut out and the disease eradicated. He ordered the dead to be cremated. Mutineers and soldiers loyal to their commander burned together. No one knew or cared on which side they had fought and died.[66]

There were now many ghosts to be exorcized from the collective memory of the Rhine legions. To re-establish an *esprit de corps* and assert his authority, Germanicus ordered an invasion of Germany, even though the campaigning season was virtually over. The soldiers focused their anger on the inhabitants across the Rhine. Thousands were slaughtered, including women and children. Plunder and blood exculpated their madness as they purified themselves at the point of the sword [67]

Germanicus now continued his father's war. He and Caecina earned renown for their military ability but also for their courage and bravery. The shades of Varus and his lost legions were also laid to rest. Six years after that defeat, Germanicus led his army to what remained of the battle site. Dismembered skeletons of Roman soldiers still littered the forest floor. In some places where the soldiers had stood, the bones were piled up; in others where they fled, they lay scattered. Skulls were nailed to tree trunks. Survivors who witnessed the massacre and still served in the ranks toured the battlefield. Varus, wounded, had taken his own life rather than be captured and sacrificed to the German gods. The eagles had been seized and, in the groves, captured officers were tortured and hung. The remains of three legions were collected and buried under a huge funeral mound. Germanicus then gathered his legions and paid tribute to the departed, connecting to their grief.[68]

They were his legions. They loved him. He had courted them, carefully protecting his image and avoided any blame that might tarnish his lustre. His reputation then spread. When he returned to Rome in AD 16, Tiberius ordered only two of the Praetorian cohorts in the capital to give him a guard of honour. However, all of them disobeyed imperial orders and marched out to meet him. Germanicus died in AD 19, never ascending the throne offered to him by the

German legions. When Agrippina returned to Italy from Syria with his ashes, she was met by a huge crowd of mourners at the port of Brundisium. Many of them were former soldiers who had served under him and were distraught with grief.[69]

The soldiers did not benefit from the new terms of service. Although Tiberius extended the concessions granted by Germanicus to the Pannonian legions in AD 14, in the following year he took advantage of a senatorial debate on taxation to declare the state was unable to bear the cost of maintaining the legions unless the soldiers served for twenty years. The revised regulations were arrogantly published on bronze tablets. Seven years later, the emperor would complain to the Senate about a lack of volunteers for the Roman Army. Tiberius also planned to go to the provinces to supervise the discharge of veterans, whose numbers were so large that the governors were reluctant to act by themselves. However, he remained in Rome. Legionaries continued to serve for twenty-five years or longer. The security of the Empire depended on these legions, but Tiberius felt his security depended upon the favour of the aristocracy. Both mutinies in AD 14 were a result of Augustus' failure to provide sufficient financial resources to maintain his military policy. Tiberius, balancing military unrest, financial constraints and a disaffected Senate, compared the governing of the Empire to 'holding a wolf by the ears'. It was an impossible challenge that few emperors ever solved.[70]

Chapter 3

The Revolt of Sacrovir and Florus (AD 20–21)

> 'For, though his campaigns in Gaul did not last for as much as ten complete years, in this time he took by storm more than 800 cities, subdued 300 nations, and fought pitched battles at various times with three million men, of whom he destroyed one million in actual fighting and took another million prisoners.'
>
> (Plutarch, *Life of Ceasar*, 15.5)

Although Plutarch may exaggerate the figures, they do indicate the true horror that the Roman conquest unleashed on the population of Gaul. A new order had arisen with Caesar's conquests between 58 and 50 BC. Hundreds of thousands were killed, and hundreds of thousands more were enslaved out of a population estimated to be between six and ten million. Many chieftains lost their lives or had their wealth confiscated. A new elite arose from the slaughter and the ashes. These were men who had supported Caesar in his conquest and were rewarded with Roman citizenship, land and wealth. They bore the name 'Julius' with pride, almost like a title, denoting their ancestor's receipt of citizenship from the dictator or his successor, Augustus. This new Gallic aristocracy was intensely loyal to the man who had given them wealth and status, a loyalty that was inherited by his imperial successors who bore his name.[1]

Seventy years of Romanization had transformed Gallic society. The fortified hill forts were rapidly abandoned for new villages at the foot of these hilltop sites or in expanded urban centres like Lugdunum, Narbonne, Arles or Vienne. These grew as trading and distribution centres for pottery, wine, olive oil and fish preserves, creating wealth for a new mercantile class. The Celtic language disappeared and was replaced by Latin, except in graffiti or potsherds. Diet, building techniques, pottery design and clothing underwent significant change. The Gallic elite no longer demonstrated their wealth in huge public feasts, but instead in traditional Roman education, public building projects, villas and banquets. They were competing for the respect of their peers and Roman officials rather than their dependants. The status and honour that was once earned in war now had to be earned in peace. Advancement for a Gallic noble no longer depended on popular approval but on the patronage of a senator, governor or procurator, or the emperor himself. This Gallo-Roman aristocracy appear to have turned their backs on their fellow tribesmen.[2]

Yet away from the heavily Romanized Narbonensis and Aquitania in the south, in the militarized zone along the Rhine and the urban centres along the Rhone Valley, older traditions remained strong. Augustus had divided Gaul into three provinces – Aquitania, Belgica and Lugdunensis. However, the Gauls never described themselves in inscriptions as either Gallic or members of a province. Instead, they defined themselves as members of the tribe or *civitas* of the Remi, or the Aedui. These areas had experienced only limited military occupation and had few developed urban centres. Some members of the Treveri and Lingones nobility continued to be buried in tumuli, whilst others were interred in mausoleums. Roman customs were not embraced by all. In these areas, the local aristocracies were reluctant to venture beyond their local power base and the tribe continued to dominate all spheres of life.[3]

Caesar had made separate treaties with these tribes. Some were made after he had defeated them, others on favourable terms to reward allies. Among these were the Lingones and Aedui. However, it is unclear which were free (*libarae*) and which were exempt from taxation (*immunes*), as the literary evidence often conflicts with the epigraphic as their status changed over time.[4] The provision of auxiliary troops was part of these terms. Gauls provided around 65 per cent of the auxiliary strength of the western provinces with twenty-eight cavalry and seventy-six infantry divisions, but most were commanded by Roman officers. Most units drew soldiers from all the Gallic provinces, the majority being recruited from Lugdunensis, Aquitania and the Treveri. Some *civitates* like the Treveri retained a cavalry division enlisted solely from their tribe.[5] Auxiliaries received less pay than Roman citizens serving in the legions, their terms of service were less favourable and they did not receive donatives or any discharge bonuses. They had little in common with the legions they served with and had not joined in the legionary mutiny on the Rhine. Germanicus even considered using them to suppress the recalcitrant legions at Vetera before they were induced to slaughter their own.

Peace brought more insidious aspects of the Roman government to Gaul. Three censuses were carried out to establish taxation in these conquered lands in 27 BC, 12 BC and finally, under Germanicus, in AD 14. This was an entirely new concept to the Gallic population. Previously, they were mainly free from taxation. Money was only paid voluntarily after a communal or tribal vote for a specific purpose and for a limited time. This freedom was replaced by the slavery of forced contributions to a distant emperor. Furthermore, the appearance of huge villas all over Gaul, supported by vast estates, possibly indicated the disappearance of independent farmers, who were forcibly evicted or had their land seized by creditors or local landowners.[6]

Roman soldiers spread over the lands. Roads were constructed, and there followed Roman traders and businessmen offering loans to a naïve and credulous population. Some would have borrowed to maintain their ostentatious lifestyle, competing with their peers. Others were exploited without the means to seek redress. In AD 28, the Frisians were forced into revolt by extortionate seizures collected by the Roman Army as tribute. The tribute was originally made in hides of domesticated cattle, but a Roman centurion decided to base the levy on the hides of much larger aurochs. Failure to pay led firstly to the confiscation of their goods and property; first 'their cattle only, next their lands, finally the persons of their wives and children, were handed over to servitude'. The governor had appointed a centurion, so any complaints would have been dismissed by a military court.[7]

Many probably struggled to meet the financial demands of Rome's officials, who were often entirely ignorant of native customs and lacked effective supervision. One of the most notorious was Julius Licinius, who used his knowledge of Gallic society to exploit its elite. He had been enslaved during Caesar's conquest of Gaul, then freed, and his services were inherited by Augustus, with whom he maintained a close relationship. At some point before 15 BC, the emperor made him procurator in Gaul, responsible for the financial administration of imperial lands in the province. Licinius plundered the country for years. Its suffering was compared to the plundering and destruction of a barbarian invasion. He 'went so far that in some cases where people paid their tribute by the month, he made the months fourteen in number, declaring the month called December was really the tenth, and for that reason, they must reckon two more (which he called the eleventh and twelfth respectively) as the last, and contributed the money that was due for these months'.[8]

This corruption only came to the notice of Augustus when he toured Gaul and the provincial nobility were able to gain access to him. Licinius gave gifts to his friends or *amici* to ensure that reports of his dishonesty never reached Rome. These recipients would no doubt have included the governors of the provinces, legates of the legions and other imperial officials. He even gave vast sums to the emperor himself. According to the rules of *amicitiae* that formed the basis of Roman society, they were obligated to him. Even when the evidence against him was overwhelming, the emperor was reluctant to take any action but eventually summoned him. Realizing that mere denial would not suffice in his defence, Licinius admitted his guilt before Augustus, claiming he 'gathered all this purposefully, master, for you and the rest of the Romans, lest the natives, by having so much money should revolt'. A donation to the imperial treasury helped his cause and the freedman was allowed to retire to Rome, surrounded by his vast riches, estates and villas. Long after his death, he remained synonymous with the archetypal greedy, corrupt and avaricious imperial freedman, who was inevitably able to retain his ill-gotten wealth. He was an extreme but by no means a unique example of corruption.[9]

Licinius had only been exposed by the emperor's visit to the province. No member of the imperial family had toured Gaul or the German provinces since Germanicus was recalled to Rome in AD 16. Furthermore, Germanicus' German campaigns had put a huge strain on the resources of Gaul. In AD 15, Caecina had lost much of his baggage train, including animals, carts and equipment in a difficult return to Roman territory. In the following year, the fleet had been destroyed in a storm whilst returning from the North Sea. Losses needed replacing quickly.[10]

The financial difficulties inherited from Augustus compelled Tiberius to amend previous treaties and privileges, '[making] many states and individuals forfeit their ancient immunities and mineral rights, and the privilege of collecting taxes'. It seems that the Aedui, Rome's oldest allies in Gaul, may have lost their immunity from taxation. They had looked to Rome for protection in their rivalry with the neighbouring Sequani, their leaders embracing Romanization. Around 13 BC, they agreed to move their capital, Bibracte, to a new location 25 miles away at Augustodunum (modern Autun), meaning 'the fortress of Augustus'. The name was chosen to honour the emperor, containing a mixture of the emperor's name and their Gallic identity. In return, they were the only town in the new Gallic provinces permitted to build a wall, with fortress towers and four gates enclosing its 200 hectares. Huge amounts of money were invested by the Aeduan nobility in this monumental architecture to rival the buildings at the provincial capital of Lugdunum (Lyons), 100 miles to the south. Any loss of financial immunities would have crippled many who had invested in a Roman future. They also established a college, which drew the children of the great Gallic nobility eager to demonstrate their new status with a classical education.[11]

Desperation fired the hearts of 'any wretch whose beggary and guilty fears made crime a necessity'.[12] News of the death of Germanicus in October AD 19 stirred hopes of success among the rebels, but eight legions on the Rhine could strike rapidly into the heartland of Gaul and so checked any thoughts of revolt. However, rumours spread from Syria that the prince had been poisoned by the governor of Syria, Calpurnius Piso, and that Tiberius played some part in his death. The German legions thus became mutinous, boosting hope that they might openly rebel. The Gallic rebels reasoned that this 'was an unequalled opportunity for regaining their independence'.[13]

Independence, however, was not the primary aim of the revolt, but rather relief from relentless taxation, debt and corruption. Support was drawn from 'the heavily indebted communities of the Gallic provinces', although Narbonensis and Aquitania remained aloof. At secret assemblies, the leaders drew upon the resentment caused by 'the continuous tributes, the grinding rates of interest, the cruelty and pride of governors'.[14] Tiberius had ignored tribal immunities, introducing a supposedly temporary tribute to pay for Germanicus' campaigns and alleviate an increasingly fraught financial crisis. This measure remained in place long after Germanicus had departed, and this hardship was now coupled with high interest rates. The two leaders of the revolt were members of the Romano-Gallic elite – Julius Florus, a noble of the Treveri, and Julius Sacrovir of the Aedui; 'each was a man of birth, with ancestors whose services had been rewarded by Roman citizenship in years when Roman citizenship was rare and bestowed upon merit only'. Their ancestors probably received citizenship from Julius Caesar, so were likely third-generation Roman citizens and therefore thoroughly Romanized. [15]

Tribal politics also played a part. Florus had a bitter rival amongst the Treveri in Julius Indus, who remained steadfastly pro-Roman.[16] Both had a large number of clients and supporters, and could raise significant tribal forces. Julius Sacrovir was also a commander of an Aeduan auxiliary unit, denoting his prestige and status in his community. Tribal leaders retained a military function seventy years after the Roman conquest of Gaul.[17]

Beneath the veneer of the Roman administration, the Gallic social and political structures remained strong but faced significant stress from pressures to adhere to Roman social, cultural and political norms. Late Iron Age institutions and religious practices survived, cloaked in Roman constructions. Sacred groves now contained statues of Roman gods, with ceremonies officiated by a *sacredos* rather than the normal *flamen*. Other Gallo-Roman officials recorded on inscriptions at the Sanctuary of the Three Gauls at Lugdunum included an *iudex* (judge), an *allectus arcae Galliarum* and an *inquisitor Galliarum* (both treasury officials). Native revolts often occurred at this point in the process of Romanization, where the old social, religious and political order was threatened but remained intact.[18]

Druids had been central to resistance to Rome. This priestly class were the noble elite of Gallic society, combining religious duties with lore keepers, political advisors and legal adjudicators. Druids were now being marginalized and suppressed. The college at Augustodunum was meant to draw the next generation of Gallic nobility into the arms of Rome by depriving the druids of their ability to educate the young and remove their influence over religion and politics.[19] Augustus banned any Roman citizens from taking any active role in the religion and Tiberius started to persecute them.[20] The Aeduan,

Julius Sacrovir, may have been particularly affected by these changes; his name translates as 'holy man'. He retained this name to publicize his proud heritage, religious authority and status in the face of the growing persecution. His estates lay close to Augustodunum, and it was here that he possibly hoped to educate the children of the Aeduan elite in the old ways but instead found his role usurped by the college in his town.[21]

The revolt began piecemeal. The Andecavi in the Loire Valley around modern Angers were the first to rebel. The governor of Gallia Lugdunensis, Acilius Aviola, was quick to respond. He commanded the urban cohort at Lugdunum, which was used to garrison the town and guard the imperial mint. He marched them 400 miles and crushed the insurgents. Soon after, the neighbouring tribe of the Turoni based around Tours also rebelled. The governor requested the support of a legionary cohort from the governor of Lower Germany, Visellius Varro. This was joined by several units raised by local Gallic chieftains. The enemy numbers were much larger. One of these auxiliary cohorts was commanded by Julius Sacrovir. His unit was probably raised from his Aeduan followers. Aviola was again victorious and Sacrovir was conspicuous in the battle, urging his men to 'strike for Rome', removing his helmet as he fought against the rebels. He followed in the way of his ancestors, who were proudly buried with their weapons and whose military renown added to their status and prestige.[22]

However, after the battle some of the prisoners identified Sacrovir as a traitor who made 'his identity clear so as to avoid becoming a target for missiles'.[23] It is logical to assume that the captured Gauls might want to incriminate Sacrovir for supporting the Romans, but these claims were taken seriously by Aviola. Sacrovir was detained and interviewed. When asked why he had removed his helmet in the midst of battle, he replied that he wished 'to let his courage be seen'. Martial valour raised the renown of the Gallic elite, who remained obsessed with privilege and rank.[24] A report was dispatched to Tiberius for him to decide on the validity of these claims. The emperor 'rejected the information'. Evidence provided by prisoners of war was untrustworthy. By removing his helmet, Sacrovir appears to have invited death, as his opponents would have been driven to kill him as he cut down their comrades, especially if he was secretly a leader of the rebellion.

Sacrovir had fought with bravery and courage for the Romans, but his reward was a formal investigation into his loyalty, followed by weeks of waiting upon the imperial judgement. If Tiberius had decided otherwise, Sacrovir would have been charged with treason and sent to Rome for trial, with an inevitable outcome. Something broke within him. The summer and autumn of AD 20 saw him take the lead in preparing for a widespread revolt.[25]

Julius Florus, a leading noble amongst the Treveri, was gathering support in his tribe. At some point they became aware of their common aims and agreed that Florus would try to gather additional support from the Belgae and Sacrovir 'amongst less distant Gauls', and probably the Sequani. They organized 'assemblies and conventicles' where they spoke against the continuous demands for tribute, the high interest rates on debts and the corruption of officials. They heard that the Rhine legions were close to revolt and that Rome, heavily reliant on Gallic auxiliaries, would be unable to defeat them. The campaign on the Loire was evidence enough of Rome's reliance on provincial auxiliaries. Sacrovir planned to organize his forces into cohorts and arm them in Roman fashion. He drew upon his experiences in the Roman Army. Weapons were secretly manufactured, which would have been costly and time-consuming. Florus appears to have relied upon native Gallic martial spirit, as his force is described as a 'rabble' and an 'orderless multitude'. Both rebel leaders probably hoped Gallic auxiliary cohorts would join them.[26]

The Treveri were closest to the legions along the Rhine, unlike the more distant Aedui. Their only hope for success was a mutiny amongst the legionaries in response to the alleged murder of Germanicus. The revolt was likely masked as a rising against Tiberius rather than Rome. Debts could be blamed on the emperor's unreasonable financial demands, and the legionaries already hated the emperor and consequently were ready to believe he had conspired with Piso to murder his adopted son. The governor of Upper Germany, Gaius Silius, and his wife had been close *amici* of Germanicus and Agrippina. He would later be charged with treason in AD 24. Was this forlorn hope part of the evidence for the later charges against him?[27]

Florus tried to use hatred of Roman businessmen and the opportunity for plunder to persuade a locally raised auxiliary cohort to join him. However, only a few were won over, the remainder of the soldiers remaining loyal to Rome. The Treveri revolt then burst into the open, but no other Roman auxiliary units joined them. The rebels were dismissed as debtors and dependants of local Gallic nobles. News of the rising took a week to reach Sacrovir at Augustodunum, who seized the town and the sons of the Gallic aristocracy who were studying there at the college. He used these as hostages to guarantee the support of those who were likely to waver or support Rome.[28]

Sacrovir also enlisted many gladiators on the promise of freedom. They were being trained as *Crupellarii*, encased in plate armour from head to foot. They wore a heavy bucket-like helmet which offered significant protection but greatly reduced visibility. In addition, 8,000 men were armed as legionaries and organized in cohorts, but were untrained. Another 32,000 were armed with hunting equipment, mostly spears. These were men from the town and dependants of chieftains who had joined Sacrovir.[29]

The Romans made no move against them, allowing the rebels time to train. This encouraged more to join their ranks; their 'forces were steadily increased: the neighbouring districts had not as yet openly committed themselves, but private enthusiasm ran high'.[30] The governors of both German provinces wanted the prestige of defeating the rebels. Failing to reach an agreement, they asked for instructions from Tiberius on how to conduct the campaign but also who should take overall command. Tiberius would later reassure the Senate that the governors had faithfully followed 'his own policy.'[31]

As it was by now the winter of AD 20/21, communication between Germany and Rome would have been difficult. Tiberius, unwilling to insult either of the two powerful commanders, deferred and allowed them to decide between themselves who should be in charge. The elderly Varro eventually conceded to Silius because he was weak and infirm. However, this was merely an attempt to save face. Varro's son inherited his father's grievance, and three years later would prosecute Silius for treason, claiming that Silius had 'long screened Sacrovir through complicity in his revolt'. He may have suggested the argument had been instigated by Silius as a delaying tactic on behalf of Sacrovir. That was untrue, but by then Tiberius suspected Silius of disloyalty and was unlikely to intervene in the trial.[32] The long delay in moving against the Gauls was used as evidence of treason.

In the meantime, the Sequani had joined the revolt, encouraged by the agents of Sacrovir and the inaction of the Romans. However, the rebel leaders received little support from the Romanized Gallic nobility and none from Gallic auxiliary cohorts. The Romans moved first against the Treveri, legions from Upper and Lower Germany descending on Florus in a pincer movement. In advance of one arm rode the Treveran noble, Julius Indus, with a squadron of cavalry he had raised. Florus retreated to avoid being caught between two armies and headed for the Ardennes. His army would have been no match for the legionaries and he probably hoped to pursue a guerilla campaign from the densely forested region. However, they never reached it. Indus' cavalry fell upon them, and they scattered over the surrounding area. Florus escaped with a small party of followers, but he was eventually trapped and committed suicide. Julius Indus was honoured for his part in the victory, and his cavalry unit was retained by the army and named the *ala Indiana*.[33]

Silius took command of two legions and some auxiliary cavalry. He also raised a detachment of cavalry, which retained his name as a mark of distinction. He advanced on the Sequani, intent on punishing disloyalty. The cavalry devasted the countryside, emptying villages of life, pillaging and raping as they marched towards the neighbouring tribe of the Aedui and their capital at Augustodunum. Archaeologists have discovered widespread destruction layers in eastern Gaul dating from this period.[34] The legionaries despised the Gauls and saw the opportunity to plunder. The two legions competed to reach Augustodunum most swiftly, hoping to be the first into the town. Twelve miles from the tribal capital, they met Sacrovir's army occupying a wide plain. He had placed his gladiators in the centre, with his recently trained cohorts on either wing. Behind was positioned the multitude of partly armed tribesmen. Sacrovir sat resplendent on a horse, surrounded by a group of chieftains.[35]

The Romans quickly moved into battle, with the cavalry on the wings and legionaries in the centre. Sacrovir's cohorts were rapidly cut to pieces on either flank, allowing the cavalry to peel around and attack the ill-armed crowd behind. Only the gladiators held the line in the centre, their armour proving impervious to sword and dagger thrusts. However, they could hardly move and resembled an iron wall rather than a line of infantry. The legionaries attacked them with their entrenching tools, axes, picks and spades, carving open the iron armour to reach the flesh beneath. Others were pushed over with poles and forks. The weight of their armour meant they were unable to rise and defend themselves. As slaves, the gladiators received no mercy.[36]

As Sacrovir's army rapidly disintegrated before his eyes, he turned and fled. Firstly, he made for the safety of the walled town. However, realizing it could not be held, he left for his villa nearby. Understanding that escape was impossible, he and his followers chose a noble death. Sacrovir stabbed himself, whilst his companions killed each other. The villa was then set on fire so their bodies would not be desecrated by the victors.[37]

The Romans then took their revenge on the Aedui. The property of the leading Gallic nobility was confiscated. Some were charged with keeping too much of their wealth as cash, which could have been used to pay troops or produce weapons.[38] Silius and his wife gorged themselves on the wealth of the area and were later charged with extortion. According to Tacitus, there was no doubt they were 'inextricably involved' with those officials exacting as much as possible from the provincials.[39] The Treveri were also punished to discourage any future tribes from resorting to insurrection, despite the role of Julius Indus in supporting the Roman cause. They lost a huge amount of land between Bingen and Koblenz.[40]

Sacrovir, and possibly Florus, were members of a militarized Romanized elite who drew their authority from their position in Gallic society. Sacrovir revelled in the ancient Gallic warrior tradition He led the attack on the Turoni and removed his helmet so all could see his prowess and bravery. However, neither leader of the revolt fought to preserve a threatened political or social order.[41] Their primary motivation appears entirely personal. Sacrovir felt his dignity and honour had been slighted after being accused of siding with the rebels after he helped the Romans achieve victory over the Turoni, whilst Florus' position amongst his tribe was threatened by a rival who had the support of Rome. Their army consisted mainly of their dependants and others who had fallen into debt or suffered at the hands of corrupt Roman officials. The revolt was not essentially anti-Roman but a reaction against exploitation and taxation. Liberty and independence were perceived as freedom from these new tributes and fiscal burdens. Sacrovir and Florus died as Gallic warriors, leaving a permanent mark in the annals.[42]

Chapter 4

The Revolt of Vindex and Galba (AD 68)

'He began by reciting a poem on the stage: then, as the crowd clamoured for him to "display all his accomplishments" (the exact phrase used), he entered the theatre, observing the full rules of the harp – not to sit down when weary, not to wipe away the sweat except with the robe he was wearing, to permit no discharge from the mouth or nostrils to be visible. Finally, on bended knee, a hand kissed in salutation to that motley gathering, he awaited the verdict of the judges in feigned trepidation.'

(Nero's performance on the lyre at the Neronia, described by Tacitus, *Annals*, 16.4)

Nero's public performances were deeply offensive to Rome's elite. Actors and musicians, along with gladiators and charioteers, were considered a low social status equivalent to criminals and prostitutes. An emperor performing on stage insulted the dignity of the imperial office and was an inversion of the established social order. Faced with increasing hostility to his art in Rome, Nero planned a tour of Greece, where he could expect a more appreciative response. In April AD 65, he had narrowly escaped death when the Pisonian conspiracy was uncovered the night before the planned murder. The plot involved one of his closest *amici*, Calpurnius Piso, one of the two Praetorian Prefects and three tribunes. Only the ineptitude of the conspirators, who were more intent on delivering a performance recreating the murder of Caesar and Gaius rather than preserving the secrecy of their designs, saved Nero. Shocked, and increasingly fearful, the emperor started to plan a triumphal tour of the Greek festivals. Increasingly, he retreated into a fantasy world of music and the stage.[1]

Another unsuccessful assassination attempt followed in AD 66, led by Annius Vinicianus, as the emperor travelled to Brundisium to take a ship to Greece. Rome was left in the hands of the imperial freedman Helius and the new Praetorian Prefect, Nymphidius Sabinus, supported by most of the Praetorian Guard. Nero divorced himself from the senatorial elite who were, for the most part, left behind. An exception was the noble Aulus Vitellius, who shared the same passions as Nero and was a close *amicus*. He travelled with men he felt he could trust. Tigellinus commanded the guard cohorts that accompanied him and the imperial freedmen. His tour was an artistic triumph. He won the four great Panhellenic festivals rearranged to coincide with his visit. Victories in all four were extremely rare and the emperor revelled in his artistic immortality. He dedicated each to the people of Rome, with no mention made of the Senate.[2]

Reality did occasionally intrude. Nero refused to visit Athens and the temple of the Mysteries at Eleusis. Guilt devoured him, for, after murdering Agrippina, he 'often admitted that he was hounded by his mother's ghost and that the Furies were pursuing him with whips and burning torches'.[3] The sanctuary of these goddesses of vengeance was in Athens. The traditional initiation into the Eleusinian Mysteries worried him, as the herald ordered the godless and wicked away before commencing the rite.[4] The gods knew the darkness that lay deep in his soul.

Guilt-ridden and anxious, he was ready to give credence to any allegations of conspiracy or treachery after the two plots against him. Rome's greatest general, Domitius Corbulo, was denounced and summoned from the East. He was not allowed to answer the charges before the emperor, but was ordered to commit suicide. His daughter was married to the conspirator Annius Vinicianus; evidence enough of treachery in Nero's estimation. Publius Sulpicius Scribonius Proculus and Publius Sulpicius Scribonius Rufus, two aristocratic brothers who governed the German provinces, were also summoned to Greece. They probably expected to be appointed to commands in Nero's planned campaign in the Caucasus. However, they had been denounced by Paccius Africanus and Vibius Crispus.[5] Neither of these were later prosecuted, suggesting there was genuine evidence to support the charge of treason. Both brothers killed themselves. The governorship of Germany Inferior was given to Gaius Fonteius Capito and Germany Superior to Lucius Verginius Rufus. Capito lacked an illustrious nobility, whilst Verginius was a 'new man', the first of his family to be ennobled through appointment to consular office in AD 63. They owed their careers to Nero and were chosen for their proven loyalty rather than ancient nobility.[6]

In Rome, the freedman Helius tried to fill the political vacuum left by Nero's absence. Informers and *delators* were given free rein in an increasingly unstable environment. Another former consul with a prestigious ancestry was accused. Q. Sulpicius Camerinus Pythicus was charged with slighting the emperor by refusing to give up his cognomen after Nero's victory at the Pythian Games in Greece. He was condemned along with his father. The executions of these Sulipcii were likely linked, and they were probably involved in a plot. Other members of the ancient Republican nobility felt threatened by an increasingly erratic and unpredictable emperor, especially those who remained in influential positions. None more so than the aged governor of Tarraconensis in Spain, Servius Sulpicius Galba, who possessed a great name and had served the state with distinction. He had been appointed in AD 61 and remained a virtual exile, awaiting an uncertain future with increasing trepidation.[7]

Galba had long been considered a candidate for the imperial throne. He had turned down a marriage proposal from Nero's mother when her husband, Domitius Ahenobarbus, died in AD 41.[8] Later the same year, he was urged to make a bid for the throne after the murder of Gaius. By then, however, Claudius had already gained the support of the Praetorians and received the recognition of the Senate. The opportunity had passed, and instead he earned the gratitude, if not the trust, of the new emperor for his loyalty. Claudius, like Nero, viewed the Republican aristocracy with suspicion. When Galba fell ill as Claudius and his army prepared to invade Britain, rather than leave him behind, the emperor postponed the invasion until he recovered so Galba could accompany him.[9]

Galba's governorship of Spain started with his usual brutal enforcement of order and discipline. He was infamous for a cruel, pitiless attitude to governing. The soldiers of Germany Superior had experienced his restoration of discipline after the lax and lenient ways of his predecessor, who had been executed for conspiring against Gaius. The legionaries composed a ditty, remembered by the legions long after he departed:

> 'Soldier, soldier, on parade,
> You should learn the soldier's trade,
> Galba's now commanding us –
> Galba, not Gaetulicus.'[10]

During his governorship of Africa, he suppressed disturbances 'ruthlessly', and when a soldier was reported to have sold his rations for an inflated price during a food shortage, Galba ordered that he be starved to death.[11] In Spain, he began his tenure with the usual ferocity, but went 'too far in his punishment of crime'. He ordered the hands of a dishonest money changer cut off and nailed to his counter, and illegally crucified a poisoner even though he was a Roman citizen. When the man appealed against this punishment, Galba ordered that his cross be whitewashed and raised higher than the others. Later, comprehending his vulnerability, he sought to win over the provincials as potential supporters.[12]

Normally diligent in his duties, Galba became increasingly 'lazy and inactive'; but this was done purposely to deny Nero any pretext for disciplining him. In his own words, 'Nobody can be forced to give an account of doing nothing.'[13] This was not true, for he was providing ample reasons for the emperor to recall him. Nero was desperately short of money, with huge amounts being spent on the rebuilding of Rome after the devastating fire in AD 64. More was spent on the construction of his huge new palace cascading down from the Palatine Hill onto land that had once been owned by Rome's elite families. Furthermore, he planned a huge military campaign in the Caucasus involving the recruitment of new troops and the movement of thousands of soldiers across the Empire. The gold and silver coinage had been debased, but income still fell well short of expenditure. The financial situation had become desperate. The emperor had fallen behind in payments to the soldiers and had been forced to postpone the discharge of time-served veterans. His financial secretaries were told, 'You know my needs', so the imperial procurators across the Empire were instructed to raise the required taxes from the provincials.[14]

In Judaea, procurator Gessius Florus made excessive financial demands which were impossible to meet. He therefore removed money from the temple in Jerusalem. In AD 66, the city rose in revolt, followed by the rest of the province. A legion sent to restore order was ambushed and 6,000 legionaries were massacred. The following year, Vespasian, another 'new man' and present in Greece, was sent by Nero to crush the revolt. It would take eight years and thousands of lives to do so. More money was needed. In Africa, six landowners were put to death and their estates that covered half the province were seized.[15]

Every province suffered from the demands of procurators and other officials. In Spain, though, Galba offered a conciliatory ear. He made 'it plain that he shared their distress and sense of wrong, [and] this somehow brought relief and comfort to those being condemned in court and sold into slavery'. In response to these exactions, derogatory and scandalous verses attacking Nero started to circulate. Galba did nothing to stop them, despite the objections of the imperial procurators. The inaction of the governor would have been reported to Nero in Greece and Helius in Rome. Galba knew he could be held to account for doing nothing, but he wanted to build the foundations for a possible bid for the throne. His newfound benevolence made him 'still more beloved by the inhabitants'.[16]

During the winter of AD 67, Helius received numerous reports of a conspiracy forming against the absent emperor. He sent several messages to Nero requesting his return, but to no avail. Reality was not allowed to intrude on the artist's invented world. Significantly, it was the imperial freedman who tried to impress upon the emperor the danger he faced, rather than Nymphidius Sabinus, who was responsible for imperial security. The Praetorian Prefect had his own agenda and had been busy securing the allegiance of the tribunes and Praetorians left in Rome.[17] Eventually, Helius was forced to travel to Greece, braving the winter storms. The freedman met with his emperor 'and frightened him by reporting that a great conspiracy against him was on foot in Rome'. Nero returned immediately. The evidence Helius possessed was convincing.[18]

Letters had been sent to all the provincial governors, legates in command of the legions, senators in Rome and exiles, sounding out their support for the overthrow of Nero. Helius probably had shown these to the emperor, as all bar one governor had passed them on. These officials 'did all they could to ruin the enterprise'. Only Galba failed to report receipt of this communication – an act of treason. Nero exploded in a fit of rage, threatening to recall all the governors and generals and execute all those exiled, and poison the entire Senate at a public banquet. Once he had regained control, the emperor prepared to return to Rome, risking the conditions at sea.[19]

These letters had been sent in secret by the governor of Gallia Lugdunensis, Gaius Julius Vindex. He was a member of the Aquitanian nobility who had made the most of the emperor Claudius' promotion of the Gallic aristocracy. He was the first Gallic senator to be honoured with the governorship of a province. He was 'powerful in body and of shrewd intelligence, was skilled in warfare and full of daring for any great enterprise; and he had a passionate love of freedom and a vast ambition'. He had been in contact with the Gallic aristocracy as well as leaders of the Batavians. The former were bearing the brunt of Nero's financial demands.[20] The Batavians were a warlike Germanic tribe whom the Romans settled in the Rhine Delta. They were obliged to provide ten auxiliary cohorts to the Roman Army and the personal German bodyguard of the emperor. The cavalry were renowned for their skill and distinguished service. The recently appointed governor of Lower Germany, Fonteius Capito, had arrested Julius Paulus and his brother, Julius Civilis, 'both of royal stock', on a charge of revolt. Paulus was executed and his brother was sent in chains to Nero. They may have been betrayed by another Batavian noble, Claudius Labeo, as Civilis later pursued him in an apparent lust for vengeance.[21] Time was running out for Vindex before the German legions would be ordered to descend on him, as they did Sacrovir.

Vindex had been using the philosopher Apollonius of Tyana as an intermediary. A puzzling meeting is preserved by his biographer, Philostratus, but it is in parts both confused and unreliable. According to this source:

> 'The governor of Baetica was very anxious to have a conversation with Apollonius, and though the latter said that his conversation must seem tedious to any but philosophers, the other insisted in his demand. And as he was said to be a worthy person and detested the mimes of Nero, Apollonius wrote to him a letter asking him to come to Gadeira [Cadiz]; and he, divesting himself of all the pomp of authority, came with a few of his most intimate friends. They greeted one another, and no one knows what they said to one another in an interview from which they excluded the rest of the company, but Damis hazards the opinion that they formed a plot against Nero. For after three days spent in private conversations,

> the governor went away, after embracing Apollonius, while the latter said: "Farewell, and do not forget Vindex.'"[22]

Damis of Nineveh is identified as a disciple of Apollonius who wrote a memoir of his teacher which was used by Philostratus. However, the governor of Baetica was later executed by Galba and probably remained loyal to Nero. This meeting is unlikely to have been with Galba as Gadeira is in Beatica, far from the provincial border of Tarraconensis, and a governor would not leave his province. Furthermore, both Plutarch and Suetonius agree that Galba made his pact with Vindex after he made his public declaration of revolt in March AD 68. Consequently, Apollonius probably met with the quaestor of the province, Aulus Caecina Alienus in Beatica, as he supported the revolt of Galba.[23]

Ceacina's motivations were not idealistic in wanting to end the tyranny of Nero. He had been using his office to embezzle funds, diverting public revenues into his pocket. He faced prosecution upon his return to Rome and hoped to avoid an inevitable conviction by obligating a new emperor.[24] Galba, governor of the neighbouring province, however, had gained additional understanding of the precarious nature of his situation. His failure to pass on the letter he had received alerted Nero to his dubious loyalty. There was only one legion in Tarraconensis, the *VI Victrix* at Legio (Leon), which guarded the gold mines in northwest Spain. There were also two cavalry *alae* and three auxiliary cohorts in his province.[25] These forces were no match for those at the disposal of Nero. However, Galba 'accidentally came across Nero's secret orders (sent to his agents) for his assassination'.[26] Nero knew that a recall to Rome would be the catalyst for revolt. The fates of the Scribonii and Corbulo made this a certainty, so he ordered imperial procurators to murder the governor in his province. Imperial communications were kept secure, yet Galba was forewarned of danger through treachery at the heart of the imperial administration.

Nero had entered Rome in triumph in January AD 68.[27] The victor's crowns were carried before him, followed by the Triumphator himself carried in Augustus' carriage used to celebrate his military victories. In his hand, Nero held the Pythian laurel, and he was crowned with a garland of wild olive. He passed through the streets in procession, with the Praetorian cohorts behind, and into the Circus to receive popular acclaim. They climbed up the Capitol and then to his palace on the Palatine. All the while, the senators and *equites* chanted in chorus, 'Hail, Olympian victor! Hail Pythian victor! Augustus! Augustus! Hail to Nero, our Hercules! Hail to Nero, our Apollo! The only victor of the Grand Tour, the only one from the beginning of time! Augustus! Augustus! O, Divine voice! Blessed are they that hear thee.'[28] Not wishing to deny his fellow citizens the opportunity to appreciate his talents, games followed, where Nero appeared as a charioteer and played the lyre on stage as well as acting in a tragedy.

The imperial *concilium* would have discussed the behaviour of Galba. This was now dominated by the freemen, including Helius, the *a libellis* (handler of petitions) Epaphroditus, the *a rationibus* (financial secretary) Phaon, Patrobius and possibly those serving his more personal needs, Phoebus, Pythagoras and Sporus. There was also the Praetorian Prefect, Tigellinus, who had found his control over the Guard supplanted by his colleague, Nymphidius Sabinus. Galba would have Patrobius, Helius and others publicly humiliated and executed when he came to power. Nymphidius Sabinus would also join them in their fate after a failed coup. Others would remarkably survive, at least in the short term.[29]

Nero had travelled to his beloved Naples by March, feeling more at home amongst the Hellenic culture of the city. News reached him there on 23 March that Vindex had risen in revolt. The date was ominous, as this was the anniversary of the murder of his mother in her villa on the Bay of Naples. The revolt began sometime after 11 March, possibly the 15th. If so, it was deliberately selected – this date was heavy with political symbolism. It was on this day in 44 BC, the Ides of March, that Julius Caesar was assassinated by the tyrannicides, including Junius Brutus and Cassius Longinus.[30]

Vindex summoned a Gallic assembly comprising the nobility of Gaul. It is unlikely this was the assembly of the Three Gauls established at Lugdunum, his provincial capital, as it was closely associated with the imperial cult and the Julio-Claudians. This assembly had no political power as its members relied on imperial patronage. Lugdunum, along with its auxiliary cohort, would remain loyal to Nero. The location of this Gallic assembly may have been Vienne, the tribal capital of the Allobroges, or Vesontio, the capital of the Sequani. Both cities would join his revolt. Vienne is the more likely, as Tacitus describes it as 'the home of war in Gaul', implying that the revolt started there.[31]

Vindex addressed the nobility gathered before him. His speech as preserved in Dio is fictional, but it bears remarkable similarity to his edicts and the propaganda carried on his coinage. Its contents may have some foundation in facts. He railed against the forced taxation and the levies imposed by Nero's procurators and governors. Then he made a personal attack on Nero as being unfit to rule: the emperor 'has despoiled the whole Roman world, because he destroyed all the flower of their senate, because he debauched and then killed his mother, and does not preserve even the semblance of sovereignty'. He went on to vilify Nero's marriage to Pythagoras, his relationship with Sporus and his performances on stage, which Vindex claims to have personally witnessed. He had seen him sing, play the lyre, act, be restrained with chains and even give birth. Nero, he declared, was unfit to bear the same titles that were held by

Augustus or Claudius. Vindex then got his supporters to 'swear to do anything in the interests of the senate and the Roman people and to slay him in case he should do anything contrary to this purpose'.[32]

Vindex clothed himself in the language of liberator, not Gallic rebel. He did not want to end Roman rule in Gaul, but instead replace Rome's ruler. His coinage was produced in the name of the Senate and the people of Rome. The most numerous issues bear the legend SPQR or SPQR OB C(ives) S(ervatos) in an oak wreath, with the other side SIGNA PR showing two standards and a legionary eagle before an altar. The oak leaf (*corona civica*) was given to honour Augustus by the Senate in 27 BC for preserving the lives of Roman citizens by ending the Civil War and sparing the lives of his defeated enemies. The legionary eagle was a direct appeal for the support of the legions, especially those on the Rhine. No coins carry the image of Vindex himself. Hercules Adsertor does appear, as he attempted to associate himself with the demi-god who protected mankind. An *adsertor libertatis* was the legal phrase for a man who defended the freedom of a man illegally enslaved. Other issues carry the image of the god Jupiter Conservator, whom Nero claimed protection from on his coinage but now appeared to have deserted the emperor. With these issues, Vindex hoped to win over the aristocracy who were the greatest landowners and leading patrons, and with them the rural population and major cities.[33]

The Gallic nobility of central Gaul joined Vindex, bringing with them their clans and clients. The Sequani with Vesontio also rose, along with the Aedui of Lugdunensis and the Arverni in Aquitania. The governor of this latter province, probably Betuus Silo, rapidly lost control and appealed to Galba for troops from his province of Tarraconensis. His appeals were ignored. Vienne was quick to support Vindex, especially as its rival city, Lugdunum, remained loyal to Nero. The war had inflamed this enmity. The two cities hated each other, the Allobroges having ejected the original colonists of Vienne during the Caesarian Civil War. They were later settled in Lugdunum, which was raised to the status of a *colonia*. Veterans from the Rhine legions were also given land there, and when a fire destroyed the city in AD 65, Nero gave four million sesterces for its renewal. One of the main patrons of Vienne was the wealthy senator Valerius Asiaticus, whose father had been executed by Claudius. His thirst for revenge on the Julio-Claudian dynasty is evident in his fervent support for Vindex and then Galba. Another patron of the city was Sex. Julius Frontinus, who had been a legate of Corbulo in Armenia. These men had powerful relatives whose support they could rely on in the city, and could use their influence as patrons of local trade and religious organizations. However, the Treveri and Lingones, who bordered the German provinces and had close commercial ties with the army, remained loyal.[34]

Galba heard of the revolt soon after 18 March whilst holding assizes at New Carthage. The request for help from the governor of Aquitania indicates how rapidly the revolt took hold. Galba's refusal to offer any assistance was an act of treason. Soon after, a letter arrived from Vindex 'asking, would he make himself the liberator and leader of humanity?' The Gallic noble recognized that he lacked the nobility and necessary *dignitas* to claim the throne. However, Galba's ancestry and service to the state made him an ideal imperial candidate, and his reluctance to crush criticism of the emperor would have been well known. Vindex claimed to already have 'a hundred thousand men under arms and could arm other thousands besides'. This was an exaggeration to win over the governor. At the Battle of Vesontio, he only commanded 20,000 troops.[35]

The figure of 100,000 soldiers may have reflected Vindex's overly optimistic hopes of support. The two provinces of Lugdunensis and Aquitania supplied most of the Gallic auxiliary cohorts garrisoning Gaul and the Germanies. As Vindex controlled their tribal homeland, he believed these units would join him. He was to be disappointed. Communications with Paulus and Civilis may have led him to think the ten Batavian cohorts would revolt as well. However, the arrest of the two brothers and the execution of Paulus had ended this expectation. Lugdunum, with its urban cohort and numerous inhabitants, including veterans, had refused to join their governor in his uprising.[36]

Vindex was an intelligent and worldly politician. He would have known that his Gallic levies were no match for the hardened legionaries on the Rhine. He may have dared to hope that the governors of the two German provinces would abandon Nero, but Capito and Verginius Rufus remained steadfastly loyal to their emperor. The support of Galba would be vital in convincing Roman governors to transfer their allegiance, but none had done so in the immediate aftermath of his declaration. Vindex issued several further edicts denouncing Nero as Ahenobarbus, his family name before his adoption by Claudius, and a poor lyre player, but this only served to stoke the anger of the emperor, who threatened to hand over Gaul to his legions for pillage and slaughter.[37]

Nero was unconcerned by the threat posed by Vindex. He remained in Naples and did not write to the Senate for eight days. Then he travelled first to Antium and from there to Rome, where he summoned his *concilium*. The news that the revolt had spread to other Gallic communities would not have been unduly worrying. The governor of Aquitania remained loyal, as did Lugdunum and the commanders of the Rhine legions. A large army was being gathered by Verginius Rufus from the garrisons of both German provinces. A price of ten million sesterces was put on Vindex's head, which was a huge sum. The financial qualification for a senator was a million sesterces. When Vindex heard of this he joked, 'The one who kills Nero and brings his head to me shall get mine in return.' Vindex had no Roman troops and relied on untrained retainers, Nero focused his attention on discussing the merits of a new water organ and evaluating several different versions, even remarking that 'he would have them installed in the Theatre "if Vindex has no objections"'. Three weeks later, news from Spain destroyed his apparent composure.[38]

Vindex's letter to Galba offering him the leadership of the revolt had its desired effect. Galba had summoned his *concilium* to discuss his options. Some suggested waiting upon events, as this offered the least risk. However, T. Vinius Rufinus, the commander of the only legion in the province, urged action. Nero already considered Galba's behaviour treasonous. He had failed to inform the emperor of his receipt of the first letter and failed to enter Aquitania to assist its governor in suppressing the revolt. Their choice was binary: either move against Vindex immediately or join him. The governor issued an edict for all those wishing to grant manumissions to slaves they owned to attend him at New Carthage on 6 April. The offer was symbolic; Galba was the liberator freeing humankind from the slavery imposed by the tyranny of Nero. The propaganda mirrored the messages of Vindex.[39]

On the appointed day, a great crowd gathered anticipating the revolt. Arrayed before the tribunal were the statues and pictures of Nero's most prominent victims. The governor ascended the platform and was acclaimed emperor by his troops and the crowd. Galba denounced Nero and the execution of the 'most illustrious men', including the Scribonii and Corbulo. Next to him stood a young nobleman who had been exiled by Nero to the Balearic Islands. This was probably Lucius Calpurnius Piso Frugi Licinianus, by birth and adoption a descendant of Pompey the Great and the Triumvir Licinius Crassus. His family had been decimated by the Julio-Claudian emperors through their almost compulsive involvement in conspiracies and treason. Nero had come close to death in AD 65 in a plot led by his relative, Gaius Calpurnius Piso. Galba rejected the title of emperor, which could only legally be bestowed by the Senate. Instead, he professed to be the legate of the Senate and the people of Rome and promised to serve his country to the best of his ability. Like Vindex, he cloaked himself in the language and image of Liberator.[40]

Also like Vindex, Galba issued coinage declaring *Roma Restitutor*, a phrase with Republican origins. Another issue had the legend *Concordia Hispaniarum et Galliarum*, with a bust of Hispania and another denoting Gallia. Below the image of Spain is a *cornucopia* and below that of Gaul an oblong shield. As well as announcing the unity of their aims, the coins advertised their desire for peace and plenty, the native shields a reference to the military reputation of the Gauls. They hoped to avoid war through the defection of the Rhine legions, with the promise of rich rewards if they abandoned Nero. The legionaries were not won over, but they understood that the Gallic rebels were part of Galba's insurrection. The soldiers hated Galba for the brutal disciplining of these legions during the reign of Gaius. This treatment remained part of their unit's collective memory. Despite continuing efforts, there was no hope of these legions abandoning Nero, the grandson of Germanicus, a name that resonated down the generations of legionaries of the German legions. In AD 69, the usurper Aulus Vitellius would hold his infant son before them and give him that hallowed name.[41]

Galba had been considering rebellion for many months. Now his plans could be accelerated, with no further need for secrecy or subterfuge. He formed an informal Senate made up of provincial notables and exiles. This gave his claims some legitimacy, as the Senate in Rome declared him a public enemy. A bodyguard of equestrians was formed to protect against assassination. Around 2 April, he began raising auxiliaries, particularly from the Basques, and a new legion from Roman citizens in Spain and areas controlled by Vindex; to reinforce its loyalty to him, he named it *VII Galbiana*. Antonius Primus from Tolosa (Toulouse) was appointed to lead it. He had been expelled from the Senate and exiled to his native city by Nero for forging a will. Revenge and poverty, not liberty, were his motivation.[42]

Galba was in no position to confront the military forces at the disposal of Nero, having only one legion, two auxiliary cavalry squadrons and three infantry cohorts. He did not send any support to Vindex, who faced a huge army being gathered on the Rhine. The Gallic rebels were left to delay the advance of Nero's forces until he had time to raise and train his new troops, or so he hoped.[43]

Galba sent a proclamation throughout the Spanish provinces seeking support. Immediately, the governor of Lusitania joined the rebellion. Marcus Salvius Otho had, like Galba, been made a virtual exile in this distant province. His crime was to have been married to Poppaea Sabina, with whom Nero had fallen in love. Otho had been one of the emperor's closest friends and had shared his enthusiasm for luxury, pleasure and the arts. Nero could not bring himself to kill his old friend, so instead, in AD 58, sent him away as governor to a territory on the very edge of the Empire and annulled his marriage to Poppaea. A popular lampoon did the rounds, only adding to Otho's humiliation:

> 'Otho in exile?' 'Yes and no;
> That is we do not call it so.'
> 'And may we ask the reason why?'
> 'They charged him with adultery.'
> 'But could they prove it?' 'No and yes.'
> 'It was his wife he dared caress.'[44]

Poppaea died in AD 65 when Nero, in a fit of rage, struck her in the abdomen when she was pregnant. She miscarried and died soon after. Otho wanted vengeance.[45]

The province of Baetica initially stayed loyal. Galba executed two senators whilst in Spain, Obultronius Sabinus and Cornelius Marcellus. These were probably the governor of Baetica and his legate. The quaestor of the province, Aulus Caecina, quickly betrayed his emperor. He was responsible for the province's finances but had been discovered embezzling funds, probably by his two superiors. Baetica was vital for Galba's war effort, having a vast reservoir of Roman citizens for his new legion, men for his auxiliary cohorts and large silver mines to pay them.[46]

Nero still commanded considerable loyalty in the army. Some Spanish cavalry, who had initially joined the revolt, rapidly came to regret ignoring their oaths of loyalty to Nero. They felt ashamed and were determined to desert. Forewarned, Galba entered their fort and, with great difficulty, persuaded them to remain at their posts.[47]

Galba also received some clandestine support from the governor of Egypt, Ti. Julius Alexander, who had been close to Domitius Corbulo, working on his staff before his enforced suicide. In the circumstances, it is surprising that Nero made him the governor of Egypt in AD 68 as Rome relied on the province's grain supply. Aexander repaid the emperor's trust with treason. At the start of April, a ship drifted miraculously into the harbour of Dertosa (Tortosa) without a crew, helmsman or any passengers. The gods appeared to be favouring Galba's endeavours. It had sailed from Alexandria and carried a large cargo of weapons. Egypt was the only province in the Empire that did not have an imperial procurator, making it easier for the governor to hide his disloyalty from the emperor; fortuitous indeed for Galba, who needed to arm his newly recruited soldiers. If Alexander had sent the ship, then Galba's revolt had been planned months before and independently of Vindex.[48]

Around 17 or 18 April, Nero received the news of Galba's revolt. His reaction underlined the serious nature of the threat. Galba, unlike Vindex, was an alternative and realistic claimant to the throne. Nero had just taken his morning bath and was at breakfast when the messenger arrived. In a fit of rage, he overturned the table. Galba should have been dead. The emperor then composed himself and remained silent for a long time before calling his *concilium*. He immediately ordered Galba's vast estates to be sold to raise money for the campaign. Galba retaliated by confiscating all the imperial estates in Spain. The Praetorian Prefect, Nymphidius Sabinus, arrested and imprisoned Galba's freedman, Icelus, who was in the capital, no doubt raising support for his master.[49]

Suetonius paints a picture of an unstable Nero, at times vacillating, panic-stricken one moment but on other occasions indifferent to the gathering storm, focusing instead on writing comic verses ridiculing the leaders of the revolt. In reality, the emperor demonstrated leadership and decisiveness. He immediately took symbolic leadership of the Senate by removing one of the two consuls and taking office himself. Orders were despatched to recall auxiliary cohorts and vexillations from the legions sent to the Caspian Gates which were in Illyricum. One of these was the *Legio XIV Gemina Martia Victrix* with its attached eight cohorts of Batavians. This legion was devoted to Nero, as he had declared them his best soldiers after they crushed the revolt of Boudica in Britain. The *I Italica*, raised in AD 67 for the expedition to the Caspian Gates, remained in northern Italy. Another, the *I Aduitrix*, was to be recruited from sailors and marines from the fleet at Misenum. Conscription was introduced and money was raised in the capital.[50]

The army gathering in northern Italy was commanded by the pliable and loyal Rubrius Gallus and P. Petronius Turpilianus. In the coming civil war, Gallus' integrity was trusted by all sides and he was used as an intermediary between rival forces. Turpilianus, consul in AD 61, had governed Britain and defeated Boudicca. He had played a significant role in suppressing the Pisonian conspiracy in AD 65 and hunting down the plotters. Nero intended to join their army.[51]

The revolt of Galba changed the dynamics of the threat facing Nero. His position was further undermined by the revolt of Clodius Macer in Africa. This legate faced prosecution and ruin on his return to Rome for plundering his province. His 'cruelty and greed had led him into robberies and murders, [and he] was clearly in a strait where he could neither retain nor give up his command'.[52] He was encouraged to rebel by Calvia Crispinilla, who had fled to her native Africa after falling from favour at court. She was the wardrobe mistress of the castrated freedman Sporus, whom she was tasked with helping play the role of Nero's dead wife, Poppaea. She urged Macer 'to bring famine on the Roman people'. Africa and Egypt were the breadbasket of the capital. Starvation from an increase in the price of grain increased unrest in Rome. If the emperor left Rome as he planned, the unstable situation could have been easily exploited by his enemies. He thus remained in his capital.[53]

Macer made a rival bid for the throne. He deposed the governor of the province in Carthage, took control of the legion, the *III Augusta*, and began raising another, along with auxiliary cohorts. To enhance its loyalty, he named the new legion *Legio I Macriana liberatrix*. Like Vindex and Galba, he probably used the provincial grievances against the taxes raised by the imperial procurators to gather volunteers. It suited his purposes to blame Nero for a situation made far worse by his rapacious corruption. His coinage also appealed to liberty and carried the legend *senatus consulto*, and he styled himself as Propraetor of Africa.

Some coins were produced with his image, but, unlike Galba, he lacked a great family name.[54]

By May, Nero faced three military threats, from Gaul, Spain and Africa. Furthermore, the consolidation of his forces in northern Italy was disrupted by the eight Batavian cohorts attached to the ultra-loyal *XIII Gemina*. These German auxiliaries 'withdrew from the Fourteenth legion in an uprising against Nero', later bragging to the legionaries 'that it was they who had checked the regulars of the Fourteenth legion, they who had taken Italy away from Nero'. The execution of the Batavian noble Paulus by Fonteius Capito in Lower Germany and the imprisonment of Civilis in Rome must have inflamed their anger. Paulus had served for twenty-five years and had probably recruited many of them. The loyalty of the legionaries to his persecutor, Nero, served to exacerbate their hatred. The two sides did not come to blows, but the Batavians 'withdrew' somewhere between Illyricum and their destination in northern Italy. But to where, and how could this lead to Italy falling from the emperor's control?[55]

Around this time, Cornelius Fuscus 'brought his own colony over to Galba's side'. At some point in Nero's reign, he had renounced his senatorial rank 'to lead a quiet life'. His rebellious actions were the antithesis of his stated aim. Noted for his 'high birth', he may have retired after Nero executed Corbulo, the Scribonii and other members of the aristocracy. His colony was probably Aquileia, which commanded the vital road from Italy to Siscia and Sirmium in Pannonia. This would block the Neronian forces in northern Italy from their reinforcements. Fuscus could not hope for any help from Galba's forces in Spain. Aquileia was surrounded by a powerful enemy gathering in preparation for the war. However, the acceptance of eight cohorts of Batavians into its walls would account for the timing of Fuscus' rebellion and his confidence in holding the city. Galba would later recognize the importance of his support by making him the procurator of Illyricum.[56]

The loss of Aquileia would have coincided with news that Lugdunum was besieged by Vindex's forces. The city lay at the confluence of the Saone and the Rhone rivers, perched on the Fourvière heights, with a population of several thousand. Fervently loyal to Nero, it stood firm against the Gallic insurgency, defended by an urban cohort and probably many veteran settlers. Although it had no city wall, its commanding position meant an attacker would expect to suffer a significant number of casualties. Vindex prepared for a long siege, supplanting his forces with volunteers from Vienne. However, he was unwilling to sacrifice his levies for a costly assault. At the end of Nero's reign, the *I Italica* and a Taurian cavalry squadron were garrisoning the city, suggesting it formed part of a large relief force from northern Italy under the command of Turpilianus. This army was probably ordered to secure the route into Italy that would be taken by the Galban army. Rubrius Gallus remained in northern Italy, to counter the threat from Aquileia. Towards the end of May, Vindex heard that Vesontio was invested by the army of Verginius Rufus. Consequently, he raised the siege of Lugdunum before any relief force arrived and moved up the Rhone Valley towards the Rhine legions. He would not have marched north if he thought Verginius supported him and Galba.[57]

Fonteius Capito in Lower Germany faced an attempt to force him to renege his allegiance to Nero. The governor had previously proven his loyalty by apprehending the two Batavian princes, who were probably working with Vindex. The situation had changed with news of the rebellion in Spain. A few of his senior commanders hoped for future rewards from Galba by suborning the garrison of the province for him. Several conflicting rumours were circulating later that deliberately mixed propaganda and facts. However, Tacitus is clear about which one was the more credible.

Though Capito's character, according to reports, 'was defiled and stained by greed and lust, he had still refrained from any thought of a revolution, but that the commanders who urged him to begin war had purposely invented the charge of treason against him when they found that they were unable to persuade him'.[58] These commanders were Fabius Valens, legate of the *Legio I Germanica* at Bonna, Cornelius Aquinus, legate of the *Legio XVI Gallica* at Novaesium, and the commander of the German fleet, Julius Burdo. Tacitus adds greater clarity when he explicitly states that Valens 'put Fonteius Capito to death after corrupting him – or it may have been because he could not corrupt him', whilst Burdo had 'plotted against' the governor and 'invented a charge against him'. The troops, however, loved their commander, and upon his death they remembered him with gratitude. After they failed to subvert Capito, Valens and vexillations of the *I Germanica* joined the army of Verginius Rufus as it moved against Vindex. Capito had then purged his officer corps, ruthlessly demoted some officers and promoted those he trusted. Valens knew what awaited him on his return to Lower Germany. A few weeks later, to earn the appreciation of the new emperor, Valens also took the lead in making the vexillations from his legion swear the oath of allegiance to Galba when Verginius and his army were informed that Nero was dead. Valens then returned to Bonna with his legion.[59]

The false charge of treason was made just after Galba ascended the throne and is recorded by Dio. Capito was alleged to have heard a legal case and found against a claimant. This man then appealed to the emperor. Capito 'changed his seat to a high chair and then said: "Now plead your case before Caesar." He then passed sentence and put the man to death.'[60] According to Dio, it was Galba who ordered Capito's execution, but this is contradicted by Tacitus. Capito was killed by a centurion named Crispinus, and Galba, who was informed after the event, posthumously approved the execution. Capito was loyal to Nero and had executed Vindex's Batavian ally, Julius Paulus, so Galba was content to leave the situation as it was, although he pointedly did not reward Valens or Burdo and replaced Aquinus. Valens had 'long been poor' and probably hoped for wealth and power by supporting a successful claimant to the throne. These commanders must have tried to persuade Capito to abandon Nero and try for the throne, failed, and then looked to hide their treachery and inevitable punishment by murdering their governor.[61]

Verginius Rufus led his forces from Moguntiacum (Mainz) against Vindex in the name of Nero. He remained loyal to his emperor to the end, despite the claims in later propaganda. This huge force was composed of the Upper German legions, *IV Macedonica*, *XXII Primigenia* – both from Moguntiacum – and the *XXI Rapax* from Vindonissa, as well as cohorts from legions in Lower Germany and auxiliaries including Belgians and two cohorts of elite Batavian cavalry from Lower Germany. Towards the end of May, they were encamped before Vesontio, the tribal capital of the Sequani. The town had refused to open its gates to them. Set in a meander of the River Doubs, it could only be approached through a narrow neck of land, making a direct assault difficult. Verginius Rufus therefore set about laying siege to the town and starving the inhabitants into surrender.[62]

Vindex's army was drawn mainly from the Arverni, the Sequani and their neighbours, the Aedui. The families of many of his soldiers would have taken refuge in the besieged town and faced slaughter if it fell. Despite the risks, Vindex marched north to confront an army that outnumbered his force and was superbly trained, unlike his levies. He possibly hoped to win over Verginius Rufus to Galba's cause, as a battle would lead to certain defeat.[63]

Vindex approached Verginius Rufus' army 'and encamped not far off, whereupon they sent messengers back and forth to each other and finally held a conference by themselves at which no one else was present and came to a mutual agreement against Nero, as was conjectured'.[64] It is surprising that Verginius Rufus agreed to meet with Vindex. What was discussed is mere guesswork. Only two people were present; one would die immediately after it, whilst the other refused ever to speak about it. According to a late source that confuses the name of Verginius Rufus with Nero's general, Rubrius Gallus, this 'Rufus Gallus' agreed with Vindex that he would 'rule the Gauls himself and that Spain should belong to Vindex, and that Galba should receive all of Italy together with the remaining provinces that owed allegiance to the Roman empire'.[65] This agreement defies reason. Vindex fought the war in Galba's name and would not renounce his agreement, nor would he allow Gaul to be ruled by Verginius Rufus.

After the meeting, Vindex's army left the safety of their camp and marched towards Vesontio. According to the sources, the army of Verginius Rufus, unaware of the supposed agreement, and without orders, marched out to meet them. The Romans fell upon the rebels 'while they were off their guard and in disarray and cut down great numbers of them'. Vindex lost 20,000 men.[66] Unfortunately, Tacitus' account of the battle has been lost; however, in his surviving books there are glimpses that Verginius had not lost control of his soldiers. Roman generals tended to send the auxiliary troops into battle first to avoid casualties to their legionaries. Civilis would later claim that 'It was the Batavian cavalry that crushed the Aedui and Averni.'[67] The Sequani were no doubt attacked by other units. Furthermore, Verginius had his forces well trained, for 'discipline was strict'.[68] It seems difficult to understand how thousands of troops could leave the camp and form up into units, as the Batavians had, without order or commands being imposed by centurions, prefects, tribunes or their general.

Vindex was struck down by grief after the slaughter of his men. Whatever had been agreed at the meeting with Verginius had led to him relaxing his guard. The forces of Nero had destroyed all hope of liberty. Vindex slew himself. His corpse was discovered and many of the victorious soldiers 'inflicted wounds on his body, and so gave rise to the false impression that they themselves had killed him'.[69] The legionaries wanted to claim a reward for killing him from Verginius Rufus. The ferocious attack on his body also reflects their hatred of Vindex and his Gallic forces. That loathing would not dissipate after their victory but intensify. The rebels were 'the enemy' or 'the defeated' and 'the Galbans.' Such was their hatred that a year later in Rome, these soldiers demanded the punishment of Asiaticus Flavius and Rufinus, Gallic chiefs who had fought for Vindex. Verginius Rufus must have known he could not control his army if he had made any agreement with Vindex.[70]

After the battle, Verginius Rufus retreated into his tent when told of the death of Vindex. He was said to 'have mourned his death greatly'.[71] However, the actions of his army speak of a man unencumbered by any sense of grief or guilt. His men revelled in their victory and that of their commander. Tacitus makes no mention of an accident or blunder that led to battle. The soldiers took immense pride in defeating the rebels, and so, 'flushed with joy over the booty and glory it had won, as was natural since it had secured a very rich victory without effort or danger, preferred to advance and fight, to secure rewards rather than mere pay'.[72] Vesontio was sacked. However, instead of retreating to Moguntiacum with his men loaded with booty, Verginius continued to attack and plunder the territory of the Sequani and Aeduans. He added to his fame through the 'prestige of victory over Vindex and his subjugation of all Gaul'.[73] There was no remorse evident. The events after the battle suggest Verginius had never any intention of forming a pact with Vindex, but led him to believe he would. Tricked, the Gallic army was annihilated.

Certain officers in his army now saw an opportunity to use their commander's glory to force a revolt against Nero. Unlike the rank and file, the legates, tribunes and centurions often chose their immediate advantage rather than keeping their oaths and loyalty to their ruler. As Tacitus notes, revolts and civil wars were instigated by the 'madness of the leading men' who wanted to exploit a crisis for their gain or ambition. One of the leaders of the unrest facing Verginius was Valens, who had command of some cohorts from his legion. Valens 'was a man of loose morals but not without natural ability, save that he sought a reputation for wit by buffoonery'. He was not only duplicitous but by now desperate. Capito and justice awaited him when he returned to Lower Germany, so 'as a legate of a legion he courted Verginius and then defamed him'.[74] His attempt to force Verginius to claim the throne, like the attempt to subvert the loyalty of Capito, appears to have failed. He was joined in his attempt by Pedanius Costa, who 'dared to move against Nero and to urge Verginius to action'. He was probably a legionary commander and, as a native of Tarraconensis in Spain, a supporter of Galba. This officer's anti-Neronian sentiments were so vehement that Vitellius later refused to make him consul so as not to alienate the supporters of the former emperor.[75]

There was a concerted attempt to coerce Verginius. According to Plutarch, 'a report was current that all the soldiers desired Verginius, in view of the great victory he had won, to assume imperial power, or that they would go back again to Nero'. Dio adds that

> 'his soldiers threw down and shattered the images of Nero and called Rufus by the titles of Caesar and Augustus. When he would not heed them, one of the soldiers thereupon quickly inscribed these words on one of his standards. He erased the words, however, and after a deal of trouble brought the men to order and persuaded them to submit the question of the throne to the Senate and the people.'[76]

The actual books of Dio have been lost, so historians are forced to rely on a summary of his work compiled by later Byzantine scholars. Plutarch infers that there were numerous attempts by the soldiers to make their commander emperor, for Verginius 'commanded the strongest legions and was often saluted by them as emperor and strongly urged by them to take the title'.[77] The summary in Dio mentions only one attempt, and appears to have condensed several attempts to coerce him into a single one. Nero was believed to be still alive in the account, his images and standards remaining in the camp as both soldiers and their commander remained loyal. Verginius refused to be forced. However, his later compromise to placate the soldiers, where he deferred to the authority of the Senate, is probably his response once he knew Nero was dead. Tacitus explicitly states that the German legions 'were slow to abandon Nero'.[78] Like their commander, they remained loyal to the end.

News arrived soon after 9 June that Nero had killed himself. This left Verginius and his army in a difficult position. They were now on the wrong side of history. Galba, when he became emperor, would not take kindly to their slaughter of his allies, nor the devastation of their lands. Verginius knew his life was in danger. There quickly followed another attempt, genuinely supported by the mass of his soldiery, to make him emperor as an alternative to Galba or Macer. After he again refused, a military tribune entered his tent and, drawing his sword, demanded that 'Verginius choose between imperial power and the steel'.[79]

His reluctance to accept was explained by Valens, who was still with the army. He said that 'Verginius had hesitated with good reason, for he was of an equestrian family, his father was unknown and he would have been unequal to the office if he had got the imperial power, but safe if he refused it.' This was the deciding factor. He was a new man, born into an undistinguished equestrian family from Mediolanum (Milan) around AD 13. He was only recently ennobled through his consulship in AD 63. Nero had greatly honoured him by making him an ordinary consul, with the year named after him and his colleague, rather than a *suffect* consul, who held office for a short period later in the year. However, his nobility paled in comparison to Galba, or indeed other members of the aristocracy. Nor did Verginius have time to canvass support amongst other governors and commanders or have enough money to fund an insurrection. Instead, he chose a safer course of action, but one which still carried a huge amount of risk. Like Galba, he deferred the decision to the Senate.[80]

Valens, with consummate skill, also chose a path to secure his safety and attain future rewards. When the Senate voted Galba the imperial powers, Verginius was expected to extract the oath of allegiance to the new emperor from his soldiers. However, he delayed, probably fearing another outbreak of unrest. Indeed, 'the armies in Germany were vexed and angry, a condition most dangerous when large forces are involved. They were moved by pride in their recent victory and also by fear, because they had favoured the losing side. They were slow to abandon Nero; and Verginius, their commander, had not pronounced for Galba immediately.'[81] Valens wrote to Galba, informing him of Verginius' hesitancy, then took the initiative himself by administering the oath to his vexillations and thus forcing his commander to do the same. This he achieved only 'with the greatest difficulty'.[82]

The army then returned to the Rhine. The legionary fortresses were full of loot from the lands they had ravaged. Valens, having gained the favour of

Galba, now felt confident in moving against the Neronian loyalist, Fronteius Capito. Meanwhile, Verginius Rufus received a letter from Galba 'inviting him to join in efforts for the preservation alike of the empire and the freedom of the Romans'.[83] Whatever he replied, it failed to convince Galba of the loyalty of his latent rival for the throne. His position was not helped by the *XIV Gemina* and *XI Claudia* legions in northern Italy, which sent representatives offering him the throne. Another refusal added to his fame and Galba's suspicions.[84]

The Upper German legions continued to show great 'attachment' to their commander,[85] so Hordeonius Flaccus was sent by Galba to relieve Verginius Rufus of his governorship. Verginius was told that Galba wished to reward him for his loyalty, a sop that was transparent in its dishonesty. Flaccus was, however, shown the greatest courtesy. Verginius introduced their new governor to his legions and left to meet Galba in southern Gaul.[86] Nevertheless, the soldiers despised their new commander; he was not Verginius Rufus. Flaccus was 'incapacitated by age and lameness, he had neither courage nor authority. Even when the soldiers were quiet, he had no control; once exasperated, the feebleness of his restraint only inflamed them further.' They took the recall of Verginius as an insult, a public questioning of their loyalty when their destruction of Vindex was deserving of praise, honours and rewards. Furthermore, the armies in Lower Germany lacked an overall commander, as the murdered Capito had not been replaced. A dangerous leadership vacuum existed on the Rhine, which invited mutiny and treachery.[87]

Verginius Rufus travelled south knowing his life was in the balance. Galba – brutal, unforgiving and vengeful – had already executed the governor of Aquitania. His crime was loyalty to Nero.[88] However, Verginius was protected by his fame and the legions on the Rhine. He had 'acquired a great name, greater, in fact, than if he had accepted the sovereignty, for refusing to receive it'.[89] An inscription reflects his greatness in the minds of ordinary Romans. A forester called Pylades, living on one of Verginius' estates near Como, dedicated an altar to Jupiter in fulfilment of a vow 'for the welfare and victory of Verginius Rufus'. To pledge this, he must have been aware that his master had been ordered by the emperor to march against Vindex.[90]

To those who feared the bloodshed inevitable with civil war, Verginius' rejection of the throne offered peace. To the former supporters of Nero, he had destroyed the allies of the rebel emperor. To all Romans, he had saved them from the threat of a Gallic invasion. Consequently, 'no man's name was greater than that of Verginius, and no man had a reputation equal to his, since he had exercised the greatest influence in ridding the Roman state alike of a grievous tyrant and of Gallic wars'.[91] He had also declared himself a servant of the Senate, in whose name Galba too had renounced his oaths to Nero. However, what ultimately saved him was the likely response of the legions in Upper Germany and northern Italy if Galba had ordered his execution.

Galba met Verginius coldly. There were no rewards, no honours, but he lived.[92] In return, he no doubt had to announce that he had been a tacit supporter of Galba all along. However, Galba's advisor, T. Vinius, wanted him removed as a potential threat to his influence. Upon his return to Rome, Verginius was brought to trial but survived. The prosecution served to further enrage his former soldiers against Galba.[93]

Verginius Rufus, a man who remained loyal to Nero to the end, would not prosper in, nor survive, the nefarious world of Roman politics after his fall unless he changed history. He cultivated men of literature and influenced their careers. Tacitus was his closest *amici* and gave the eulogy at his funeral many years later. He was a guardian to Pliny the Younger, whose uncle, Pliny the Elder, wrote a lost history of these years.[94]

Towards the end of his long life, Verginius Rufus had a revealing conversation with the historian Cluvius Rufus which was witnessed by Pliny the Younger. The historian observed to his host: 'You know, Verginius, that truthfulness is required from history. I beg you to forgive me if you read in my histories things you would not like.' To which Verginius Rufus replied: 'Cluvius, don't you know that I did what I did in order that the rest of you would feel free to write as you please?'[95] Cluvius' truth evidently contradicted the prevalent belief that the Battle of Vesontio was brought on by the ill-discipline of the Roman troops, which would undermine the old general's assertion that he gave tacit support to Galba.

Verginius Rufus would die in contented old age in AD 97 after being rewarded with two further appointments as consul by two different emperors wishing to bask in his reflected glory; an almost unique honour outside members of the imperial family. He spoke rarely about the events surrounding the Battle of Vesontio, and when he did, his words were guarded and ambiguous. His epitaph reflected his desire to hide his loyalty to his emperor, Nero: 'Rufus is buried here, who, Vindex having been defeated, restored the Empire – to the fatherland, not to himself [*hic situs est Rufus, pulso qui Vindice quondam, imperium adseruit non sibi sed patriae*].' There is no mention of the constitution or *Libertas* or fighting in the name of the Senate and the *res publica*. Verginius made war for his *patria*, for Rome.[96]

In May AD 68, just before the Battle of Vesontio and the apparent destruction of Galba's hopes, Nero's position was militarily strong. He may have lost control of Africa, Spain and Gaul, but the forces ranged against him were weak. Vindex had only 20,000 untrained levies, whilst Galba and Macer had two legions each, but half of these were recently recruited and had little training. Nero could count on the seven Rhine legions, at least three legions in northern Italy and vexillations drawn from other legions of Britain, Germany and Illyricum. There was also the recently raised legion of marines and sailors, the *I Adiutrix*. There were an equivalent number of auxiliaries too. Then there were the twelve cohorts of the Praetorian Guard and six Urban cohorts. The legions of Pannonia, Moesia and the whole of the East remained loyal. And yet, a man ruthless enough to murder his mother and members of the elite after the Pisonian conspiracy abandoned all hope and killed himself.[97]

Nero was deceived, Tacitus concluding that he 'had been driven from his throne rather by messages and rumours than by arms'.[98] Rumours of defections had led Nero to prepare to abandon Rome and flee to Alexandria, hoping to live as a private citizen, devoting himself to the lyre. His German bodyguards, who were fervently loyal to him, had already been sent in advance.[99] A few days before the crushing defeat of Vindex, Nero had been informed that Verginius Rufus had betrayed him,[100] which was untrue. The final straw came when he was told the commander of his forces in southern Gaul, Petronius Turpilianus, had deserted to Galba. This was another lie. After the emperor's death, Turpilianus reappeared in Rome, 'bare and unarmed' as a private citizen. He was ordered by Galba to commit suicide when he entered the city as he 'was faithful to Nero'. Turpilianus 'was hated merely because he would not betray nor show hatred to Nero in spite of all the emperor's crimes, but apart from this had participated in not one serious offence'.[101] He likely left his command upon learning of the emperor's suicide and hoped to prepare support and allies for his inevitable prosecution. However, this 'helpless old man' was not given the chance to defend himself.[102]

Nero had been fed falsehoods. He was made to believe in betrayals that had never occurred. He was persuaded to send his German bodyguard away when they would have been duty-bound to defend him. The two Praetorian Prefects were prominent in his small circle of advisors. Tigellinus was, however, seriously ill with consumption at this time. His life was painfully ebbing away from bodily diseases.[103] Nevertheless, his influence over the Praetorians had been undermined by his colleague, Gaius Nymphidius Sabinus, during his absence with the emperor in Greece. Nymphidius had shown favours to high-ranking Praetorian officers, probably tribunes and centurions, who were as a consequence indebted to him. Illness now deprived Tigellinus of any opportunity to restore his control. However, he betrayed Nero by failing to inform the emperor of his suspicions. Tigellinus took out an insurance policy, protecting the daughter of Galba's close advisor, T. Vinius, from Nero's vengeance.[104]

Nero's trust in Nymphidius Sabinus was absolute. He had played a crucial role in unveiling the Pisonian conspiracy in AD 65, earning consular honours and the post of Praetorian Prefect alongside Tigellinus. He was the son of a freedwoman courtesan, Nymphidia, the daughter of the imperial freedman, Callistus. Such humble origins precluded him from the throne, and he owed his advancement and position solely to the patronage of his emperor. However, his ambition was all-consuming. He had tasted unfettered power in Rome during Nero's absence in Greece, constrained only by the presence of Nero's freedman, Helius.[105]

Nymphidius Sabinus used his position and influence to panic his emperor. He used the same tactic with the absent and newly proclaimed emperor, Galba, sending him 'messages intended to alarm him – now, that there was much-hidden distemper and unrest in the city, now that Clodius Macer was holding back the grain supplies in Africa; again, that the legions in Germany were mutinous, and the like news came concerning the forces in Syria and Judaea'. Galba, made of sterner mettle than Nero, ignored them, 'putting no confidence in his reports'.[106] He knew the Praetorian Prefect was repeating the same strategy he had used to undermine Nero's confidence.

The Praetorian Prefect had no intention of murdering Nero. He planned to retain his office under Galba by placing him in his debt as having removed Nero. However, no emperor would retain an officer who was directly responsible for the death of his predecessor. On the evening of 8 June, Nymphidius Sabinus had withdrawn the cohort of guards on night duty in the palace once the emperor had retired to his private chambers. Waking from his disturbed sleep, Nero found the palace empty except for four imperial freedmen: Epaphroditus, the *a libellis*, Phaon, the *a rationibus*, Neophytus and his young slave boy, Sporus. Nero had asked for some poison, which he placed in a golden box, and crossed to the Servilian Gardens, where he tried to persuade some Praetorian tribunes and centurions to flee with him, but they gave evasive responses. He was then persuaded to flee to Phaon's villa on the outskirts of the capital. This was in the opposite direction to Ostia, where ships were waiting to take him to Alexandria and where 'his most faithful freedmen had gone ahead to equip the fleet'.[107]

Suspiciously, three of Nero's four final companions are known to have survived the fall of the emperor, despite many of his other leading freedmen being hunted down and brutally executed. Sporus was protected by Nymphidius Sabinus and Phaon lived out his days in peace on his vast estates. Phaon's movements before Nero's suicide suggest a preplanned course of action to ensure the emperor killed himself. After persuading Nero to hide in his villa and initially accompanying him, the freedman left on the pretext of discovering what was happening in Rome as the new day dawned. Then, when Nero hesitated to end his life, he received a message from Phaon informing him that the Senate had ordered his death 'in the ancient style'. The emperor had never heard of this form of execution and no doubt wished he hadn't asked what it was. The executioners were said to strip 'their victim naked, thrust his head into a wooden fork, and then flogged him to death with rods'. Nero was now determined to die by his own hand. Epaphroditus retired in luxury and survived into his 70s until he was exiled and then executed by the emperor Domitian in AD 95. Domitian was concerned by the corruption and loyalty of his leading freedman and made an example of Epaphroditus, who failed to protect his master. However, it is equally possible that he was instrumental in the death of Nero, which fits into the historical context surrounding the last years of Domitian's rule. Suetonius uses the Latin word *necum* in describing the charges against the freedman, which implies the case did not involve the suicide of his master, but his murder.[108]

As Nero made his way through Rome, disguised by a faded cloak and hat, holding a handkerchief over his face, he had passed the Praetorian fortress. A huge shout rang over its walls that terrified the fleeing emperor. Inside, the Guard was being addressed by Nymphidius Sabinus. His authority was augmented by a group of senators who had conspired with him. The Praetorian Prefect claimed that Nero had already left Rome for Egypt and had abandoned them, a deceit to weaken their loyalty. As their commander-in-chief, Nero had obligations to them. They now believed he had forfeited their oath of loyalty to him by abandoning his position and responsibilities. The soldiers would later avenge themselves for the Prefect's lie. To win their support, Nymphidius promised in Galba's name a huge donative of 30,000 sesterces each, which was double what Claudius and Nero had given upon their accessions and equivalent to ten years' pay. The shout that Nero heard was the Praetorians' enthusiastic response to the money. The promise had not been agreed with Galba, but was credible as he was the richest man ever to ascend the throne.[109]

Had Nero shown greater courage and entered the fortress, the Praetorians would probably have returned to their former allegiance. Tacitus admits that 'the city garrison, for its part, had a long tradition of sworn allegiance to the Caesars, and had been induced to desert Nero more by cunning and suggestion than from any inclination of its own'. Even as Nero rushed from the walls of the fortress, he was recognised by a Guard veteran and saluted.[110]

Courage deserted Nero then, and in his last moments, he faltered again. He asked his freedmen to kill him, but they refused. The sound of a large troop of cavalry was heard approaching the villa. The emperor's whereabouts had either been disclosed by Phaon or it had been planned for him to hide there. Riding with the soldiers was Icelus, Galba's freedman. He had been arrested by Nymphidius Sabinus and imprisoned in the Praetorian fortress. There, the two were able to plot unobserved. When Nero left his palace, Icelus was released. He wanted confirmation that the emperor was dead.[111]

Thinking of the eternal realm, Nero made his freedmen promise that they would not allow the soldiers to cut off his head. He wanted to live the next life whole. With that, he declared, 'What an artist dies with me' and plunged a dagger into his throat. His death was slow. To put a stop to his suffering, Epaphroditus drove the blade into his neck a second time. A centurion rushed into the room and tried to stop the flow of blood. Was this an act of loyalty or a callous charade? Nero knew which. With his dying breath, he muttered, 'Too late! But, ah, what fidelity.' Icelus granted his final wish, and his body was not mutilated but cremated on the Pincian Hill, high above Rome. His shade could thus still sing in the underworld. The death of the last of the Julio-Claudian dynasty made any noble a potential emperor. War would ravage the Empire, cities fall and Rome would burn before a new dynasty arose.[112]

Chapter 5

The Praetorian Revolt and Murder of Galba (15 January AD 69)

'He seemed too great to be a subject so long as he was a subject, and all would have agreed that he was equal to the imperial office if he had never held it.'

(Tacitus, describing Galba, *Histories*, 1.49)

Proud, austere and despotic, Galba was incapable of flexibility or exhibiting agility in adjusting his position to the needs of the moment. But most of all, he was perceived as a temporary occupant of the throne. He was over 70 years old and childless when he bid for the imperial purple. He had curvature of the spine and was bowed with age, which inspired ridicule and scorn. As a young man, he was pleading a case before Augustus and kept saying, 'Set me straight if you find any fault', to which Augustus replied, 'I can advise you, but I cannot set you straight.' Younger men, eager and ambitious, quickly joined his revolt, knowing he would soon have to choose an heir. The 37-year-old Marcus Salvius Otho quickly threw caution to the wind and left his governorship of Lusitania to join Galba and make himself indispensable.[1]

Otho was one of the first to support Galba and was acknowledged as 'the most brilliant of all Galba's immediate supporters'.[2] He brought with him all his silver and other valuables, which he donated to the cause. There was only a small inner circle of close advisors that surrounded the usurper, and he allied himself with one, the legionary commander T. Vinius Rufinus. It was rumoured that their alliance was cemented with the promise that Otho would marry Vinius' daughter.[3]

Vinius' great rival to the ear of Galba was Cornelius Laco, a legal advisor to the governor. Neither possessed any great nobility. Only Piso Frugi Licinianus, who had escaped his exile and joined Galba in Spain, stood as a potential rival to the aspirations of Otho. He was slightly younger than Otho and his family was one of the greatest in Rome. He was a descendant of the triumvirs Pompey and Crassus. His family had been involved in numerous conspiracies against the imperial family. His father, mother and one brother had been executed by Claudius, and another brother by Nero. However, he had held no offices and his reputation, great as it was, revolved around the Julio-Claudian destruction of his family. He possessed a great name, but although intelligent, his 'look and manner' soon alienated many for although 'he had justly been called stern; those who took a harsher view regarded him as morose' and 'caused the anxious to suspect him'.[4] Piso remained on the periphery of Galba's circle and took no active role in Galba's rise to power; only his fall.

Otho was at the very heart of Galba's revolt. Favoured and honoured, he soon 'conceived the hope of being adopted by Galba, he desired it more keenly every day that passed'.[5] In June, however, his hopes and dreams were crushed when news arrived that Vindex and his army had been utterly destroyed. The German legions were busy quashing the last vestiges of Gallic resistance and would soon descend on Spain, reinforced by the Neronian forces at Lugdunum and in northern Italy. In despair, Galba and his followers retreated to Clunia. There, Galba 'spent time regretting what he had done but doing nothing else'.[6] Nero would show no mercy. Then news arrived from Rome, carried by Icelus, Galba's freedman, that Nero was dead and the Senate had conferred imperial authority on Galba. The new emperor set out for Rome accompanied by the *VII Galbiana*, under the command of Antonius Primus, and his entourage.[7]

Progress was slow as the towns and cities emptied to greet their new ruler as he passed through. Galba also had to reward loyalty and punish those who had remained firmly wedded to Nero's cause. The governor of Aquitania was executed and replaced, and the murder of Fonteius Capito was authorized after the event. Verginius Rufus was summoned and his fate was hotly discussed in the emperor's *concilium*, where Vinius urged his destruction. However, the threat of his Rhine armies saved his life and he was allowed to retire to Rome.[8]

Galba replaced the vigorous and admired Verginius Rufus with a senator whose age, indolence and lack of any martial quality or ambition meant he presented no threat to the new regime. Hordeonius Flaccus was despised by the soldiers in Upper Germany. He was incapacitated by gout, so he rarely left his headquarters. He lacked any authority and discipline declined. The legionary commanders were also replaced. The corrupt former quaestor of Baetica, Caecina Alienus, was appointed legate of the *IV Macedonica* at Moguntiacum (Mainz). At the same time, the Spanish provincial Dillius Vocula was probably given command of the *XXII Primigenia* that also garrisoned the provincial capital. The soldiers' respect was shifted to these new commanders. Lower Germany was left without a governor for a considerable time after the murder of Fonteius Capito. Fabius Valens, legate of the First Legion at Bonna, expected a promotion for his services to the new emperor, but his expectations were frustrated and he resented Galba's ingratitude.[9]

Those Gallic tribes that supported Vindex were also rewarded with a reduction of their taxes and the grant of Roman citizenship to nobles who had lent their support to the rebellion. Vesontio was also raised to the status of a *municipium*. This served to fuel the anger of the German legions. The Treveri and Lingones, who had remained loyal to Nero and had close ties with the army on the Rhine, were punished for their constancy. They had their taxes increased and some of their lands were confiscated and given to their victorious neighbours. Lugdunum had its revenues diverted to the imperial treasury, whilst the African rebel, Clodius Macer, was also dealt with by the blade of an imperial procurator.[10]

Whilst the situation in the German provinces was incendiary, the flames of revolt were ignited in Rome. The Praetorian Prefect, Nymphidius Sabinus, believed Galba owed him the throne. As his reward, he expected to be retained as the sole Praetorian Prefect for life. His power and future safety lay in his control over the Guard. Many would want to avenge his betrayal of Nero. Nymphidius forced his fellow Prefect, Tigellinus, to resign his office and, in Galba's name, invited former consuls and commanders to extravagant banquets. He was the power in Rome, so the aristocracy attended his morning *salutatio* and granted him the right to initiate and confirm senatorial decrees. These were not acts of treachery, but an attempt to establish himself as the right hand of Caesar. He saw himself as a Sejanus or Macro, but he should have heeded their fates.[11]

As Nymphidius had to remain in Rome, he sent Gellianus to Spain to act as his agent and win the ear of the emperor. However, Galba did not allow Gellianus to stand near him, nor did he receive him in private. This was a public demonstration of mistrust and contempt. Gellianus returned to Rome to inform Nymphidius that Vinius and Laco dominated the new court, and Laco had been made Praetorian Prefect. Galba was never going to retain a Praetorian Prefect who had betrayed his oath to protect his ruler, as the reward for such behaviour would be an open invitation for others to do the same. The best he could hope for was *adlection* to the Senate or, more likely, retirement. Without imperial protection, it would not be long before he faced prosecution, exile or death. It was better to take control of his destiny.[12]

He made a final bid to force Galba into agreeing to his demands. Nymphidius called a meeting with the Praetorian officers and informed them that Galba refused his advice due to the influence of Vinius and Laco. He then attempted to persuade them to send a delegation to Galba demanding these be removed from the imperial *concilium*, and that he would be 'more acceptable and welcome on his arrival'.[13] However, the tribunes were unconvinced. They did not want to dictate terms to the new ruler, who could easily dismiss them upon his arrival in Rome. Their confidence in the Praetorian Prefect would have been damaged, possibly fatally, as most of the Guards 'were conscious of their guilt' in the overthrow of Nero and the deceit of their commander. The promised donative was all that kept them tied to Nymphidius, and now they faced the possibility that the guaranteed amount would not be granted.[14]

Nymphidius next attempted to unsettle Galba as he had Nero with exaggerated and disturbing reports, in this instance that the German legions had broken out in mutiny and were joined by those in Syria and Judaea and there were riots in the capital as Clodius Macer had cut the grain supply from Africa. There was some truth to these reports, but the threat was amplified. He wanted to present himself as indispensable, but Galba knew the Prefect could not be trusted. He had already replaced officers in the German legions with his men, Macer would soon be assassinated, and Vespasian in Judaea and Mucianus in Syria had got their legions to take the oath to Galba. As the emperor 'gave no heed to him whatever and put no confidence in his reports', Nymphidius knew his position was untenable.[15]

Nymphidius grew desperate. His survival now lay in becoming emperor himself. He thus propagated a rumour that he was the illegitimate son of the emperor Gaius, who he claimed had an affair with his mother, Nymphidia, the daughter of the powerful imperial freedman Callistus, who had served Gaius and Claudius.[16] Another rumour that had greater traction was that he was the son of a famous gladiator with whom his mother fell in love.[17] He hoped that this tenuous link to the Julio-Claudian dynasty would be enough to kindle the loyalty of the Praetorians to him and provide a veneer of legitimacy. He had the support of his *amici* 'and certain women and men of senatorial rank', including the consul designate Cingonius Varro and the deposed client king, Mithridates of Pontus.[18]

One friend tried to dissuade the Prefect from his senseless plan. Clodius Celsus, a senator from Antioch, bluntly pointed out that 'in his opinion, not a single precinct in Rome would give Nymphidius the title of Caesar'.[19] Some of his adherents were probably motivated by greed, others by fear. A contemporary observed that 'no one, you realise, fears Caesar himself, it is death, exile, dispossession, jail and disenfranchisement that they are afraid of. Nor is Caesar loved, unless by chance he is personally deserving; we love money, a tribuneship, a military command or consulship.'[20] Mithridates would look to a time when he was restored to his ancestral kingdom, while Varro, as a designated consul nominated by Nero, knew the honour would likely be rescinded by the new ruler, who had his own followers to reward.

Others feared Nymphidius as commander of the Guard. These soldiers symbolized imperial power and authority. In the absence of Galba, many saw the Prefect as emperor in all but name. Their appearance denoted power over life and death. They and the Prefect were the only ones permitted to carry arms in the presence of the emperor, so audiences with Nymphidius would have bristled with weapons. Epictetus, an imperial freedman, witnessed their fear and imagined their response: 'Show me the swords of the guards. See how big they are, and how sharp. What then do these big swords do? They kill.' The philosopher elaborated: 'What makes the tyrant formidable? The guards, you say, and their swords, and the men of the bed chamber and those who exclude them who would enter.'[21] Nymphidius acted and behaved as an emperor; however, the soldiers were not loyal to him but the man who paid them.

The plan was simple. At midnight, Nymphidius would enter the Praetorian fortress and deliver the speech written for him by Varro. The Guard would then acclaim him emperor, and at dawn their choice would be confirmed by the Senate. The tribunes were given their orders, but one held firm to his oath to Galba. That evening, Antonius Honoratus called his cohort together and denounced the actions of his Prefect. The betrayal of Nero was justifiable for murdering his mother, his wife and his appearances on the stage, but how could they justify betraying another? He contrasted the aristocratic inheritance of Nero and Galba to the lowly origins of Nymphidius. It was Nymphidius who had tricked them into abandoning Nero. They now had an opportunity to avenge the death of Nero and win the favour of Galba. The cohort was won over and they quickly dispersed to gather support from the other cohorts.[22]

Around midnight, Nymphidius approached, escorted by his supporters carrying torches. As he reached the fortress, he saw the gates closed and armed soldiers manning the ramparts. Realizing his coup had failed before it had begun, he attempted to restore his authority, demanding to know who had issued orders to arm the Guard. The soldiers responded with a shout hailing Galba as their emperor. Nymphidius joined the acclamation and told his followers to do the same. Negotiations followed and he was permitted to enter with some of his escort. The gates opened and, as he set foot inside, a javelin was thrown towards him. The quick reactions of his bodyguard, who raised his shield, saved him. However, this was the signal for the rest of the soldiers to fall upon him. Nymphidius fled into a barrack block, where he was found and hacked to death. His body was then dragged out and surrounded by a fence for the public to view.[23]

His supporters faced prosecution for treason and a certain death. Most committed suicide, hoping to save their estates from confiscation so their children could inherit them. A few hoped to appeal to Galba's mercy. They were to be disappointed. When Galba heard of the attempted coup, he ordered the execution of all Nymphidius' surviving supporters without trial. Cingonius Varro and Mithridates of Pontus were put to death. This was the action of a tyrant, not a man who claimed to restore constitutional freedom.[24] Their blood, like that of Fonteius Capito and the Neronian general Petronius Turpilianus, stained the new emperor's reputation. Galba, the champion of senatorial liberty and freedom, would soon spill rivers of blood.

Galba continued to make slow progress towards Rome. Otho used the time to ingratiate himself with the legionaries. He addressed them as a fellow soldier, deliberately using the personal names of the veterans in conversation as they held the greatest influence and respect. He considered himself Galba's heir and was preparing for the succession.[25]

Eventually, Rome came into sight. Galba's army approached the Milvian Bridge to the north of the city. The city had emptied to honour their new emperor, including the Praetorian Guard and the legion of marines raised by Nero which had remained in the capital. It was here, at the very start of his reign, that he brought about its rapid end. The legion of marines had not received their eagle, nor had its status as a legion been formally acknowledged. Galba could have secured the loyalty of these men by simply granting this request.

The magistrates, leading senators and equestrians came forward to greet the emperor, but their welcome was drowned by the shouts of the marines, who demanded their standards and garrison quarters. Galba put them off by saying he needed to take the advice of his *concilium*. The soldiers took this as a refusal and followed his entourage, shouting and venting their anger. Some drew their swords, probably to demonstrate their status, but Galba took this as a threat to his position as commander-in-chief. He had always met threats of mutiny with brutality, and now he ordered his cavalry to charge and cut them down. The soldiers fled, as most were unarmed, but there was no quarter. Thousands were slain, with the survivors rounded up and their leaders imprisoned. As they had fled, they could technically be charged with cowardice and so suffer the ancient punishment for this. They were ordered to be decimated, with every tenth man selected to be beaten to death by his comrades. The Praetorians witnessed the atrocity and slaughter of their fellow soldiers. Such injustice would not be forgotten by these men, nor the legions stationed around the Empire.[26]

Galba's enemies had dismissed him as a weak old man, but 'now all regarded him with shuddering fear'.[27] He already had a reputation amongst the army for unwarranted brutality and harsh discipline. He had been despised, now he was hated for unjustly reviving a cruel punishment. He took up residence in the palace, guarded by men whose loyalty was already faltering. Taking their allegiance for granted, he immediately dismissed four tribunes – two from the Praetorian Guard and one each from the Urban cohorts and *Vigiles*. He believed they were too closely associated with Nymphidius, but this act served to arouse the fears of the remaining officers, who felt they 'were being driven from office craftily and cautiously one by one because they were all suspected'. They were replaced with men who were unfalteringly loyal to Galba.[28]

The dismissed officers were experienced men whose careers inspired widespread respect. The career of one of these officers, Lucius Antonius Naso, has been preserved on an inscription from Heliopolis in Syria. He rose through the grades of legionary centurion to *Primus Pilus* and then tribune in the *I Italica*, and was raised by Nero to tribunates in the *Vigiles*, Urban cohorts and then the Praetorian Guard. He had been 'awarded honours by the emperor Nero with a rampant crown, a golden crown, two standards, and two untipped spears'. These were probably won for exceptional valour in combat during the Vindex revolt or, less likely, in the suppressing of the Pisonian conspiracy in AD 65. He was then dismissed by Galba, but would be recalled to the Guard by Vespasian, serving again as a tribune, then commander of veterans in Rome before being made imperial procurator in Pontus and Bithynia. He was recognized as being intelligent, talented and courageous. The sacking of such a man could only undermine the emperor's authority.[29]

Reports soon reached the emperor that the Praetorians were complaining that they had not received the promised donative. In the circumstances, they accepted that Galba would not give the full amount, but probably thought he would provide the amounts distributed by Nero,[30] it being customary to follow established precedents. However, Galba was desperately short of money and looked to make savings by refusing to provide any donative. This broke with tradition. Augustus, Tiberius and Gaius had given voluntary bequests on behalf of their predecessor, but Claudius' payment established the idea that a gift be made in his own right. It now became a virtual obligation that tied the emperor to his troops, and them to him.[31] Galba had broken that bond. He further insulted the soldiers by declaring that 'it was his custom to enrol soldiers, not to buy them; whereupon they began to cherish a dire and savage hatred towards him'. Furthermore, he had set a new precedent where future emperors were no longer obligated to provide largesse upon their accession.[32]

Nero and his predecessors also kept a personal bodyguard of 500 Germans, mostly Batavians. These were utterly loyal to the Julio-Claudian emperors. Nero had sent his German cohort to Alexandria in anticipation of his flight to Egypt. Upon his death, they had made the long journey back, but suffered greatly from seasickness and other illnesses. When they landed in Italy, Gnaeus Cornelius Dolabella allowed them to recuperate on one of his estates. Dolabella probably harboured imperial aspirations, as he was the grandnephew of the emperor. Galba reacted by dismissing the Germans from his service without a bounty, but they were in no condition to return to their homeland, so he allowed them to recuperate in the Hall of Liberty in Rome. There, as they were an elite group of soldiers, Galba took 'great pains to care for them'.[33]

Otho was very aware of the effect of Galba's actions on the Guard, for the 'majority of the soldiers were still conscious of their guilt, and there were plenty of men to comment unfavourably on Galba's age and greed. His strictness, which had once been esteemed and had won the soldiers' praise, now vexed them, for they rebelled against the old discipline.' His comment that he selected his soldiers rather than buying them was 'dangerous to himself'.[34] His revival of decimation angered all military men. The emperor was old and unlikely to live long; his death would usher in more instability, which his successor would struggle to deal with unless he had the support of the Praetorians. Otho expected to be the heir, so took steps to mend the fractured relationship with the Guard. Many others also understood that Otho would be chosen as Caesar. Vinius had secured his future influence by agreeing to marry his daughter to Otho 'when he had been adopted by Galba and declared his successor'. In return, Vinius would support his cause. Galba, however, kept delaying the decision, but the expectation grew that he would announce his successor when both he and Vinius became consuls on 1 January.[35]

Otho knew many of the Praetorians well from his time in Nero's court. He focused his energy on winning their respect and indebting individuals to him. Those he knew he approached in casual conversation, using their name and recalling their time together serving Nero. Others 'he asked after and helped with money or influence', and knowing their deep-seated hatred of Galba, distanced himself from the emperor's actions as 'oftentimes he let drop words of complaint and remarks of a double meaning concerning Galba, and did other things that tended to disturb the common soldiery'.[36] He was always ready to win the support of the guardsmen, many of whom he supported in their careers by using his influence with the emperor, Vinius or the imperial freedmen Icelus and Asiaticus. These soldiers were advanced 'to places of command', probably as leading centurions in the legions or commanders of auxiliary prefectures. Other guardsmen knew he was a sympathetic patron of their interests.[37]

Public acts of generosity were expected in Roman society. When he invited Galba to a banquet at his house, Otho 'used the dinner as an excuse for distributing one hundred sesterces to each member of the cohort that stood on guard. This was a kind of gift from the state, but Otho added to it by secret gifts to individuals.'[38] The gifting of money to the imperial bodyguard on a private occasion was seen as a way of honouring the emperor and was probably commonplace among the emperor's *amici*.[39] However, private gifts to soldiers were not.

Otho took a huge risk in intervening on behalf of Cocceius Proculus, a Praetorian in the *speculatores*, an elite and prestigious unit with close links to the emperors. Augustus had often used the villa of one of them to escape the demands of his office and honoured him with a private banquet. A diploma dated AD 76 listing guardsmen and soldiers in the Urban Cohorts honours *speculatores* by placing them at the top of the list, denoting their status and importance. They were commanded by a *trecenarius*, which implies a unit of 300 men and ranked equal to the *Primus Pilus* of the Guard. Originally recruited as scouts and imperial messengers, they would have been asked to report on the reaction of the recipient of imperial communication. Their role evolved into service as imperial spies and they ran a network of informants, becoming 'all the eyes with which the government sees'. They sometimes wore plain clothes and infiltrated crowds or observed suspects. They attended imperial banquets observing the guests, whilst the emperor was served by other guardsmen. As part of the role, they were efficient and effective executioners.[40]

Otho was asked by his *amicus*, Proculus, to arbitrate on a boundary dispute with a neighbour whose land bordered his estate. Otho settled the disagreement by secretly buying the whole of the lands and gifted them to Proculus.[41] Estates near Rome were worth a fortune and beyond the reach of virtually all but the wealthiest Romans. Furthermore, it is significant that Otho was prepared to risk being denounced by his enemies to the emperor to obligate this Praetorian to him. Proculus may have been the commander of the *speculatores*.

Laco, the Praetorian Prefect, should have been aware of Otho's activities. Galba's former legal advisor is described as stupid, intolerably arrogant, lazy and 'unacquainted with the soldiers' spirit'. He remained close to Galba's side day and night, living in the palace along with Vinius and the former freedman Icelus, who had been elevated to equestrian status. All three were solely concerned with undermining each other. Icelus plotted against Laco as he desired the Praetorian Prefecture, whilst Laco hated Vinius and stood opposed to the succession of Otho.[42] With his focus on the Palatine, it is doubtful that the Praetorian Prefect spent much time in his headquarters in the fortress on the outskirts of the city. He would have relied on reports from the tribunes, who were Galba's appointees and probably were no more aware of their soldiers' festering anger than the Prefect.

Grievances flourished. Many felt guilt or anger at the abandonment of Nero, others feared their close association with Nymphidius Sabinus, and some bristled at the treatment of the former Praetorian Prefect Tigellinus. The latter had received no imperial recognition for his role in Galba's seizure of the throne but instead lived every day in fear of the executioner. Vinius endeavoured to protect him as he had saved his daughter's life, but he lived on his estate near Sinuessa awaiting death. Maevius Pudens, one of his closest friends who remained in the Praetorians, worked to undermine support for Galba amongst his comrades by further inflaming their anger.[43]

Many of the imperial freedmen wanted nothing more than the death of Galba. The emperor had executed many of their colleagues who were closely associated with Nero. These men 'were dragged through the forum to their doom', with the crowds applauding and baying for their blood. The old Neronian freedmen were displaced by Galba's household, who rapidly enriched themselves through bribery and gifts in return for favours.[44]

Against this background, the news from the German provinces grew increasingly grave. The Lower German legions under Fonteius Capito had remained loyal to Nero, with detachments fighting against Vindex. Capito had been loved by his men and his murder went unpunished. Furthermore, Galba had rewarded those Gallic tribes that had fought against them whilst they had received nothing. To add insult to injury, Galba had also freed the Batavian noble Julius Civilis, who had returned to his people on the Rhine delta. The emperor then hesitated and delayed in appointing a successor. Eventually, in November, he settled on Aulus Vitellius, a man in the same mould as Hordeonius Flaccus, whom he had appointed to replace Verginius Rufus in Upper Germany. Vitellius arrived in his province around 1 December. These nobles were considered so languid that it was believed they could never appeal to the military spirit of the legionaries.[45]

Unlike Flaccus, Vitellius was one of the leading nobles in Rome. To all appearances, he was an amiable socialite, but he was adept at hiding his true thoughts and abilities. He was a close friend of every emperor from Tiberius onwards, a former consul and governor of the prestigious province of Africa. The choice of such an illustrious aristocrat was surprising, and was probably suggested by Vinius. However, he was renowned for his love of food, which was reflected in his physique. Galba declared 'that a glutton was the sort of rival whom he feared least, and that he expected Vitellius to cram his belly with the fruits of the province, [and thus] the appointment must have been made in contempt, not approval'. The new governor had no interest in imposing any form of discipline on his already mutinous forces, so resentment and loathing of Galba was allowed to go unchecked, with inevitable consequences. Galba was no judge of character.[46] Anyone who survived court was a supremely gifted and ruthless courtier and politician. Galba had spent most of his public career in the provinces and lacked those skills that Vitellius possessed in abundance.

Reports of increasing ill-discipline in the armies were repeatedly sent to Rome. Antonius Primus was sent with the loyalist VII *Galbiana* to Pannonia to shore up support in the province, whilst the *X Gemina* was sent to garrison Clunia in Spain.[47] Galba had appointed men to govern the military provinces whom he felt lacked ambition or leadership to make a bid for the throne as they were old and rich. At the twilight of their careers, he felt Tampius Flavianus in

lose-up of the front face of the so-called Portonaccio sarcophagus decorated with scenes of battles between omans, Sarmatians and Germans carved in marble. Roman work, AD 180–190, from the vicinity of Via iburtina, Museo Nazionale Romano, Palazzo Massimo alle Terme, Rome. (*Jean-Pol GRANDMONT via ʼikimedia Commons/CC BY 4.0*)

harles-Gustave Housez, The Death of Vitellius, 1847. (*VladoubidoOo via Wikimedia Commons/ C BY-SA 4.0*)

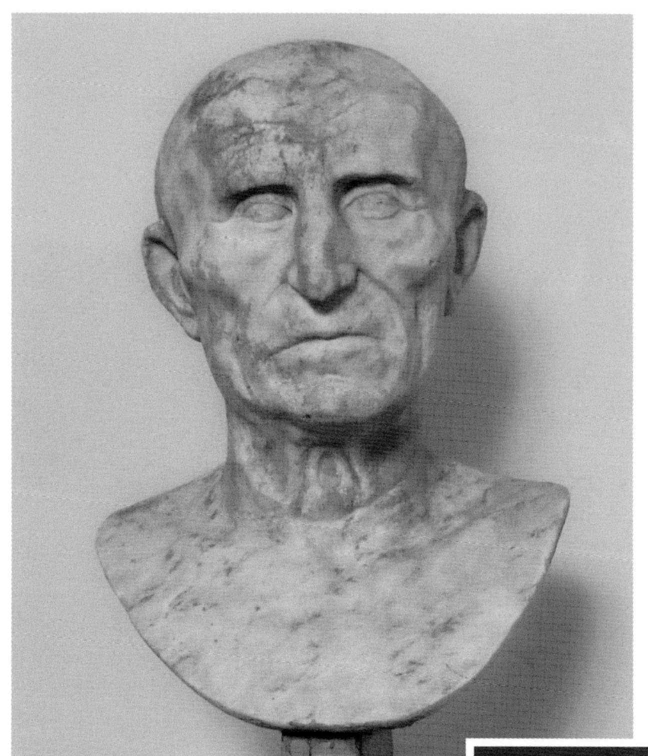

Bust of Emperor Galba in Gustav III's Museum of Antiquities, Stockholm. (*Richard Mortel via Wikimedia Commons/CC BY 2.0*)

Bust of Emperor Augustus, wearing a civic crown in the Glyptothek, Munich. (*Dan Mihai Pitea via Wikimedia Commons/ CC BY-SA 4.0*)

Reconstruction of a Roman fluvial boat, a *navis lusoria* of the *classis germanica* (Rhine flotilla). It is based on the discovery of five Roman boats at Mainz in the early 1980s. The boat above, denoted Mainz Type A, was designed as a rapid-intervention launch, with a long, narrow shape and shallow keel. It would be rowed by the troops themselves (thirty-two oars, with sixteen on each side). The mounted shields protected the oarsmen from missiles shot from the riverbanks. At the time of Civilis' revolt, most of these boats were manned by Batavian crews. Museum für Antike Schifffahrt, Mainz, Germany. (*Martin Bahmann via Wikimedia Commons/CC BY-SA 3.0*)

Medallion signifying the possession(s) of Gaius Aquillus Proculus, Centurion of the *Leg VIII Augusta*. This has been connected to a passage in Tacitus' *Historiae* by Professor Bogaers, on 8 May 1995 during a lecture for Numega. The silver-plated bronze medallion was found in the fire-layer attributed to the Batavian Revolt of AD 69–70. Nijmegen, Netherlands. AE 1998, 966 = AE 2000, 1011, EDH:HD049059. C(aii) AQVILLI PROCVLI/ C(enturionis) LEG(ionis) VIII/ AUG(ustae). (*Museum Het Valkhof via Wikimedia Commons/ CC BY-SA 3.0*)

Bust of the Emperor Tiberius in the Musée Saint-Raymond, Toulouse, France. (*Musée Saint-Raymond via Wikimedia Commons/ public domain*)

Bust of Drusus, the son of the Emperor Tiberius. Located in the Musée Saint-Raymond, Toulouse, France. (*Musée Saint-Raymond via Wikimedia Commons/public domain*)

Marble bust of Germanicus in the Getty Museum, Los Angeles. (*Getty Villa via Wikimedia Commons CC0 1.0/ public domain*)

Bust of Agrippina the Elder, wife of Germanicus, in the Archaeological Museum of Istanbul, Turkey. (*Eric Gaba via Wikimedia Commons/CC BY-SA 3.0*)

Bust of the Emperor Nero in the Capitoline Museum, Rome. (*Cjh1452000 via Wikimedia Commons/CC BY-SA 3.0*)

Portrait bust of Emperor Otho in the Louvre, Paris. (*Fred Romero via Wikimedia Commons/CC BY 2.0*)

Bust of a man traditionally identified as the Emperor Vitellius. Located in Venice's Museo Archeologico Nazionale. (*Mark Landon via Wikimedia Commons/CC BY-SA 4.0*)

'ortrait bust of the Emperor 'espasian, now in the Vatican Auseum, Rome. (*Rabax63 'ia Wikimedia Commons/CC 'Y-SA 4.0*)

Marble bust of Emperor Titus, located in the Castello Barbacane on the island of Pantelleria. (*Rabax63 via Wikimedia Commons/CC BY-SA 4.0*)

Bust of Emperor Domitian in the Capitoline Museum, Rome. (*Steerpike via Wikimedia Commons/ CC BY-SA 3.0*)

Carving of six Praetorian guardsmen in parade armour that decorated Claudius' triumphal arch in Rome, commemorating his conquest of Britain. (*Jamie Heath via Wikimedia Commons/CC BY-SA 2.0*)

·lief showing Roman legionaries ›m the Fourvière Gallo-Roman useum, Lyon. (*Photograph by ıma via Wikimedia Commons/ C BY-SA 2.0 FR*)

Relief of a Roman legionary erected in honour of Emperor Trajan from Pozzuoli, Italy. Located in the Neues Museum, Berlin. (*Carole Raddato via Wikimedia Commons/CC BY-SA 2.0*)

Virtual reconstruction of legionary barrack blocks around AD 179. (*Dr Christof Flügel via Wikimedia Commons/CC BY-SA 3.0*)

tail from Trajan's Column depicting the emperor addressing his soldiers (*adlocutio*), and in another scene ionaries construct a fort. (*Attributed to Apollodorus of Damascus, public domain via Wikimedia Commons*)

tail from Trajan's column showing Roman legionaries attacking an enemy fort using a *testudo*, whilst :orious auxiliaries offer the heads of the slain to the emperor. (*Attributed to Apollodorus of Damascus, lic domain via Wikimedia Commons*)

Awards for bravery included *phalerae*, gold, silver or bronze sculpted discs worn on the breastplate dur parades. (*Roland zh via Wikimedia Commons/CC BY-SA 3.0*)

Replica in the Colosseum, Rome, of *lorica segmentata* worn by Roman legionaries. (*Dennis Jarvis via Wikimedia Commons/ CC BY-SA 2.0*)

Tombstone of the centurion Marcus Caelius, who died in the Battle of Teutoburg Forest in AD 9. He holds his vine staff, which signifies his rank, and wears his *phalerae*, awarded for bravery. The inscription reads: 'To Marcus Caelius, son of Titus, from the tribus Lemonia, from Bononia, centurion 1st order of the 18th legion, 53 years and a half old. He died in the war of Varus. The bones of the freedmen may be buried here. Publius Caelius, son of Titus, from the tribus Lemonia, his brother, made [this tombstone].' (CIL XIII 8648 = AE 1952, 181 = AE 1953, 222 = AE 1955, 34.) *(Agnete via Wikimedia Commons/public domain)*

eplica of a column base, probably n the pillar hall of the Praetorium in legionary fortress at Mogontiacum. relief depicts two legionaries in le order. (*Martin Bahmann via imedia Commons/CC BY-SA 3.0*)

Aerial view of the Principia of the legionary fortress at Vetera. The fortress was abandoned after Batavian revolt for a less exposed position about a mile from its original location. (*Baoquan Song Wikimedia Commons/CC BY-SA 4.0*)

A reconstructed inscription probably records the construction of the defensive walls of Emona da between the autumn of AD 14 and the spring of AD 15, as it refers to the joint rule of Augustus and Tibe The legionaries involved in its construction mutinied upon hearing news of the death of Augustus. ' inscription is based on the grey fragment discovered in 1887 and is located in the National Muse Ljubljana. The inscription reads: 'The ruler Caesar, son of the divine (Caesar), Augustus, pontifex maxir thirteen times consul, twenty-one times proclaimed commander-in-chief (imperator), thirty-seven ti confirmed as tribune, and Tiberius Caesar, son of the divine (?) Augustus, Augustus, pontifex maxi (?), twice a consul, six times appointed commander-in-chief, sixteen times confirmed as tribune, they g (the city) [?].' (*Slovenščina: Preslikava, dokumentacija Muzeja in galerij mesta Ljubljane; English: Mapp documentation of the Museum and Galleries of the City of Ljubljana, via Wikimedia Commons/CC BY-SA*

etail from Trajan's Column showing Roman auxiliary infantry crossing a river on a pontoon bridge. hey were equipped with oval shields (*clypeus*), rather than the rectangular *scutum* carried by legionaries. *ristianChirita via Wikimedia Commons/CC BY-SA 3.0*)

Bust of the Emperor Nerva in the National Museum, Rome. (*Livioandronico2013 via Wikimedia Commons/CC BY-SA 4.0*)

Bust of the Emperor Trajan wearing the civic crown in the Glyptothek of Munich. (*Laci3 via Wikimedia Commons/CC0*)

The remains of the Lacus Curtius in the Roman Forum. This was a ceremonial pool whose origins dat back to the founding of the city. This was where Galba was murdered. (*MM via Wikimedia Commo CC BY-SA 3.0*)

Pannonia and Pompeius Silvanus in Dalmatia had little to gain and much to lose from disloyalty. Instead, their quiescence only encouraged the ambitions of men with little to lose and much to gain from harnessing the unrest.[48]

The situation had become so ominous that by 22 December, Galba was forced to recognize as a legion the marines whom he had decimated. Diplomas of the newly formed *I Aduitrix* suggest they were formed by the emperor whom they despised and hated.[49] On 1 January, soldiers across the Empire were assembled by their commanding officers to retake their oath to the emperor before the standards and the gods. Galba went to the Praetorian fortress to receive it, but there was no expected announcement on his successor. Instead, the emperor and Vinius then attended the Senate, where they performed the traditional ceremonies as new consuls.

A few days later, a message arrived from the imperial procurator in Belgica that the legions of Hordeonius Flaccus in Upper Germany had refused to take the oath to Galba, thrown down his statues and removed his portrait from their standards. Instead, they swore allegiance to the Senate and the people of Rome. The rebels had sent a message to the Praetorians asking that they join them and choose another emperor. The crisis rapidly grew as the legions in Lower Germany joined in by acclaiming their governor, Vitellius, emperor.[50]

Galba called together his *concilium* to seek advice. He had decided that the emergency demanded the selection of a successor. Vinius argued for Otho, whilst others backed Galba's relative Cornelius Dolabella. However, Icelus and Laco opposed an heir who was indebted to their rival and so supported the claims of Piso Frugi Licinianus. The latter had formed an alliance with Laco in opposition to Otho. Galba surprised many in the room by choosing Piso, for his nobility rather than ability. This choice would elevate the prestige of his dynasty over most of the aristocracy in the Senate and guarantee the support of that august and impotent body. Had he chosen Otho, the Praetorians and those legions loyal to the memory of Nero would probably have remained faithful.[51]

On 10 January, Galba presented his adopted heir and nominated successor to the Praetorians in their camp. This was done to honour the Guard rather than presenting his heir to the Senate. It was an empty gesture. The heavens poured with rain and lightning flashed across the horizon as the gods gave their judgement on the decision. The emperor's reception was utterly underwhelming. Galba, already lacking confidence in the Praetorians' loyalty, kept his speech short. Rumours of the revolt on the Rhine were dismissed as exaggerations. The tribunes, centurions and soldiers nearest the tribunal gave the customary shout, but from the rest there was a sullen silence. Piso stood forward and did his best to win their support. However, there was no mention of a donative that was normally given on such an occasion. From that moment, all was lost. Galba and his adopted son would be murdered within five days.[52]

Otho made no effort to hide his anger. His situation was perilous. Many had assumed he would be chosen as emperor and consequently loaned him vast amounts of money, to the sum of five million sesterces. These creditors would soon demand repayment, effectively bankrupting Otho. He declared that he 'might as well fall to some enemy in battle as to my creditors in the Forum.' Furthermore, he was a threat to Piso as an alternative imperial candidate, so he anticipated that either exile or death awaited him upon the demise of Galba. He had spent ten years as a virtual exile in Lusitania and had no wish to repeat the experience. He feared Piso, blamed Galba and hated Vinius for betraying him. Consequently, two choices were available to him: attempt to seize the throne or die trying.[53]

Otho was encouraged to act by those who were closely associated with Nero, Tigellinus or Nymphidius. His household freedmen and slaves looked to the riches and influence that could be gained as members of the imperial bureaucracy. They too urged him on. The astrologers he employed who had predicted that he would outlive Nero, now prophesized his rise to the throne.[54] His first plan was to go to the Praetorian fortress, win over the Guard and then capture Galba during dinner. This was rejected, as 'the same cohort that happened to be on guard duty as when Gaius had been assassinated, and again when Nero had been left to his fate', were on palace duty and 'he felt reluctant to deal their reputation for loyalty a further blow'.[55] It would be surprizing that Otho would have considered the blemished reputation of this cohort in his calculations, but it is more likely the tribune and centurions of this unit were fixed in their loyalty to Galba.

Most of the Praetorian tribunes and centurions were Galba's appointees or could not be trusted to keep the plot secret. Instead, Otho targeted the *speculatores*, who had the freedom to move between cohorts and held the respect and admiration of their comrades. In the circumstances, he could not be seen associating with Praetorians, so he worked through his freedman, Onomastus. Otho had recently received 10,000 gold pieces from one of Galba's slaves for securing him a stewardship, and this was all he had to fund his conspiracy.[56]

Onomastus approached two junior officers in the *speculatores*: Barbius Proculus, a *tesserarius*, and Veturius, an *optio*.[57] The *tesserarius* and *optio*, along with the *signifer* or standard bearer, were a self-contained group whose career was on the rise. They could normally expect promotion to centurion, but Galba might have overlooked them. Their responsibilities, however, made them ideal plotters to assess comrades as potential conspirators and recruit them. The *tesserarius* passed on the watchword to the Guards on duty, whilst the *optio* assisted the centurion in passing on orders and messages. Their frequent contact with members of their unit made them the perfect vehicle to drive an uprising.[58]

Onomastus met the two officers several times, winning their support for his master's plan, and through various conversations learned 'that they were clever and bold'.[59] He must have accompanied Otho on his visits to the palace and met them in a darkened corner of the huge complex. They were given most of the money and loaded with promises of future rewards, being told to use it to win over more of the Guard. They kept the number of active plotters small; only twenty-three initially accompanied Otho in his march on the Praetorian camp. All these were themselves *speculatores*, trusted by Barbius and Veturius through shared clandestine activities and trained for secrecy.[60]

Other members of the Praetorians were approached to undermine any vestiges of loyalty they might possess towards Galba. No tribunes or centurions were enlisted; instead, they targeted junior officers and the ranks 'by various devices, [and] they worked on the anxieties of the rest – on the soldiers of higher rank by treating them as if they were suspected because of the favours Nymphidius had shown them, on the mass of the common soldiers by stimulating their anger and disappointment that the donative had been so often deferred. Some were kindled by their memory of Nero and a longing for their former licence: but all had one common fear of some change in their conditions of service.'[61] Galba's refusal of their donative could be easily used to suggest a decrease in their pay, extension of the sixteen years of service or the possibility of retirement without the discharge bounty.

The two *speculatores* were confident that once the revolt started, most of the Guards would join them. This was a mutiny from below. The *I Aduitrix* also remained in Rome and had vengeance on their minds, whilst other legionaries stationed in the capital remembered the decimation of their comrades and the lack of a donative upon Galba's accession. The Batavian bodyguard had been dismissed from imperial service, whilst the three urban cohorts were stationed in the Praetorian fortress and surrounded.

It took four days to organize the plot, with 15 January set as the day Galba would die. Otho had been invited to accompany the emperor as he sacrificed in the palace. He was the only senator to receive the honour, and a refusal would be both disrespectful and suspicious. The offer was probably an attempt at reconciliation by Galba. An excuse would be manufactured to allow Otho to leave the ceremony early. From there, he would join with his Praetorians in the Forum and then march to the Praetorian fortress to be acclaimed by the cohorts. However, Galba had to be drawn out of the palace, which could be easily defended by the cohort on duty and the thousands of freedmen and imperial slaves on the Palatine.

Unbeknown to Otho, another conspiracy had formed to place him on the throne. This was organized by legionaries from the Rhine and Pannonian armies stationed in the capital. It was now widely known that the German legions had revolted against Galba, and they faced fighting a civil war. They may not have been aware that Vitellius had been acclaimed and hoped to reap the rewards of placing their own candidate on the throne.

They planned to abduct Otho at night as he returned home from a banquet and present him to the troops. Luckily for Otho, they decided against the move at the last minute. Some wiser heads pointed out that the attempt would end in chaos. Most of them did not know what Otho looked like, and there was the possibility they might kidnap the wrong man and acclaim him as emperor. Furthermore, they knew the dark streets would add to the confusion, especially as many of the soldiers around the capital would be drunk by the time Otho emerged from his revelry. Finally, the legionary and auxiliary troops were dispersed around Rome, making it difficult to gather them together without revealing the plot. The Praetorians were not approached, probably because the legionaries despised their pampered and closeted comrades. The newly formed *I Aduitrix* were garrisoned somewhere in the city, with vexillations from the Illyrian legions in the Vipsanian portico on the Campus Agrippae. They would have eagerly joined any rising against Galba, but the opportunity to gain their support was dismissed. Rivalries and the First Legion's former status as marines may have coloured their thinking.[62]

Before dawn broke on the fifteenth, Otho made his way to the Forum, where he left his escort and fellow conspirators at the gilded milestone in front of the Temple of Saturn. It was here that he later planned to meet the Praetorians who would join him as he made his way to the fortress. He then walked up to the palace on the Palatine, high above Rome. He was admitted by the Guards and conducted to the emperor, who embraced him. They made their way to the altar in front of the Temple of Apollo, and as the sun rose, standing next to Galba, he watched as the emperor sacrificed to the god. Close by stood Vinius, Laco and the imperial household. The sacrificial victim was handed over to Umbicius, the officiating priest, who inspected the entrails. He then declared to Galba 'that the omens were unfavourable, that a plot was imminent, and that the enemy was in his house'. The priest then appeared to gesture towards Otho and warned Galba not to leave the palace.[63]

There was no ambiguity. The seer was clearly aware of a plot and used his position to warn the emperor, as Galba had been dismissive of earlier warnings. Even in a tight-knit group, secrecy was a problem. Umbicius may have suspected Laco was also involved, as 'some things reached Galba's ears, but the prefect Laco made light of them'. The Praetorian Prefect was responsible for the emperor's security. Rather than taking the reports seriously, Laco saw them as attempts to undermine the emperor's confidence in his ability. Nor was he fully aware of the discontent in his troops and, almost on a point of principle, 'he was opposed to any plan, however excellent, which he did not propose himself, and obstinate against those who knew better than himself'.[64]

The priest's divination was met with confusion. Treachery hung in the air; Otho was terrified. At this moment, Onomaestus arrived with a prearranged message. Otho made his excuses and made to leave, when someone asked where he was going. Calmly, he explained that he was buying some property which he felt was in poor condition and his architects had arrived to value the building. The appearance of the freedman actually signified that the *speculatores* were waiting for him in the Forum.[65]

Otho, taking the arm of his freedman, calmly passed through the Palace of Tiberius, down the western slope of the Palatine Hill and into the market in the Velabrum to the golden milestone. Here, his hopes of success were dashed, as he had expected to see a huge throng of Praetorians but instead was met by just twenty-three. The soldiers saluted him as emperor, drawing attention from the crowds. Otho's courage now faltered and he grew frightened. He repeated to himself that he was a lost man but allowed the *speculatores* to place him in a litter. The bearers then lifted him whilst the soldiers drew their swords and escorted him through the Forum towards the distant Praetorian fortress. Another twenty or so soldiers joined them; some were aware of a plot and attached themselves to the small party, while others sensed an opportunity and joined. Then the small group announced that they were going to make Otho emperor.[67]

The crowds were at first astonished that an attempt on the throne could be made by so few. But Otho and his men were quickly joined by more and more soldiers, in groups of three and four, as news spread. They crowded around the litter, saluting Otho as emperor, but slowed his progress. Otho repeatedly urged his bearers to quicken their pace, but the narrow streets were now full of people. He abandoned the litter and began to run through the streets. When he paused to tie a lace on his shoe, he was picked up and carried on people's shoulders and hailed as emperor.[68]

Martialis was the tribune on duty at the gate to the Praetorian fortress. Unaware of the conspiracy that engulfed him, he lost his nerve as a huge mob approached the walls. Some of the Praetorians called from the street below for him to open the gates. Intimidated by the sheer numbers and fearful that the soldiers on duty and those already inside the camp were involved, he gave the order for the doors to be opened. The crowd swarmed in. Those soldiers who were not involved either ran or stood in confusion, whilst others who knew, surrounded their comrades and urged them to join the revolt. All resistance was crushed through fear or persuasion.[69]

Galba was still attending the sacrifice at the Temple of Apollo when news of the revolt first arrived – a senator was being hurried to the Praetorian fortress. Soon more information followed, confirming it was Otho. Vinius and Laco had armed some freedmen, who now acted as imperial bodyguards as the Praetorians were not trusted. Then, as the city population divided, those who sided with Galba arrived at the palace, some exaggerating the numbers who had joined Otho while others underestimated them.[70]

It was decided to test the loyalty of the cohort on duty in the palace, and they were assembled in the open space in front of the palace steps. Rather than risk the authority of the emperor, it was decided that Piso should give a speech to inspire loyalty and adherence to their oath. Their reputation remained unblemished, they were told, for it was Nero who had betrayed them and they had not betrayed him. Nor should they be swayed by the efforts of a deceitful senator supported by less than thirty common soldiers. Furthermore, Piso promised that their loyalty would be rewarded but any treachery punished. With this, the cohort gave their cry of approval and raised their standards that carried the image of Galba. However, the *speculatores* amongst them took the chance to steal away and join their comrades in the fortress.[71]

Once their immediate safety appeared secured, Galba and his advisors decided to test the support of other units around the city and see if the Praetorians could be persuaded to return to their former allegiance.[72] Marius Celsus, a man admired by all and designated consul for AD 69, was sent to the Illyrian legionaries, whilst first-ranking centurions of the Guard were ordered to summon the German cavalry from the Hall of Liberty where they were convalescing. The most difficult task was assigned to three Praetorian tribunes – Cetrius Severus, Subrius Dexter and Pompeius Longinus – who were to attempt to win over the Praetorians. These were brave men who risked death in confronting the rebels.

Celsus was driven away with spears by the Illyrian soldiers when he ordered them to join Galba, but the centurions had better luck. The German horsemen were divided. Some were too ill to lend any assistance, whilst the others argued over whether to aid the man who had disbanded them but had demonstrated genuine concern for their welfare. The Praetorians in the camp were, however, enraged by the appearance of the tribunes. They attacked all three and beat them up. Pompeius Longinus was disarmed and imprisoned, as he owed his office to the patronage of Galba whilst the other two had attained their promotions through merit and service. Their courage, though, drew admiration. Celsus would later be saved by Otho from certain death and become one of the commanders of his army, only to suffer defeat, then serve Vitellius as an advisor and later be appointed governor of Lower Germany by Vespasian. Pompeius Longinus also survived. His son would become governor of Judaea, a *suffect* consul in AD 90 and command armies in Trajan's conquest of Dacia. Such a distinguished career was made possible by the firm foundations built by his father.[73]

Two choices were left to Galba. Vinius advocated fortifying the palace, arming the slaves and defending it until the revolt had time to die down and dissipate. Laco naturally opposed this sensible option by his rival, instead encouraging Galba to take a proactive step and seize the initiative. He argued that they should enter the Praetorian fortress and confront Otho before he had time to organize his supporters. The argument grew personal, with threats exchanged, whilst Icelus added his spite and goaded Vinius. A well-considered and logical decision was impossible. Instead, it was decided to send Piso to the fortress to win over the Guard without risking the life of the emperor. Vinius, having supported the claims of Otho, would have been happy to see the chosen heir murdered by the soldiers. Perhaps he suggested it. However, Vinius' vehement insistence that Galba remain in the palace suggests he had no part in Otho's plot.[74]

A deception ended the arguing, a rumour being spread that Otho was dead. It was embraced by the crowd around the palace and, as Piso passed through, he was fed this lie. No doubt filled with relief, he hungrily accepted its truth and returned to Galba. Others claimed to have seen Otho's murder in the fortress. Some of his advisors asserted the crisis was over and speculated that the rebels were on their way to offer their surrender. Piso was despatched again to confirm the accounts, which were fed to a gullible audience. Congratulations were offered. Many of the senators and equestrians who had gone to the Palatine to be seen offering their support burst into applause. Some were more guarded and did not believe the story, suggesting that Otho's partisans had spread it in the crowd outside. Then the gates were forced and the crowd entered the palace, eager to be the first to greet the emperor. Galba put on his armour and was raised high in a chair to protect him from the crowd that surrounded him.[75]

Then one of the *speculatores* arrived, his sword drenched in blood, and demanded to meet the emperor to gain his reward. Julius Atticus raised the blade high and claimed to have killed Otho. Exhibiting his usual arrogance, Galba angrily demanded to know who gave him the order to do so. His response was well thought out – Atticus said he acted to uphold his fidelity and his oath. The crowd shouted out that he had done well and broke into another round of applause. All doubt vanished and the emperor prepared to go down into the Forum with his advisors and the Praetorian cohort. He intended to show himself to his people and sacrifice to Jupiter on the Capitol. They had been outplayed by a small group of soldiers of low social status but possessing greater ability and intelligence.[76]

Another huge crowd had filled the Praetorian fortress, but these were not senators and equestrians armed with bold words and savage tongues; they were legionaries and guardsmen eager for blood. Otho ascended the tribunal, where the golden statue of Galba had once stood. It now lay in the dust, trampled by his soldiers. They raised standards no longer adorned with portraits of the emperor. A guard had been formed around him and no tribunes or centurions were allowed to approach. These officers were not trusted. The new emperor owed his throne to the rank and file, not the equestrians or senatorial classes. All took a new oath of allegiance, whilst Otho 'stretched out his hands and did obeisance to the common soldiers, threw kisses', and the bond was sealed. Then the *I Aduitrix* entered and immediately swore allegiance to Otho. Rome was his.[77]

Otho then addressed his army from the ramparts and, with the legion of former marines before him, railed against the excesses of Galba, the man who had massacred his soldiers, then decimated them, the man whose wealth was second only to the imperial house but refused a donative, the man now defended by a single cohort of Praetorians in civilian dress. The roar from the soldiers rolled down the streets to warn the approaching Piso that they had been fed lies and it was pointless to enter the fortress. Piso returned with his Praetorian escort to meet Galba's entourage as they entered the Forum. Marius Celsus had already brought Galba the news that Otho was still alive and commanded the army. The imperial party came to a stop, paralyzed by indecision. Some argued for returning to the Palatine, others for occupying the Capitol, whose high ground was a more defendable position. Others advocated Galba address the crowd from the Rostra to rally men to his cause. Again, nothing was decided.[78]

Amid this crisis, Laco contemplated using his last moments to murder Vinius. Either he blamed him for their present position, considered him a part of Otho's plot or simply because hated him from the very heart of his being. However, Laco's attendants melted away into the crowd and, unwilling to deliver the blow himself, he gave up the attempt.[79]

Otho and the conspirators were decisive in their actions. The armoury was opened and all those who had not brought weapons were armed. It was then announced that Galba too was arming his supporters. The time had come to exact vengeance. The soldiers streamed out of the gates, heading towards the Forum, at their head a squadron of cavalry. These were probably *speculatores*, who as scouts and messengers were expert horsemen. At the same time, a group of German cavalry had finally decided to help Galba and charged towards the palace. However, they were not well acquainted with the streets of the capital and got utterly lost.[80]

The crowd, thousands strong, swept Galba's litter first one way then another, like a ship caught in a storm. Then the news spread that Otho's soldiers were descending on the Forum. Suddenly, the thousands fell silent. All strained to hear the sound of hooves or hobnails on the stone flags of the surrounding streets. First one person heard it, then another, and there was panic. The cavalry burst into the open space from the Basilica of Paulus next to the Senate House, trampling any who got in their way. They drew up and ordered everyone out of the way. Anyone who stood frozen to the spot through fear was threatened with a spear point.[81]

The crowd ran in one direction then another as all sought the safety of the temples, porticoes, public basilicas or entrances. Galba's chair was swept away. The imperial party, his advisors and the Praetorian cohort were left alone, surrounded by statues of Rome's great men, with the gods looking on from their temples. The mob had climbed any vantage point to watch the spectacle unfold. The Praetorian cohort was ordered to form up around the emperor's litter. The standard bearer from the imperial escort carrying Galba's portrait tore it down and threw it on the ground. The cohort, unwilling to die for a man they despised, then ran.[82]

The horsemen had by now been reinforced with infantry. Knowing they could attack without injuring their comrades, they released a volley of javelins at the litter. Galba and Piso were wounded, but the litter bearers managed to avoid the missiles and ran towards the Lacus Curtius, a small enclosed pool in the middle of the Forum. Piso ran in the opposite direction towards the Temple of Vesta. One Praetorian centurion stood firm, holding to his oath. Galba had ordered Sempronius Densus and his century to protect Piso. His men had gone, but Densus was determined to allow Piso time to escape. He held up his vine rod and ordered the advancing rebels to spare the emperor. They drew their swords and, coming to close quarters, he fought them off until he fell with a cut into his groin. Piso had managed to reach the Temple of Vesta, where he was hidden by a slave attendant in his quarters.[83]

Galba was not so lucky, the litter bearers stumbled in their haste to escape and the emperor was sent sprawling. He was unable to get up, constrained and weighed down by his body armour. Within seconds he was surrounded by the rebel soldiers. The emperor shouted, 'What is all this, comrades? I am yours, you are mine!'[64] Then, realizing they only had one intent, he stuck out his neck and ordered them to do their duty if they felt it was for the good of the state. With that, one thrust his spear into his neck. The rest vented their hatred by stabbing his unprotected arms and legs. Galba's head was cut off, placed on top of a spear and spun around to gratify the crowds of soldiers who had gathered to share in the deed.[84]

Otho was brought the head, but he demanded that of Piso as well. Men were banned from entering the Temple of Vesta. However, a great reward was expected from Otho, so two were willing to brave the anger of the gods and enter. Sulpicius Florus, a British auxiliary, and Statius Murcus from the *speculatores* eventually found Piso and dragged him out of the temple grounds before murdering him. Otho took great delight in studying his decapitated head, satisfying his hatred for the man who replaced him as heir. Laco's and Vinius' heads were also brought. Vinius had reached the steps of the Temple of Julius Caesar before he was surrounded. He shouted out that he was part of the plot and Otho wanted to preserve his life. The soldiers did not believe him, and one brought him down with a cut across the back of the knee before a legionary ran him through.[85]

The heads were placed alongside the standards in the Praetorian fortress. Eventually, that of Vinius was sold to his daughter and Piso's given to his wife. Galba's head was sold to the servants of Nero's freedman Patrobius, who had been executed on Galba's orders. After abusing it, they threw it into the Sessorium, where their master had died. Galba's body was interred in the family tomb. Icelus, as a former slave, was executed, whilst Laco, who had been captured, was initially exiled. However, Otho sent an *evocatus*, a time-served soldier who volunteered to remain with the army, to murder him. An officer was not to be trusted.[86]

The Praetorian soldiers remained devoted to their emperor and guarded his safety. However, they distrusted the tribunes and centurions who were retained by Otho. A few weeks later, Otho ordered one of the tribunes to transfer the urban cohort stationed at Ostia to return to Rome. The streets were crowded during the day with people, animals and waggons, so he chose to move the weapons stored in the armoury at night. Some Praetorians, already deep in their cups, saw slaves removing the contents of the armoury into waggons. Rumour and supposition soon became truth. The Praetorian officers were arming the slaves of the senators to kill Otho. Disorder erupted, and 'when the tribune attempted to stay the mutiny, they killed him and the strictest centurions'. They then seized their weapons and got on their horses to ride to the Palatine to save their emperor.[87]

Otho was giving a banquet to the senatorial elite when the doors of the palace were forced. The Guardsmen demanded to be taken to Otho. In the meantime, his guests had fled, knowing the Senate was hated and distrusted by the soldiers. The Praetorians were opposed by Martialis, who had allowed Otho into the fortress on the day of his insurrection. The tribune was wounded, along with a prefect of a legion. Threats were made against the other tribunes and centurions until order was restored when Otho climbed onto a couch to show he was alive and unharmed.[88]

The next day, the two Praetorian Prefects addressed the Praetorians to restore their authority. They could also ascertain the mood of the soldiers. Otho had remained outside the fortress. This was for safety and also acted as a public demonstration of imperial anger at their behaviour. Would they betray a third emperor? The Praetorian Prefects told the soldiers that each was to receive a donative of 5,000 sesterces. This was less than that given by Nero. The stretched finances of the state and the need to raise money for war had precluded even Otho from promising a donative, but circumstances had changed. Otho then entered, surrounded by tribunes and centurions, 'who tore away the insignia of their rank and demanded discharge and safety from dangerous service'. The emperor had shown his trust in the officers by standing alongside them as well as showing disapproval of the indiscipline of their men. Otho praised their 'excessive loyalty' but demanded the two instigators of the mutiny be punished. The monetary reward and limited punishment appeased the assembly and order was restored.[89]

Otho was the Praetorian emperor, just as Galba was the Spanish one and Vitellius the German, as he was made by the German legions. He was theirs and they were his. Otho would maintain their privileged position against the threat posed by the Rhine legions of Vitellius and Rome's elite. The soldiers saw the tribunes as part of the elite and the centurions as their allies. They continued to distrust the senators, for although they did not 'engage in any general riot, they nevertheless distributed themselves in disguise among the houses and suspiciously kept watch on all whom had high birth or wealth, or some distinction had made the object of gossip'.[90] This suspicion was not due to envy or greed, as the senatorial historian Tacitus would have his reader believe, but from an understanding that this elite burned to avenge the murder of Galba.

They were right to do so. Otho was to be badly served and advised by these nobles and aristocrats. The Praetorians accused three of his commanders of treachery even before Otho left Rome for northern Italy.[91] Before the first Battle of Cremona, two Praetorian tribunes approached the enemy commander, Caecina, but their proposal was never heard as the news of the Othonian advance ended the interview.[92]

The battle was a disaster for Otho. The two wings of his army were pushed back, whilst the five cohorts of Praetorians in the centre were enveloped after holding their ground against the far superior numbers of the *I Italica*. His army then broke, and the slaughter was even greater as the survivors attempted to make for the security of their camp 14 miles away.[93]

Upon hearing the news, Otho decided to end his life despite large numbers of men urging him to fight on. He addressed an assembly of the remaining Praetorians to explain his reasoning. He said that 'it was far better and far more just that one should perish for all than many for one, and that I should refuse on account of one man alone to embroil the Roman people in civil war and cause so great a multitude of human beings to perish'. They attempted to dissuade him, as legions from Pannonia and Moesia were approaching to support his cause. 'Upon thee our lives depend,' they said, 'and for thee we will all die.' Those at the front fell on their knees and kissed his feet, while those at the back saluted him. Otho asked for a dagger from his servants and retired to his chambers, where he managed to get some sleep. As dawn broke, he stabbed himself through the heart.[94]

His funeral was quickly arranged, as Vitellian forces were approaching. He had not wanted his body mutilated and abused like that of Galba's. The 'Praetorians bore his body to the pyre, praising him amid their tears and kissing his wound and hands. Some soldiers slew themselves near his pyre not because of any fault or from fear but prompted by a desire to imitate his glorious example and moved by affection for their emperor.' Afterwards, other Othonian soldiers of all ranks killed themselves in the same way.[95]

Soon after, the Praetorian Prefect, Plotius Firmus, tried to administer the oath of allegiance in the name of Vitellius to the Praetorians; some took it and others rioted, whilst a group seized Verginius Rufus who had accompanied Otho to again try to make him emperor. If he had been uncertain but reluctant in AD 68, he was certain the following year and now fled.[96] Many of Otho's senior commanders were pardoned by Vitellius, including the Praetorian Prefect Licinius Proculus and Suetonius Paullus, who had defeated Boudicca. They defended themselves before Vitellius by convincing him they had deliberately made mistakes before the battle, and their treachery saved them.[97]

Tacitus believed that soldiers were primarily motivated by greed and desired nothing more than the opportunity to pillage and commit murder. However, they repeatedly demonstrated greater loyalty to their ruler than many of the officer class. Nero was betrayed by a conspiracy headed by his Praetorian Prefect. The soldiers in the Rhine legions remained faithful to his death and were punished for it. His guardsmen were made to believe he had already fled for Egypt, deserting them. Romans believed relationships were reciprocal, and loyalty had to be earned. Consequently, at a 'spectacle, when the military tribunes and centurions, after the Roman custom, invoked health and happiness upon the emperor Galba, the mass of the soldiery raised a storm of dissent at first, and then, when the officers persisted in their invocation, cried out in response, "If he deserves it."' In their estimate, he didn't.[98]

Galba ignored his duties to the soldiers. He massacred and then decimated a legion, breaking bonds that tied a soldier to his commander, then refused any donative when precedent demanded it. Otho treated the soldiers with respect, imposed discipline with a light touch and gave them a donative. He was their emperor. His coup was centred on a small core of skilled and determined soldiers driven by vengeance. However, when Otho died less than three months later, he had earned the admiration and devotion of thousands.[99]

Chapter 6

The Revolt of Vitellius (January AD 69)

> 'But discipline which is stern in time of peace is broken down by civil strife, for there are men on both sides ready to corrupt, and treachery goes unpunished.'
>
> (Tacitus, *Histories*, 1.51)

After the destruction of Vindex, the armies of the two German provinces retired to their garrison duties bitter and angry. They had won a great victory over Rome's enemy and had remained steadfast in their loyalty to their now-dead emperor. These legions had been late in taking the oath to Galba and fell under the cloud of imperial suspicion. So instead of reaping the rewards that were their due, they saw the tribes that had fought against them awarded lands and tax benefits whilst their allies, the Treveri and Lingones, were punished. Vindex's allies were the enemy, 'the defeated' or 'the Galbans', despised like their new emperor.[1]

The legions of Upper Germany fumed at the insulting treatment dealt to their commander, Verginius Rufus, which also affronted their honour. In his place, Galba imposed a commander, Hordeonius Flaccus, who added further offence through his lack of presence and authority, and exhibited an undignified subservience. Consequently, 'the soldiers in the Germanies who had been under the command of Rufus became more and more exasperated because they could not obtain any favours from Galba'. Furthermore, they were denied a donative normally given upon the accession of an emperor.[2]

Galba's appointments reflected his poor judgment and inability to assess character. Into this void of authority he placed Aulus Caecina Alienus, who was given command of the *IV Macedonica* based at Mogontiacum (Mainz). At the same time, the Spaniard Dillius Vocula was given command of the *XXII Primigenia* which garrisoned the same fortress. Caecina had been one of the first to join Galba's revolt to escape prosecution for embezzling funds as quaestor in Baetica. The very antithesis of Hordeonius Flaccus, he quickly filled the vacuum created by his superior's lack of authority. This 'handsome young man of towering stature and boundless ambition, had won over the support of the soldiers by his clever speech and dignified carriage'. Vocula was a strict disciplinarian and thus hated by the soldiers.[3]

Galba drew from a small pool of people he trusted from personal acquaintance. However, it was often misplaced. When he discovered Caecina's corruption, he 'ordered him to be prosecuted for peculation' upon his return to Rome. Ceacina had no intention of accepting this, as he faced inevitable conviction because he had lost imperial favour. However, he lacked nobility, whilst his governor, despite his many faults, was loyal to Galba. He awaited an opportunity to change his future.[4]

The situation in Lower Germany was no better. The governor, Fonteius Capito, had been murdered in a conspiracy headed by Fabius Valens, legate of the *I Germanica* based at Bonna (Bonn). The Neronian loyalist Capito had been falsely accused of plotting against Galba and executed. Galba was quite happy to accept the situation, but then he failed to appoint a new provincial governor for several months. The emperor also released Vindex's ally, Civilis, the leading Batavian noble, who had been imprisoned in Rome and now returned to his home. As in Upper Germany, the new emperor allowed a disaffected and treacherous legionary commander to effectively take control. Valens had first attempted to undermine the loyalty of Capito to Nero, then tried to do the same with Verginius Rufus. Failing a second time, he was the first commander in Rufus' army to get his vexillations to take the oath to Galba to undermine Rufus' reluctance. However, the new emperor had in his view failed to reward his deceit, so he was 'hostile to Galba because Galba had treated with ingratitude his disclosure of Verginius' hesitancy and his crushing of Capito's plans'.[5]

Both Valens and Caecina 'were men of boundless greed and extraordinary recklessness',[6] bound together despite their mutual hatred in the desire for a regime change to save themselves from an uncertain future. Discipline in the Rhine legions was gradually eroded. In Upper Germany, Flaccus could not exert any authority, whilst Caecina wanted to build on his popularity with the troops. In Lower Germany 'the soldiers remembered Capito with gratitude' and wanted vengeance. Their anger was focused on Julius Burdo, commander of the Rhine fleet, and Crispinus, a centurion, who had slain Capito. There were many others as well; no doubt Valens was one of them. Consequently, the centurions struggled to impose order, and by December many troops had been punished and had their rank and privileges removed. Others were awaiting trial, whilst more still had been convicted and suffered penalties.[7]

The Treveri and Lingones shared the German army's hatred of the new emperor. They too had suffered and had lost land to Vindex's allies, the Aedui and Sequani. Many of the veterans had settled in the area, especially around the colony of Colonia Agrippinensium (Cologne). This was also the tribal capital of the Ubii. There were close commercial ties with the army, as local communities provided crops, food and other services to the soldiers, many of whom had married locally and their sons had followed in their father's footsteps. The local population appreciated the military presence, and their ties were close.[8]

The Lingones took the initiative and, 'according to their ancient custom, had sent clasped right hands, as an emblem of friendship, as gifts to the legions of Upper Germany'. Their envoys took on the appearance of poverty and mourning at their receptions in the headquarters of each legion. Then they remained in the locality to visit the inns and taverns frequented by the soldiers to complain about the wrongs they had suffered, and 'when the soldiers were ready to lend a listening ear, of the dangers and the insults suffered by the army itself, and so inflamed the temper of the troops'. Hordeonius Flaccus was either unaware of their presence or unwilling to take decisive action until his legionaries were close to mutiny. Only then did he order the envoys to leave at night so that their departure would not be used to initiate further unrest,[9] a poor decision born from his precarious hold over his soldiers.

The next day, the rumour was spread that Flaccus had ordered the envoys killed. They had won a considerable following, and their disappearance further inflamed the troops. Another story spread amongst the soldiers, no doubt propagated by Caecina and his allies, that 'the most energetic among them and those who complained of present conditions would be put to death under cover of darkness without the knowledge of their fellows'. These rumours brought auxiliary cohorts to Mogontiacum, where they were stationed close to the legionary fortresses. There had always been hostility between legionaries and auxiliaries over differences in status, pay and terms of service. The legions believed they were about to be attacked, but it transpired the auxiliaries had gathered to support their fellow soldiers in their time of danger. The soldiers bound themselves together in secret oaths against the threat posed by their emperor and governor.[10]

Galba's actions had unified an army against him. His massacre and then decimation of the marines and sailors who had asked to be recognized as a legion had horrified their comrades around the Empire. His excessive brutality made others fear a similar fate, the German legions most of all. The news from Rome was used to add credence to another rumour that the Rhine legions were also going to be decimated and 'the most active centurions dismissed'. The soldiers were filled with hatred for Galba and fear for their own lives. However, the loyalty of the centurions was essential to maintain discipline and order. Their opportunities for promotion were minimal with Galba as emperor, even if they managed to stay in post. Their interests were aligned with the rank and file, not the emperor in Rome.[11]

Into this cauldron of discontent, Galba added the final ingredient. He made two appointments in an attempt to restore the situation on the Lower Rhine, one of them utterly disastrous. He firstly appointed Pompeius Propinquus as procurator of Belgica and effectively the paymaster of the Rhine armies. He was another Spaniard whom Galba felt he could trust from personal acquittance.[12] He also made the surprising choice of placing Aulus Vitellius as governor of Lower Germany in place of the murdered Capito. This illustrious noble had been one of the foremost courtiers under Claudius and Nero, but his wealth, status and influence had rapidly dissipated under Galba. The patron of innumerable cities and other aristocrats, he now relied on the patronage of Vinius to gain the governorship. He had already held the prestigious governorship of Africa in AD 60, which ranked equal to that of Asia, but he needed to escape Rome, and quickly.[13]

Once, basking in long-lost imperial benevolence, he had been ranked amongst the richest men in the Empire. By AD 69, however, he faced the humiliation of threatening bankruptcy and needed to escape his creditors. He had been forced to rent out his townhouse in Rome and find modest accommodation for his wife and children to raise enough money to cover his travelling expenses to his new province. He had raised more money by selling some of the family jewellery, but he was still besieged by 'the huge crowd of creditors he kept at bay through threats of litigation including [the] towns of Sinuessa and Formiae from whom he had embezzled funds'. He had, however, been forced to provide security for his debts, probably mortgaging his estates in Italy. In a humiliating legal victory, he managed to win compensation from a former slave who had punched and kicked him, such were the depths to which he had descended in dignity and power. He had become a figure of ridicule.[14]

Galba knew Vitellius was financially compromised and would therefore fill himself 'with the fruits of the province'.[15] It never occurred to the emperor that desperation and humiliation would spur the man on to raise the standard of revolt to save himself from inevitable poverty when he returned to Rome. Otho too would move against Galba when financial ruin became inevitable after he failed to be chosen as the imperial heir. Yet Germany was not a wealthy province, unlike those in the East. Vitellius was unlikely to restore his finances by fleecing the provincials of Colonia Agrippinensium, Bonna, Vetera or Noviomagus. Furthermore, their close links to the already volatile army and veterans settled in the surrounding area made this an extremely dangerous proposition. The Batavians, who were the largest tribe in the province, were obligated by their treaty with Rome only to provide men, not money or resources.[16] Vitellius had just one purpose in seeking the governorship of Germania Inferior – rebellion.

It would take a month to travel from Rome to the distant province on the edge of the Empire, meaning there was plenty of time to corrupt the legionaries and baggage handlers sent to escort him from their bases on the Rhine. On the march, 'he would greet even private soldiers with an embrace, and at wayside inns behave most affably towards the muleteers, inquiring whether they had yet breakfasted, and then belching loudly to prove that he had done so'. This was remarkable behaviour for a man of his exalted social status. An embrace denoted equality, while an inferior kissed an offered hand or, in subjection, a foot. Vitellius presented himself as a fellow soldier, a comrade, just as Germanicus had done and as the infant Gaius had been dressed as a mini-legionary.[17]

Around 1 December, the army of Lower Germany received him 'as a gift from the gods'.[18] He was no Germanicus, but he was noble enough to be accepted as emperor. They had their imperial candidate, and he was willing.[19] Immediately he inspected the winter quarters of his legions and 'many of the troops had their ranks restored, their disgrace removed, the marks against them cancelled'. He emptied the military prison and cancelled legal actions for those awaiting trial. These were the most vocal opponents of Galba. To counter the anger of officers, 'he granted any favour that was asked of him' and 'gave away his own property without limit and without judgement and squandered what belonged to others'.[20] This was no great loss to him, as most of his estates stood as security to his creditors and were already lost.

All knew what lay behind their governor's generosity. His 'partisans called it affability and kindness', but his actions 'were not regarded as those simply of a consular legate, but without exception were taken to be more significant'.[21] As he did not have a large retinue of *amici* and advisors to draw upon, the core of his revolt would have been built around the legates and tribunes in the army. Valens was at the forefront, driving the pace. He 'had long been poor' and 'his desires had been increased by long poverty'. These men would be assured of rapid promotion when their candidate ascended the throne, followed by immense wealth, power and influence. As emperor on the Rhine, Vitellius would require an imperial bureaucracy staffed by equestrian officers in the army and Lower Germany rather than freedmen.[22]

From this inner core, contact was extended to wider circles using trusted agents, often carrying coded letters as Vindex had done. These communications were risky but necessary to build a support network in other provinces and armies. In Upper Germany, Hordeonius Flaccus was probably ignored, but his officers like Caecina were approached instead. Others such as the procurator of Belgica, Pompeius Propinquus, who were known for their loyalty to Galba, remained ignorant of the conspiracy that grew around them. However, Galba's recently appointed governor of Belgica, Valerius Asiaticus, was won over with the promise of a consulship and the hand of Vitellius' daughter. Membership of the imperial house was too great an opportunity to dismiss. The presence of four potentially hostile legions on his border also swayed his decision. Contact would also have been made with the tribal leaders of the Treveri and Lingones, with their support assured.[23]

Vitellius would need vast amounts of money to give a donative to his soldiers when they proclaimed him emperor. He would also need to pay for food, wagons, houses and oxen purchased from allied tribes. Moving an army was expensive. Pillaging these resources would undermine his support. Auxiliary soldiers would need to be raised from these native communities to protect the frontier when he removed his experienced troops to fight against Galba. These also would need to be paid and weapons produced. Time was needed to build the organizational logistics and assess his level of support in the provinces, especially those he intended to march through.[24]

Centurions were selected as agents and messengers, accompanied by a few select soldiers. These were intelligent and literate officers. They would also be closely aligned with their immediate commanders and enthused with the promises of a lucrative career. The Helvetians who remained loyal to Galba 'intercepted some letters which were being carried in the name of the army in Germany to legions in Pannonia, and they kept the centurions and certain soldiers in custody'. They would pay a heavy price when Caecina led the German legions through their territory.[25]

Vitellius had only been in post for a month when he was obliged to supervise the customary oath of allegiance to the emperor on 1 January. He was not yet ready to raise the standard of revolt, for 'it was a slow and laborious task to set in motion civil war'. The legionaries were united in their hatred of Galba but divided on the action to take. The words were shouted out by the legates and repeated by a few of the front ranks. The majority remained silent, not wishing to offend the gods by breaking their vow but determined not to promise their allegiance to Galba. Afterwards, some of the legionaries expressed their true feelings. The *I Germanica* under Fabius Valens and *V Alaudae* garrisoning Vetera (Xanten) 'were so mutinous that some stoned Galba's images'. The perpetrators remained unpunished, providing a clear message to their comrades. The *XV Primegenia* which also held Vetera and the *XVI Gallica* at Novaessium (Neuss) did 'nothing worse than murmur and threaten' but remained on the brink of revolt.[26]

The oath of allegiance (*sacramentum*) was taken very seriously by the soldiers. They swore to place the safety of the emperor above all else, undertook personal allegiance to him and promised to obey all his instructions. It was considered *nefas* (forbidden) to break it, as to do so brought the vengeance of Jupiter upon them. To break it offended divine law. Consequently, most of the soldiers of Lower Germany remained silent rather than risk punishment in this life and the next.[27]

Most of the soldiers had little or no education, and their political consciousness was as basic and unpretentious as their religious beliefs. The gods had to show their displeasure with the ruling emperor for them to relinquish their oath. All citizens took the oath, and the Stoic Philostratus warns that for any magistrate or official

> 'who designs to depose a tyrant, the first requisite is plenty of deliberation, with a view to conceal his plans till they are ripe for action; and the second is a suitable pretence to save him from the reproach of breaking his oath. For before he dreams of resorting to arms against the man who appointed him general and whose welfare he swore to safeguard in the council chamber and on the field, he must surely in self-defence furnish heaven with proof that he perjures himself in the cause of religion.'[28]

Events at Mogontiacum in Upper Germany, however, forced Vitellius' plans. The *IV Macedonica* commanded by Caecina took the lead in refusing to give the oath to Galba, followed by the more hesitant *XXII Primigenia* led by Vocula, another of Galba's appointees. The governor, Hordeonius Flaccus, stood impotent on the platform, with his legates and tribunes equally powerless or covertly supporting the mutiny. The men then stormed the platform to tear down Galba's images from their standards. Only four centurions stood in their way, and they were quickly overcome and imprisoned. The reluctant were swiftly swayed by the number of mutineers and a lack of leadership from their officers.[29]

The soldiers wanted to express their loyalty to Rome, rather than its emperor, and so, recalling the oath they swore under Verginius Rufus, they again made their pledge to the Senate and people. The soldiers could feel they were not being disloyal to the state. However, their relationship with their emperor, like that with their gods, was reciprocal. Before battle, a soldier would offer Mars a sacrifice in return for divine protection. If he survived, then the offering had been accepted, but if he was wounded, the sacrifice would not have been adequate; possibly the gift was too little.[30]

Galba had not fulfilled his obligations and duties to the German legions, the victors of Vindex. There had been no rewards, no donative, no titles, no honours. Their comrades in Rome had been decimated, and the shadow of this horror now lay over them. Galba had made no effort to hide his suspicions, so they were not willing to promise to protect his safety. The oath was also a symbol of their potential rewards and safety under the emperor. The German legions had none of these.[31]

The soldiers retired to their quarters when some of their officers recalled them. The governor was not present, so the legionary legates, Caecina and Vocula, must have given the command. They wanted their legions to take the oath to Vitellius. They undermined what was left of the authority of Hordeonius Flaccus by denigrating him as 'a shadow and image of Galba'. Then they commended the nobility of Vitellius to the assembled soldiers. However, Vitellius did not cut an inspirational figure, his poverty making the probability of a substantial donative unlikely.[32]

The legionaries were divided, so it was decided to force their decision. Vitellius' coup was still emergent, and he had developed few links to other provinces. A standard bearer was despatched to Colonia Agrippinensium (Cologne) from Mogontiacum to inform Vitellius that an opportunity for revolt was presenting itself and should be seized immediately. The messenger arrived that night, travelling 111 miles, no doubt by boat along the Rhine. Vitellius was entertaining guests when the standard bearer arrived. Bedecked on his couch, Vitellius was told the Fourth and Twenty-second legions had destroyed the images of Galba and taken their oath to the Senate instead.[33]

Vitellius knew the attitude of his legions from their reluctance to take the same oath. He immediately sent messengers to both the legions and their legates. If the commanders attempted to remain loyal, their men would force them to back down. Vitellius presented a simple choice to the soldiers, knowing already what their response would be. They could either fight for Galba against their comrades in the neighbouring province or acclaim him as emperor.[34] Later Vitellian propaganda presented him as a reluctant usurper, forced out of his bedroom half-asleep by a mob of soldiers and carried around Colonia Agrippinensium in his night attire. It was a standard motif but was undermined by his message to his officers.[35]

The first to receive the news was Fabius Valens 18 miles away at Bonna. He is described as 'the most energetic of the commanders', just as he had been in getting his vexillation to give the oath to Galba when his superior, Verginius Rufus, hesitated. His ambition and grievances were matched only by his energy. He also wanted the prestige of being the first to acclaim him, so he gathered his legionary and auxiliary cavalry and arrived early in the morning to salute Vitellius as emperor. Soon after, Vitellius was presented with a sword once owned by Julius Caesar that was in the Temple of Mars, the god of war, in Colonia Agrippinensium. A man with no military experience or martial reputation would need the favour of the two gods, Jupiter and the divine Caesar. His soldiers could take comfort from this. Galba was famed for the prestige he had won in campaigns beyond the Rhine, but Vitellius owed 'his elevation to no campaigns or reputation as a soldier, but solely to men's hatred of Galba'.[36]

Initial celebrations were marred by an ill omen. A stove had been knocked over in the headquarters building and the dining room burnt down before the fire could be extinguished. The gods appeared to be showing their anger at the soldiers breaking their oath to Galba. This 'apparently unlucky portent caused general concern and alarm'. Vitellius was forced to call an *adlocutio* to restore the men's faith in the support of the gods to his cause. He addressed the ranks and 'told them: "Courage, my men. Light is given us!"' This was the only speech he gave to the soldiers. The courtier was well out of his comfort zone in front of thousands of hardened legionaries. When the army of Upper Germany received the news that their comrades in Lower Germany had acclaimed Vitellius, they readily did the same on 3 January.[37]

Their new emperor was given the official name Germanicus by his men. The fame and renown of their long-dead prince was remembered in the tradition of the German legions. Furthermore, the name reminded their new emperor that he was theirs. The Vitellian coinage produced at Lugdunum at first bears the legend IMP. GERMAN. rather than GERMAN. IMP., suggesting the emperor was made by the German armies.[38] Galba had been made by the Spanish army and provinces, and later Otho by the Praetorians recruited mainly from Italy. Now the German army and its provinces had their emperor.

The provincials of Colonia Agrippinensium were quick to recognize their governor as emperor. Veterans, settled in the hinterland, married local women, had families and farmed the land. The city's declaration was followed by the Treveri and Lingones. The 'chief men' of these communities 'offered their personal services, horses, arms, or money according to the physical strength, wealth, or talent that each possessed'. Many of these were the tribal elite, important landowners and great merchants whose commerce was based on providing crops and materials to the legions. With their support, the local population and individual towns would be committed to his cause. Trading clubs were formed on a tribal basis, linked with neighbouring forts and garrisons. The merchants' clubs of the Remi and the Lingones, for example, were associated with the legionary base at Vetera. The wealthiest group were the long-distance traders who transported goods along the Rhine, Rhone and inland waterways. Their affluence was reflected in the huge warehouses built next to the river at Vienne and Lugdunum, or their mausoleums and monuments in Mogontiacum or on the shores of Lake Geneva.[39]

News of the revolt spread along these waterways, which carried Vitellius' messengers and agents. Lugdunum continued its bitter rivalry with Vienne by declaring for Vitellius. It was a veteran colony, so was closely allied to the German army whose former soldiers were settled in the area. More importantly, it possessed a mint and was still garrisoned by the *I Italica*, which Galba had negligently left there after the death of Nero. The legion had been raised by the last of the Julio-Claudians, and the colony had been fervently pro-Nero and was thus punished by Galba whilst he had honoured Vienne.[40]

When Valens led one of Vitellius' armies through the city, its inhabitants urged his soldiers to slaughter their rivals in Vienne, reminding them that they had supported Vindex and Galba. Lugdunum was, they said, 'part of their army', whilst Vienne was full of booty. The Vitellian soldiers were so enraged that the officers lost control of their men as they advanced on Vienne. The city was partially sacked before being saved from destruction by Valen's promise of 300 sesterces to every soldier and the provisioning of his troops without charge.[41]

The reluctance of Valens to see the city sacked was not borne from a newfound compassion or consideration for unarmed civilians. Rumours spread that the commander had received a huge bribe from the town's wealthy elite. However, one of its great patrons was Valerius Asiaticus, who governed Belgica and had been betrothed to Vitellius' daughter. The sacking of Vienne would make an enemy of his emperor's future son-in-law.[42]

The two armies led by Vitellius' generals, Caecina and Valens, left a trail of devastation as they passed through the territories of Vindex's former allies. This was partly to exact revenge but also to compensate the legionaries who had not received a donative from Vitellius upon his accession. The soldiers understood that it would be paid when they had been victorious and possessed Rome. The money was paid to the legionaries on the Rhine in late AD 69. By then, it was clear Vespasian would be victorious in his war against Vitellius, so Hordeonius Flaccus made the grave mistake of distributing it in Vespasian's name. The soldiers remained fixed in their loyalty to their emperor, and the governor was dragged from his bed and murdered.[43]

Many of the senior officers remained fluid in their loyalty, ready to shift and move to whoever appeared to be most likely to win. Caecina, who along with Valens defeated Otho's forces at the first Battle of Cremona, would later turn traitor again and, along with his leading centurions, attempt to force their army to switch their allegiance to Vespasian. The Vitellian legionaries were incensed, and led by the *V Alaudae*, threw him into chains. Governors, legates and tribunes could be well rewarded for bringing over their province or army despite a sullied reputation. Individual soldiers, however, had everything to lose in the defeat of their chosen leader and nothing to gain. Otho's Praetorians were devoted to him, unlike his leading generals. Vitellius' legionaries had no thought of abandoning their emperor, even when all was lost.[44]

Vitellius had few funds or resources for the march into Italy. His men would live off the land of their enemies, but money was still needed to pay for crops, carts, oxen, waggons and metal to forge weapons. These had to be provided by the communities that had immediately supported him. Consequently, in their enthusiasm, 'common soldiers, prompted by excitement and enthusiasm and also by greed, contributed their own spending money, or in place of money their belts and bosses, and the decorations of their armour adorned with silver'. These were the symbols of their courage and bravery, which they willingly donated to secure victory. The silver was melted down into coins. Levies were also held amongst local tribes, including the Batavians, who would garrison the frontier in the absence of a third of the Rhine army. Furthermore, an enormous number of Gallic auxiliaries were raised, and these would need to be paid.[45]

The German army had a fearsome reputation. In February, they learnt that Galba had been murdered and deposed by Otho and his Italian-born Praetorians. However, the die had already been cast. In March, the snows melted early, allowing them to advance through the Alpine passes into Italy. A cavalry *ala* raised in Upper Germany but operating in the Po Valley changed its allegiance after its officers who had served under Vitellius when he was governor of Africa 'kept extolling the strength of the approaching force and the reputation of the army in Germany'. Their motivations to rebel were diverse. The decurions hoped for rewards from Vitellius, so they secured Milan, Novara, Ivrea and Vercelli for him. With treachery, it was always best to bring something tangible to the table. The soldiers had ties to their kin among the Treveri and Lingones, whilst they all considered that defeat was a distinct probability if they opposed the invading army that included their tribesmen.[46]

The overall impression is that the dominant force behind Vitellius' revolt came from the ranks, which was exploited by some senior commanders holding grievances or burdened by debts or lost influence. Otho's revolt was also an uprising from below. These Rhine legionaries were not returning home when they invaded Italy; most had been born in the German provinces to fathers who had fought under the standards of the legions. The stories of their exploits were passed from father to son down the generations. The charisma of Germanicus came alive in their tales, as did the brutality and cruelty of Galba.[47]

The Rhine legionaries were feared. More barbarian than Roman, these soldiers 'presented a sight that was equally savage, dressed as they were in shaggy skins of wild beasts and armed with enormous spears'.[48] And yet they remained faithful to Vitellius, their new Germanicus. They had given their oath to him and he rewarded their loyalty. The legionaries knew that they would replace Otho's Praetorians. The guardsmen who were not slaughtered at Cremona were later dismissed by Vitellius. Twenty thousand Vitellian legionaries were recruited into sixteen new Praetorian cohorts and four Urban cohorts, each 1,000 strong.[49]

The legionaries also did not forget injustices. For this reason, they hated Galba. In Germany, they demanded the arrest and execution of Fonteius Capito's murderers. They wanted justice served on all those who supported Vindex and Galba. Vitellius was in no position to oppose the wishes of the soldiers. Many men of lesser rank were offered up. The four centurions who had attempted to defend Galba's images on the legionary standards were also expendable. In Rome, they demanded the arrest of four of Vindex's tribal leaders who remained at large. Other leaders, though, were too important and influential to surrender to their bloodlust. Consequently, the centurion who had slain Capito was executed, but Julius Burdo, who commanded the Rhine fleet, was merely imprisoned and then released once victory was won and 'the hatred of the soldiers for him was now appeased'. Valens was untouchable. The Batavian noble, Julius Civilis, was not, so he was arrested again but later released as Vitellius needed the support of the eight Batavian cohorts that had remained in the territory of the Lingones after their withdrawal from the fervently Neronian *XIV Gemina*.[50]

For all his intelligence in winning and retaining the backing of the Rhine legions, Vitellius would quickly lose the support of other soldiers across the Empire by repeating the cruelties and injustices perpetuated by Galba. When victory was won and he was able to appease the defeated armies, he took vengeance. Otho's Praetorians were dismissed without any gratuity and in disgrace, until he was forced to give them all an honorary discharge. Most would fight for Vespasian. Then 'those centurions who had been most active in supporting Otho were put to death, an action which more than anything else turned the forces in Illyricum against Vitellius, [and] at the same time the contagion spread to the rest of the legions'. The *XIII Gemina* that had fought bravely for Otho at Cremona was deliberately humiliated. The survivors were forced to build two amphitheatres close to the site of their defeat for games to celebrate the Vitellian victory. They too would embrace Vespasian.[51]

As Vitellius followed in the wake of his victorious army, he insisted on seeing the site of this battle. The dead of both sides still lay strewn across the vineyards and ditches of the battlefield. The slaughter had been too much for Otho, who declared, 'Enough, quite enough, has already happened. I hate civil war, even though I conquer; and I love all Romans, even though they do not side with me.' The stench of 40,000 rotting corpses polluted the air. The smell was so overpowering that it 'caused some consternation, [and] Vitellius cheered his companions with the brazen remark: "Only one thing smells sweeter to me than a dead enemy, and that is a dead fellow citizen." Nevertheless, he took a good swig of neat wine to counteract the stink and generously passed the flagon around.'[52]

The soldiers who were with him were all too aware of the horror and pity of war, and many 'were moved to tears'. But not Vitellius. He never turned his eyes away from the mutilated corpses and severed limbs, 'ignorant of his own fate which was so near'. Eight months later he would be dragged from his hiding place in the palace to the Forum, and after being tortured by Vespasian's soldiers, he would be executed and his body thrown into the Tiber like that of a common criminal.[53]

His soldiers understood better than to gloat. They knew death and recognized that fortune often came full circle. Their bodies too would litter the same ground, covering the fields up to the walls of Cremona, cramming its streets and polluting the temples. The second Battle of Cremona was a night battle and was even more vicious, more chaotic, with the slaughter even greater.[54]

Vespasian's forces were led by Antonius Primus, a noble possessing ample political agility. Exiled for fraud by Nero, he became a fervent supporter of Galba, who gave him command of his Seventh Legion. He then attempted to join Otho before leading the Pannonian army into Italy on behalf of the eventual victor, Vespasian. By then the Vitellians were without the equally duplicitous Caecina, whom the soldiers had imprisoned after he attempted to change sides. His life had only been saved by his tribunes. Vespasian would spare his life, and in gratitude he would try to overthrow his new emperor by inciting a revolt. He was executed in AD 79 whilst Antonius Primus was sent to his native town of Tolosa to enjoy an abrupt and premature retirement.[55]

Tacitus, like Dio, was a proud member of the nobility who held the common people in contempt. He believed that the mob was governed by base instincts. They were an ignorant mass who lacked moral responsibility. The soldiers were recruited from the common people, so consequently they too lacked loyalty to the state and their emperor. Only harsh discipline kept in check their insatiable greed and desire for pillage. Rightful grievances and legitimate causes of discontent are fleetingly passed over in the histories. However, Tacitus is at times more nuanced, recognizing that there were both good soldiers who accepted their position and bad ones who led the rabble in demanding change. The historian blamed the civil war on 'the madness of the leading men' who 'held their honour cheap'. The officers and commanders were often deceitful in their oaths and allegiance, in contrast to the fervent loyalty and devotion of the rank and file Praetorians to Otho or the 'the unshaken loyalty of centurions and soldiers towards Vitellius'. Their loyalty was a personal relationship with their chosen emperor, who identified with them and showed consideration for their wellbeing.[56]

The soldiers were the victors and victims in this conflict. Tacitus does recognize the futility and misery of war. Amid the second Battle of Cremona, a father and son met on opposing battle lines. The father had enrolled in the *XXI Rapax* based at Vetera in Lower Germany and had left his child behind in Spain. The young man decided to follow his father into the legions and volunteered in the

Seventh, raised by Galba. Now they met in the darkness and the son struck down his father, mortally wounding him. As the son moved to make the killing blow they 'recognised each other; the son embraced his expiring father and prayed with tears in his voice that his father's spirit would forgive him and not abhor him as a parricide. "The crime," he cried, "is the State's; and what does a single soldier count in civil war?"' He then dug his father's grave and his comrades, struck with grief, helped him. Once his duty was performed, the battle continued and they did not 'slacken in their murder of relatives, kinsmen, and brothers'.[57]

Chapter 7

Vespasian's Rising in the East (July AD 69)

'It is not the man who has too little who is poor, but the one who hankers after more.'

(Seneca, *Letters from a Stoic*, 2.4)

The main players in this political game were dissatisfied with their present state. Nymphidius, Valens, Caecina, Vitellius and others conspired to take control of events to forge a better future for themselves. However, Roman politics was a watching game. A safer course was to adapt to changing circumstances and wait for events.

Vespasian had learnt this under Gaius, Claudius and Nero. He was always cautious and reluctant even to start a senatorial career, unlike his more ambitious and well-connected elder brother, Titus Flavius Sabinus. He was initially supported by the great imperial freedman, Narcissus. After holding the command of a legion in Germany, Vespasian led the *II Augusta* during Claudius' invasion of Britain in AD 43 and was awarded an honorary triumph for conquering the southwest of the country. However, he fell from favour when his patron, Narcissus, misguidedly supported Britannicus Claudius' biological son, as heir. Agrippina the Younger, the emperor's wife, had similar aspirations for her son, Nero. Narcissus was sent to Baiae in Campania to recuperate from gout, where he learned of the death of his emperor. Claudius had probably been poisoned by Agrippina, who had Narcissus executed a few weeks later. Vespasian fled to his country estates, awaiting a similar fate. He survived but learnt from the experience to wait, watch and observe.[1]

Britannicus did not live much longer. His murder served to teach Vespasian's 16-year-old son, Titus, a similar lesson. Titus had grown up in the imperial court and had become a close friend of Britannicus. Nero had decided to remove his rival. He held a banquet the night before Britannicus' 14th birthday which was attended by his friend, his sister Antonia, Agrippina and various honoured and distinguished guests. Suddenly, Britannicus fell to the floor, convulsing after taking a drink from a cup he was sharing with Titus, who also fell seriously ill. The experienced courtiers watched, waited and observed but made no outward move, concealing their horror, whilst 'those sitting nearby were thrown into confusion; the imprudent fled, but those with deeper understanding remained rooted to the spot and watched Nero'. Politics was a battleground.[2]

Britannicus died immediately, but his friend slowly recovered. As emperor, Titus remembered his young friend and set up two statues of Britannicus, a golden one erected in his palace and an ivory one carried in processions before the games. Yet 'he did not forget what had happened'. Father and son held no love for Nero, but remained loyal. He was the source of all power, influence, honours and offices. Nero's murder of his mother led to Vespasian's rehabilitation. He was honoured with the prestigious governorship of Africa and then given command of three legions to crush the Jewish rebellion in Judaea in AD 66. Titus became legate of one of them.[3]

The accession of Galba offered opportunity and threat. Vespasian's brother, Sabinus, was removed from the city prefecture and his nephew lost his promised consulship. His own command was under threat as he had been appointed by Nero. However, Vespasian ensured his soldiers took the oath of allegiance to Galba and sent Titus to Rome with King Herod Agrippa II, to receive further instructions for the Judaean campaign and secure a praetorship from the new emperor. In the meantime, the war was put on hold, although only Jerusalem and a few scattered strongholds held out against the Romans.[4]

In early February at Corinth, Titus learnt of the death of Galba and the accession of Otho. Soon after, merchants reported that Vitellius and the German army had risen in revolt. Titus called his friends together to seek their advice. To continue his journey to Rome seemed perilous, but to return to Judaea without paying his respects to Otho invited suspicion. His advisors realised that 'if he should go on to Rome, he would enjoy no gratitude for an act of courtesy intended for another emperor, and he would be a hostage in the hands of either Vitellius or Otho; on the other hand, if he returned to his father, the victor would undoubtedly feel offence'. He would be forgiven, though, if Vespasian brought his legions over to the winning side before the outcome was settled. However, delaying the choice or choosing the losing side would bring catastrophe down upon his family. Titus's younger brother, Domitian, remained in Rome, along with his uncle, Flavius Sabinus, whom Otho reinstated as City Prefect, ostensibly at the request of the Praetorians but partly as a conciliatory gesture to Vespasian. Furthermore, Sabinus could not abandon his office and leave the capital, effectively becoming a captive for his brother's loyalty.[5]

Titus, however, had already made his decision, and his actions betray his ambition. The accession of Otho, descended from a family of recent nobility, had changed the imperial landscape. Many members of the aristocracy could claim an equal or better nobility than that of the new emperor; what they lacked was the opportunity to lay claim to the throne. Vespasian didn't lack that opportunity. Titus made a slow and protracted return journey to his father. 'He coasted along the shores of Achaia and Asia, leaving the land on the left, and made for the islands of Rhodes and Cyprus', where he visited the oracle of Venus at Paphos. He was ostensibly asking the goddess for a safe journey, but the priest then asked for a private interview after examining the entrails of the sacrificial victim. Titus made public what was said. He had 'heard his own prospects of wearing the purple mentioned again'. A rumour was already circulating that Galba had sent for him so he could adopt him as his son. The soldiers would need persuading that the gods favoured Vespasian and Titus, which negated their previous oath of allegiance.[6]

By the time Titus returned to Judaea, his father's legions had already taken the oath to Otho, as had Tiberius Alexander's two legions in Egypt and the four in Syria commanded by Gaius Licinius Mucianus. The three legions in Judaea were not enough to win a civil war. Titus' imperial ambitions rested on these three men. He knew the ever-cautious Vespasian would need convincing. The 60-year-old general 'was never inclined to be rash, and he hesitated very much about involving himself in such troublesome affairs'. Life had taught him that the wise sought anonymity while fools sought the throne. However, he was convinced otherwise.[7]

Vespasian knew he would be recalled to Rome. He was Nero's man, but his son's decision to return to Judaea made recall inevitable. His army had taken the oath to Otho, whose forces were no match for the German legions. Vitellius would win the war and he would view Vespasian with suspicion. With no army to protect him and in imperial disfavour, his prospects in Rome were bleak. He had been in this position before and had no desire to experience the anxiety and insecurity again. He was a man of 'modest antecedents' who lacked the ancient Republican ancestry of Galba, but stood equal to the nobility of Otho and possessed greater military repute.[8]

Both Mucianus in Syria and Tiberius Alexander in Egypt faced the same stark future. The Prefect of Egypt was an early supporter of Galba. Alexander had been a close friend of Domitius Corbulo and served on his staff. Nero's execution of the great general had alienated many of those who had admired and served Corbulo on his eastern campaigns. Alexander had secretly sent a shipload of weapons to Spain to aid Galba's revolt and his province was amongst the first to acknowledge him as emperor. The hatred of the German legions for any ally of Galba meant disgrace, exile or death under Vitellius. Mucianus had also served with Corbulo, and in AD 67 had been appointed governor of Syria by Nero.[9]

A major obstacle in forming this coalition was Mucianus and Vespasian's mutual hatred. Vespasian was an austere military man who revelled in danger and enjoyed sharing the hardships of his men. By contrast, Mucianus 'was eminent for his magnificence and wealth and by the complete superiority of his scale of life to that of the private citizen'. The Syrian governor was also known for his homosexual appetites and theatrical manner. He knew his soldiers admired his neighbouring governor, which added to their fraught relationship. However, necessity and their shared danger first brought dialogue, then trust. Titus, who had a close, positive friendship with Mucianus, would cement their alliance.[10]

Mucianus and Vespasian, both highly intelligent men and consummate politicians, had, at Nero's death, 'laid aside their hostilities and consulted together, at first through friends as go-betweens; and then Titus, the chief bond of their concord, had ended their dangerous feud by pointing out their common interests; both by his nature and skill he was well calculated to win over even a person of the character of Mucianus'.[11] Tacitus' hostility is couched, yet Mucianus proved loyal to Vespasian as he led his armies across the Roman world to make him emperor. He had no children so had no dreams of founding an imperial dynasty. Furthermore, he knew Vespasian's debt to him would bring him untold wealth, influence and power without the risks inherent in holding the imperial throne. He was a wise man and no fool.

Tiberius Alexander was probably already willing to join them, but the proximity of seven legions in Judaea and Syria made his decision a certainty. Rome was entirely dependent on Egypt's grain, and holding back the grain fleet at the start of the sailing season would result in starvation and food riots in the capital. The grain could also be used to provision his army, while the vast wealth of the province could pay the soldiers and buy the resources needed to fight a war. The fighting in Judaea remained on hold as the focus moved to preparing for revolt and civil war. Preparations took from February until July. Galba had taken time to emerge from Spain, even failing to support his ally, Vindex. Otho's Praetorian revolt was confined to Rome itself, whilst Vitellius' incipient plans were overtaken by events in Upper Germany. Vespasian's preparations were protected by secrecy and distance. He was cautious, methodical and thorough. Vitellius' forces would ultimately be overwhelmed by a tsunami that emerged from various regions of the East.[12]

The troops were persuaded that they could break the oath without impiety. They had promised before the gods to protect the life of Nero, then Galba, followed by Otho and finally Vitellius. Vespasian showed that he had been destined by the gods to rule. A series of religious portents and signs were manufactured, and the reports were fed to the men. Rumours, supposedly originating from Rome, confirmed his destiny was divinely blessed, for 'Nero, it seemed, had been warned in a dream shortly before his death to take the sacred chariot of Jupiter Best and Greatest from its shrine to the Circus, calling at Vespasian's house as he went'. During the brief reign of Galba, 'a statue of Julius Caesar turned of its own accord to face east', and then 'when the Battle of Bedriacum [Cremona] was about to begin, two eagles fought in full view of both armies, before a third appeared from the rising sun and drove off the victor'. The omens were manufactured at regular intervals to reassure the committed and persuade the wavering that the gods encouraged them to abandon their previous oaths without divine retribution.[13]

To confirm his divine favour, 'in Judaea, Vespasian consulted the oracle of the God of Carmel and was given a promise that he would never be disappointed in what he planned or desired, however lofty his ambitions'. The historian Josephus also used the situation to his advantage. He had commanded the rebel Jewish garrison at Jotapata in AD 67, surrendering to Vespasian's Fifth Legion after a six-week siege. The defenders committed suicide, but Josephus hid and was brought before Vespasian and Titus. He said he was a seer and claimed that the ruler of the world would rise out of Israel. This was an ancient Biblical prophecy foretelling the Messiah, but Josephus used it to save himself from execution. Instead, he was imprisoned and became a friend of Titus. Aware of all the preparations for the revolt, he decided to use the situation to his advantage. He claimed to have received another vision and 'insisted that he would soon be released by the very man who had put him in fetters, and who would then be Emperor'. Josephus was rewarded with his freedom and Roman citizenship.[14]

There were a multitude of omens, prophecies and predictions that circulated the camps and forts, and when the moment came for revolt, the leading men 'became bolder; they gathered about Vespasian, encouraged him, and recalled the prophecies of seers and the movements of the stars'. Later, Flavian propaganda portrayed the revolt as a movement growing from the soldiers, who forced a reluctant Vespasian to accept their demands for him to seize the throne. There was indeed a groundswell of support for revolt amongst the soldiers, but this was exploited and encouraged by the senior officers and commanders. The news that Spanish and German legions had acclaimed their imperial candidates encouraged a similar feeling in members of the eastern legions, who 'began to murmur and examine their own resources, that the rewards of empire might not fall to the rest, to them only the necessity of servitude'. War meant plunder and donatives.[15]

The soldiers admired Vespasian. It did not matter to them that he lacked a great name: he had led armies to victory in Britain and Judaea. Leading 'the assault on one fortress he was wounded on the knee by a stone and caught several arrows on his shield'.[16] The role of fellow soldier came naturally to him, being 'energetic in war. He used to march at the head of his troops, select a place for camp, oppose the enemy night and day with wise strategy, and, if occasion demanded, with his own hands. His food was whatever chance offered; in his dress and bearing he hardly differed from the common soldier.' He shared their dangers and endured their hardships. They knew that he would not risk their lives needlessly. Titus also had a great military reputation, having captured the Judaean fortresses of Tarichaeae and Gamala, where 'he had a horse killed under him, but mounted another belonging to a comrade who fell at his side'.[17]

Vespasian and Titus, as well as Mucianus in Syria, first targeted the legates and tribunes, and then the centurions in their legions. Promises of promotion, senatorial status, governorships or procuratorships were the currency of betrayal. The centurions were an important means of gaining the support of the soldiers. It was they who were used as a conduit for rumours and messages. Their position and rank would add credence and validity to these reports. The most effective was the assertion 'that Vitellius had decided to transfer the legions of Germany to Syria, where they could enjoy a profitable and easy service, while in exchange he would assign to the troops in Syria the wintry climate and laborious duties of Germany'.[18]

The threat would have enraged the soldiers, not because they jealously guarded a comfortable and cosseted lifestyle, but because most of them had been born in the East, had married local women and had families that they would be forced to abandon. Even their gods were Syrian. The *XII Fulminata* and *VI Ferrata* had been in Syria for decades. Another Syrian legion, the *III Gallica* that fought in the night battle at Cremona, had been transferred to Moesia by Nero in AD 68 after garrisoning Syria for over a century. The soldiers were all devotees of the eastern religious cult that worshipped the sun. As dawn broke over the battlefield of Cremona, they turned as one to face the first rays and in one shout hailed their god.[19]

As part of this campaign, a forged letter supposedly from Otho was also circulated. In it, the dead emperor begged Vespasian 'most earnestly to avenge his death and come to the aid of the empire'. This added further justification for ignoring their recent oath of allegiance to Vitellius by legitimising the accession of the dead Otho. However, when the oath to Vitellius was read out to the armies in Syria and Judaea, 'they listened in complete silence'. There was no attempt by the officers to make the soldiers repeat the words. The oath had been administered and as such was reported to the much-relieved Vitellius, but the eastern soldiers had not taken it. They were free of obligations to the emperor in Rome or the gods. Tellingly, the imperial mint at Antioch never produced any coinage carrying the image of Vitellius.[20]

Vespasian, Titus and Mucianus had been just as prepared to wage war against Otho as they would against Vitellius. They were content to see their two adversaries destroy each other, knowing the forces of the defeated side would later be willing to join them. All three 'knew that the victors and vanquished in civil war never unite in any complete good faith and that it made no difference whether it was Vitellius or Otho whom Fortune allowed to survive'. Time was on their side, so they 'postponed the war until a more favourable opportunity'.[21]

The soldiers had little understanding of imperial politics or conceptual grasp of the state. Their allegiance was personal. Vexillations of three Moesian legions – the *III Gallica*, *VIII Augusta* and *VII Claudiana* – had marched from their bases on the Danube towards Italy to support Otho. They reached Aquileia in late April, where they received news of Otho's defeat at the first Battle of Cremona and his suicide. They also learnt that 'the centurions who had been most active in supporting Otho were put to death'. These were officers from the *I Aduitrix*, the *XIII Gemina* from Pannonia and vexillations of the *XIV Gemina*.[22]

When they heard the news, the 6,000 Moesian legionaries attacked Vitellius' envoys who had brought the message, seized the camp treasury and took to plundering the area. Then, led by the vexillation from the *III Gallica*, they replaced Otho's name on their standards with that of Vespasian. Soldiers from this legion had fought in Judaea before its transfer and had come to admire Vespasian's military acumen. The readiness of these soldiers to support him was later pivotal in convincing Tiberius Alexander, the Prefect of Egypt, that his neighbour would win a war against Vitellius. But the legionaries lacked support from elsewhere, and facing certain defeat they reluctantly took an oath to Vitellius and returned to their garrison fortresses. Vespasian was probably informed of the insurrection after it had ended, but he knew the *III Gallica* would join him, and the other two in Moesia were likely to join his revolt when he had finalized his preparations three months later.[23]

The interlude was spent extending his support and gathering resources. Otho's defeated Praetorians were eager for revenge. Vitellius had initially dismissed them without any discharge bonus or gratuity, and their former posts were taken by Vitellian legionaries. They had been kept separate from the other troops as they were already mutinous and would inflame the passions of the other defeated forces. A revolt was imminent, so Vitellius gave them an honourable discharge along with land to settle on around Aquileia and the Maritime Alps. The process had already started by June, with the guardsmen handing over their weapons to their tribunes. However, Vespasian's agents were already circulating amongst them, promising a return to their former posts if they took up arms against Vitellius. When they heard of Vespasian's revolt in July, 'they resumed their former service and formed the backbone of the Flavian party'.[24]

Contact was made with the governors, officials, patrons and great landowners in all the eastern provinces, as well as the allied kings of Emesa and Commagene. Equestrians were offered prefectures and procuratorships in the new regime, while others were promised senatorial status. Those of higher status would be rewarded with influence and access to the new emperor, along with the great offices of the state. Catlius Longus, for example, was an equestrian officer in command of an auxiliary unit of horse archers. Once Vespasian ascended the throne, he was adlected into the Senate at praetorian rank, probably for bringing over his city of Apamea in Bithynia. As the city's patron, he no doubt influenced its ruling council and trades guilds, and owned a significant proportion of the surrounding land.[25]

The allied kings were faced with no choice. If they remained loyal to Vitellius, they would be quickly overwhelmed by Vespasian's forces and deposed. However, by supporting the usurper they would retain their throne and acquire rewards, tax benefits or territorial expansion of their kingdom. Emesa was strategically important as it stood at the headwaters of the Tigris and Euphrates, but more importantly, it could supply regiments of mounted archers. Commagene was ruled by Antiochus IV, who had inherited the enormous wealth of the Seleucids. He would contribute generously to Vespasian's war chest, but three years later would be charged with treason, deposed and his kingdom absorbed into the Roman Empire.[26]

Time was also needed to warn King Herod Agrippa II, who had continued onwards to Rome after receiving news of the murder of Galba, whilst Titus had returned to his father. Titus had fallen in love with the king's sister, Berenice. His friends were instructed to send private messages to him to return whilst Vitellius remained unaware of the plot. In the East, Berenice used all her wealth and influence to further Vespasian's cause. Herod Agrippa retained his kingdom of Judaea after supporting Vespasian and providing Titus with 2,000 soldiers to crush the Jewish revolt.[27]

Critically, Vespasian's brother, Sabinus, had to remain in Rome as City Prefect, as did his younger son, Domitian. Sabinus had command of the Urban cohorts, but they were heavily outnumbered by the Vitellian forces in the city. He used his position to win the support of eminent individuals on behalf of his brother, but once the revolt began, his life and that of Domitian would be at risk. In July, he recruited the Vitellian generals Ceacina and Rubrius Gallus to Vespasian's cause. When the fleet at Misenium attempted to mutiny, a praetorian senator was fortutiously close by, ostensibly holidaying in the area. However, neither Sabinus nor Domitian could leave Rome, as it would give advanced warning of Vespasian's planned revolt. For this reason, Vespasian wanted to convince Vitellius that he faced inevitable defeat. In these circumstances, Vitellius would preserve the lives of Sabinus and Domitian as a bargaining chip to preserve either his own life or that of his infant son.[28]

Sabinus targeted officers who had been cashiered by Galba and had fought for Otho. Aemilus Pacenius had been released from the Urban cohorts, then commanded Othonian forces in the Maritime Alps and Gallia Nabonensis and would die alongside Sabinus in Rome. The centurion Claudius Faventius, who had been discharged by Galba, would attempt to subvert the imperial fleet at Misenum on behalf of the Flavians. Lucius Antonius Naso was dismissed as a tribune in the Praetorian Guard by Galba but later joined Vespasian's forces to be reappointed to the same post, followed by promotion to commander of the veterans in the capital.[29]

Plans and preparations reached a point where secrecy hindered further progress. On 25 June, Titus travelled to Syria to meet Mucianus to make the final arrangements for the acclamation of Vespasian. Messages were also sent to Tiberius Alexander in Alexandria. Vespasian wanted to present to the world the picture of a reluctant general forced by his troops to accept the throne to save the Empire from a tyrant. The same propaganda had been employed by Galba when he rose against Nero, and also by Vitellius.[30]

On 1 July AD 69, Alexander addressed the two Egyptian legions in their fortress at Nicopolis, on the outskirts of Alexandria. The *III Cyrenaica* and *XXII Deiotariana* enthusiastically gave their oath of allegiance to Vespasian. The Prefect of Egypt then returned to the Hippodrome, where the populace had been told to gather. There, the crowds endorsed the proclamation of the troops. On 3 July, Vespasian was proclaimed emperor at his provincial capital of Caesarea. A ship then travelled between the two provinces with a message confirming proceedings had gone to plan. [31]

According to the official account, Vespasian was surprised one morning as he stepped out of his private quarters. The commander was greeted by his guard, but instead of saluting him as legate, they did so using the imperial title of *imperator* and 'then the rest ran up and began calling him Caesar and Augustus; they heaped upon him all the titles of emperor'. History is written by the victors. From the coast, Vespasian travelled to Jerusalem, where the majority of his legionary troops were besieging the city. There, on 11 July, in another carefully choreographed event, the soldiers 'surrounded his tent and hailed him as emperor'. The legions and auxiliary cohorts were then assembled for a formal *adlocutio* and 'the army in Judaea swore allegiance to Vespasian in person'. The physical presence of their commander was important to reinforce the personal bond that existed between their emperor and his legions.[32]

Like a wave, the neighbouring province of Syria discarded their loyalty to Vitellius and swore to obey Vespasian. Each acclamation increased the confidence of the soldiers in the next province. Mucianus had waited to receive the news from Judaea before he administered the oath 'to his own eager troops'. The hard work had already been done to ensure their commitment to Vespasian's revolt. Only a modest donative was promised, as resources were to be focused on war. Nor was there any promise to improve pay or conditions of service. This is surprising, as both Otho and Vitellius had promised to pay the bribes normally paid by soldiers to centurions for a reduction in duties and fatigues. Vespasian's soldiers accepted this, recognizing there would be opportunities for plunder. Then, mirroring the actions of Tiberius Alexander, Mucianus ordered the populace of Antioch to gather in their theatre. Acknowledging the heritage and cultural pride of his audience, he spoke in Greek. The same lies and rumours that had worked so well on the legionaries were repeated to an enthusiastic and receptive crowd.[33]

Their governor again claimed that Vitellius was about to transfer the Syrian legions to Germany, knowing that there was nothing that angered the provincials more as 'they were accustomed to live with the soldiers, and enjoy association with them; in fact many civilians were bound to the soldiers by ties of friendship and of marriage, and the soldiers from long service had come to love their old familiar camps as their very hearths and homes'. The *XII Fulminata* and *VI Ferrata* had been in Syria since the reign of Augustus, most of the legionaries had been born there and their families lived in the province. Mucianus had personalised the civil war. Now, all had a vested interest in defeating Vitellius.[34]

By 15 July, all of Syria had taken the oath of allegiance to Vespasian, followed rapidly by the provinces in Asia Minor which were garrisoned by auxiliary troops. Across the Aegean, Achaia soon followed. Messengers were despatched to provinces across the Empire, addressed to the legions, the commanders and governors. To carry these letters and Vespasian's proclamations, soldiers and centurions were chosen who had contacts or family in the area they were instructed to visit. Vitellius placed guards on the roads, particularly on the passes through the Pannonian Alps. Some agents were captured in Rhaetia and Gaul, and sent to Rome for interrogation and execution, but the majority escaped detection, 'being concealed by faithful friends or escaping by their own wits'. They sent information back to Syria too, detailing Vitellius' strength and preparations for the coming war.[35]

Vitellius had for months heard rumours of Vespasian's preparations, but he had put too much confidence in the oath taken by the eastern legions. The presence of Sabinus and the young Domitian in Rome reassured him. However, once the revolt had broken out he was ignorant of his enemy's plans. The Bosphorus and ports along the Aegean coast would have been guarded as 'this was the season of the etesian winds, the sea was favourable for vessels sailing to the East, but unfavourable to those coming from that quarter'. Vespasian's agents spread far and wide over the western provinces, undermining Vitellius' support. Even

Hordeonius Flaccus in Upper Germany secretly spoke of changing sides, but the fervent loyalty of the soldiers towards Vitellius prevented him from openly expressing support. However, he did all he could to slow the levies, and in a private meeting encouraged Civilis and the Batavians to prevent reinforcements being sent to Rome from the Rhine. The governor of Britain, Vettius Bolanus, and a legate, Agricola, were also turned.[36]

The governor of Britain and officials in Spain wavered in their allegiance to the emperor, but the proximity of the German legions kept them loyal. However, they too slowed the dispatch of reinforcements from their provinces so they could claim they had discreetly supported the Flavian cause. Africa was vital to Vitellius, as Rome was now dependent on its grain supply, especially as Egypt was lost. The provincials remembered Vitellius' benevolent governorship of their province, in contrast to Vespasian's administration. Vitellius had also reconstituted Clodius Macer's legion and auxiliary cohorts that had been discharged by Galba. Consequently, they too remained fixed in their loyalty to Vitellius. Their governor continued to issue edicts and public letters in Vitellius' name, 'but by secret messages he fostered Vespasian's interest and was ready to take whichever side that prevailed'. Most, who were not forced to commit by the presence of large numbers of troops close by, remained unattached; they watched and waited, eager to present a favourable face to both sides but loyal to none. The danger in this was waiting too long. Once the victor became clear, committing too late imperilled future rewards.[37]

The plotters could now operate openly. Governors, commanders, officers and officials who had switched allegiance could leave their province for the first time and meet. A conference was called at Beirut. Hundreds attended, but foremost among them was Mucianus 'with all his lieutenants and tribunes, as well as his most distinguished centurions and soldiers; the army in Judaea also sent its best representatives'.[38] The contribution of the first-rank centurions and junior officers was vital in putting the provinces on a war footing. These were the professional elements in the army, unlike their tribunes and legates.

Client kings arrived to show their support but also demonstrate their power, thereby ensuring a place at the table once Vespasian was established in Rome. They came escorted by a 'great concourse of foot and horse, with princes who rivalled one another in splendid display'. Herod Agrippa would have attended alongside Antiochus of Commagene and other client kings. Their main concern was the defence of their kingdoms from a potential attack by the Parthian king once the bulk of the eastern Roman garrison was removed to overthrow Vitellius.[39]

As emperor, Vespasian sent envoys to Parthia and Armenia to secure peace. The embassies were so successful that the Parthian king, Vologaeses, offered to support Vespasian's forces with 40,000 cavalry. These were prudently declined to avoid the embarrassing position of a Roman emperor being indebted to a Parthian king.[40]

The inner circle of advisors decided that Titus should continue the siege of Jerusalem, with the rest of the province largely pacified. Vespasian's heir would thereby acquire a military reputation, victory already being assured. Titus was advised by Tiberius Alexander, the Prefect of Egypt, who had served under Corbulo. This removed the Prefect from blame for the forthcoming fleecing of his province for money and resources to support the campaigns. It was hoped he would later be able to return to govern Egypt without culpability. Vespasian toured Syrian towns and cities to review the production of weapons and ensure the gathering of materials proceeded efficiently before travelling to Alexandria. There he would guarantee that the wealth of Egypt was harnessed effectively for the Flavian cause. Nor did Vespasian wish to be in Italy or Rome when war visited the capital. There would need to be executions of prominent nobles who were a potential threat to the new dynasty. Vitellius' 7-year-old son would also be marked for death. The new emperor wanted to avoid the mistakes made by Galba and Vitellius. Any unpalatable measures would be enacted by Mucianus, not the new emperor.[41]

Mucianus was to cross the Bosphorus, land at Byzantium and advance towards Dyrrachium. The fleet would use this as a base to blockade Italy and threaten an invasion on the southern coast. The legions in Moesia were already wavering and would probably join the Flavians. Mucianus' army would consist of the *VI Ferrata* and another 13,000 legionary veterans drawn from the other legions in the East. Vespasian would cut Rome's grain supply from Egypt, causing the price of bread to rise beyond the means of its inhabitants, creating food riots. Vitellian commanders, facing inevitable defeat, would be encouraged to abandon their emperor, bringing their forces with them. Formal letters from Vespasian were sent to all the armies and their commanders offering retention in their posts and rewards for transferring their allegiance. Otho's former Praetorians were told that they would be recalled to their former service if they took up arms in Vespasian's name. They were initially used to feed unrest in the capital by spreading news of the revolt and Vitellius' imminent defeat.[42]

Some of Vitellius' officers had been sent to Syria and Judaea as emissaries carrying similar letters. However, their arrogance had served to inflame the anger of their eastern counterparts. The rivalry between legions was stoked by their pride in the emperor they had made, and, 'though savage in appearance and barbarous in speech, they constantly mocked at all the others as their inferiors'.[43] These men would not have survived long after Vespasian's proclamation.

The vast wealth of the East was harnessed in a unified movement to overthrow Vitellius. Firstly, levies of local inhabitants were held and veterans were recalled to replace units heading west. A multitude of auxiliary cohorts bore the name Flavian, binding them to their emperor. At the same time, 'the strong towns were selected to manufacture arms; gold and silver were minted at Antioch'. The coastal towns were busy constructing ships. Vespasian toured the area, inspected the work and rewarded his officials with prefectures, procuratorships and the promise of admission to the Senate. He then journeyed to Alexandria to finance this production. '"Money," Mucianus kept saying, "is the sinews of civil war."' Knowing that victory would bring limitless rewards, Mucianus and many of the leading men in the East donated much of their wealth, forcing the less willing to replicate their generosity.[44]

Mucianus did not need to worry about the threat posed by the three Moesian legions who heard of the gathering of the Flavian forces and the imminent crossing of the Bosphorus. The former Syrian legion, *III Gallica*, took the lead in throwing off its nominal allegiance to Vitellius in early August. The centurions remembered the treatment of their fellow officers and were pressured by the legionaries. The discontent was conveyed to their legate, T. Aurelius Fulvus, who saw an opportunity to win the favour of the likely victor in the civil war and declared for Vesapsain. He would be well rewarded for his treachery. The grandfather of the future emperor Antoninus Pius was summoned to Alexandria after the death of Vitellius to be an imperial advisor. This was followed by consular office and elevation to patrician status.[45]

The governor of Moesia, Aponius Saturninus, at first remained loyal to Vitellius. However, in attempting to protect his position, his report to Rome was both vague and untruthful. It was reported that the revolt was limited to one legion, with the other two remaining faithful. Initially, this may have been so, but they too revolted soon after. Saturninus then declared for Vespasian and decided to use the situation to settle a feud with the commander of the *VII Claudiana*, Tettius Julianus. Saturninus hated this man and accused him of remaining loyal to Vitellius. A centurion was sent to murder Julianus, who, 'learning of the danger, took some men who knew the country and escaped through pathless stretches of Moesia to districts beyond Mt. Heamus'. There he remained until the war was over and Vespasian guaranteed him safety.[46]

The Moesian legions sent a letter to their comrades in Pannonia asking that they join them, whilst also preparing to invade the province should they refuse. Again, the governor was ignored and instead it was a legionary commander who seized the initiative. Antonius Primus, legate of the *VII Galbiana*, had been amongst the first supporters of Galba and his legion was one of the few which remained faithful to the memory of their founder. After Galba's murder,

Antonius Primus offered his support to Otho. Vitellius would soon recall him and, once deprived of his legion, he would be prosecuted in Rome for his past and present corruption. The other Pannonian legion, the *XIII Gemina*, had been humiliated by Vitellius after its defeat at Cremona and thirsted for revenge. There was no doubt these would join with their comrades from Moesia.[47]

The Dalmatian legions soon followed their lead, and again, the governor 'took no lead in the revolt. Tampius Flavianus was the governor of Pannonia, Pompeius Silvanus of Dalmatia, both rich and old.' More importantly, they already held a surfeit of honours to add as much lustre to their dignity as they desired. Both had been consuls and had held the prestigious governorship of Africa during the reign of Nero, whilst Flavianus had been awarded an honorary triumph. It was the commander of the *XI Claudia*, L. Annius Bassus, who provided the impetus and energy in Vespasian's name. These men were ambitious, wanting the honours and offices that had been awarded to their superiors in times of peace. Whilst Silanus stood at the head of the Dalmatian legions, the 'actual guiding spirit was Annius Bassus, the legionary legate. Silvanus displayed no energy in war, but wasted in mere talk the days for action. Bassus directed him by pretending to defer to him, and continually attended to all necessary operations with unobtrusive activity.' His reward would be consular office in November AD 70.[48]

The leaders of these legions met at Poetovio to decide on their next move. These included the procurator of Dalmatia, Cornelius Fuscus, who had been appointed to this post by Galba for bringing over his colony. He 'contributed all the fire of his enthusiasm to the war' and would rise to become Praetorian Prefect in the reign of Domitian. The senior centurions and junior officers also attended. Some urged caution, but Antonius Primus argued for a more aggressive strategy and a rapid move on Italy. He had the support of the Pannonian soldiers, who wanted to restore their damaged reputations after their defeat fighting for Otho at the Battle of Cremona.

Antonius Primus' fervour and enthusiasm for the Flavian cause had elevated him to supreme command of these forces. When he received the letter from Vespasian, he had called an *adlocutio* to address his legion. Rather than a noncommittal, guarded speech, he acknowledged the mood of the soldiers before him and launched into a venomous attack on Vitellius while warmly praising Vespasian. He was their leader from that moment on. The governor, Tampius Flavianus, fled to Italy. He was appointed by Galba and was related to Vitellius. Later, he was persuaded by Cornelius Fuscus to return as the Flavians needed the dignity of a man of consular rank to add prestige to their cause. However, he failed to regain the trust of his soldiers, who would later accuse him of treachery, and it required the protection of Antonius Primus to save his life.[49]

Letters were sent in Vespasian's name to the *XIV Gemina*, which had been sent to Britain, and to the *I Aduitrix*, which had been ordered to Spain. The Gallic provinces were also swamped with messages which 'burst into flame'. It was evident to all that Vitellius' cause was damned.[50]

Antonius Primus grasped the leadership of these armies. He was a man whose vaulting ambition matched his propensity to sell his allegiance to the winning side. He sent a letter to the Vitellian governor of Upper Germany, asking him to hinder the dispatch of reinforcements to Italy. Hordoenius Flaccus believed that Vitellius would lose but was constrained by the fervent loyalty of the Rhine legions to their choice of emperor. Consequently, he secretly urged the Batavian prince, Civilis, to organize a revolt amongst his tribe in the Rhine Delta. Antonius Primus had already approached him, knowing he was a longstanding *amicus* of Vespasian, so the Batavian Revolt began.[51]

Antonius Primus led a flying column of auxiliary cavalry past Aquileia and into the north Italian plain. He was followed by six legions from Pannonia, Moesia and Dalmatia. The Danube had been left virtually undefended. Vespasian had instructed him to stop at Aquileia and await the forces commanded by Mucianus. He received further messages explaining the reason for not invading Italy. As Vespasian held the wealth of the East, the grain of Egypt and commanded the seas, the invasion of Italy was deemed unnecessary, it being anticipated that Vitellian generals would surrender knowing they faced inevitable defeat. Vespasian also wanted to protect his brother, Sabinus, in Rome and his young son, Domitian, from Vitellian reprisals. This insubordination would not be forgiven.[52]

Antonius Primus ignored these instructions, invoking the anger of both Mucianus and the distant Vespasian. He forced a battle at Cremona, winning a decisive victory which resulted in the deaths of thousands of soldiers and the sacking of Cremona itself. As his army advanced on Rome, Vitellius attempted to abdicate but was forced to continue as emperor by his soldiers. Inevitably, the Vitellians turned on Sabinus, who fortified the Capitoline Hill. His grandchildren and nephew, Domitian, were smuggled in during the night. However, their position was taken after a fire was started that consumed a long portico that had been used by the defenders to throw tiles and stones onto the attackers below. The defenders set fire to neighbouring apartment blocks in their desperation to hinder attacks. The religious centre of Rome was consumed by flames. The temples of Jupiter, Juno and Minerva were burned to the ground as a tall pillar of smoke rose above the capital. The chaos and confusion allowed Domitian to escape, but Sabinus was captured and dragged to face Vitellius in his palace.[53]

Vitellius had lost all control over the soldiers who claimed to be fighting his war. He tried desperately to persuade his men to show mercy to Sabinus, knowing his life would only be spared if he saved Vespasian's brother from death. However, his authority now did not even extend beyond the limits of the palace steps. Sabinus was hacked to death and decapitated, his body given a criminal's fate by being thrown down the Gemonian Steps. With that, Vitellius knew his fate was sealed. Forty miles to the north, Antonius Primus had paused his victorious army to celebrate the Saturnalia. This would add to Vespasian's anger at the behaviour of his ally.[54]

Two days later, Flavian forces entered Rome. After brief resistance in the narrow streets of the capital and around the Praetorian fortress, the Vitellian soldiers were overwhelmed. The old Praetorian cohorts were especially determined to recapture their barracks and exact vengeance. The civilian populace enjoyed the slaughter as they would a gladiatorial show in the amphitheatre. Perched high above on roofs, windows or balconies, they pointed to where the defeated Vitellian soldiers were hiding and clapped and cheered as they were dragged out and slain.[55]

Vitellius was found hiding in the empty and abandoned palace. He was bound with his arms drawn behind his back and dragged to the Forum to observe the destruction of his statues, kneel before the Rostra and witness the place where Galba had been slain. After enduring this macabre tour, he was hauled to the Gemonian Steps, where the body of Sabinus had lain, exposed and abused. There he suffered insults and humiliation, but retained some dignity. When a tribune insulted him, he replied, 'Yet I was your emperor'. With that, he fell under a shower of blows and his corpse was left brutalized.[56]

Chapter 8

The Batavian Revolt (AD 69–70)

> 'The various peoples of Germany are separated from the Gauls by the Rhine, from the Raetians and Pannonians by the Danube, and from the Sarmatians and Dacians by mountains – or, where there are no mountains, by mutual fear.'
>
> (Tacitus, *Germania*, 1)

The Roman mind divided the world between the civilized and the barbarian. Everything depended upon this distinction, as it both justified and legitimized their rule. The barbarians not only existed beyond the Rhine, the Danube and Rome's other frontiers, but also within the Empire. The civilized were citizens or they were imbued in Graeco-Roman culture and heritage. The rich also demonstrated their membership of the ruling elite through their villas, their clothes, their banquets, their townhouse and especially their knowledge of classical literature, rhetoric and Roman law.

Even a low-born citizen soldier in the legions with no education or property felt superior to a wealthy Gallic farmer, Germanic merchant or auxiliary soldier. The rivalry and hatred between the citizen legions and the auxiliary cohorts were evident to all. There were graduations to this attitude; it was not binary. The Roman senator Tacitus admired barbarians for their warlike spirit and bravery. They were the noble savage, but still savages, for the barbarian thought 'it tame and spiritless to accumulate slowly by the sweat of his brow what can be got quickly by the loss of a little blood'.[1]

Into this world came men who lived an uneasy co-existence. They were leaders of their communities, educated, and their families had held Roman citizenship for generations. They were proud of their tribal heritage but not yet fully accepted by their Roman peers or even social inferiors. The Aeduan noble and Roman citizen Julius Sacrovir was one. His treatment may in part reflect Roman arrogance. He was a Gallic warrior whose status was amplified through bravery in war. Arrested after having decisively crushed the rebellion of the Andecavi and accused of treason, his life hung on the decision of a distant emperor. He neither forgot this treatment nor forgave it.

The Batavian noble Julius Civilis was another.[2] In Roman eyes, the Batavians were Germanic and thus barbarians. Civilis' family were descended from the early kings of the Batavians who were settled on the Roman bank of the Rhine after they split from the Chatti between 50 and 40 BC. The area had previously been occupied by the Eburones, but their numbers had been decimated in a brutal campaign led by Julius Caesar. They occupied an island formed by the River Rhine, the Mass and Waal, whilst the western part was settled by the Canninefates. Other smaller sub-tribes, such as the Sturii, Marsaci, Frisiavones and Texuandri, made their home in the neighbouring areas. These were clients of the Batavians, so the Romans considered them to belong to the same tribal group. The Ubii, another Germanic tribe, were settled around Colonia Agrippinensium, modern Cologne.[3]

The Batavians acted as a bulwark against German attacks across the Rhine and were bound by a treaty giving them federate status. Consequently, as Tacitus explained to his contemporaries, 'they are not subject to the indignity of tribute or ground down by the tax-gatherer. Free from imposts and special levies, and reserved for employment in battle, they are like weapons and armour – "only to be used in war."' The loyalty of the Batavian elite was bound to Rome by the grant of citizenship, probably gifted by Augustus, and their king given the title and rank of prefect.[4]

The ruler probably had responsibility for raising the levy amongst the Batavians and its client tribes. Eight Batavian cohorts of 500 soldiers were associated with the *XIV Gemina* legion. These were uniquely deployed together and constituted a fierce fighting force. They had served in the Claudian invasion of Britain and played a vital role in crushing Boudica's revolt, before being transferred by Nero to Illyria in preparation for an attack on the kingdoms in the Caucasus. More Batavians also served as oarsmen in the Rhine fleet.

There was also a *cohors equitata* based in its homeland, along with the prestigious *ala Batavorum* commanded by the Batavian leader. This was probably based at a fort on the Kops plateau near the tribal capital. The treaty also obliged the recruitment of men for the German imperial bodyguard employed by the Julio-Claudian emperors. Many of these were probably members of the Batavian elite. A funerary monument preserves the memory of one of them: 'Indus, a bodyguard of Nero Claudius Caesar Augustus, decury of Secundus, Batavian nation, lived 36 years. His brother and heir Eumenes, from the *collegium* of the Germans, dedicated this.' Both were probably members of the Batavian elite who were devoted to the emperors they served until disbanded by Galba. The Batavians were an elite force, renowned for their bravery and horsemanship, being able to swim across rivers with their horses in full armour. Most, however, were retained by the Romans as infantry.[5]

The island which formed the Batavian homeland was 60 miles long and supported a population of around 40,000 people. With 6,000 men under arms, the Batavian cohorts must have also drawn from sub-tribes and possibly from the free Germans across the Rhine, such as the Bructeri and the Frisians, who belonged to the same ethnic group. Their contribution to the Roman Army was massive, although most units operated close to their homeland. Ultimately, virtually every family will have contributed a father, son or brother to Rome's war machine, and some families more.[6]

Romanization remained marginal in the Batavian territory. Only their capital at Batavodurum (also called Oppidum Batavorum) could be described as a *civitas*. It was settled by Roman traders, veterans and craftsmen who lived in long wooden strip houses, with some containing stone cellars. The town was protected with a wooden palisade and ditch. Archaeologists have discovered a stone monument to Tiberius and a marble statue of Julius Caesar, which may imply the presence of a forum. However, only 3 per cent of the town has been excavated. The statue associated the Julian aristocracy with the great Roman general, and the Batavian nobility will have had residences here as well as the headquarters of the prefect. The surrounding countryside was bereft of Roman influence. Most of the tribe lived in small native settlements, rearing cattle and horses.[7]

The slow progress of Romanization is shown by a stone altar from Ruimel dating to the first half of the first century, dedicated by Flavus, son of Vihirmas, supreme magistrate (*summus magistratus*) of the *civitas* Batavorum. The office was probably an old native magisterial post held by a tribal elite who did not possess Roman citizenship but had a significant influence over the native population. They had more in common with their fellow tribes across the Rhine than with their more Romanized Gallic neighbours to the south. Tensions would exist between these two supreme offices, one held by a Romanized noble and the other by members of the native lesser nobility.[8]

Julius Civilis lived in this hybrid world, in some ways distinct from the culture and heritage of his fellow tribesmen and women. He may have grown up as a hostage in Rome, which was often a condition in treaty arrangements with client tribes. He will have received an elite education, along with his brother, Paulus. He was then made a commander of a Batavian cohort and became an *amicus* of the future Emperor Vespasian. He later confessed that 'toward Vespasian my respect is of long-standing and when he was still a private citizen, we were called friends'. This bond may have been formed when Vespasian was appointed in AD 41 as commander of the *II Augusta* at Mogontiacum, or possibly Civilis served under him in the conquest of the Durotriges and Dumnonii tribes during the conquest of Britain in AD 43. Civilis probably lost an eye at this time, possibly in combat, as he later associated this disfigurement with the illustrious generals Hannibal and Sertorius. This was a mark of courage better than any crown or torc awarded by the Roman Army.[9]

Civilis had served over twenty-five years as prefect of the Batavians, alongside older brother Paulus. Both 'were by far the most distinguished among the Batavians', and through that time controlled the recruitment of thousands of Batavian auxiliaries. Then in May or June AD 68, Paulus was executed by the governor of Lower Germany, Fonteius Capito, and Civilis was sent in chains to Nero. They were linked to Vindex's revolt, but as a Roman citizen, Paulus had been entitled to a trial in Rome. The injustice wrought on two members of the Batavian royal family would have burned deep. Galba released Civilis when he entered Rome, and the Prefect returned to his homeland. However, the legionaries hated any allies of Vindex. This led to their demand from the newly acclaimed Vitellius that Civilis be arrested again. Consequently, Civilis admitted that 'there was nothing but hatred between him and me – he began the quarrel, I increased it'.[10]

Vitellius later released Civilis, as he needed the support of the eight Batavian cohorts which 'would have great weight as allies or opponents', nor did he want to start a revolt on the Rhine as he advanced on Italy with most of its legionary garrison. Civilis 'had great influence with the Batavians so that Vitellius did not wish to alienate this savage people by punishing him'. The Batavian, though, wanted vengeance for the murder of his brother and his treatment at the hands of the legionaries in Lower Germany and their acquiescing new emperor.[11]

The eight Batavian cohorts had originally been associated with the *XIV Gemina*, which took immense pride in its reputation as Nero's most effective fighters. However, the treatment of Paulus and Civilis caused a rupture between the auxiliaries and the legion that erupted into outright conflict. With the brothers' execution and arrest in May, the Batavians withdrew from the legion in an uprising against Nero. Nero's death and the accession of Galba brought them back into line, and they had been ordered to Britain. Nonetheless, Galba had added further insult to their tribal pride by discharging the Batavian imperial bodyguard, which returned to the Rhine disgruntled and resentful. There, Civilis would have greeted his comrades and shared in their anger. His command of the *ala Batavarorum* had been given to his rival, Claudius Labeo, who was based near Mogontiacum. To add fuel to his hostility, it was probably Claudius Labeo who had denounced his treasonous contact with Vindex, which had led to the execution of his brother.[12]

The eight Batavian cohorts had camped in the territory of the Lingones rather than march to Britain as instructed. There, they learnt of the revolt of Vitellius in Lower Germany, followed by news of the re-arrest of Civilis at the demand of the legions in the province. His later release was probably part of a bargain entailing the incorporation of the Batavian cohorts into the army of the Vitellian general, Fabius Valens. In the circumstances, Civilis and the auxiliaries had to acquiesce, but they were far from willing or loyal allies. Instead, the Batavians remained violent and aggressive. Soon, 'a quarrel arose between the Batavians and the legionaries, and then a brawl. Finally, as the soldiers took sides with one or the other, they broke out almost into open battle, and in fact, would have done so had not Valens, with the punishment of a few men, reminded the Batavians of the authority which they had forgotten.'[13] However, the preferential treatment of the legionaries only added to the Batavians' sense of injustice.

A few weeks later, the conflict was resumed by the Batavians, who

> 'began to be insolent, going up to the quarters of each legion and boasting that it was they who had checked the regulars of the Fourteenth legion, they who had taken Italy away from Nero, and that in their hands lay the whole fortune of the war. Such action was insulting to the legionaries, bitterly offensive to the commander; discipline was ruined by quarrels and brawls; finally, their insolence began to make Valens suspect even their loyalty.'[14]

These legionaries had fought against Vindex and remained loyal to Nero until his death. They continued to revere his memory. The Batavians also claimed through their insults to be superior in valour and skill to the German legionaries. Both took immense pride in their elite reputation. This slur hit hard at the Roman sense of martial superiority. There had always been a deep-seated rivalry bordering on hatred between the two types of soldiers. Auxiliaries received less pay than the legionaries, and they received no donatives nor any gratuity or land upon retirement. They were, however, given Roman citizenship as a reward for their services, which often stretched beyond the stipulated twenty-five years.[15]

Yet ironically, when Valens tried to divide the Batavians by sending some cohorts to southern Gaul to counter an incursion by Othonian troops, these same legionaries rioted, demanding their return, as the soldiers 'declared that they were losing the help of their bravest troops; that it looked as if the Batavians, veterans in so many victorious campaigns, were being withdrawn from the line after the enemy was in sight'. It was auxiliaries, rather than legionaries, who were sent into combat first, whilst the citizen soldiers were often held in reserve. The legionaries believed it better for Batavian blood to be shed in the coming battles, rather than their own. The legionaries then mutinied and stoned Valens, who fled his camp disguised as a slave. The resentment towards their commander had been growing for a while. His soldiers believed Valens had taken an unfair share of the plunder extracted from the Gallic provincials and gold extorted from the people of Vienne. However, once their ardour had cooled, Valens returned to his command after treating the mutineers leniently, as 'he was well aware that in civil wars the soldiers have more liberty than the leaders'. They did not trust Valens but did trust the courage and bravery of their Batavian comrades.[16]

The defeat of Otho's forces at the Battle of Cremona (Bedriacum) brought more unrest. The *XIV Gemina* was at the forefront, declaring it had never been defeated as only a vexillation of its veterans had been present at the battle. Its soldiers sowed seeds of unrest in other units. Vitellius decided to send this legion back to Britain. The equally disruptive Batavian cohorts were to accompany it, knowing they 'had had a difference of long-standing with [the] Fourteenth'. Both groups would act as a check to the other.[17]

Putting two volatile and mutually antagonist forces together had inevitable consequences: 'Peace did not last long among armed men who hated one another so violently.' The soldiers had been quartered within the town of Turin. There 'a Batavian charged a workman with being a thief, while a legionary defended the workman as his host; thereupon their fellow soldiers rallied to the support of each and matters soon passed from words to blows. There would have been a bloody battle if two Praetorian cohorts had not taken the side of the soldiers of the Fourteenth and inspired them with courage while they frightened the Batavians.' The Praetorians and legionaries had both supported Otho and were now united as citizens against the effrontery of the auxiliaries. The Batavians would have struggled to understand the logic of billeting them with their hated rivals and seen the decision as another deliberate insult. Vitellius belatedly recognized the stupidity of his decision and kept the Batavians in Italy whilst ordering the *XIV Gemina* to continue its march to Britain. As a parting gesture, the legionaries set fire to Turin.[18]

The civil war continued in the Vitellian army, with the auxiliary ranged against the legionary. At Ticenum, the victorious emperor decided to entertain an important senatorial delegation from Rome that included Verginius Rufus. As after-dinner entertainment, a wrestling match was staged between a legionary from the *V Alaudae* legion and a Gallic auxiliary. This legion, based in Lower Germany, had played a key role in the defeat of Vindex. The emperor and his advisors were either blind to the hostile currents that divided his army or, with typical arrogance, chose to ignore them. The soldiers, their passions already inflamed by the presence of their former commander who refused their offer of the throne, flocked to watch the contest. Drink further liberated their passions.[19]

The contest was close, but 'when the legionary was thrown and the Gaul began to mock him, the crowd of spectators that had gathered took sides and the legionaries started to kill the auxiliaries, and two cohorts were wiped out'. The chaos bred more chaos. A cloud of dust was seen in the distance, and it was rumoured that the *XIV Gemina* was returning to exact vengeance on all. However, it was soon reported that the marching soldiers were the rearguard of their own army. The lull in the violence was ended by a report that a slave in Verginius' household was an assassin aiming to murder their emperor. As a body, the legionaries stormed the dinner, demanding the execution of Vitellius' guest. Vitellius was able to calm the situation, but the soldiers remained volatile.[20]

The next day, the emperor addressed the army in a formal *adlocutio* to reassert his authority. He praised the loyal devotion of his army, clearly meaning his legionaries who had slaughtered a thousand auxiliaries. The latter understandably complained that 'the legionaries were allowed to enjoy such impunity and to display such impudence'. Knowing this would incur a reaction from the Batavians, they were immediately ordered to return to their bases in the German provinces, whilst thousands of Gallic auxiliaries were also dismissed back to their homes. There was no donative, no thanks; merely empty words to compensate for their blood spilt at Cremona. The eight Batavian cohorts returned as one to Mogontiacum, intent on rectifying the wrongs done to them and their leader, Civilis.[21]

The arrival of the Batavians added to the problems facing the governor of Upper Germany, Hordeonius Flaccus. He knew their loyalty was suspect but had been left with few reliable soldiers to garrison both German provinces. In Upper Germany, there was the *IV Macedonica* and the remains of the *XXII Primigenia*, both at Mogontiacum, along with the remnants of the *XXI Rapax* at Vindonissa. Lower Germany was held by the *XVI Gallica*, based at Novaesium, the double legionary fortress of Vetera was held by the remnants of the *XV Primigenia* and the *V Alaudae*, whilst the *I Germanica* garrisoned Bonna. These much-reduced legions were augmented with recently recruited levies raised from the German and Gallic provincials.[22]

There was trouble in the Batavian tribal area in May as Hordeonius Flaccus attempted to comply with Vitellius' demands for more recruits to counter the impending invasion of Italy by Flavian forces. However,

> 'this burden, which is naturally grievous, was made heavier by the greed and licence of those in charge of the levy: they hunted out the old and the weak that they might get a price for letting them off; again, they dragged away the children to satisfy their lust, choosing the handsomest – and Batavian children are generally tall beyond their years.'

The breach of Rome's treaty with the Batavians was exacerbated by the brutality of the levy. This was a threat to the structure of their society and the independent position and status of their leaders. The Batavians themselves, under their prefect, were solely responsible for raising soldiers and had already met their obligations in providing the eight cohorts now at Mogontiacum. This unlawful action transformed the proud Batavians from allies into slaves of Rome. Nor was there enough manpower in the tribal area to satisfy Vitellius' demands without affecting the ability of the civilian population to farm their marginal lands. Traditionally, these cohorts had served close to their homeland, which was no longer the case. Young men were conscripted knowing they would never see their families again. The local leaders rapidly organized opposition to the levy, probably leading to increased brutality. A revolt became inevitable.[23]

Civilis had already received a letter in early September from Antonius Primus in the name of Vespasian, urging him to lead a revolt to ensure Vitellius received no reinforcements from his German provinces. It was well known that the Batavian noble was bound by ties of friendship to the usurper in the East. Hordeonius Flaccus had also met Civilis in person to persuade him to do the same. It was evident to all that Vitellius was doomed and the governor probably hoped these actions would preserve his life and estates when the new regime came to power. However, the German legionaries remained fanatically loyal to their emperor, unlike their officers, who hoped to retain their careers and fortunes.[24]

Civilis called an assembly of native tribal and religious leaders at a sacred grove 'under the pretext of giving a banquet'. Their support was vital in raising enough soldiers to match the power of the German legions, even though their manpower was much depleted. The support of the old gods was sought to assure the fainthearted that victory was guaranteed. For this, Civilis needed to discard his Roman heritage and embrace his tribesmen's Germanic traditions and Batavian beliefs. He vowed to destroy the Romans based at Vetera who had left his homeland a wasteland. He dyed his hair red with ochre and refused to cut it until he had fulfilled this promise before his god. This symbolized a blood feud. He now promised to deliver vengeance upon their enemies.[25]

The principal deity worshipped in the Rhine Delta was Hercules Magusanus. This god, part-Roman and part-Germanic, mirrored the heritage of Civilis himself and was based on an older cult that was subsumed into that of Hercules. This religious worship would have been linked to the tribal senate called by Civilis and administered by native magistrates. The major sanctuaries of the Batavians are found outside the main towns in rural sites where the tribal leaders gathered on feast days. One such site has been discovered at Elst, where a small first-century temple was excavated underneath a larger one dating from the reign of Trajan. In the sanctuary at Emphel, excavations revealed a bronze figurine depicting Hercules, as well as many items of military equipment left as votive offerings. Both sites revealed extensive evidence of ritual feasting, including drinking cups. The largest ritual site was discovered at Kessel/Lith on the south bank of the Meuse. Remains of early Roman military equipment, horse gear and weapons were also unearthed alongside human and animal bones and pottery. Late Roman fortifications had been constructed from the remains of a monumental Gallo-Roman temple, suggesting this was the principal site of the militarist cult.[26]

Hercules stood for masculine power and courage. He was the protector of humanity. The cult was also a unifying force, with other groups who shared ties with its worship including sub-tribes like the Canninefates, the Ubii and Frisians. The Germans claimed that the demi-god visited them on his travels, and they sang 'of him as the foremost of all the heroes when they are about to engage in battle'. His heroic deeds made him a shining example for all Germanic warriors, and he had a reputation as a protector and keeper of cattle. These attributes were close to the heart of all Batavians, and Civilis drew upon his association with the cult as a leading magistrate and warrior who had waged war in many lands in his twenty-five years in the Roman Army.[27]

Civilis also used his facial disfigurement to identify himself with Rome's protagonists of the past, Hannibal, and Sertorius. The link to the Carthaginian Hannibal is understandable, as he was famous for coming close to destroying Rome. However, Sertorius was a more nuanced figure, probably known only to the well-educated Romanized elite in the provinces. He was a Republican general who was outlawed by the dictator Sulla for supporting his rival Marius in a civil war. He fought a protracted guerrilla-style war in Spain against his Roman enemies, with the support of the native tribes, until he was murdered in 73 BC. Civilis had to appeal to different groups to gather and retain support. His presentation of himself as the new Hannibal, a 'barbarian' and leader of a people subjected to the injustices of Rome, would have appealed to his native tribal warriors. Conversely, his association with Sertorius would encourage the Romanized provincial elite and Roman commanders to perceive him as a man who remained loyal to Rome but had been ostracized by a tyrant who had seized control of his *patria*. He had not betrayed Rome; Rome had betrayed him.[28]

Civilis initially hid his role as leader of the mutiny behind his position as a senior Roman officer and a representative of imperial power. He had already been secretly approached by Antonius Primus and by his commander, Hordeonius Flaccus, to support his patron, Vespasian, by organizing a revolt against Vitellian forces in Lower Germany. The Frisians across the Rhine were already in revolt and Civilis despatched messengers to the Canninefates in the northern part of the island, and others to Batavian cohorts from Britain and the eight cohorts formerly attached to the *XIV Gemina* that had moved to Mogontiacum. This was a military revolt that utilized tribal anger at an illegal levy of men.[29]

The leader of the Canninefates was a client king. He was 'a man of brute courage named Brinno, who was of illustrious descent; his father had dared to commit many hostile acts and had shown his scorn for Gaius' absurd expeditions without suffering for it'. As a sub-tribe of the Batavians, the Canninefates had treaty obligations to Rome and were also suffering from the depredations caused by the illegal recruitment of their men. However, unlike the Batavian elite, their leaders were not granted Roman citizenship nor did they serve as officers in the Roman Army. The treachery of the Batavian cohorts and their officers was to remain concealed from the Vitellian forces. Instead, Brinno was to take command of a native revolt whilst Civilis would lead the Roman soldiers against him. Therefore, Brinno was publicly recognized as the leader of the revolt after being raised high on a shield carried on the warriors' shoulders and acclaimed by them.[30]

In April, two auxiliary forts on the island were attacked by the Canninefates and Frisians. These were undermanned and the soldiers were caught utterly by surprise. They were assaulted by land and sea. One was the military fort near Katwijk, described as Lugdunum in the land of the Batavians although located in the territory of the Canninefates. The other fort was probably Praetorium Agrippinae, located slightly inland on the Rhine. Both were destroyed. Next, Roman traders and soldiers foraging for food and materials were massacred across the island.[31]

The commander of Roman forces on the island was a lead centurion, C. Aquilius Proculus. All forts in the area were only partly garrisoned and vulnerable to attack, so he ordered all the auxiliary prefects to retreat to the upper part of the island after burning their forts. Most of these cohorts were recent recruits drawn from the Nervii and Germans, as Vitellius had used the regular soldiers for his invasion of Italy.[32]

Civilis now faced a large, unified force when he had planned to destroy the enemy piecemeal. Consequently, he used his rank as a senior Roman commander to reprimand the prefects for abandoning their forts 'and declared that he would crush the revolt of the Canninefates with the cohort under his command; they were to return each to his winter quarters'. The orders were insane and revealed his treachery. The forts were destroyed, and the cohorts would have been defenceless had they returned to their garrison quarters. Aquilius Proculus ordered his forces to remain where they were.[33]

With the obvious failure of his deception, Civilis took over the leadership of the revolt, advancing to meet the Romans before reinforcements arrived. He organized his native supporters into three tribal units – Batavians, Canninefates and Frisians – along with his cohort of Batavian cavalry who may have been the former imperial bodyguard. The Roman force drew up close to the Rhine, supported by the archers of twenty-four river galleys drawn up with their bows facing the bank. Treachery destroyed all hope of a Roman victory. Almost at the moment when the battle was joined, a cohort of Tingri transferred their allegiance to Civilis and attacked their former comrades in the flank. At the same time, the Batavian oarsmen hindered the archers and marines on their galleys and then rowed to the banks occupied by the Batavians. Any helmsman or centurion who resisted was cut down. All the ships were captured. The remaining Roman force capitulated and surrendered to Civilis.[34]

The captured auxiliaries and their prefects were treated with dignity. The soldiers were allowed to return to their tribes or enlist with Civilis. The officers were offered the same choice, but those who chose to leave met Civilis in private before being loaded with gifts. Tacitus produces a fictional account of this conversation, but Civilis continued to act in the name of Vespasian. News of his victory crossed the Rhine, and he soon received offers of alliance from the free Germans. Close tribal links existed between them, especially with the Bructeri, who may have volunteered to fight in the Batavian cohorts.[35]

Hordeonius Flaccus continued to undermine the Vitellian war machine. He had initially refused to acknowledge the extent of the revolt by the Canninefates and attacks by the Frisians, but the defeat and expulsion of Roman forces on the island forced his hand. When Civilis emerged as leader, his son was arrested in Cologne but 'treated with honour while in custody'. Then Flaccus ordered the remaining detachments of the two legions at Vetera to advance under the command of Munius Lupercus and recover the territory. They were augmented by cohorts of Ubii and a Treviran cavalry detachment. The *ala Batavorum* led by Civilis' rival, Claudius Labeo, also joined, but unbeknown to its commander, the Batavians planned to desert once battle was joined. Civilis had been their commander before. He wanted his position back.[36]

Civilis allowed the enemy to advance onto the island and met them in battle. He placed the captured auxiliary standards before them, and behind his army he positioned the wives and children of his men so they could observe the valour of their men, who also knew their families would be slaughtered if they fled. They raised the traditional war cry, which was feebly matched by the response of the legionaries and auxiliaries. The *XV Primigenia* and *V Alaudae* in the centre were understandably concerned about the loyalty of the troops on their flanks. On the left, the *ala Batavorum* immediately turned and attacked their former comrades. On the right wing, the Ubii and Treveri fled. The legionaries, however, made a disciplined retreat, the Germans and Frisians hunting down the auxiliaries, who were easier prey. The two legions escaped and found safety in their camp at Vetera.[37]

Claudius Labeo was captured, but Civilis could not execute him as this would have divided the Batavians when he was desperate for unity. Instead, Labeo was taken to the land of the Frisians and kept as a prisoner, guarded by the allies, where he couldn't sow the seeds of dissent in his homeland.[38]

Meanwhile, a messenger reached the eight Batavian cohorts with the news that Civilis and the Batavians had risen in the name of Vespasian. The cohorts were marching towards Italy to reinforce Vitellius' army. The emperor had promised them double pay and the enrolment of many of the soldiers as cavalry. They had grown up with their horses and wanted the higher status and pay as cavalrymen. Hordeonius Flaccus had followed the imperial instructions, glad no doubt to remove the proud but unruly soldiers from his province. They may have demanded the pay that had been promised, which the governor was unable to provide. Probably reasoning that neither Flaccus nor Vitellius could be trusted, they turned around and marched towards their homeland.[39]

The governor of Upper Germany was in a dangerous military position. He summoned a *concilium* composed of his tribunes and centurions. He was told that the auxiliary cohorts were unreliable, and his legions were depleted and weakened by recent recruits with no experience of war. He ordered the soldiers to remain behind their walls, and in doing so he secretly complied with Vespasian's instructions. However, the Vitellian legionaries were outraged that rebels were allowed to pass under their fortifications without challenge. Flaccus appeared to be either a coward or a traitor. The governor was soon forced to change his instructions. He sent orders to the legate of the *I Germanica* at Bonna to prevent the Batavians from passing, whilst he said he would advance from Mogontiacum and catch them in a vice.[40]

Again, Hordeonius Flaccus was hesitant, then changed his mind again and sent another order to Bonna ordering its legion to let the Batavians pass. The governor was accused of treason and siding with the Batavians. The Batavian cohorts approached Bonna and sent a message to the commander, Herennius Gallus. They said they did not want conflict, having fought alongside their Roman comrades on many occasions. They reassured the Romans that they wanted to return home to their farms and families and enjoy peace after completing a long and profitless service. Many had probably served over twenty-five years like their former commander, Civilis.[41]

Gallus was reluctant to ignore his latest orders, but the 3,000 legionaries demanded blood. He also commanded 'some cohorts of Belgians, which had been hastily raised, as well as a band of peasants and foragers, unwarlike, but bold until they met actual danger'. They burst out of the gates and surrounded the 4,000 Batavians, who closed ranks and formed a square. Discipline and training soon prevailed against superior numbers. The numbers of the attackers were thinned, and their initial courage drained away as the Batavians started to cut through their line. The Belgian cohorts broke first, followed by the legionaries. All fled towards the gates, which were soon blocked with panicking, desperate men. Others attempted to cross the ditch and climb the ramparts to safety. Many were crushed to death; others were wounded and killed by their comrades as they battled to get inside, but more died on the end of Batavian swords and spears.[42]

The Batavian auxiliaries later attempted to excuse their slaughter of Roman soldiers, saying they had asked for peace and had merely defended themselves when attacked. They continued on their march, avoiding Cologne, and joined forces with Civilis. Before, his was a native force, but with the arrival of the auxiliary cohorts he had an experienced, disciplined core to his army. All his forces, both auxiliary and tribal warriors, were made to take the oath of allegiance to Vespasian. He also sent messengers to Vetera, asking the two legions there to do the same. Defeated but resilient, they declined. They retorted that their emperor was Vitellius, to whom they had pledged their lives.[43]

Soon, huge numbers of Germans from across the Rhine joined the Batavians, drawn by messengers carrying news of victories and the chance of glory and plunder. The Frisii, Bructeri and Tencteri crossed the river in September and joined Civilis in the siege of Vetera. Civilis had sworn before the tribal leaders and Hercules Magusanus that he would wage war until Vetera fell. His hair remained uncut and red to remind him and his warriors that this oath had to be fulfilled. A prophetess of the Bructeri named Veleda had also helped with recruitment by prophesizing that the Germans would be victorious and Rome's legions would be destroyed. She 'enjoyed extensive authority, according to the ancient German custom, which regards many women as endowed with prophetic powers and, as the superstition grows, attributes divinity to them'. Vetera had to fall with its legions.[44]

The double legionary fortress of Vetera lay on the bank of the Rhine, vulnerable to attack on three sides, where it could be easily approached up a gentle slope. Archaeologists have confirmed its unsuitable location, and it was moved in AD 70. Designed to be held by around 12,000 men, its garrison was reduced to around 5,000 supported by armed servants, traders and other civilians who had taken refuge in its ramparts along with their families. The settlement surrounding the fort had been demolished to give clear lines of sight from the strengthened ramparts. The surrounding area was plundered for provisions, but with the enemy approaching, the soldiers consumed much of the food themselves rather than adding it to the fortress's supplies.[45]

Civilis employed the knowledge and expertise of the soldiers drawn from the Roman army to build scaling ladders and siege towers, and trained soldiers in the use of the tortoise (the *testudo*), a shield wall formation. Civilis was overly confident that the defeated remnants of the garrison would be unable to resist a direct attack. The Rhine was filled with captured ships and both banks echoed with the German war cry: 'On one side were the standards of the veteran cohorts, on the other the images of wild beasts taken from the woods and groves.' The Batavians and their allies launched their assault on the palisade, first firing waves of arrows which stuck in the wooden battlements or towers. The Romans countered with a hail of stones that killed at a greater distance. Then, with a roar, the main attack began. Siege towers were pulled up to the walls, allowing the Batavians to clear the ramparts of defenders, whilst below their comrades undermined the bank. Groups also formed several tortoises to act as a bridge, which allowed others to climb up and reach the battlements.[46]

The legionaries moved in for the close-quarter fighting. The Germans were thrown down as they climbed to the top, whilst *ballistae* fired stones through the sides of the siege towers, demolishing them. The Batavians also failed with another assault using sheds and screens to get close to the ramparts. These were quickly destroyed using blazing darts fired from crossbows. Frustrated, Civilis surrounded the fortress and decided to starve the legionaries into submission, knowing they had few provisions and had admitted 'a great crowd of non-combatants; at the same time they counted on treachery as a result of want, and on the uncertain faith of the slaves and the chances of war'.[47]

News of the siege soon reached the legions at Mogontiacum. Hordeonius Flaccus immediately requested reinforcements from auxiliary cohorts in all the Gallic provinces and Spain. Then he instructed the *IV Macedonica* and the remains of the *XXII Primigenia* to mobilize and march along the Rhine to relieve Vetera. He placed the force under the command of Dillius Vocula, the legate of the Twenty-second Legion. He decided not to march with the army, excusing his lack of leadership on age and poor health. The real reason was that his soldiers had lost all confidence in his ability and his loyalty either to Vitellius or them. The legionaries 'murmured against him in no uncertain tone, saying he had let the Batavian cohorts go from Mogontiacum, had concealed his knowledge of the undertakings of Civilis, and was making allies with the Germans'. Their distrust had firm foundations. Then a letter arrived from Vespasian, addressed to their governor. The army forced him to read it out at an assembly. The messengers were then sent in chains to Vitellius.[48]

Hordeonius Flaccus had more to fear from his army than did the enemy. When he reached Bonna by ship, he found the *I Germanica* even more vehement in their hatred of him. They 'placed the blame for their disaster on Hordeonius:

they declared that it was by his orders that they had given battle to the Batavi, under the assurance that the legions were following from Mogontiacum; that by his treachery their comrades had been killed since no help came to them'. Accusations, rumours and falsehood brought the army close to mutiny. It was believed that the governor had not sent messengers for reinforcements, so he was forced to 'read to the army copies of all the letters that he had dispatched throughout the Gauls, Britain, and the Spains asking for aid'.[49]

His position became untenable when he was forced to hand over all written orders and instructions to the eagle bearers, which were then read to the soldiers before being despatched to officers, magistrates and commanders. The legionaries saw the centurions as firmly allied with their officers, dependent as they were on their commander's recommendation for promotion.[50]

The civil war divided the German legions. The soldiers no longer trusted their officers, who had lost all authority. Orders and commands were obeyed only if the soldiers saw the benefit in carrying them out. The truth was evident to all that 'undoubtedly the common soldiers were faithful to Vitellius, but all the officers inclined to favour Vespasian'. The German legionaries had nothing to gain from Vespasian, whilst their officers knew the Flavians would be victorious and hoped to gain future favour by bringing the German legions over to his cause.[51]

Upon arriving at Cologne, Hordeonius Flaccus made one last attempt to reassert his authority, ordering the arrest of one soldier who had instigated the mutiny. He hoped his leniency would lessen the reaction of his soldiers. Instead, 'the angry temper of the legions increased'. This soldier claimed that he had been a messenger between Flaccus and Civilis, and the governor knew the revolt was imminent and did nothing to avert it. The allegations were both credible and believed. It was Vocula who restored order. With admirable bravery, he assembled the army and from the tribunal ordered the mutineer to be arrested. Despite his cries, the man was seized and dragged away for punishment. The common soldier admired courage. Vocula had their respect, so the assembled soldiers demanded that he take over supreme command. Flaccus, humiliated but no doubt relieved, abdicated the responsibilities bestowed on him by the emperor and the Senate.[52]

Surrounded by enemies, the legionaries looked for leadership and Vocula provided it. He may have served as a tribune with the *I Germanica* earlier in his career, so this legion might have been instrumental in urging their comrades to elevate him to overall command. He had been appointed to commander of the *XXII Primegenia* by Galba and must have demonstrated considerable political dexterity in retaining his post under Vitellius. The present emergency required a commander with proven military ability, but he did not trust the constancy of the legionaries, nor would they trust his.[53]

Despite his position as the chosen commander of the relieving force, Vocula had to share command with Herennius Gallus, the legate of the *I Germanica* at Bonna. Both were equal in rank but not ability. The army marched down the Rhine, passed Colonia Agrippinensium and entered Novaesium (Neus) to join with the *XVI Gallica*. However, the advance stopped 40 miles from Vetera. A summer drought had reduced the depth of the Rhine, allowing the Chatti and Tencteri to raid Roman territory. Large numbers of auxiliary cohorts were diverted to patrol the banks. Several cohorts of Ubii had been cut to pieces near Marcodurum (Düren), west of Cologne, whilst the Cugerni, a tribe located between the Ubii and the Batavians, had joined Civilis.[54]

The legionaries were increasingly mutinous, having not received their pay due to the disruption caused by the civil war. They were hungry as well: the grain ships that brought supplies down the Rhine were unable to sail, whilst Civilis had captured most of the river galleys and prevented grain from Britain from reaching the beleaguered troops. It was decided to divide the army, as it was increasingly difficult to find food and provisions. Half, under the leadership of Gallus, marched 13 miles down the Rhine towards Vetera and constructed a fort at Gelduba (Gellep). After building fortifications, discipline was restored through drills and training whilst they plundered and gathered food from enemy territory. The remainder, under Vocula, attacked the territory of the Cugerni, pillaging their villages and gathering supplies.[55]

A grain ship soon arrived at Gelduba, but became grounded in the narrows. The Germans swam the river and started to drag it to their bank. Gallus ordered a cohort to rescue the ship, but the enemy committed more men. Other Roman troops came to the assistance of the cohort, which was struggling against superior numbers, until both sides were engaged in a full battle. The Romans suffered heavy losses and the ship with its cargo was lost. Frustration, hunger and anger fired the legionaries, who dragged Gallus from his tent, then stripped and beat him. This was the degrading punishment used on slaves and soldiers. They demanded to know how much he had been bribed and who his accomplices were, suspecting he had received instructions from Hordeonius Flaccus. His incompetence had cost many lives. Gallus, fearing for his life, denounced the governor. Flaccus, who was probably at Novaesium, was put in chains but his life was saved by the arrival of Vocula.[56]

Order was quickly restored, the ringleaders being executed the following day. The legions were in enemy territory and accepted that the restoration of discipline was paramount; division and disorder would result in defeat and death. The territory of the Ubii and Treveri was then inundated by huge numbers of

Germans, who took advantage of the absence of the legionary garrisons, whilst the Menapii and Morini south of Boulogne were also attacked. The mutiny had allowed Civilis another opportunity to fulfil his vow and destroy Vetera and its defenders before the relief force arrived.[57]

Roman *ballistae* and slingers had defeated the previous attempts to storm Vetera, so Civilis decided to use the cover of night to sow confusion and hide his attackers until they were on the ramparts. The Batavian auxiliaries supervised the construction of more siege works and machines. To his German allies, hiding inside towers or behind screens was cowardice. They wanted to demonstrate their bravery with a frontal assault. Civilis let them, knowing the most belligerent would be killed and failure would cow the remainder into following his orders. The assault failed, but his authority was thereafter accepted without question.[58]

Night fell. Huge fires were lit using the wood from the demolished settlement and the men drank and feasted, toasting comrades and the gods. Then the assault was launched, but the attackers were silhouetted against the firelight, allowing the *ballistae* crews to target the most courageous and those warriors illuminated by their glittering decorations for valour. They were cut down with bolts and stones. Civilis soon realized his mistake and the fires were extinguished, casting the battlefield into darkness.[59]

The defenders waited in silence on the ramparts until the presence of the enemy was revealed as they climbed the wooden walls or a scaling ladder appeared on the parapet. The Germans, struggling for balance on the rungs, were hit in the face with shield bosses, whilst a hail of javelins struck those below waiting in the ditch. Those few that struggled over the parapet felt the cold point of a *gladius*. Repulsed, they withdrew and waited for dawn.[60]

The legionaries manning the Praetorian gate were the first to see the two-storey siege tower being dragged across the level ground towards the fortress. However, the defenders were already prepared. Strong poles were thrust out from the towers, fixing it, while beams were swung out to pulverise it. Then the gates were opened and the legionaries rushed out to complete the destruction. At the same time, the defenders had devised a machine to terrify the attackers. A large beam was swung out from the wall with a net that fell on the Germans below. A counterweight was then released, and the beam swung upwards, sending those unfortunates who had been ensnared high into the air and into the fort. The attackers fell back. Civilis returned to starving the defenders out.[61]

In late October, news of the second Battle of Cremona reached the Rhine. The Vitellian forces had been destroyed in the night battle and their emperor in Rome faced certain defeat. The recently raised Gallic auxiliary cohorts immediately returned home, leaving the remaining Rhine legions and the Ubii, Treveri and Lingones isolated. The news came 'through a letter from Primus

Antonius, to which was added a proclamation issued by Caecina; and a prefect of a cohort from the defeated side, one Alpinius Montanus, acknowledged in person the misfortune of his party'. Too eager to gain the approval of Vespasian, Hordeonoius Flaccus ordered his tribunes to take the new oath of allegiance from the legions. He lacked the authority to lead the assembly himself and hoped his subordinates would. The officers responded enthusiastically, seeing it was to their advantage to switch their support as soon as possible.[62]

The legionaries were despondent. The illustrious reputation of the German legions lay buried in the mud around Cremona, their comrades dead, wounded or captured. Their emperor waited upon his fate in Rome and Vespasian would exact his revenge for their part in the civil war. They were alone, surrounded by enemies. Thus, as the tribunes read out the words, the soldiers 'took an oath which neither their looks nor wills quite confirmed: and while they repeated the greater part of the usual formula, they hesitated at Vespasian's name, some murmuring it faintly, most passing over it in silence'. The centurions did not attempt to enforce the vow. A promise made before the gods was not to be taken lightly. Despite the dire situation and the destruction of their cause, the rank and file remained loyal to Vitellius.[63]

The resentment and anger of the soldiers soon erupted into mutiny. Some letters written by Antonius to Civilis were read out to the assembled troops. In them, Antonius addressed Civilis as an ally, whilst the German legions were described as enemies. Perhaps Flaccus hoped the conflict would end, as both legionaries and Batavians were now on the same side. It was a naïve and forlorn hope. The letters were then read to the soldiers at Gelduba who had recently suffered a humiliating defeat at the hands of an enemy they were now expected to embrace as friends and allies. They too responded with anger, fury and hostility.[64]

Montanus was then sent to Civilis to convey news of victory to Vespasian's ally and instruct him to end the war, as 'his efforts had already been sufficient'. In reply, Civilis was evasive and ambiguous, giving a 'crafty answer': afterwards, when he saw that Montanus was of an impetuous nature and inclined to revolt, he began to complain of the dangers which he had passed through for twenty-five years in the camps of the Romans. The two met in private, however, and Tacitus imagines Civilis' response before Montanus was sent 'away with orders to make a mild report' but 'bearing himself as though he had failed in his embassy'.[65]

The account of Civilis' initial response to news of the Flavian victory is both confused and contradictory. It was in the interests of the Flavian emperors to depict Civilis' revolt as purely a native insurrection against Rome, history being written to avoid giving any real substance to the suspicion that Vespasian had supported native Batavians and their Gallic allies in a war against citizen legions. Tacitus drew chiefly from a lost history of Pliny the Elder, who was a contemporary. The core of Civilis' support came from the Batavian auxiliary cohorts, supplemented with tribesmen from sub-tribes. However, they had gained nothing from their support for Vespasian. There was no mention of rewards for their endeavours, merely a demand for them to cease fighting. The Batavians revolted after the Romans broke their treaty with the tribe, and they treated their leader, Civilis, with disdain and contempt. For all the blood they had shed in Vespasian's name, they were offered nothing.[66]

On a personal level, Civilis had made an oath to Hercules Magusanus to avenge the destruction wrought on his homeland by the legionaries at Vetera and capture the fortress. His hair remained uncut; his vow unfulfilled. He could not remain the leader of the tribe if Vetera did not fall. The German prophetess had foreseen the destruction of the legions there. To return to his allegiance with Rome was a betrayal of all the gods and those countless thousands who had fallen before Vetera's walls. Therefore he continued the war.

Vocula had expected Civilis to agree to the Flavian demands. Civilis remained with his German allies besieging Vetera, whilst he 'dispatched the veteran cohorts and the best of the Germans under the leadership of Julius Maximus and Claudius Victor, his own nephew, to attack Vocula and his army'. In early December, the fort at Asberg was sacked and then he led a surprise attack on the Romans at Gelduba. The Romans had posted few scouts or pickets. Vocula managed to form up the legionaries in the centre of his line but the auxiliaries on either wing were caught up in the chaos. To buy time, Vocula ordered his cavalry to attack the Batavians, but they were met by a disciplined, well-formed line of infantry and broke, fleeing back to the Roman line, adding to the disorder. The Nervian cohorts on either wing fled and the legionaries attempted to retreat to the safety of their fort. Attacked on all sides, their standards were lost and the Batavians broke inside the ramparts. A massacre began.[67]

Civilis failed to take advantage of the collapse of Vocula's line. He held back his reserve, and then chance played its part. Several cohorts of Vacones, summoned earlier by Hordeonius Flaccus, were approaching the Roman camp and heard the noise of battle. They fell upon the rear of Civilis' forces, who panicked, believing that the troops from either Novaesium or Mogontiacum had arrived, whilst Vocula's forces rallied. Many Batavians were trapped in a vice, and the slaughter continued as the tide turned. Civilis, probably concerned that more Romans were about to arrive on the battlefield, failed to commit his reserve. His cavalry escaped, along with the standards and captives they had captured earlier, but he lost the Batavian infantry cohorts. The Romans also suffered large numbers of casualties.[68]

Civilis quickly returned to Vetera, hoping to trick the garrison into surrender. He displayed the captives and standards before the rampart and offered terms, pretending that their cause was lost and their relief force destroyed. However, one of the prisoners 'had the courage to do a heroic deed, shouting out the truth, for which he was at once run through by the Germans: their act inspired the greater confidence in his statement, and at the same time the harried fields and the fires of the burning farmhouses announced the approach of a victorious army'.[69]

Civilis was obsessed with capturing Vetera. Instead of retreating, he decided to position his army between Vocula's advancing force and the garrison. Caught between the two, his army was already buckling when Civilis was thrown from his horse. His army, believing he had been killed, broke. Vocula, however, failed to follow up his success and allowed Civilis to escape. The siege was relieved, the wounded, sick and starving were evacuated to Novaesium and supplies were called for. The Rhine was controlled by the Batavians using the captured river galleys, so food and provisions had to be transported by land. The first baggage train made it to Novaesium and back without a problem, but the second was attacked upon its return journey. Nightfall ended the battle, and the supply train made it to Gelduba. The next day the escort and army servants refused to move, terrified that loaded with heavy waggons they would be easy prey. Vocula was forced to order 1,000 of the best soldiers from Vetera's garrison to march to Gelduba and retrieve the supplies.[70]

Discipline now started to collapse. The veteran legionaries had no doubt believed that Civilis was dead, and the successful return of the first baggage train added credence to this belief. But this had now been shattered. Those not chosen to march to Gelduba grew desperate at the prospect of remaining behind. More than half-starved, surrounded and facing no hope of relief, the order to remain was a death sentence As the column marched out, large numbers of unselected men joined them. Those that remained 'complained that they had been abandoned', whilst those who marched to Gelduba 'began to murmur openly that they could no longer endure hunger or the plots of their commanders'. Roman losses in the battle at Gelduba had shaken the soldiers' belief in Vocula's ability, and his carelessness had indeed cost many lives. Furthermore, the letters from Antonius Primus confirmed that Civilis had been allied with Vespasian, whilst Hordeonius Flaccus and their senior officers had provided illicit support. The army had selected Vocula as its leader solely on his reputation as a competent commander who would not risk their lives. That was no longer the case. With all trust in Vocula now gone, a mutiny became inevitable.[71]

Vetera was besieged again. Vocula, unable to risk another battle, abandoned his attempt to reprovision Vetera and withdrew to Novaesium. The legionaries from the *V Alaudae* and *XV Primigenia* knew that the comrades they had left behind stood little chance. Then the soldiers learnt that Vitellius' donative had arrived at around the same time news of his death reached the Rhine. The legionaries demanded the donative be distributed, which the governor immediately did in the name of Vespasian. The coins that soldiers received under their standards that now carried the image of Vespasian, carried the face of Vitellius. Their old emperor had kept his agreement with them, and they had accepted his coins. The soldiers, flush with money, took to the inns to enjoy their newfound wealth. Anger, resentment and rumour mixed with alcohol to create a toxic brew. Mutiny erupted amongst former members of Vetera's garrison. Hordeonius Flaccus was dragged from his bed and murdered; Vocula managed to escape disguised as a slave.[72]

Although the legionaries of Upper Germany immediately repudiated the actions of their comrades, the die had been cast. Leaders, unnamed but respected, took control. The army of Civilis was approaching, Vetera's much-depleted garrison was again besieged, and the Chatti, Usipi and Mattiaci had crossed the Rhine and laid siege to Mogontiacum. They had also plundered the territory of the Treveri, who had built a huge earthwork and a palisade along 'their borders and fought the Germans with great losses on both sides'. The Rhine legions lacked a commander, officers and an emperor.[73]

The *I Germanica* at Bonna, *IV Macedonica* and *XXII Primigenia* took the lead in rescuing the situation. Vocula was found and placed at their head. He made them retake their oath to Vespasian. The emperor's imperial image was reinstated on the standards and discipline was restored. They were ready for war. Centurions were sent to their old provincial allies, the Treveri and Lingones, requesting help. Then they marched down the Rhine and defeated the Germans besieging Mogontiacum, catching them whilst they were scattered plundering the local area, inflicting significant losses before driving them back across the river.[74]

This was the moment when the interests of the Treveri and Lingones, and Civilis and the Batavians, aligned. They all faced the threat of Vespasian's forces, having rejected the hand of friendship, the Batavians most of all. The Treveri were led by Julius Classicus, a prefect of the Treveri cavalry who had led the Vitellian advance against Otho up to the Maritime Alps. He 'was superior to the others in birth and wealth; he was of royal family and his line had been famous in both peace and war, and he himself boasted that more of his ancestors had been enemies than allies of the Romans'. Classicus was joined by Julius Tutor, who had been appointed prefect of the Rhine bank by Vitellius, a position traditionally held by members of the Treverian Julian elite. They were both high-ranking Roman officers whose careers and aspirations had been destroyed by the fall of Vitellius. They wanted to create a Roman Empire for the Gauls, but had no aspirations of reasserting Gallic supremacy.[75]

The Lingones were led by Julius Sabinus, a Romanized noble who claimed descent from Julius Caesar and adopted the title of 'Caesar'. He and Tutor offered their tribes a view of *imperium* that would be their own. In the absence of a senator as a viable candidate for the throne, they were the only alternative. Each were chiefs who first drew upon the support of their clients and then their *amici* through private interviews. They met in Cologne. They were joined by representatives of the Ubii and Tungri. Julius Classicus had already attempted to win over Civilis to their cause for, according to Tacitus, 'before the murder of Hordeonius Flaccus nothing came to the surface to make the conspiracy known'.[76] There had been no evidence of contact between Civilis and the Treveri, apart from Tacitus' fictitious dialogue between the prefect Montanus and the Batavian leader. Civilis must have rejected these overtures, as it was agreed to provide Civilis' rival and enemy, Claudius Labeo, with 'a small force of foot and horse' to attack the Canninefates and Marsaci. Labeo had managed to escape from the Frisians after bribing his guards.[77]

The rebels believed the Roman Empire was on the brink of collapse. The Batavians had broken their allegiance to Rome, whilst German tribes had crossed the Rhine and plundered the countryside. Italy itself was pillaged by Roman armies and the legions were slaughtering one another. The Capitol and the Temple of Jupiter in Rome itself had been burned to the ground. Vitellius was dead, whilst Vespasian remained in Egypt. Rumours – credible but false – added to this impression. It was said that legions in Moesia and Pannonia were besieged by Sarmatians and Dacians, whilst Britain had been overrun. The Druids, long persecuted but resilient, prophesized that this was 'proof from heaven of the divine wrath and presages the passage of sovereignty of the world to the peoples beyond the Alps'. Rome was about to fall, and they stood on the verge of a new dawn.[78]

The Treveri and Lingones had a close association with the legionaries and needed their support in countering the German incursions. However, their commanders were not trusted. It was decided to isolate the Rhine army in enemy territory and then use the threat of imminent destruction to pressure the soldiers into betraying their officers. An offer of alliance was sent to Vocula and the garrison troops of Upper Germany. His forces were weak, and he did not trust his legionaries. However, Classicus and Tutor offered to join him in relieving Vetera. Warily, he marched his force to Cologne, from where they all advanced towards Vetera.[79]

A few miles from Vetera, the Treveri separated from the main army and constructed a camp. Vocula had used Classicus and Tutor's cavalry as scouts to reconnoitre the land ahead. They used this opportunity to contact Civilis and gain his agreement with their plan. This is the moment their alliance was formed. The Roman army was forced again to withdraw and returned to the nearby fortress at Novaesium, whilst the Treveri built a camp 2 miles away. The centurions took the lead. They and other 'soldiers frequently visited them, and attempts were made to tamper with their loyalty'. A deal was struck. The legions would arrest or kill 'their chief officers' and then swear a new oath of allegiance to the Gallic empire. After all, many legionaries were recruited locally and had grown up amongst the Treveri, even though their neighbours may not have been Roman citizens.[80]

Vocula was made aware of the plot but refused to flee. He had done so once before, and that humiliation was too much. He now preferred death to dishonour. Instead, he assembled his legions and attempted to shame them into rejecting the offer. Their treachery distorted the boundaries between Romans and barbarians. The soldiers as always were divided. Some felt shame at deserting their officers, renouncing their oath and pledging loyalty to the Gauls. Others – the majority – took the safer course and chose to do nothing. Classicus sent a deserter from the *I Germanica* into the fort and Vocula was murdered. The legates of the *I Germanica* and *XVI Gallica*, Herennius Gallus and Numisius Rufus, were imprisoned. Classicus then entered the camp wearing the insignia of a Roman general and took the *adlocatio*. The legionaries swore allegiance to the 'Empire of the Gauls'.[81]

The capital of Upper Germany, Cologne, and the rest of the legions in the province soon made the same oath. However, the tribunes of the *IV Macedonica* and *XXII Primigenia* at Mogontiacum refused and were executed, whilst a Prefect of the Camp was expelled. The besieged legions at Vetera received the news that there would be no further attempts to relieve the siege. To crush their hopes, the news was given by fellow legionaries sent from Novaesium.[82]

The depleted garrison of the *XV Primigenia* and *V Alaudae* had withstood hell for months. Reduced to eating the grass and roots that grew inside the fortress, they had held out for as long as feasibly possible. Further resistance was futile, so they sent a delegation to Civilis begging for their lives. Tacitus criticizes their decision, yet other legions who had freely taken the oath to the Gallic Empire escaped this censure. Civilis refused to consider their terms until they had taken the oath themselves. Then they were allowed to march out of the fortress, leaving behind all their possessions, servants and civilians. The column was led by their commander, Munius Lupercus. It marched about 5 miles before being attacked by the Germans. Some stood their ground and fell facing the enemy, but most turned, scattered and attempted to make it back to their fort and were cut down. The few who made it inside the ramparts were killed as the camp was plundered and then burned.[83]

Civilis assembled his army and criticized them for breaking his agreement with the slain legionaries. This pretence was necessary if he still hoped to be granted a pardon from Vespasian. He must have known his army wanted revenge for the losses they had suffered at the swords and spear points of these soldiers. His oath had now been fulfilled. He cut his hair short. Until then, he had allowed his hair to cover his face, as was the custom of the Chatti,

> 'in accordance with a vow pledging them to the service of Valour; and only when they had slain an enemy do they lay it aside. Standing over the bloody corpse they have despoiled, they reveal their faces to the world once more, and proclaim that they have at last repaid the debt they owe for being brought into the world and have proved themselves worthy of their native land and parents. The coward who will not fight must stay unshorn.'

Civilis stood before the bodies of thousands.[84] He showed no mercy. Some captives were used for target practice by his young son. Civilis also had another debt to repay. Lupercus was sent as a prize to Veleda, but he was killed before he met a horrendous end, sacrificed to the German gods. The captured forts along the Rhine, with the exception of Mogontiacum and Vindonissa, were burned. These two were considered strategically important as Flavian armies gathered to recover the lost provinces.[85]

Civilis had no interest in the concept of a Gallic Empire – 'he did not bind himself or any Batavian by an oath of allegiance to Gaul'. The Ubii settled around Colonia Agrippinensis were Germans and, threatened by the Tencteri across the Rhine, looked to the protection of Civilis, who sent the *ala Batavorum* to garrison the city. In return, Civilis left his wife and sister in the city 'as pledges of fidelity to the alliance'. The Treveri and Lingones served a useful purpose as allies against the inevitable attempt by the Flavians to restore Roman authority along the Rhine. For this reason, he kept a few centurions and tribunes of Gallic birth 'as hostages to assure the alliance'.[86] No attempt was made to help or assist these tribes as various Roman armies descended on them. Instead, Civilis focused on hunting down Claudius Labeo, whom he blamed for the death of his brother.[87]

The Gallic revolt was limited in scope, restricted mainly to the tribes closely associated with the Rhine legions. Julius Sabinus led the Lingones against the Sequani and was soundly beaten.[88] Other Gallic tribes had reluctantly joined the revolt, but as Rome reasserted itself, they quickly renounced their brief and temporary alliance with the Treveri. A huge army from Italy advanced over the Alps. The Flavian legions – *VIII Augusta*, *XI Claudia* and *XIII Gemina* – with the *II Adiutrix* enlisted from the Ravenna fleet and the Vitellian *XXI Rapax* from Vindonissa, were to fall upon the Lingones. Two legions were summoned from Spain, the *I Adiutrix* and VI *Victrix*, and later they were joined by the *X Gemina*. From Britain came the *XIV Gemina*, who hated the Batavians. They were transported across by the Channel fleet and threatened the 'island'. No auxiliaries were called upon, only veteran legionaries intent on revenge or plunder.[89]

Faced with inevitable defeat, many of the Gallic tribes quickly abandoned the cause, but Civilis focused on exacting revenge. He 'ranged the pathless wilds of Belgium in his efforts to capture Claudius Labeo or drive him out of the country'.[90] Soon Flavian forces drew close. The *XXII Rapax* had advanced past its base at Vindonissa, whilst the procurator of Noricum advanced on the Treveri with his auxiliary cohorts and an elite cavalry unit, an *ala Singularium* which had been raised by Vitellius but had gone over to Vespasian. They 'were commanded by Julius Briganticus, the son of a sister of Civilis, who was hated by his uncle and who hated his uncle in turn with all the bitter hatred that frequently exists between the closest relatives'. Tutor and the Treveri waited with Roman veteran infantry and cavalry. However, when the Flavian army drew near, they deserted, forcing Tutor to retreat towards Trier. To prevent the Treveri from abandoning them, Tutor and fellow leader Valentinus murdered the two captured legates, Herennius Gallus and Numisius Rufus. The Treveri were cut to pieces at Riol and their capital fell. Briganticus later died defending Vada, a Batavian town. Another grievance was settled.[91]

The former Vitellian legions – *I Germanica* and *XVI Gallica* – were encamped nearby. They had sworn an oath of allegiance to the Gallic Empire but were not trusted to fight for it. These legionaries felt the shame of defeat and treason; they 'stood there, downcast by the consciousness of their own guilt, their eyes fixed on the ground: when the armies met, there was no exchange of greetings; the soldiers made no answer to those who tried to console or to encourage them; they remained hidden in their tents and avoided the very light of day'. Both had a proud history. The *I Germanica* had been raised by Julius Caesar, fought against Pompey the Great and was awarded its title for distinguished service fighting the Germans. In the name of Rome, it had destroyed Vindex and remained fixed in its oath to Nero when others abandoned him. Their love of Germanicus and loyalty to Vitellius had brought no rewards.[92]

The *XVI Gallica* had been raised by Caesar's adopted son, Octavian, to recover Sicily from Pompeian forces. It had probably campaigned against the Chatti under Galba in AD 40/41 and suffered under his strict discipline. They too had campaigned against Vindex for Nero and were eager to acclaim Vitellius when their former commander became emperor. They had remained loyal too long to escape some form of punishment. The Flavian commander, Q. Petillius Cerialis, assembled the conquered and conquerors before him. The sullen and humiliated stood side by side with the proud and arrogant victors. Cerialis quietened the anger and fears of the defeated by blaming their current situation on the Fates, the treachery of their allies and, significantly, 'the differences between the soldiers and their commanders'. In acknowledging the dubious loyalty and fickleness of their governor, *legates* and officers, Cerialis recognized they had genuine grievances. There was none of the brutal imposition of severe punishment of a Drusus or Galba or the vengeance of a Vitellius. Through compromise and clemency, the Flavians won the support of their former enemies. With that, the *I Germanica* and *XVI Gallica* again took the oath of allegiance to Vespasian.[93]

Military discipline required some form of punishment. The two legions ceased to exist: their titles, honours and proud history were gone. However, the legionaries escaped the humiliation of dishonourable discharge and a social death. Instead, the *I Germanica* joined the *VII Galbiana* to form the *VII Gemina*, or 'Twin', and garrisoned Legio (Leon) in Spain. The retention of its number and return to Spain rewarded the legionaries of the *VII Galbiana* who were raised there and had rapidly joined the Flavian cause under Antonius Primus. However, the German legionaries lost their homes, family ties and connections. The same was true of the *XVI Gallica*, which was reconstituted as the *XVI Flavia Firma*, the 'Steadfast Flavian Sixteenth', but transferred to Satala on the River Euphrates. The legion remained loyal to its appellation and carried it with pride through a distinguished history of service.[94]

The Batavians were at first pushed back to 'the island', which they attempted to defend by cutting its bridges and flooding the area by destroying the dykes dug by Drusus the Elder. It delayed rather than frustrated the Roman invasion of their homeland, which was laid waste, apart from the properties and land owned by Civilis. Cerialis sowed division and death. Victories, however, were hard-won and countered by minor reverses. The fleet sent from Britain was destroyed by the Canninefates, so Civilis retained control of the Rhine, making provisioning the Roman army slow and difficult. However, the Ubians treacherously destroyed Civilis' remaining elite unit. They invited the cavalrymen of the *ala Batavorum* to a banquet and glutted their guests with abundant quantities of wine. The doors to the hall were then shut and the building was set on fire, incinerating this outstanding regiment. They then handed over Civilis' wife and sister, who had lived there as guarantors of Batavian loyalty.[95]

The Batavians grew weary of war. The human cost was devastating. The Romans too suffered huge casualties. In one battle, 'so great a multitude of Romans and barbarians were slain that the river flowing nearby was dammed up by the bodies of the fallen'. Winter was approaching and the Romans struggled to impose their control on 'the island'. Batavian ships blockaded the mouth of the Rhine and patrolled the river, preventing grain and supplies from reaching the Roman garrisons. Civilis had withdrawn his main forces across the Rhine, and using his captured ships he was able to attack Cerialis' army with impunity and then retreat over the river. The war had reached a stalemate. The Romans admired the bravery, skill and tenacity of their enemy. It was in the interests of both Civilis and Cerialis to reach an agreement.[96]

The two met on the remains of a destroyed bridge on either the river Ijssel or Vecht. Cerialis had already offered peace to the Batavians and a renewal of their treaty with Rome. Secretly, he offered Civilis a pardon. Envoys were also sent to the prophetess Veleda and her relatives, asking her 'to change the fortunes of a war, which repeated disasters had shown to be averse to them, by rendering a timely service to the Roman people'. She appears to have done so, as she was later captured by the Romans and, instead of executing her, they took her to Italy and made her a priestess in the Temple of Ardea. Civilis, for his part, claimed that he could have destroyed all the captured legions, and his German allies wished to do so, but he had dissuaded them, which, Tacitus acknowledged, 'seems not far from the truth, since his surrender followed a few days later'. The Batavians retained their federate status under the same terms, although the old military elite disappeared, replaced by landowners, merchants and shipping agents. The Batavian Julii faded into history.[97]

Civilis acted as the hand of vengeance. His people wanted to avenge the rape, extortion and suffering caused by the two legions based at Vetera, who acted on the orders of Vitellius in breach of their long-established treaty with Rome. To cement his tribe to this cause, he took an oath before Hercules Magusanus and the leaders of his tribe. To renege on this vow was an act of cowardice and sacrilege. As a man of honour, he would keep his pledge. The veteran legions were destroyed and their fort burned, fulfilling the visions of Veleda and his promise.

He also burned with personal grievances against the men whom he blamed for the execution of his brother and his arrests, trials and humiliations, the emperors Nero and Vitellius, as well as Claudius Labeo. There was incriminating evidence that he had conspired with Vindex, otherwise he would not have been arrested and his brother executed. He does appear to have received a pardon, although the account in Tacitus frustrating breaks off. His revolt certainly began under the Flavian banner, urged on by Hordeonius Flaccus and Antonius Primus. He prevented the Rhine legions from sending reinforcements to support Vitellius. If he was a traitor, it was to Nero and Vitellius, not Vespasian. He had reasons enough to hope for clemency from the Flavians. Civilis probably lived the remainder of his life across the Rhine. A traitor to Nero, he remained steadfastly loyal to his people and his code of honour. The Batavian cohorts and people, though, paid a heavy price for their loyalty to him.[98]

Chapter 9

Revolt of Saturninus (1 January AD 89)

> 'Domitian also dreamed that Minerva, whom he worshipped with superstitious reverence, emerged from her shrine to tell him that she had been disarmed by Jupiter and could no longer protect him.'
>
> (One of the omens foretelling the murder of the emperor; Suetonius, *Domitian*, 15)

Death stalked the emperor Domitian. He lost his mother as a child, and then his uncle, Flavius Sabinus, when the forces of Vitellius stormed the Capitol. He had escaped after disguising himself as a worshipper of Isis. His father, Vespasian, had died in AD 79, and death cut short his brother Titus' reign after just two years. Domitian sought divine protection from Minerva, the goddess of wisdom, justice and the law. She was the goddess 'he revered most', and he kept a shrine to her in his private chamber. He established a college of priests in her honour who officiated over a five-day festival. This he celebrated 'on a magnificent scale; on these occasions, he held contests of poets and orators and gladiators almost every year at his Alban villa'. He demanded that he be addressed as 'Lord and God', as well as the son of Minerva. She was the mother he had lost; however, his devotion was not enough. Her favour was dependent upon his protection of Rome's laws and religious moralities.[1]

Domitian was ferocious in hunting out dishonesty, injustice and corruption. He was the custodian of Rome's traditional religion and laws. Intolerant, an inflexible authoritarian and obsessive in restoring traditional morals, he looked to ancient precedents to restore respect for the law and began a 'campaign for improving public morals'.[2] Domitian revived the Republican-era *lex Scantinia* as part of this drive, which criminalized Roman citizens who engaged in a passive role during homosexual intercourse or with Roman boys. The cases were likely heard before the emperor, and although the punishment appears to have been a fine, Domitian acting as censor would remove those convicted of their senatorial or equestrian status.[3] Consequently, he 'sentenced many members of both orders under the Scantinian Law'.[4]

The Flavians had rewarded Lucius Antonius Saturninus, but he would fall foul of Domitian's attempt to re-establish the traditional religion and the illusory moral standards of Rome's past. He was a new man without a noble ancestry and owed everything to the emperor's favour. He was adlected into the Senate by Vespasian, appointed governor of Judaea *c.* AD 78–81, and attained nobility through a suffect consulship in AD 82. He may have been governor of Macedonia before becoming governor of Upper Germany between AD 86 and 88. This post was only given to experienced senators of proven loyalty to the regime. He commanded four legions along the Rhine, facing the hostile Chatti. The double legionary fortress at Mogontiacum was held by the *XXI Rapax* and *XIV Gemina*, whilst the *XI Claudia* garrisoned Vindonissa (Windisch) and *VIII Augusta* was at Strasbourg. He may also have commanded the *I Adiutrix*, which was also stationed at Mogontiacum until being transferred in AD 86 to the Danube. Such a powerful army, along with its vast numbers of auxiliary cohorts, would only be given to a man held in the highest imperial confidence and trust.[5]

On 1 January AD 89, Saturninus suddenly raised the standard of revolt, with the support of only the two legions at Mogontiacum. Ranged against him were the two other legions in Upper Germany, the legions of Lower Germany and Pannonia, and the Praetorians at Rome. An act of such suicidal idiocy by the governor and the two legions is difficult to explain. So too is the hostility of the ancient sources to a senator who rose against an emperor many denounced as a tyrant. Late accounts are full of venom. He is described as an 'infamous and despicable' man, whose consulship 'enveloped him in evil dignity'.[6] The reason for this hostility is provided by Aelian, who declares he was infamous for 'while living he used to approach no sacred [place], for they drove him [out] as accursed and infamous'. Elsewhere, Aelian says 'he was infamous for pederasty'. 'Having lived a life infamous and abominable, he was entrusted with no authority over imperial funds.' Yet he was given control over four legions, so the allegations only became public after his appointment to the governorship of Upper Germany.[7]

Domitian must have believed the accusations. After the revolt was crushed, an investigation was launched to determine the extent of Saturninus' support. Evidence was extracted from suspects using a unique and vile form of torture which the emperor felt matched the crime. This involved

> 'scorching his prisoners' genitals to make them divulge the whereabouts of other rebels still in hiding and cut[ting] off the hands of many more. It is a fact that only two leaders of the revolt – a colonel of senatorial rank and a centurion – earned a pardon, which they did by the simple expedient of proving themselves to have been so disgustingly immoral that they could have exerted no influence at all over either their commander or the troops.'[8]

The dubious reputation of the young tribune, Julius Calvaster, saved him. Calvaster stood accused of treason, as 'he had had frequent meetings alone with Antonius, and he had no other way to free himself from the charge of conspiracy, he declared that he had met him for amorous intercourse; and in fact, he was of an appearance to inspire passion'.[9] Reports, rumours and allegations concerning the governor's activities probably became public knowledge in Rome after his appointment: 'inflamed by these depravities of his and most of all by an injury of words, as a result of which he used to suffer to be called a male prostitute, Antonius, supervisor of Germania Superior, seized imperium.'[10] His recall and prosecution were inevitable, followed by loss of status, humiliation and ruin. He could expect no mercy from Domitian, nor a fair hearing. The emperor's alliance with Minerva did not allow for leniency.

The former governor of Lower Germany, Vitellius, had a similar fate, although he faced financial ruin. It was no coincidence that Saturninus chose the twentieth anniversary of Vitellius' acclamation for his own.[11] The soldiers had spent a heady seven days celebrating the Saturnalia. The drinking, gambling and revelry culminated on 23 December with celebrations including a public banquet, paid for from the soldiers' savings. However, in the circumstances, Saturninus no doubt contributed and joined in with the festivities. A significant relaxation of discipline probably marked the following eight days, with the party atmosphere allowed to continue.[12]

The officers and centurions would have made plans to ensure that the legionaries assembled on 1 January transferred their oath of allegiance from Domitian to Saturninus. As the officers and centurions of the two legions at Mogontiacum suffered mass execution following the failure of the revolt, it is clear that they took the lead, whilst the rank and file avoided severe punishment. When Domitian arrived at Mogontiacum, he 'proceeded to commit a series of murders'; all those condemned had their names removed from inscriptions and official records, and he 'sent their heads as well as that of Antonius to Rome and caused them to be exposed in the Forum.' These punishments were reserved for the elite, not ordinary soldiers. The legates and tribunes of the two legions were executed, apart from Calvaster, and probably most of the leading centurions.[13]

The legionaries were prepared to support their governor by donating their savings stored in the vaults. The sums were significant, as 'the large amount of soldiers' savings laid up in the joint winter headquarters of the two legions on the Rhine had provided Lucius Antonius with the necessary funds for launching his rebellion'. Neither the local merchants and landowners nor the Treveri appear to have been approached. They were either hostile or Saturninus' decision was forced upon him unexpectedly by news of imminent recall to Rome. Funds were needed to purchase grain, fodder, wagons and horses. It was costly to move an army and too risky to rely on plunder to serve its needs.[14]

If Saturninus took the revolt of Vitellius as his model, we can conjecture that various rewards were offered to his commanders and officers. As he was acclaimed emperor, the offices of Praetorian Prefect, tribunates and centurion posts in the Guard, procuratorships, governorships and heads of the imperial bureaucracy were offered to elicit treachery. The soldiers in the *XXI Rapax* and *XIV Gemina* could expect a transfer to the Praetorians and a comfortable life in Rome. There was also the opportunity to plunder the wealthy Gallic provinces on their march and the towns of Italy. Furthermore, the transfer of the *I Aduitrix* to the Danube after garrisoning Mogontiacum for sixteen years added an element of resentment and fear. The *XXI Rapax* had already been moved from Bonn to Mogontiacum. Domitian was gradually transferring legions from the Rhine to the Danube because Rome faced threats from the Marcomanni, Quadi and Dacians. The *XXI Rapax* was sent to Pannonia immediately after the revolt, so preparations were no doubt already underway. The dislocation from their families, communities and ancestral land provided further motivation to support the imperial claims of their governor.[15]

To add lustre to his imperial claims, Saturninus may have claimed descent from the famous opponent of Augustus, Marcus Antonius. This may be the context of Martial's poem addressed to Saturninus:

> 'While, puffed up beyond measure by an empty name, you were entranced with delight, and were ashamed, unfortunate man, of being merely Saturninus, you stirred up war under the Parrhasian Bear, like he who bore arms for his Egyptian consort. Had you so entirely forgotten the ill-fortune of that name, which the fierce rage of the sea at Actium overwhelmed? Or did the Rhine promise you what the Nile denied to him, and were the northern waters likely to be more propitious? Even Antony fell by our arms, who, compared with you, traitor, was a Caesar.'[16]

Saturninus had no great deeds to add lustre to his claim, nor military victories or great ancestors. The nobility in Rome would have known of his undistinguished heritage, but the soldiers standing before him in the *adlocutio* may have believed he was descended from Mark Antony.[17]

Domitian left Rome with the Praetorian cohorts on 12 January, the date the Arval Brethren offered for his victory and safe return. He must have been forewarned in late AD 88 to be able to march north so soon after the revolt broke out. Saturninus would have approached the commanders of the *XI Claudia* at Vindonissa and the *VIII Augusta* at Strasbourg to gain their support. He failed, these legions remaining loyal to Domitian. The legates would then have sent a message to Rome warning Domitian of the imminent revolt.[17]

The army was indeed loyal to Domitian. He had raised their pay by more than a third, the first emperor to do so since Augustus. Around this time, the emperor issued an edict establishing a series of benefits for veterans, including freedom from public taxes and harbour dues, as well as conferring citizenship on them, their married wives and their children. Upon his murder in AD 96, the soldiers demanded his deification, whilst a legion in Pannonia came close to mutiny. The Praetorians eventually took vengeance on the conspirators, hunting down and killing them in the palace.[19]

The refusal of the legions to join the revolt was a severe blow to Saturninus. He must have kept the news from the legionaries at Mogontiacum. Instead, he made an agreement with the Chatti across the Rhine. In AD 82, Domitian had led the legions against this tribe, destroying their territory and advancing the frontier of the Empire 120 miles further north. The war ended in AD 85 with the capitulation of the Chatti. Domitian took the title 'Germanicus' and possibly issued a donative to the soldiers. The *XXI Rapax* had fought in the war, but it was not returned to its base at Bonn, instead moving to Mogontiacum. The donative may not have compensated them for their lost home. Bonn was garrisoned by a newly raised legion named after Domitian's divine protector, the *I Minerva*. This legion remained loyal to the emperor who raised and named it. The Chatti, however, wanted revenge for their defeat and the opportunity to plunder the wealthy provinces. The Rhine froze, as was normal in midwinter, and they were to cross it on 1 January to support Saturninus' revolt.[20]

Fate undermined Saturninus' rapidly reducing chance of victory. A sudden warm spell thawed the ice on the Rhine, leaving the Chatti on the far bank. The bridges across the river must have been held by units loyal to Domitian.[21] Saturninus was forced to face the legions of Lower Germany alone. Its governor, Aulus Lappius Maximus, gathered his troops at Colonia Agrippinensis. The *X Gemina* arrived from Nijmegen, where it had been stationed after the Batavian revolt, whilst the *XXII Primigenia* was summoned from the newly built fortress at Vetera. These legions were joined by the *VI Victrix* from Noveasium and *I Minervia* from Bonn. Saturninus was also threatened by the auxiliary forces of Rhaetia, led by its procurator, T. Flavius Norbanus. The *VIII Augusta* at Strasbourg and *XI Claudia* holding Vindonissa remained loyal to Domitian, who was marching north with the Praetorians. The emperor had also summoned Trajan from Spain with the *VII Gemina*.[22]

Lappius Maximus rapidly marched south along the Rhine and met Saturninus in battle near Remagen or Andernach around 15 January. Saturninus was defeated and killed. The victorious legions from Lower Germany, all the auxiliary cohorts and the Rhine fleet were awarded the title *pia fidelis Domitiana* by the emperor. Even after the emperor's murder, they continued to carry the appellation, Pius and Faithful. Mogontiacum was captured and the revolt was over. A story later emerged that Lappius Maximus came across incriminating letters in the chests of Antoninus and burnt them to save the lives of co-conspirators in Rome. However, this was probably a story created by Lappius Maximus after the murder of Domitian in AD 96 in an attempt to disassociate himself from the emperor he had served so loyally. Domitian continued to demonstrate utmost trust in him. In AD 89 he was made governor of Syria, with its huge military garrison, and then in AD 95 he was given the rare honour of a second consulship. Lappius Maximus remained loyal and true to his emperor, which he attempted to hide upon the accession of Nerva, who had aided and abetted the killers of Domitian.[23]

The poet Martial also praises the loyalty of his patron, Norbanus, to Domitian: 'when your affectionate fidelity, Norbanus, was standing in defence of Caesar against the raging of sacrilegious fury, I, the well-known cultivator of your friendship, was amusing myself with the composition of these verses, in the calm security of Pierian retreats.'[24] Norbanus too was well rewarded, rising to become Praetorian Prefect. However, he betrayed his benefactor in AD 96 by failing to warn Domitian of the conspiracy that was forming against him.[25]

Trajan was also compensated for his loyalty in rapidly marching his legion from Spain, receiving another singular honour with an ordinary consulship in AD 91. It was a remarkable rise, as he had only been appointed as legate of a legion in AD 89. The ordinary consulship was normally reserved for members of the imperial house. Trajan arrived at Mogontiacum in February, just before Domitian. They united their forces, as the Chatti had invaded and destroyed some forts along the newly established *limes*. An inscription describes Lappius Maximus as the 'German warmaker'. The officers of the two defeated legions would also be purged.[26]

The future conspirator, Nerva, however, was granted the greatest award. He was given a second consulship in AD 90, which he shared with the emperor. He had remained in Rome whilst Domitian departed for the Rhine in January AD 89. The emperor did not return to the capital until November, as he took the *XXI Rapax* to Carnuntum to counter a threat from the Marcomanni and then travelled to Moesia to fight the Dacians. Nerva's reward was greater than that given to Lappius Maximus, who secured his four legions for Domitian and crushed the revolt. There were no plots, executions or trials in Rome during the emperor's protracted absence. Nerva was possibly tasked with ensuring the Senate remained compliant and obedient.[27]

Events had made Domitian deeply suspicious. On 22 September AD 87, the Arval Brethren recorded a sacrifice to the gods in response to 'the detected crimes of the wicked'. The plot may have involved a group of eminent senators, including Mettius Pompusianus, who was exiled around this date and later executed. The governor of Asia, C. Vettulenus Ciuica Cerealis, was also executed at this time. He may have been linked to the plot or condemned for a failure to crush a rising in the East led by a man claiming to be Emperor Nero.[28]

The emperor, however, had many supporters in the Senate. Dio records one senator who came out of retirement to join the emperor's entourage as he marched to the Rhine:

> 'Lusianus Proculus, an aged senator, who spent most of his time in the country, had set out with Domitian from Rome, feeling constrained to do so, that he might not appear to have deserted him in his peril and so be put to death. But when the news came [of the defeat of Saturninus] he said, "You have conquered emperor, as I always prayed; restore me therefore, to my country estate." Thereupon he left him and retired to his farm; and after this, though he survived a long time, he never came near him.'

There was evidently no compulsion to demonstrate his public backing of the emperor, and this should be interpreted as an expression of genuine support. His son was rewarded with a suffect consulship in August AD 93.[29]

However, there remained opposition that potentially could have used the revolt and the absence of the emperor to ferment unrest in Rome. The revolt of the Rhine legions conjured up memories of Vitellius' march on the city, the slaughter on its streets and the burning of the Capitol. Consequently, 'Rome was in consternation, expecting great wars from the quarter of Germany.' This was quashed 'all of a sudden, and nobody knows upon what account, the people spontaneously gave out a rumour of victory, and the news ran current through the city, that Antonius himself was slain, his whole army destroyed, and not so much as a part of it escaped; nay, this belief was so strong and positive, that many of the magistrates offered up sacrifice'. The involvement of officers of state and priests in thanking the gods implies the rumour itself had its origins in the palace. Domitian then marched north with the Praetorians, only to receive the news a few weeks later that Saturninus was already dead.[30]

All emperors were beset by threats – seen and unseen The emperor Tiberius hesitated to take the reins of government, fearing 'the dangers that threatened him from many quarters, and often led him to declare that he was holding a wolf by the ears'.[31] Domitian returned to Rome in November. Saturninus was dead, the Chatti had been defeated and forced to sign a peace agreement, the

Dacians had become clients of Rome and he had led his armies against the Marcomanni and Quadi across the Danube.[32] To prevent further revolts, he forbade soldiers from keeping more than 1,000 sesterces in savings in their legionary chests and ended the practice of double legionary fortresses. The date for the annual renewal of the soldiers' oath of allegiance was also moved, from 1 January to the 3rd, probably to allow the revelry and indiscipline promoted by the festivities of the *Saturnalia* to dissipate and provide time for the restoration of order. The *XXI Rapax* had already been moved to Moesia and would be destroyed by the Sarmatians in AD 92. Furthermore, Saturninus was not replaced by a military man, but a jurist with little military experience. Domitian also nominated eleven suffect consuls for AD 90, alongside himself and Nerva as the ordinary consuls at the start of the year. There were many men whose loyalty needed to be recognized and rewarded.[33]

In Rome, though, there remained a disenchanted and ambitious few whose imperial aspirations remained hidden. Some would have secretly prayed for the victory of Saturninus. The emperor was now deeply suspicious of the loyalty of many leading senators.[34] Domitian felt the foremost senators and *equites* needed reminding of the prospective rewards for loyalty and the inevitable fate for those who contemplated treason. With dark humour, the emperor wanted them to feel what it was like to live under the threat of imminent death. This was his existence. They were invited to the palace for an imperial banquet. Once settled, their servants and slaves waiting in the atrium were sent away. Everything was based on a funeral feast, ostensibly to honour those who had fallen in the Dacian war. They entered a dark room and reclined on black couches, their places identified by a slab shaped like a gravestone with their name on, illuminated by a small lamp similar to those that hung in tombs. Out of the darkness came naked boys painted black, who danced like ghosts around them and then sat at the feet of each guest. The food was then served on black plates, consisting of dishes served at funerals and used to make sacrifices to the spirits of the departed.[35]

All were terrified: 'consequently every single one of the guests feared and trembled and was kept in constant expectation of having his throat cut the next moment. On the part of everybody but Domitian there was dead silence, as if they were already in the realms of the dead, and the emperor himself conversed only upon topics relating to death and slaughter.' Finally, they were dismissed, only to find their escorts had been sent away and instead, each was allotted imperial slaves to carry them home in their litter or carriage. Isolated and alone, their journey home was filled with fear. Once they arrived back in the bosom of their family and had started to recover from their ordeal, 'word was brought to them that a messenger from Augustus had come'. Immediately, each believed their executioner had arrived.[36]

Domitian had put a great deal of thought into the performance, playing with their emotions, from the delight at the honour of an invitation to an imperial banquet to their anticipation of imminent death. The evening ended with imperial gifts that symbolized the wealth they might acquire in loyal devotion to their emperor. Imperial servants 'brought in the slab, which was of silver, and then others in turn brought in various articles, including the dishes that had been set before them at the dinner, which were constructed of very costly material; and last of all (came) that particular boy who had been each guest's familiar spirit, now washed and adorned. Thus, after having passed the entire night in terror, they received the gifts.' The banquet added to the fear and terror that permeated the atmosphere at court.[37]

Domitian never again had to deal with a military revolt. The army remained loyal to their commander-in-chief, who led his armies in the war zones. There were no immediate prosecutions of senators until AD 93, and then only directed at the inflexible Stoic opposition. Those aristocrats who were exiled or executed fell for good reason. Minerva protected her imperial devotee until AD 96, when he was stabbed to death in a conspiracy led by imperial freedmen whose corruption was about to receive imperial justice. Their candidate for the throne was the aged but ambitious friend of the emperor, Nerva. The Praetorians would have vengeance. In AD 97, they took Nerva hostage, demanding the death of those who had murdered Domitian. The leader of the conspiracy had been retained by Nerva as his principal advisor. He was hunted down within the palace and his genitals were cut off and forced into his mouth. Stripped of authority and held in contempt by the soldiers, Nerva was forced to adopt as his heir a military man of proven ability and loyalty: Trajan.[38]

Conclusions

The Roman Army reflected the social hierarchy of Roman society. Status and privilege were closely guarded, and the social divide between the commanders and the common soldiers was substantial. The provincial governor was superior in *dignitas* and *auctoritas* to his immediate subordinates, but they all belonged to the senatorial class. His legates who commanded his legions were senators like him, as was one of the five legionary tribunes. The *laticlavian*, or broad-stripe tribune, completed a one- or two-year period of military service before entering the Senate at 25. His fellow narrow-stripe tribunes were drawn from the equestrian class, so ranked below him in status, although they had far more military experience. Whilst the former were politicians in military guise, the latter were military men who had formerly served as prefects of auxiliary infantry cohorts, before promotion to a cavalry cohort and then tribune in a legion.

Appointment was arranged on patronage and recommendation based on the rules surrounding *amicitiae*, where favours were granted to *amici* or friends of equal status and clients of lesser rank, which obligated the recipient to return it when called upon. Military ability or experience was irrelevant; the tribunes who acted as advisors and administrators were young and inexperienced, and their common focus was on the political intrigues in Rome, not the battlefield. A gulf existed between the upper and lower ranks, separated as they were by wealth, status and experience. In times of stress, this disparity manifested itself in distrust, hostility, repression and mutiny. The professional soldiers were the centurions and the rank and file, whose trust in the ability of the officer class was not given; it had to be earned. A commander who made mistakes that needlessly cost the lives of his soldiers rapidly lost the confidence of the men. Hordeonius Flaccus paid with his life.[1]

The senatorial and equestrian officers, with their common interests, shared culture, education and opportunities for advancement and wealth, saw the common soldiers under their command as a potential threat, comparable to the unruly mob in Rome, who endangered political order. The ancient historians and biographers were drawn from the Graeco-Roman elite which perpetuated the jaundiced view of the soldiers as governed by base instincts, unconstrained through ignorance and motivated by greed. According to this interpretation, the soldiers were prone to emotional instability bordering on madness and possessed an insatiable desire for plunder. In times of mutiny or revolt, their leaders are undeserving of names, or like Percennius, are vilified as demagogues drawn from the lowest strata of society. This was a view shared by the aristocratic elite and many commanders. It was reflected in the savage brutality of Drusus during the Pannonian revolt and Galba throughout his military career.[2]

The aristocratic elite responded to threats as they would a peasant rising in the countryside or on the streets of Rome where the soldiers were recruited. They believed in the imposition of old-fashioned discipline, which resulted in punishments that were often excessive, unjust and completely unacceptable to the common soldier. The German legionaries despised both Tiberius and Galba for the measures they used to establish order in the ranks. The severe punishment of decimation was revived by Galba to symbolize the tradition of *virtus* and engender support from the old Republican nobility. His treatment of the newly raised legion of marines horrified soldiers across the Empire, led directly to the German legions acclaiming the unworthy Vitellius and added to unrest amongst the Praetorian guardsmen. This was perceived by the rank and file as illegitimate and unjust cruelty in executing innocent men and an attack on the status of the remainder. His enemies were quick to use this violent act to gather military support.[3]

The common soldiers were categorized as *humiliores*, who were still subject in law to most forms of capital and corporal punishment, unlike the elite *honestiores* who composed the upper social strata. The legionaries, as soldiers, citizens and free men, were protected from torture or the crueller forms of execution such as crucifixion. However, the interpretation of this prohibition was subjective and military law served to preserve the authority of the officers. The centurions' use of the vine rod to beat soldiers was perceived by the legionaries as both a form of torture and an assault on their status. They denounced their cruel beatings, echoing the language of the 'struggle of the orders' at the birth of the Roman Republic. This punishment was *iniuriae*, an attack on their status and honour, as slaves who possessed no status could be beaten. The centurions were not subject to this treatment yet used it, and so were the focus of the rage felt by the legionaries. Mutiny often led to centurions being beaten with rods to rob them of their dignity and status.[4]

Status pervaded everything. The senatorial and equestrian officer class guarded their standing against threats by the lower classes. The military career progression established by Claudius confirmed these graduations. A tribune began his career in command of non-citizen auxiliary infantry, was then commander of a cavalry *ala* and finally tribune in a legion composed of citizens. Legionaries protected their superior status over auxiliaries, who received less pay, no donative and served for longer. This caused conflicts between the auxiliary and legionary troops under Vitellius. Cavalry possessed superior rank to infantry, leading to the Batavian infantry cohorts' demand to be raised to the status of cavalry. Below the infantry came sailors and marines, hence the fervent demands of the *I Aduitrix* to gain legionary recognition from Galba. Outranking all in status, pay and conditions of service were the Praetorians, engendering envy and jealousy. This hierarchy bred unit pride and bitter rivalry. Even legions competed with each other for honour and prestige, which was important on the battlefield but undermined co-operation when working to improve their service conditions. The German legionaries took pride in their status as citizens but felt disdain for Gallic and Batavian auxiliaries and hatred of the provincials who supported Vindex and Galba. This culminated in a desire to exact vengeance and plunder from rebels who, in their view, were no better than German barbarians from beyond the Rhine.[5]

Ordinary soldiers possessed a higher social status than the peasants, which was reflected in certain legal privileges, especially those protecting their wills. They owned slaves, reserved the right not to be beaten and had freedom from taxation and requisitions upon retirement. However, until Domitian's pay increase, their wages were roughly equivalent to a farm labourer. The demands of the Pannonian mutineers for four sesterces a day put them on a par with a workman in Rome, but from their wage, there were compulsory deductions for clothing, equipment, the *Saturnalicium leastrense* (dinner to celebrate the *Saturnalia*), the burial club and the ever-increasing bribes to centurions. Added to this was the need to support their partners and children, from whom Augustus' reforms had removed legal recognition until the soldiers were discharged from the army. Soldiers would have increasingly relied on donatives to supplement their income, exacerbating Galba's error in refusing to grant one. Half of every donative was placed in the regimental savings bank and half was given to the soldier. Significantly, neither Otho, Vitellius nor Vespasian offered to increase pay to win the support of the troops. Otho and Vitellius did, however, promise to pay the bribes demanded by the centurions. Plunder was also seized during war or unrest. The enormous wealth of the Gallic provinces and Italy was especially attractive.[6]

The demands of the AD 14 mutineers were entirely legitimate, especially as their years of service had been increased to the Republican maximum of sixteen years in 13 BC, then in AD 5 to twenty years, with a further five in the reserve, which in practice was no different to active service. Many of the veterans in the Rhine and Danube legions in AD 14 found the terms they had enlisted under had been radically altered. The Pannonian veterans had also expected to be given land in Italy around Aquileia or a cash gratuity, not barren and unfertile lands around Emona. It is little wonder that this group formed the nucleus of the mutiny in these legions. It was the primary demand of the legions encamped near Emona and the time-expired veterans were quickly discharged in Germany, whilst those in the reserve were sent to Raetia to counter an imaginary threat.[7]

Both mutinies in AD 14 were well-planned and organized, undermining the assertion that it was a collective madness that overwhelmed the simple-minded soldiers. However, after initial successes, the mutinies were undermined by unforeseen factors beyond the control of Percennius. In Pannonia, it was the arrival of the unruly Vibulenus and soldiers who had assaulted the Camp Prefect and pillaged the local villages. Their actions crossed boundaries that would require punishment once order was restored. This inevitability released the guilty from norms of behaviour, and with nothing to lose they used lies to spread mayhem. In Germany, the arrival of a senatorial delegation at Cologne was used to disrupt the calm that had descended. Again, false rumours and inherent distrust of the senatorial aristocracy were used by a group dissatisfied with the settlement agreed with Germanicus to enrage the drunken soldiers, leading to a violent attack upon the delegates. Again, these actions would require inevitable punishment for discipline to be restored.[8]

Mutinies were rare in times of peace. The legionaries remained steadfastly loyal to the Julio-Claudian dynasty to the very end. Germanicus himself was the son of Drusus the Elder, whose reputation as a supreme commander in his German campaigns between 12 BC and his death in 9 BC passed to his son, who was married to the granddaughter of Augustus. He was seen as a dynastic alternative to the hated strict disciplinarian, Tiberius, who had ascended the throne on condition that he adopt Germanicus. The army of Verginius Rufus only attempted to raise him to the throne once they heard the news that Nero had committed suicide. They knew they would receive no honours or rewards from Vindex's ally, Galba. The Praetorians did not attempt to remove Nero; instead, they were told by their traitorous Prefect, Nymphidius Sabinus, that the emperor had betrayed them by setting sail for Egypt. Nero received his last salute from a retired Praetorian who recognized him on the darkened streets of the capital. The ultra-loyal *XIV Gemina* legion's conflict with its Batavian auxiliary cohorts was a miniature civil war. Nero's fall was an orchestrated palace plot by Nymphidius Sabinus, who worked to undermine the confidence and assurance of the last Julio-Claudian emperor. Galba was the undeserving beneficiary. All was lost and, despairing for the future, Galba retreated to Clunia to await the arrival of the legions gathering in northern Italy and those from Germany.[9]

There were attempted revolts before AD 69, but these were initiated by 'the madness of the leading men'. The emperor Claudius faced a revolt in Dalmatia by the aristocratic Arruntius Camillus Scribonianus in AD 42. His claim was based solely on an illustrious ancestry, which may have impressed his *legates* and tribunes but not his men. After a few days, the revolt was ended when the soldiers, 'repenting of having been led by their officers to join Camillus' rebellion, killed them'.[10] The elite moved in a different world to the common soldier. Their primary concern was to add to the lustre and dignity of their name through the accumulation of magistracies, culminating in consular office or a position at court close to the emperor, where they could use their influence to accumulate wealth and extend their network of clients and friends (*amici*). The soldier's world was limited to their legion, camp and the civilian settlement.[10]

Scribonianus was descended from Pompey the Great and the legendary figure of Camillus, whilst Claudius was not related to Augustus. His claims rested on descent from Livia as well as a daughter of Augustus' sister. A great name mattered to the nobility. Consequently, Verginius Rufus rejected the pressure to seize the throne from his legate, Fabius Valens. The aristocratic officers would have potentially received huge rewards for supporting Scribonianus, as many did who supported the revolts of Galba, Otho, Vitellius and Vespasian. Cornelius Laco, a lowly legal advisor to Galba in Spain, became his sole Praetorian Prefect, and the freedman Icelus received equestrian status and a place in the imperial *concilium*. Vespasian was urged to revolt 'by his officers and friends and especially by Mucianus'. Governor of Syria and Vespasian's conquering general, Mucianus was awarded an almost unprecedented second and third consulship in AD 70 and 72. The reciprocal nature of relations in Roman society made such aspirations certainties, should their claimant ascend the throne.[11]

The failure to adequately reward an *amicus* for their *gratia* was considered a just reason for breaking a bond of friendship. Fabius Valens felt unrewarded by Galba for forcing Verginius Rufus to make his reluctant legions take the oath of loyalty to Vindex's ally. He would be instrumental in Vitellius' successful revolt. Nymphidius Sabinus rightly considered Galba owed him the throne and expected to be retained as sole Praetorian Prefect. Shocked at the ingratitude of Galba, he plotted to overthrow him. Otho was the first governor to support Galba's revolt, and was instrumental in organizing the revolt. He expected to be adopted as Galba's heir, but instead his place was supplanted by a noble whose main contribution to the revolt was to be exiled by Nero and possess a great name. This ingratitude was met with swords.[12]

Some commanders looked to restore their social and economic status using their military position to gain the *amicitiae* (friendship) of a claimant once it was clear they had lost the favour of the ruler. Fabius Valens, legate of *I Germanica* at Bonna in Lower Germany, had 'long been poor'. In the long term, he believed he would be enriched through gifts from Vitellius and contributions for influencing the emperor; however, in the short term, he was able to pillage the Gallic provinces his army marched through, communities like Vienne that had supported Vindex and Galba. Plunder and pillaging were not just the desire of the soldiers but also instigated by their commanders. Valens was attacked by his own men for keeping most of the loot from Gaul and Vienne for himself. The future rebel Vitellius left Rome for the governorship of Lower Germany hounded by his debtors, whilst Otho had bankrupted himself distributing gifts in the expectation of being named the imperial heir. Financial ruin meant humiliation. Saturninus, the governor of Upper Germany in AD 89, faced another form of humiliation in a recall to Rome and trial before Domitian under the draconian *lex Scantinia* which the emperor had revived. Aulus Caecina, questor of Beatica and early supporter of Galba, faced prosecution for embezzling provincial funds so joined Vitellius. Antonius Primus also joined Galba, having been expelled from the Senate by Nero for forging a will, and later, having lost imperial favour a second time, become a fervent supporter of Vespasian after the accession of Otho. These men were desperate to avoid a social death.[13]

Galba, however, believed Nero was plotting his actual death. Other nobles who led revolts harboured personal injuries and grievances. Sacrovir had raised an auxiliary cavalry cohort from his tribe and had fought for Rome to crush a rebellion by the Turoni. His conspicuous bravery in the battle brought a charge of treason from the defeated warriors, who resented his vital contribution to their defeat. Instead of rewards, he was charged and imprisoned, and forced to await judgement from Tiberius in distant Rome, contemplating a possible death sentence. Similar treatment led the Batavian Prefect, Civilis, to seek revenge and justice for the unlawful execution of his brother and his own transportation to Rome in chains. The insult and injustice were also borne by the Batavian cohorts and his tribe. They waged their war, firstly against Nero and then Vitellius, who ordered his arrest for a second time. Otho wanted revenge for his decade-long exile in Lusitania and Nero's virtual abduction of his wife.

The allegiance and loyalty of the senatorial and equestrian officers and commanders were based on the expectation of future rewards from the emperor. They were a mercenary class. Their military posts were temporary; the common soldiers and centurions were the professional soldiers. Understandably, they often lacked trust and confidence in the ability of their civilian superiors. In times of peace, this was not a problem, but in war, mistakes cost lives – thousands of lives, as the incompetence of Varus proved in the Teutoburg Forest in AD 9. This often led to a breakdown in the structure of command. The rank and file did not tolerate incompetence. Hordeonius Flaccus, appointed by Galba to command the Rhine legions because of his lack of military bearing, was overweight and often bedridden with goat, and so appeared a safe political choice. Galba applied the same reasoning in appointing Vitellius to Lower Germany. However, Flaccus' inertia inspired contempt in his men, leading to a power vacuum that was exploited by the ambitious Aulus Caecina. He was ultimately forced to renounce his command for Vocula, legate of the Twenty-second Legion and a commander whom the soldiers trusted. Flaccus was dragged from his bed and murdered by the soldiers.[14]

Conversely, in times of war, the soldiers were willing to follow commanders whose political allegiance to their emperor was suspect but who had demonstrated proven military ability. In AD 70, Vocula, Herennius Gallus – legate of the *I Germanica* – and Hordeonius Flaccus were believed to be conspiring with Vespasian and Civilis to prevent reinforcements from being dispatched to Vitellius in Italy. However, their hold over their army was tenuous and conditional on military success. Defeat at the hands of Civilis led to a humiliating beating for Gallus and the murder of Vocula.

In AD 14, a detachment of legionaries mutinied deep in the territory of the Chauci. The Camp Prefect had attempted to restore order by executing two of their number, resulting in a 'wave of disorder'. The unjust execution of comrades was a sure way of enraging mutinous soldiers. He saved himself and restored discipline by seizing their standard and marching out of camp, declaring that any who refused to follow him would be punished as deserters. The legionaries rallied around him and made their way to safety on the Rhine. The legionaries did not want the dishonour of losing their standard to the enemy, nor to face charges of cowardice and a dishonorable discharge. Both events would result in the loss of their retirement gratuity, land and privileges. Most importantly, they knew division would result in death at the hands of the Germans who surrounded them. So they rallied under the leadership of an officer they hated and despised but who possessed the military ability to save them.[15]

The legionaries firmly believed in loyalty and tended to be more steadfast than their officers. It was the legate Fabius Valens who tried to pressurize Verginius Rufus into abandoning Nero. The Vitellian legionaries on the Rhine and in Italy remained fervently loyal to their emperor. The Othonian Praetorian guardsmen fought to the very end, some burning themselves alive on his funeral pier. Upon his acclamation, they kept Otho separated from the tribunes and centurions whilst he blew kisses to the crowd. Later, a group of guardsmen burst into the palace, fearing the senators had allied with the Praetorian officers to murder their emperor. Their bond was personal, as a small group of *speculatores* had made him emperor for the rank and file. Vitellius likewise owed his throne to the German legions, and Vespasian to those who had served under him in Syria and Judaea. Most importantly, the suspicions of the common soldiers were justified. The Vitellian commanders on the Rhine were conspiring with

Vespasian and Civilis, whilst the Othonian generals were spared by Vitellius, who was convinced by their shambolic campaign that they had deliberately led Otho's army to defeat.[16]

The Julio-Claudian emperors had been remarkably successful in personalizing their relationship with the soldiers. They saw their benefits as originating with their emperor, not the state. Promotion to centurion was sanctioned by the emperor, probably based on a recommendation from the commander. The coins they spent bore his crowned head, showing the number of times he had been acclaimed *imperator*, their commander-in-chief. They gathered for their pay before his image, which stood proudly on their standards. The standards were worshipped, kept guarded in the imperial shrine. They took the oath in his name upon enlistment, every January and again on the anniversary of his accession. Their gratuity and land on retirement came from him. One of the arguments used by Drusus to undermine the Pannonian mutiny was to ask the soldiers whether they would 'swear fealty to Percennius and Vibulenus? Will Percennius and Vibulenus give the soldier his pay – his grant of land on discharge?'[17]

The fate of Galba shows that loyalty was partly based on the anticipation of reciprocity which was embedded in all aspects of Roman society and religion. A donative had been promised in his name and established through precedent by Claudius. The failure to provide even a small amount of money and the decimation of the legion of marines compromised the loyalty of the soldiers. Germanicus was made to say to the mutinous troops in AD 14 that 'if you are willing to restore to the senate its deputies, to the emperor your obedience, and to me my wife and children, then stand clear of the infection and set the malignants apart: that will be a security of repentance – that a guarantee of loyalty'. Nero broke his obligation to the Praetorians by supposedly deserting Rome for Alexandria, whilst Domitian sought the protection of Minerva in return for restoring Rome's traditional religious and moral codes.[18]

The relationship worked both ways. At the end of the mutinies in AD 14, the soldiers wanted to restore their relationship with the emperor by murdering the leaders of the mutinies in exchange for a return to imperial service. The violence unleashed was horrific. In Pannonia, there was a 'hue and cry', with most ringleaders cut down while 'others were handed over by the companies themselves as a certificate of their loyalty'.[19] At Mogontiacum, they threw the ringleaders into chains before they were executed in front of the assembled ranks. The slaughter at Vetera by the 'loyal' troops was much worse, moving Germanicus to tears. Tacitus blames the slaughter on the madness that infected the soldiers, but the insanity originated with their commanders, who knew exactly what the outcome of their orders would be.[20]

The oath sworn by soldiers and officers alike was reciprocal. The soldiers took them seriously, otherwise the Vitellian legionaries would not have muttered or passed over the name of Vespasian when Hordeonius Flaccus foolishly issued Vitellius' donative in his successor's name. The oath was made to Jupiter, and to break it was considered *nefas*, inviting divine vengeance. Some German legions refused to make one to Galba, and for want of a better alternative made it to the Roman state in the form of the Senate and people of Rome. Later, they transferred it to Vitellius, which they kept until his death. The brave Praetorian centurion, Sempronius Densus, stood alone before Galba's litter in the Forum, facing certain death, not for any love of the emperor, but 'in defence of honour and the law'. Others put their immediate survival before the wrath of the gods and fled.[21]

The soldiers could be convinced by religious portents to renounce an oath if they were persuaded that the gods wished it. The revolt of Camillus Scribonianus was ended when a rumour was spread that the standards were fixed, 'for on being ordered to march off and rally around their new emperor, they found that some divine intervention prevented them from dressing the Eagles with garlands and perfumes and that the standards resisted all attempts to pull them out of the ground'. Titus made it known that the oracle of Venus at Paphos foretold he would wear the imperial purple, even though the eastern legions had given their oath to Otho. His father, Vespasian, later 'consulted the oracle of the God of Carmel and was given a promise that he would never be disappointed in what he planned or desired, however lofty his ambitions'. The promise of divine favour assured the legions that the gods wanted them to renounce their oath to Vitellius. The priestess Veleda supported Civilis by prophesying the destruction of the legions in Vetera, which in return the Batavian fought to achieve to boost her power and reputation as well as fulfil his blood oath.[22]

Revolts took time to arrange, increasing the risk of discovery before the rebels were fully prepared. They initially centred on a small core of supporters. At first, Galba's associates were limited to his immediate staff and advisors in Tarraconensis. These were the men he trusted. Legionary legates took the lead in Vitellius' revolt, while Otho relied solely on his leading freedman. Vindex was far less circumspect in his arrangements, sending messages to numerous governors and administrators, probably due to the proximity of the loyal legions in the German provinces and Dalmatia. He had less time to gather an army. Vespasian was protected by distance, so was able to send his agents far and wide across the Empire. These were brave soldiers and centurions with family or friends in the area they were sent to who could hide them and help. They also had an excuse to travel there.[23]

The soldiers and centurions would be intelligent, literate, resourceful and loyal. Vespasian probably employed men occupying junior posts, such as *tesserarii*, *optiones* and headquarters staff who were known to his senior officers. The centurions would command respect and deference on their travels, and could use the roads and service stations with the necessary documentation. Most centurions were promoted from the ranks at the recommendation of their commander. Vespasian had commanded legions fighting in Judaea since AD 66, and Mucianus, the governor of Syria, since AD 67. Unlike Vitellius, they had time to establish personal bonds with the troops. Promotion to the centurionate brought a huge improvement in pay, which amounted to five times that paid to a Praetorian guardsman, and status. This separated them from the ordinary troops and elevated them to membership of the officer class. They were a closely knit group who would not normally risk their position or prospects.[24]

Although they were indebted to their patron, their rewards would have to equal the risks. Few of these centurions could normally expect a prefectorship or procuratorship, but a successful revolt offered unique opportunities. Transfer to centurion posts or greater in Vespasian's Praetorian Guard was a distinct probability. 'Vitellius had appointed as prefects of the praetorian guard Publilius Sabinus, prefect of a cohort, and Julius Priscus, a centurion at the time. Priscus owed his position to the favour of Valens, Sabinus to that of Caecina.'[25] Vespasian drew support on promises of advancement – 'many he rewarded with prefectures and procuratorships; large numbers of excellent men who later attained the highest positions he raised to senatorial rank'.[26] Cities were enlisted by promises of tax exemptions or being raised to an official status above that of their nearest rivals. Patrons like Valerius Asiaticus of Vienne were also important in recruiting their client communities. The earlier the support, the greater the risk and the reward.

An army on the move required weapons, money, wagons, horses, ships, food and fodder, and most of all soldiers raised in levies on the provincials. Gold and silver were vital, not just for payment of the donative and materials, but also as a vehicle to spread propaganda advertising the support of the army and propagate conservative messages that did not alarm the landowners and elite. Consequently, 'it was slow and laborious to set in motion civil war'. The men who organized and facilitated the revolt were well rewarded if victory was won. The time between Vitellius' acclamation and the march on Italy was short to prevent Otho from receiving reinforcements from Moesia and Dalmatia. Consequently, there was less time to procure the necessary resources for war, and instead it was plundered from Vindex's former Gallic allies.[27]

Vespasian's revolt began by winning over the tribunes and centurions, and then the soldiers. The initial impetus came from Titus, Mucianus and the legionary legates. Vitellius found willing conspirators in Valens and Caecina, both commanders of legions. The narrow-stripe tribunes had military experience as auxiliary prefects, but their influence over the legionaries was minimal. The centurions were the key. They had regular contact with their centuries, enforced discipline and had their troops' respect. In the Judaean war, it was the centurions who stood in the front rank, led the charge and stood firm when others faltered. The war also allowed Vespasian to earn the respect of his soldiers, leading from the front and sharing their dangers. To them, he was a fellow soldier.[28]

Commanders and emperors often used the term 'fellow soldier', or *commilito*, when addressing their men. Galba's last words to his attackers addressed them as fellow soldiers, asking why they wanted to kill him as he was theirs and they were his. Yet it was a commander's performance and actions that persuaded the soldiers to accept him as one of their own. Vespasian did not need to perform; he was a gifted general, being 'energetic in war. He used to march at the head of his troops, select a place for camp, oppose the enemy night and day with wise strategy and, if occasion demanded, with his own hands. His food was whatever chance offered; in dress and bearing he hardly differed from the common soldier.' Germanicus dressed his small son, Gaius, in miniature uniform and military boots, so the soldiers gave him the affectionate name Caligula, 'little boots'. The departure of Agrippina and the officers' wives from Cologne to shame the troops was an extraordinary performance. Vitellius, unwarlike and hardly the physical specimen to inspire martial valour, had to perform. On the march, 'he would greet even private soldiers with an embrace, and at wayside inns behave most affably towards muleteers and such like whom he met in the morning, inquiring whether they had breakfasted, and then belching loudly to prove he had done so himself'. Galba, an accomplished general, would never demean himself with such behaviour.[29]

The term *commilito* was a term used exclusively by aristocratic officers when addressing common soldiers. Soldiers did not use it themselves. On their epitaphs, they employed the terms *commanipularis* or *contubernalis*. The latter is a highly emotional word, denoting comrade or brother, men who shared their tents or barrack room, or close friends. The former term encompasses men in their century. This was the social world of the soldiers, men they fought and died beside. The centurion who had daily contact with these units was vital in leading them into revolt.[30]

As part of this performance, a commander had to allow discipline to relax. Strict disciplinarians like Galba could never curry favour with the common soldiers. As Vitellius already planned to raise a revolt, 'immediately he came into camp he granted every favour asked of him, and actually of his own accord cancelled the black marks of men who were in disgrace, the legal actions against those awaiting trial in the morning, and the penalties of people already convicted'. In AD 39, the governor of Upper Germany, Cornelius Lentulus Gaetulicus, planned to use his legions to support an assassination plot targeting Gaius. He had been in post since AD 26 and 'had gained an extraordinary hold on their affections as an officer of large clemency, chary of severity'. His plans were only thwarted by the dispatch of Sulpicius Galba with a force of Praetorians. Despite this relaxation of discipline, the soldiers stood, fought and died in their ranks, as demonstrated by the bravery and courage at both battles of Cremona.[31]

Rumours, misinformation and lies were another way of convincing the soldiers to rebel. Galba's brutal decimation of the legion of marines allowed his enemies in the Rhine legions to claim they would be next. The most effective rumours had a kernel of truth. Nero's confidence and self-assurance was destroyed by a drip-feed of bad news and embellishments fed to him by Nymphidius Sabinus, who exaggerated minor setbacks or described the worst consequences. This culminated in the Praetorian Prefect's outright lie that Nero had fled to Egypt. Vespasian won the support of the legions through two deceits: 'First, the copy of a letter (possibly forged) in which Otho begged him most earnestly to avenge his death and come to the aid of the Empire. Second, a persistent rumour that Vitellius had planned, after his victory, to re-station the legions, transferring those in Germany to the Orient, a much softer option.'[32]

The forged letter was probably read to the soldiers in assemblies and, to the credulous, it provided a reason to break their recently taken oath of allegiance to Vitellius. The threat of moving the Syrian and Judaean legions to Germany cut deep. Vitellius had sent some of his Rhine legionaries to the East as his agents to monitor Vespasian's legions. It would have been easy to suggest they were preparing for the transfer. The eastern legionaries were already angry 'over the arrogance of the soldiers of Vitellius who came to them, because though savage in appearance and barbarous to speech, they constantly mocked all the others as their inferiors'.[33] The legions of Vespasian and Mucianus had been in the East for decades, some for generations. They were not going to abandon their families and friends, their homes and neighbourhoods where they grew up, and hoped to someday return.

The story was repeated time and again. The governor of Syria administered the oath of allegiance to Vespasian, then addressed the people of Antioch, for 'there was nothing that angered the province and army so much as the assertion of Mucianus that Vitellius had decided to transfer the legions of Germany to Syria'.[34] Saturninus probably employed a similar rumour to enrage his legions in Mogontiacum, as the *XXI Rapax* had recently been moved from Bonna and preparations were probably underway for another move to Pannonia.

The Treveri and Lingones who lived alongside the Rhine legionaries acted as their allies and fought alongside them in the wars against Vindex and then Otho, and finally Vespasian. By the mid-first century, most legionaries were no longer recruited in Italy but were raised in the provinces. They were the sons and grandsons of veterans whose homes were the banks of the Rhine that swept past Colonia Agrippinensium, the mayhem of Antioch's streets, the heights above Lugdunum or the thin-soiled farmland around Emona: 'For the provincials were accustomed to live with the soldiers, and enjoyed association with them; in fact, many civilians were bound to the soldiers by ties of friendship and of marriage, and the soldiers from their long service had come to love their old familiar camps as their hearths and homes.'[35]

Notes

Chapter 1

1. Velleius Paterculus, *The Roman History*, trans. Yardley, J. C. and Barrett, Anthony A. (Hackett Publishing Company, 2011), 2.96.2; Šašel Kos, M. (2014), *Kaj se je leta 14/15 dogajalo v Emoni–cesarski napis in upor panonskih legij/What Was Happening in Emona in AD 14/15? An Imperial Inscription and the Mutiny of the Pannonian Legions*. V: M. Ferle (ed./ur.), Emona. Mesto v imperiju/Emona. A City of the Empire. Ljubljana, pp.79–95. He argues that the summer camp was located near Siscia, p.80.
2. Wilkes, J. J., 'A Note on the Mutiny of the Pannonian Legions in A. D. 14', *The Classical Quarterly*, Vol. 13, No. 2 (Nov. 1963), pp.268–71; Radman-Livaja, Ivan and Dizdar, Marko, *Archaeological Traces of the Pannonian Revolt 6–9 AD: Evidence and Conjectures,* Imperium Varus und seine Zeit Beiträge zum internationalen Kolloquium des LWL-Römermuseums am (28 & 29 April 2008).
3. Velleius Paterculus, *The Roman History*, 2.110.
4. Cassius Dio, *Roman History*, 56.12.2, 16.4.
5. Wilkes, J. J., 'A Note on the Mutiny of the Pannonian Legions in A. D. 14', pp.268–71; Dando-Collins, Stephen, *Legions of Rome, The Definitive History of Every Imperial Roman Legion* (Quercus, 2010), pp.152–53; Kos, M. Šašel, *The 15th Legion at Emona, Some Thoughts* (Zeitschrift für Papyrologie und Epigraphik, Bd. 109, 1995), pp.227–44; Keppie, Lawrence, 'The Army and the Navy', in A. Bowman, E. Champlin & A. Lintott (eds), The Cambridge Ancient History (Cambridge University Press, 1996), pp.371–96, p.359.
6. Cassius Dio, *Roman History*, 54.25.6.
7. Cassius Dio, *Roman History*, 55.24.8.
8. Cassius Dio, *Roman History*, 55.23.1; Phang, Sara Elise, *Roman Military Service: Ideologies of Discipline in the Late Republic and Early Principate* (Cambridge University Press, 2008), p.17; Keppie, Lawrence, *The Making of the Roman Army, From Republic to Empire* (Batsford, 1991), pp.147–48; Keppie, Lawrence, 'The Changing Face of the Roman Legions (49 BC–AD 69)', *Papers of the British School at Rome*, Vol. 65 (1997), pp.89–102.
9. Suetonius, *Life of Augustus*, 25; Keppie, Lawrence, *The Making of the Roman Army*, p.168.
10. Keppie, Lawrence, *The Making of the Roman Army*, p.170.
11. Keppie, Lawrence, *The Making of the Roman Army*, p.148; Campbell, J. B., *The Emperor and the Roman Army 31 BC–AD 235* (Clarendon Press, 1984), p.158.
12. Dio, 55.31.4, 56.28.4; Campbell, J. B., *The Emperor and the Roman Army 31 BC–AD 235*, pp.162–63.
13. Keppie, Lawrence, *The Making of the Roman Army*, p.150.
14. Tacitus, *Annals*, 1.17.

15. Wilkes, J. J., 'A Note on the Mutiny of the Pannonian Legions in A. D. 14', pp.268–71, citing CIL iii. 3845 = I.L.S. 2264, CIL 3847 ILS 10757, CIL 3848; Kos, Marjeta Šašel, *What Was Happening in Emona in AD 14/15? An Imperial Inscription and the Mutiny of the Pannonian Legions*, p.81, https://www.academia.edu/11150509.
16. Wilkes, J. J., 'A Note on the Mutiny of the Pannonian Legions in A. D. 14', pp.268–71.
17. Tacitus, *Annals*, 1.17.
18. Tacitus, *Annals*, 1.20; Wilkes, J. J., 'A Note on the Mutiny of the Pannonian Legions in A. D. 14', pp.268–71; Phang, Sara Elise, *Roman Military Service: Ideologies of Discipline in the Late Republic and Early Principate*, p.16; Kos, M. Šašel, *The 15th Legion at Emona, Some Thoughts*, pp.227–244; Kos, Marjeta Šašel, *What Was Happening in Emona in AD 14/15? An Imperial Inscription and the Mutiny of the Pannonian Legions*, p.81, https://www.academia.edu/11150509. Keppie, Lawrence, The Changing Face of the Roman Legions (49 BC–AD 69), pp.89–102, citing AIJ 303; Wilkes, J., 'The Danubian and Balkan provinces' in A. Bowman, E. Champlin & A. Lintott (eds), *The Cambridge Ancient History*, pp.545–585.
19. Watson, G. R., *The Roman Soldier* (Thames and Hudson, 1981), pp.77–78, citing P.Mich. VIII 466, 18ff; *Digest* 50.6,7.
20. Phang, Sara Elise, *Roman Military Service: Ideologies of Discipline in the Late Republic and Early Principate*, p.16; Campbell, J. B., *The Emperor and the Roman Army 31 BC–AD 235*, pp.101–02; Syme, R., *The Praetorian Guard*, The Roman Papers Vol VI (ed. Birley, Anthony R.) (Clarendon Press, Oxford, 1991), pp.25–34).
21. Campbell, J. B., *The Emperor and the Roman Army 31 BC–AD 235*, pp.103, 109.
22. Pliny, *Letters*, 6.25, writes that he secured the post of centurion for a young man from his town with no previous military experience and bought his equipment and dress for him, even though his client was rich enough to own a horse. Also see MacMullen, Ramsay, 'The Legion As Society', *Historia: Zeitschrift für Alte Geschichte*, 4th Qtr, Bd. 33, H. 4 (1984), pp.440–56.
23. Tacitus, *Annals*, 1.18.
24. Phang, Sara Elise, *Roman Military Service: Ideologies of Discipline in the Late Republic and Early Principate*, p.130.
25. Campbell, J. B., *The Emperor and the Roman Army 31 BC–AD 235*, pp.310–11, citing Macer 16.13.4; Phang, Sara Elise, *Roman Military Service, Ideologies of Discipline in the Late Republic and Early Principate*, p.130.
26. Tacitus, *Annals*, 1.17, 1.23.
27. Campbell, J. B., *The Emperor and the Roman Army 31 BC–AD 235*, pp.161, 177.
28. Watson, G. R., *The Roman Soldier*, pp.104, 107; Campbell, J. B., *The Emperor and the Roman Army 31 BC–AD 235*, p.179.
29. Campbell, J. B., *The Emperor and the Roman Army 31 BC–AD 235*, p.180, citing BGU 814.
30. Tacitus, *Annals*, 1.18, 1.19.
31. Tacitus, *Annals*, 1.16; Watson, G. R. *The Roman Soldier*, p.103.
32. Campbell, J. B., *The Emperor and the Roman Army 31 BC–AD 235*, pp.90–91.
33. Augustus died on 19 August at Nola. Tiberius first received the oath from the Praetorian Guard at the imperial villa, then sent messages to the Senate in Rome and the governors and commanders in the provinces. These would have been by horsemen, using the imperial post, and would probably have taken three days to reach the summer camp near Emona. See McHugh, J. S., *Sejanus, Regent of Rome* (Pen & Sword, 2020),

pp.26–27. Levick, Barbara, *Tiberius the Politician* (Routledge, 1999), p.72, suggests Blaesus was informed of the death of Augustus around midday on 25 August.

34. Campbell, J. B., *The Emperor and the Roman Army 31 BC–AD 235*, pp.71–73.
35. Tacitus, *Annals*, 1.16; Dio 57.4.1; Lammers, Cornelis J., 'Strikes and Mutinies: A Comparative Study of Organizational Conflicts between Rulers and Ruled', *Administrative Science Quarterly*, Vol. 14, No. 4, 'Conflict within and between Organizations' (Dec. 1969), pp.558–72; Brice, Lee L., 'Indiscipline in the Roman Army of the Late Republic and Principate', pp.113–26, in *New Approaches to Greek and Roman Warfare* (John Wiley & Sons, 2020), p.120.
36. Tacitus, *Annals*, 1.17; Kajanto, Iiro, 'Tacitus' Attitude to War and the Soldier', *Latomus*, T. 29, Fasc. 3 (July–September 1970), pp.699–718.
37. Tacitus, *Annals*, 1.16.
38. MacMullen, Ramsay, *Enemies of the Roman Order* (Routledge, 1992), pp.170–71.
39. Tacitus, *Annals*, 1.16, 4.4; Dio 52.27.4; *Digest* 49.16.4.8; Pliny the Elder, *Natural History*, VII. 149; Keppie, Lawrence, *The Making of the Roman Army*, p.170; MacMullen Ramsay, 'The Legion as a Society', *Historia: Zeitschrift für Alte Geschichte*, Bd. 33, H. 4 (4th Qtr., 1984), pp.440–56; Fulkerson, Laurel, *Staging a Mutiny: Competitive Roleplaying on the Rhine (Annals 1.31–51)* (Ramus), pp.169–92, 183.
40. Velleius Paterculus, *The Roman History*, 2.124.1.
41. Keppie, Lawrence, *The Making of the Roman Army*, p.170.
42. Tacitus, *Annals*, 1.17; Dio 57.4.2. Suetonius, *Tiberius*, 25, states that the mutineers demanded the same pay as Praetorians. See also Keppie, Lawrence, *The Making of the Roman Army*, p.170. For Augustus' promise of a cash gratuity immediately on release, see Dio 54.25.5.
43. Tacitus, *Annals*, 1.17; MacMullen Ramsay, 'The Legion as a Society', pp.440–56; Brice, Lee L., 'Indiscipline in the Roman Army of the Late Republic and Principate', pp.113–26.
44. Syme, R., *The Augustan Aristocracy* (Oxford University Press, 1986), p.163; Wiedemann, T. E., Bowman, A. K. and Champlin, E., *Tiberius to Nero*, The Cambridge Ancient History 10, The Augustan Empire, 43 BC–AD 69, pp.198–255, 206.
45. Tacitus, *Annals*, 1.18.
46. Tacitus, *Annals*, 1.19; Dio 57.4.3.
47. Velleius Paterculus, *The Roman History*, 2.125.2.
48. Tacitus, *Annals*, 1.20.
49. Tacitus, *Annals*, 1.21.
50. Tacitus, *Annals*, 1.21; Breeze, David J., 'Pay Grades and Ranks below the Centurionate', *The Journal of Roman Studies*, Vol. 61 (1971), pp.130–35; Watson, G. R., *The Roman Soldier*, pp.52, 79; Eaton, Jonathan, 'The Political Significance of the Imperial Watchword in the Early Empire', *Greece & Rome* 58, no. 1 (2011), pp.48–63.
51. Tacitus, *Annals*, 1.21–22.
52. Tacitus, *Annals*, 1.23; Dio 57.4.2; Phang, Sara Elise, *Roman Military Service, Ideologies of Discipline in the Late Republic and Early Principate*, p.123.
53. Dio 57.4.3; Williams, Mary Frances, Four Mutinies: Tacitus 'Annals' 1.16–30; 1.31–49 and Ammianus Marcellinus 'Res Gestae' 20.4.9–20.5.7; 24.3.1–8, *Phoenix*, Vol. 51, No. 1 (Spring 1997), pp.44–74.
54. Tacitus, *Annals*, 1.23; Lammers, Cornelis J., 'Strikes and Mutinies: A Comparative Study of Organizational Conflicts between Rulers', pp.558–72.

55. Tacitus, *Annals*, 1.23; Bingham, Sandra, 'The Praetorian Guard in the Political and Social Life of Julio-Claudian Rome', University of British Columbia, PhD Thesis (1997), pp.126–27; Toit, Lois Du, 'The Senatorial Debate on 17th September AD 14 and Drusus' journey to Pannonia', *Acta Classica*, Vol. 23 (1980), pp.130–33.
56. Tacitus, *Annals*, 1.23, 1.28.
57. Tacitus, *Annals*, 1.24, 1.27; Seager, Robin, *Tiberius* (Blackwell, 2005), p.49.
58. Tacitus, *Annals*, 1.27–29; Seneca, *Moral and Political Essays,* trans. Cooper, John M. (Cambridge University Press, 1995), pp.233–34; Seager, Robin, *Tiberius*, p.51, Syme, R., *The Roman Revolution* (Oxford University Press, 1979), p.400 n.4.
59. Tacitus, *Annals*, 1.24.
60. Bingham, Sandra, 'The Praetorian Guard in the Political and Social Life of Julio-Claudian Rome', pp.126–27.
61. Tacitus, *Annals*, 1.25; Dio 57.4.2.
62. Tacitus, *Annals*, 1.25; Lammers, Cornelis J., 'Strikes and Mutinies: A Comparative Study of Organizational Conflicts between Rulers', pp.558–72; Campbell, J. B., *The Emperor and the Roman Army 31 BC–AD 235*, p.31.
63. Velleius Paterculus, *The Roman History*, 2.105.3–4; Tacitus, *Annals*, 1.26; Campbell, J. B., *The Emperor and the Roman Army 31 BC–AD 235*, pp.32, 34, 175–76.
64. Tacitus, *Annals*, 1.26; Campbell, J. B., *The Emperor and the Roman Army 31 BC–AD 235*, p.159.
65. Tacitus, *Annals*, 1.26; Kajanto, Iiro, *Tacitus' Attitude to War and the Soldier*, pp.699–718.
66. Tacitus, *Annals*, 1.27; Dio 57.4.4.
67. Tacitus, *Annals*, 1.28; Dio 57.4.4.
68. Campbell, J. B., *The Emperor and the Roman Army 31 BC–AD 235*, p.30.
69. Tacitus, *Annals*, 1.28.
70. Tacitus, *Annals*, 1.28; Breeze, David J., 'Pay Grades and Ranks below the Centurionate', pp.130–35; Rogers, Robert Samuel, *Studies in the Reign of Tiberius* (The Johns Hopkins Press, 1943), pp.109–10.
71. Tacitus, *Annals*, 1.28; MacMullen, Ramsay, 'The Legion as a Society', pp.440–56.
72. Tacitus, *Annals*, 1.29.
73. Tacitus, *Annals*, 1.30; Woodman, A. J., 'Mutiny and Madness: Tacitus "Annals" 1.16–49', *Arethusa*, Vol. 39, No. 2 (Spring 2006), pp.303–29; Brice, Lee L., 'Indiscipline in the Roman Army of the Late Republic and Principate', pp.113–26, 121.
74. Velleius Paterculus, *The Roman History*, 2.125.3; Woodman, A. J., 'Mutiny and Madness: Tacitus "Annals" 1.16–49', pp.303–29; Williams, Mary Frances, 'Four Mutinies: Tacitus "Annals" 1.16–30; 1.31–49 and Ammianus Marcellinus "Res Gestae" 20.4.9–20.5.7; 24.3.1–8', pp.44–74; Phang, Sara Elise, *Roman Military Service, Ideologies of Discipline in the Late Republic and Early Principate*, p.111.
75. Dio 57.4.5; Tacitus, *Annals*, 1.29–30; Shotter, David, *Tiberius Caesar* (Routledge, 1992), p.23.
76. Tacitus, *Annals*, 1.30; Williams, Mary Frances, 'Four Mutinies: Tacitus "Annals" 1.16–30; 1.31–49 and Ammianus Marcellinus "Res Gestae" 20.4.9–20.5.7; 24.3.1–8', pp.44–74.
77. Tacitus, *Annals*, 1.52.
78. Dio 57.22.1; Tacitus, *Annals*, 4.1, 4.3; Suetonius, *Tiberius*, 48; Mchugh, J. S., *Sejanus, Regent of Rome*, pp.92–93.
79. Wilkes, J. J., 'A Note on the Mutiny of the Pannonian Legions in A. D. 14', pp.268–71, citing Pliny, *Natural History*, 3.146, CIL 3.4235, 4247; AE 1914, 5, 6, 7 and from east of Sopron at Répceszemere, CIL 3.4229; Kos, Marjeta Šašel, *What Was Happening in*

Emona in AD 14/15? An Imperial Inscription and the Mutiny of the Pannonian Legions, p.87; Brice, Lee L., 'Indiscipline in the Roman Army of the Late Republic and Principate', pp.113–26, 123.
80. Tacitus, *Annals*, 4.4; Brice, Lee L., 'Indiscipline in the Roman Army of the Late Republic and Principate', pp.113–26, 119.
81. Fulkerson, Laurel, *Staging a Mutiny: Competitive Roleplaying on the Rhine (Annals 1.31–51)* (Ramus), pp.169–92, 181.

Chapter 2

1. Dio 56.19.1–56.22.2; Velleius Paterculus, *The Roman History*, 2.119.1–4; Dornberg, John, 'Battle of the Teutoburg Forest', *Archaeology*, Vol. 45, No. 5 (September/October 1992), pp.26–32.
2. Pagán, Victoria E., 'Beyond Teutoburg: Transgression and Transformation in Tacitus Annales 1.61–62', *Classical Philology*, Vol. 94, No. 3 (July 1999), pp.302–20.
3. Velleius Paterculus, *The Roman History*, 2.120.2; Dio 56.22.2–4.
4. Levick, Barbara, *Tiberius, the Politician*, p.62.
5. Velleius Paterculus, *The Roman History*, 2.121.6; Seager, Robin, *Tiberius* (Blackwell, 2005), p.36.
6. Dio 56.24.4–5, 57.5.4; Keppie, Lawrence, 'The Army and the Navy', in Bowman, A., Champlin, E. & Lintott, A. (eds), *The Cambridge Ancient History* (Cambridge University Press, 1996), pp.371–96, 385.
7. Tacitus, *Annals*, 1.31.
8. Kajanto, Iiro, 'Tacitus' Attitude to War and the Soldier', *Latomus*, T. 29, Fasc. 3 (July–September 1970), pp.699–718.
9. Suetonius, *Tiberius*, 19.
10. Phang, Sara Elise, *Roman Military Service, Ideologies of Discipline in the Late Republic and Early Principate* (Cambridge University Press, 2008), pp.112–13.
11. Suetonius, *Tiberius*, 18.
12. Dio 56.25.2–3.
13. Suetonius, *Tiberius*, 18.
14. Tacitus, *Annals*, 1.31, 1.35; Velleius Paterculus, *The Roman History*, 2.121.1, 2.123.1, 2.125.1; Dio 57.5.1; Wiedemann, T. E. J., 'Tiberius to Nero', in Bowman, A. K., Champlin, E. & Lintott, A. (eds) *The Cambridge Ancient History*, Vol. 10 (Cambridge University Press, 1996), p.209.
15. Powell, Lindsay, *Eager For Glory, The Untold Story of Drusus The Elder, Conqueror of Germania* (Pen & Sword, 2011), pp.61, 64, 66, 81, 93 & 102; Sparavigna, Amelia Carolina, *The Orientation of the Plan of Novaesium, a Roman Fort on the Rhine* (6 July 2021), available at SSRN: https://ssrn.com/abstract=3392789 or http://dx.doi.org/10.2139/ssrn.3392789; Williams, Mary Frances, 'Four Mutinies: Tacitus "Annals" 1.16–30; 1.31–49 and Ammianus Marcellinus "Res Gestae" 20.4.9–20.5.7; 24.3.1–8', *Phoenix*, Vol. 51, No. 1 (Spring 1997), pp.44–74; Shotter, D. C. A., 'Tacitus, Tiberius and Germanicus', *Historia: Zeitschrift für Alte Geschichte*, Bd. 17, H. 2 (April 1968), pp.194–214.
16. Dio 57.5.4; Tacitus, *Annals*, 1.31; Velleius Paterculus, *The Roman History*, 2.125.2; Williams, Mary Frances, 'Four Mutinies', *Phoenix*, Vol. 51, No. 1 (Spring 1997), pp.44–74; Sumner, G. V., 'Germanicus and Drusus Caesar', *Latomus*, T. 26, Fasc. 2 (April–June 1967), pp.413–35.

17. Brice, L. L. (ed.), *New Approaches to Greek and Roman Warfare* (John Wiley & Sons, 2020), p.121.
18. Tacitus, *Annals*, 1.32; Campbell, J. B., *The Emperor and the Roman Army 31 BC–AD 235*, p.383.
19. Tacitus, *Annals*, 1.31; Suetonius, *Gaius*, 1; Velleius Paterculus, *The Roman History*, 2.125.1; Williams, Mary Frances, 'Four Mutinies', *Phoenix*, Vol. 51, No. 1 (Spring 1997), pp.44–74; Campbell, J. B., *The Emperor and the Roman Army 31 BC–AD 235*, p.40.
20. Suetonius, *Gaius*, 4 & 9; Dio 57.5.1.
21. Tacitus, *Annals*, 1.32; Phang, Sara Elise, *Roman Military Service, Ideologies of Discipline in the Late Republic and Early Principate*, p.129.
22. Dio 59.29.2
23. Tacitus, *Annals*, 1.32, Josephus, *Jewish Antiquities*, 19.18, 105–107; Suetonius, *Gaius*, 56–58.
24. Tacitus, *Annals*, 1.16.
25. Tacitus, *Annals*, 1.64–68.
26. Tacitus, *Annals*, 1.32.
27. Tacitus, *Annals*, 1.61–62, 65.
28. Tacitus, *Annals*, 1.31.
29. Tacitus, *Annals*, 1.34.
30. Tacitus, *Annals*, 1.34.
31. Tacitus, *Annals*, 1.31; Suetonius, *Tiberius*, 25; Velleius Paterculus, *The Roman History*, 2.125.2.
32. Tacitus, *Annals*, 1.34.
33. Tacitus, *Annals*, 1.34.
34. Velleius Paterculus, *The Roman History*, 2.97.4.
35. Tacitus, *Annals*, 1.35.
36. Tacitus, *Annals*, 1.35.
37. Tacitus, *Annals*, 1.35; Dio 57.4.2; Shotter, David, *Tiberius Caesar* (Routledge, 1992), p.21.
38. Tacitus, *Annals*, 1.35.
39. Dio 57.5.1; Woodman, A. J., 'Mutiny and Madness, Tacitus "Annals" 1.16–39', *Arethusa*, Vol. 39, No. 2 (Spring 2006), pp.303–29.
40. Tacitus, *Annals*, 1.35; Dio 57.5.2–3; Suetonius, *Tiberius*, 25.
41. Williams, Mary Frances, 'Four Mutinies' , *Phoenix*, Vol. 51, No. 1 (Spring 1997), pp.44–74.
42. Tacitus, *Annals*, 1.36; Williams, Mary Frances, 'Four Mutinies', *Phoenix*, Vol. 51, No. 1 (Spring 1997), pp.44–74; MacMullen, Ramsey, 'The Legion as a Society', *Historia: Zeitschrift für Alte Geschichte*, Bd. 33, H. 4 (4th Qtr.,1984), pp.440–56 n.54.
43. Tacitus, *Annals*, 1.36; Phang, Sara Elise, *Roman Military Service, Ideologies of Discipline in the Late Republic and Early Principate*, p.144; Williams, Mary Frances, 'Four Mutinies', *Phoenix*, Vol. 51, No. 1 (Spring 1997), pp.44–74; Seager, Robin, *Tiberius*, p.55.
44. Tacitus, *Annals*, 1.36; Dio 57.5.3; Williams, Mary Frances, 'Four Mutinies', *Phoenix*, Vol. 51, No. 1 (Spring 1997), pp.44–74.
45. Tacitus, Annals, 1.37.
46. Tacitus, *Annals*, 1.37, 1.60; Dio 57.5.4.
47. Woodman, A. J., 'Mutiny and Madness', *Arethusa*, Vol. 39, No. 2 (Spring 2006), pp.303–29; Williams, Mary Frances, 'Four Mutinies', *Phoenix*, Vol. 51, No. 1 (Spring 1997), pp.44–74; Rutland, Linda W., 'The Tacitean Germanicus: Suggestions for

a Re-Evaluation', *Neue Folge*, 130. Bd., H. 2 (Rheinisches Museum für Philologie, 1987), pp.153–64, argues that his excessive mildness and readiness to avoid conflict made the situation worse. His actions, though, imply careful planning that led to logical conclusions and, when the occasion demanded, a readiness to embrace ruthless aggression.

48. Tacitus, *Annals*, 1.38; Levick, Barbara, *Tiberius the Politician*, p.74.
49. Tacitus, *Annals*, 1.49; Dio 57.5.5; Suetonius, *Gaius*, 48; Watson, G. R., *The Roman Soldier*, p.129.
50. Tacitus, *Annals*, 1.39; Dio 57.5.6.
51. Breeze, David J., 'Pay Grades and Ranks below the Centurionate', *The Journal of Roman Studies*, Vol. 61 (1971), pp.130–35; Brunt, P. A., 'Pay and Superannuation in the Roman Army', *Papers of the British School at Rome*, Vol. 18, (1950), pp.50–71; Campbell, J. B., *The Emperor and the Roman Army 31 BC–AD 235*, p.85.
52. Campbell, J. B., *The Emperor and the Roman Army 31 BC–AD 235*, p.85; Woodman, A. J., 'Mutiny and Madness', *Arethusa*, Vol. 39, No. 2 (Spring 2006), pp.303–29.
53. Tacitus, *Annals*, 1.39; Phang, Sara Elise, *Roman Military Service, Ideologies of Discipline in the Late Republic and Early Principate*, p.127.
54. Tacitus, *Annals*, 1.39; Williams, Mary Frances, 'Four Mutinies', *Phoenix*, Vol. 51, No. 1 (Spring 1997), pp.44–74; Fulkerson, Luke, *Staging A Mutiny: Competitive Role Playing On The Rhine (Annals 1.31–51)* (Cambridge University Press), pp.173, 178; Shotter, D. C. A., 'Tacitus, Tiberius and Germanicus', *Historia: Zeitschrift für Alte Geschichte*, Bd. 17, H. 2 (April 1968), pp.194–214.
55. Tacitus, *Annals*, 1.40; Malloch, S. J. V., 'The End of the Rhine Mutiny in Tacitus, Suetonius, and Dio', *The Classical Quarterly*, Vol. 54, No. 1 (May 2004), pp.198–210; Brice, L.L. (ed.), *New Approaches to Greek and Roman Warfare*, p.123; Kajanto, Iiro, 'Tacitus' Attitude to War and the Soldier', *Latomus*, T. 29, Fasc. 3 (July–September 1970), pp.699–718.
56. Tacitus, *Annals*, 1.41; Dio 57.5.5–6.
57. Tacitus, *Annals*, 1.42–43. Suetonius, *Gaius*, 9; in Dio 57.5.6–7, both Agrippina and Gaius are seized by the soldiers, who agree to release them on the condition Gaius remains in the fort. Malloch, S. J. V., 'The End of the Rhine Mutiny in Tacitus, Suetonius, and Dio', *The Classical Quarterly*, Vol. 54, No. 1 (May 2004), pp.198–210, believes that Suetonius, Tacitus and Dio draw upon the same account, but due to the length of his work, Dio omitted much of the detail. These were probably the lost *Histories of the German Wars* by Pliny the Elder and Agrippina the Younger's memoirs. See Wiedemann, T. E. J., 'Tiberius to Nero', in Bowman, A. K., Champlin, E. & Lintott, A. (eds) *The Cambridge Ancient History* (Vol. 10) (Cambridge University Press, 1996), p.207. Also, Woodman, A. J., 'Mutiny and Madness', *Arethusa*, pp.303–29.
58. Tacitus, *Annals*, 1.44; Phang, Sara Elise, *Roman Military Service, Ideologies of Discipline in the Late Republic and Early Principate*, p.127; Brice, L.L. (ed.), *New Approaches to Greek and Roman Warfare*, p.123; Fulkerson, Luke, *Staging A Mutiny: Competitive Role Playing On The Rhine (Annals 1.31–51)*, p.179.
59. Tacitus, *Annals*, 1.44; Dio 57.5.7.
60. Williams, Mary Frances, 'Four Mutinies', *Phoenix*, Vol. 51, No. 1 (Spring 1997), pp.44–74.
61. Brice, L.L. (ed.), *New Approaches to Greek and Roman Warfare*, p.120; Fulkerson, Luke, *Staging A Mutiny: Competitive Role Playing On The Rhine (Annals 1.31–51)*, p.179; Watson, G. R., *The Roman Soldier*, pp.115–16.

62. Tacitus, *Annals*, 1.45; Levick, Barabara, *Tiberius the Politician*, p.74.
63. Tacitus, *Annals*, 1.45, 1.49; Garzetti, Albino, *From Tiberius to the Antonines, A History of the Roman Empire AD 14–192* (Methuen and Co Ltd, 1974), p.22.
64. Tacitus, *Annals*, 1,48; Fulkerson, Luke, *Staging A Mutiny: Competitive Role Playing On The Rhine (Annals 1.31–51)*, p.181; Lammers, Cornelius J., 'Strikes and Mutinies: A Comparative Study of Organizational Conflicts between Rulers and Ruled', *Administrative Science Quarterly*, Vol. 14, No. 4, 'Conflict within and between Organizations' (December 1969), pp.558–72.
65. Tacitus, *Annals*, 1.49; Levick, Barbara, *Tiberius the Politician*, p.74.
66. Woodman, A. J., 'Mutiny and Madness', *Arethusa*, Vol. 39, No. 2 (Spring 2006), pp.303–29.
67. Tacitus, *Annals*, 1.49–51; Dio 57.6.1.
68. Tacitus, *Annals*, 1.61–62; Dio 57.18.1; Rutland, L. W., *The Tacitean Germanicus: Suggestions For A Re-evaluation*, Rheinisches Museum für Philologie, 130 (H. 2), pp.153–164.
69. Tacitus, *Annals*,1.78, 3.1, 4.4; Dio 57.6.2, 57.18.1; Suetonius, *Tiberius*, 25.1.
70. Rothenhöfer, Peter, 'Emperor Tiberius and His *praecipua legionum cura* in a New Bronze Tablet from AD 14', *Gephyra*, 19 (2020), pp.101–10; Wiedemann, T. E. J., 'Tiberius to Nero', in Bowman, A. K., Champlin, E. & Lintott, A. (eds), *The Cambridge Ancient History* (Vol. 10) (Cambridge University Press, 1996), p.209; Campbell J. B., *The Emperor and the Roman Army 31 BC–AD 235*, p.173; Keppie, Lawrence, *The Making of the Roman Army: From Republic to Empire*, p.173.

Chapter 3

1. Henige, David, 'He Came, He Saw, He Counted: The Historiography and Demography of Caesar's Gallic Numbers', *Annales de Démographie Historique*, no. 1 (1998), pp.215–42; Drinkwater, J. F., 'The Rise and Fall of the Gallic Iulii: Aspects of the Development of the Aristocracy of the Three Gauls under the Early Empire', *Latomus*, T. 37, Fasc. 4 (October–December 1978), pp.817–50; Goudineau, C., 'Gaul', in Bowman, A. K., Champlin, E. & Lintott, A. (eds), *The Cambridge Ancient History* (Cambridge University Press, 1996), pp.489, 492, 499; Woolf, Greg, 'Generations of Aristocracy: Continuities and Discontinuities in the Societies of Interior Gaul', *Archaeological Dialogues* 9(1) (July 2002), pp.2–15; Raaflaub, Kurt A., 'Caesar and Genocide, Confronting the Dark Side of Caesar's Gallic Wars', *New England Classical Journal*, Vol. 48, Issue 1, pp.54–80.
2. Goudineau, C., 'Gaul', in Bowman, Champlin & Lintott (eds), *The Cambridge Ancient History* (Cambridge University Press, 1996), pp.481, 493; Woolf, G., 'Generations of Aristocracy', *Archaeological Dialogues* 9(1) (2002), pp.2–15; Seager, Robin, *Tiberius*, p.141.
3. Woolf, G., 'Generations of Aristocracy', *Archaeological Dialogues* 9(1) (2002), pp.2–15; Goudineau, C., 'Gaul', in Bowman, Champlin & Lintott (eds), *The Cambridge Ancient History* (Cambridge University Press, 1996), p.501.
4. Goudineau, C., 'Gaul', in Bowman, Champlin & Lintott (eds), *The Cambridge Ancient History* (Cambridge University Press, 1996), p.498.
5. Goudineau, C., 'Gaul', in Bowman, Champlin & Lintott (eds), *The Cambridge Ancient History* (Cambridge University Press, 1996), p.500; Drinkwater, J. F., 'The Rise and Fall of the Gallic Iulii', *Latomus*, T. 37, Fasc. 4 (October–December 1978), pp.817–50.
6. Royen, R. V., 'Slavery and Conquest', *Actes du Groupe de Recherches sur l'Esclavage depuis l'Antiquité*, 29(1) (2007), pp.39–54.

7. Tacitus, *Annals*, 4.72.
8. Dio 54.21.2; Suetonius, *Augustus*, 67.
9. Dio 54.19.1, 54.21.6–8, 54.22.1; Macrobius, *Saturnalia*, 2.4.24; Seneca, *The Apocolocyntosis of the Divine Claudius*, 6 (Penguin Classics, 1986; trans. J. P. Sullivan); Juvenal, *Satire*, 1.108–09; Perseus, *Satire*, 2.36; Martial, *Epigrams*, 2.12.
10. Drinkwater, J. F., 'The Rise and Fall of the Gallic Iulii', *Latomus*, T. 37, Fasc. 4 (October–December 1978), pp.817–50; Dyson, Stephen L., 'Native Revolts in the Roman Empire', *Historia: Zeitschrift für Alte Geschichte*, Bd. 20, H. 2/3 (2nd Qtr, 1971), pp.239–74; Seager, Robin, *Tiberius*, p.141.
11. Suetonius, *Tiberius*, 49; Tacitus, *Annals*, 3.43; Levick, Barbara, *Tiberius the Politician*, pp.133–34; https://www.archaeology.org/issues/445-2111/features/10049-autun-roman-town#art_page2; Goudineau, C., 'Gaul', in Bowman, Champlin & Lintott (eds), *The Cambridge Ancient History* (Cambridge University Press, 1996), pp.493–94.
12. Tacitus, *Annals*, 3.60.
13. Tacitus, *Annals*, 2.43, 2.69, 2.72, 2.73, 2.82, 3.2, 3.10, 3.60. Despite Tacitus asserting that the revolt started in AD 21 and concluded by the March when Tiberius was in Campania, events appear to have been compressed to fit into the historian's chronological framework, so some events must belong to AD 20. See Bellemore, Jane, 'Cassius Dio and the Chronology of A.D. 21', *The Classical Quarterly*, New Series, Vol. 53, No. 1 (May 2003), pp.268–85.
14. Tacitus, *Annals*, 3.40.
15. Tacitus, *Annals*, 2.5, 3.40; Velleius Paterculus, *The Roman History*, 2.129.3; Drinkwater, J. F., 'The Rise and Fall of the Gallic Iulii', Latomus, T. 37, Fasc. 4 (October–December 1978), pp.817–50; Christopherson, A. J., 'The Provincial Assembly of the Three Gauls in the Julio-Claudian Period', *Historia: Zeitschrift für Alte Geschichte* , Bd. 17, H. 3 (July 1968), pp.351–66.
16. Tacitus, *Annals*, 3.42.
17. Drinkwater, J. F., 'The Rise and Fall of the Gallic Iulii', *Latomus*, T. 37, Fasc. 4 (October—December 1978), pp.817–50.
18. Dyson, Stephen L., 'Native Revolts in the Roman Empire', *Historia: Zeitschrift für Alte Geschichte*, Bd. 20, H. 2/3 (2nd Qtr, 1971), pp.239–74; Goudineau, C., 'Gaul', in Bowman, Champlin & Lintott (eds), *The Cambridge Ancient History* (Cambridge University Press, 1996), p.499.
19. Aldhouse-Green, Miranda, *Caesar's Druids: Story of an Ancient Priesthood* (Yale University Press, 2010), p.47.
20. Last, Hugh, 'Rome and the Druids: A Note', *The Journal of Roman Studies*, Vol. 39, Parts 1 and 2 (1949), pp.1–5.
21. Tacitus, *Annals*, 3.46; Seager, Robin, *Tiberius*, p.140; Weidemann, T. E. J., 'Tiberius to Nero', in Bowman, Champlin & Lintott (eds), *The Cambridge Ancient History* (Cambridge University Press, 1996), pp.212, 233.
22. Tacitus, *Annals*, 3.41, 3.46; Woolf, Greg, 'Generations of Aristocracy', *Archaeological Dialogues* 9(1) (July 2002), pp.2–15.
23. Tacitus, *Annals*, 3.42.
24. Goudineau, C., 'Gaul', in Bowman, Champlin & Lintott (eds), *The Cambridge Ancient History* (Cambridge University Press, 1996), p.491.
25. Bellemore, Jane, 'Cassius Dio and the Chronology of A.D. 21', *The Classical Quarterly*, New Series, Vol. 53, No. 1 (May 2003), pp.268–85.
26. Tacitus, *Annals*, 3.40, 3.42, 3.43.

27. Tacitus, *Annals*, 4.18.
28. Tacitus, *Annals*, 3.43.
29. Tacitus, *Annals*, 3.43, 3.46.
30. Tacitus, *Annals*, 3.43.
31. Tacitus, *Annals*, 3.47; Bellemore, Jane, 'Cassius Dio and the Chronology of A.D. 21', *The Classical Quarterly*, New Series, Vol. 53, No. 1 (May 2003), pp.268–85.
32. Tacitus, *Annals*, 3.43, 4.19; Shotter, D. C. A., 'The Trial of Gaius Silius (A.D.24)', *Latomus*, T. 26, Fasc. 3 (July–September 1967), pp.712–16; Rogers, Robert Samuel, 'Notes on the Gallic Revolt, A.D. 21', *The Classical Weekly*, Vol. 36, No. 7 (30 November 1942), pp.75–76.
33. Tacitus, *Annals*, 3.42; Bellemore, Jane, 'Cassius Dio and the Chronology of A.D. 21', *The Classical Quarterly*, New Series, Vol. 53, No. 1 (May 2003), pp.268–85; Garzetti, Albino, *From Tiberius to Nero* (Methuen, 1974), p.65.
34. Tacitus, *Annals*, 3.45, 4.19; *Histories*, 1.70, for the Silian cavalry squadron. Goudineau, C., 'Gaul', in Bowman, Champlin & Lintott (eds), *The Cambridge Ancient History* (Cambridge University Press, 1996), p.491.
35. Tacitus, *Annals*, 3.45.
36. Tacitus, *Annals*, 3.46.
37. Tacitus, *Annals*, 3.46.
38. Suetonius, *Tiberius*, 49.
39. Tacitus, *Annals*, 4.19; Rutledge, Steven H., *Imperial Inquisitions: Prosecutors and Informants From Tiberius to Domitian* (Routledge, 2001), pp.141, 210–12.
40. Rüger, C., 'Roman Germany', in Bowman, Champlin & Lintott (eds), *The Cambridge Ancient History* (Cambridge University Press, 1996), p.529.
41. Dyson, Stephen L., 'Native Revolts in the Roman Empire', *Historia: Zeitschrift für Alte Geschichte*, Bd. 20, H. 2/3 (2nd Qtr, 1971), pp.239–74.
42. Woolf, Greg, 'Generations of Aristocracy', *Archaeological Dialogues* 9(1) (July 2002), pp.2–15.

Chapter 4

1. Griffin, Miriam, T., *Nero, The End of a Dynasty* (Routledge, 1984), pp.161–64; Wallace-Hadrill, Andrew, 'Civilis Princeps: Between Citizen and King', *The Journal of Roman Studies*, Vol. 72 (1982), pp.32–48.
2. Holland, Richard, *Nero: The Man Behind the Myth* (Sutton Publishing, 2000), pp.215–16; Griffin, Miriam T., *Nero, The End of a Dynasty*, p.180.
3. Suetonius, *Nero*, 34.
4. Dio, 62.14.4; Griffin, Miriam T., *Nero, The End of a Dynasty*, p.164.
5. Dio 62.17.2–6; Rutledge, Steven H., *Imperial Inquisitions: Prosecutors and Informants from Tiberius to Domitian* (Routledge, 2001), loc. 3286, 4138.
6. Dio 63.17.2–3; Tacitus, *Histories*, 4.41.3, 5; Rutledge, Steven H., *Imperial Inquisitions*, loc. 4127; Vervaet, Frederik Juliaan, 'Domitius Corbulo and the Senatorial Opposition to the Reign of Nero', *Ancient Society*, Vol. 32 (2002), pp.135–93; Campbell, Brian, 'Who Were the "*Viri Militares*"?', *The Journal of Roman Studies*, Vol. 65 (1975), pp.11–31.
7. Dio 62.18.2; Pliny, *Letters*, 1.5.3; Tacitus, *Histories*, 4.42; Rutledge, Steven H., *Imperial Inquisitions*, loc. 4160; Griffin, Miriam T., *Nero, The End of a Dynasty*, p.118.
8. Suetonius, *Galba*, 5.
9. Suetonius, *Galba*, 7.
10. Suetonius, *Galba*, 6.

11. Suetonius, *Galba*, 7.
12. Suetonius, *Galba*, 9.
13. Suetonius, *Galba*, 9.
14. Suetonius, *Nero*, 32, 42; Holland, Richard, *Nero: The Man Behind the Myth*, p.199; Brunt, P. A., 'The Revolt of Vindex and the Fall of Nero', *Latomus*, T. 18, Fasc. 3 (July–September 1959), pp.531–55; Garzetti, Albino, *From Tiberius to the Antonines* (Methuen, 1974), p.168.
15. Dio 63.22.1a; Plutarch, *Galba*, 4; Pliny, *Natural History*, 18. 35; Josephus, *Jewish War*, 2.293; Griffin, Miriam T., *Nero, The End of a Dynasty*, p.187.
16. Plutarch, *Galba*, 4.
17. Griffin, Miriam T., *Nero, The End of a Dynasty*, p.180.
18. Dio 62.19.1–2.
19. Suetonius, *Nero*, 43; *Galba*, 9.2; Plutarch, *Galba*, 4.3; Dio 63.22.3–6; Shotter, D. C. A., 'A Time-Table for the "*Bellum Neronis*"', *Historia: Zeitschrift für Alte Geschichte*, Bd. 24, H. 1 (1st Qtr, 1975), pp.59–74. For the involvement of exiles, see the late source, John of Antioch, fragment 91 Muell. V. 6–10: 'And having associated with himself many of the senate who were in exile, he appointed Galba king.'
20. Plutarch, *Galba*, 4.2; Dio 63.22.1[2]; Josephus, *The Jewish War*, IV 440; Drinkwater, J. F., 'The Rise and Fall of the Gallic Iulii: Aspects of the Development of the Aristocracy of the Three Gauls under the Early Empire', *Latomus*, T. 37, Fasc. 4 (October–December 1978), pp.817–50; Vervaet, Frederik Juliaan, 'Domitius Corbulo and the Senatorial Opposition to the Reign of Nero', *Ancient Society*, Vol. 32 (2002), pp.135–93.
21. Tacitus, *Annals*, 4.13; Siofstra, J., 'Batavians and Romans on the Lower Rhine. The Romanisation of a Frontier Area', *Archaeological Dialogues*, vol. 9, no. 1 (2002), pp.16–38; Keppie, L., Bowman, A. K., Champlin, E. & Lintott, A. (eds), 'The Army and Navy', *The Cambridge Ancient History* (Vol. 10) (Cambridge University Press, 1996), p.387.
22. Philostratus, *Life of Apollonius of Tyana*, 5.10, 5.35.
23. Tacitus, *Histories*, 1.53.1; Shotter, D. C. A., 'A Time-table for the "*Bellum Neronis*"', *Historia: Zeitschrift für Alte Geschichte*, Bd. 24, H. 1 (1st Qtr, 1975), pp.59–74.
24. Tacitus, *Histories*, 1.53.
25. Hirt, Alfred M., *Gold and Silver Mining in the Roman Empire*, pp.1–22. https://livrepository.liverpool.ac.uk/3066254/; Levick, Barbara L., 'Verginius Rufus and the Four Emperors', *Rheinisches Museum für Philologie*, Neue Folge, 128. Bd., H. 3/4 (1985), pp.318–46.
26. Suetonius, *Galba*, 9.
27. Shotter, D. C. A., 'A Time-Table for the "*Bellum Neronis*"', *Historia: Zeitschrift für Alte Geschichte*, Bd. 24, H. 1 (1st Qtr, 1975), pp.59–74.
28. Dio 62.20.5.
29. Griffin, Miriam T., *Nero, The End of a Dynasty*, p.180.
30. Suetonius, *Nero*, 40; Griffin, Miriam T., *Nero, The End of a Dynasty*, p.131; Shotter, D. C. A., 'A Time-table for the "*Bellum Neronis*"', *Historia: Zeitschrift für Alte Geschichte*, Bd. 24, H. 1 (1st Qtr, 1975), pp.59–74; Hainsworth, J. B., 'Verginius and Vindex', *Historia: Zeitschrift für Alte Geschichte*, Bd. 11, H. 1 (January 1962), pp.86–96.
31. Dio 63.22.2; Tacitus, *Annals*, 1.64; *Histories*, 1.65; Christopherson, A. J., 'The Provincial Assembly of the Three Gauls in the Julio-Claudian Period', *Historia: Zeitschrift für Alte Geschichte*, Bd. 17, H. 3 (July 1968), pp.351–66.
32. Dio 63.22.2–3; Zonaras, 11, 13, p.41, 12–19 D.

33. Christopherson, A. J., 'The Provincial Assembly of the Three Gauls in the Julio-Claudian Period', *Historia: Zeitschrift für Alte Geschichte*, Bd. 17, H. 3 (July 1968), pp.351–66; Kraay, Colin M., 'The Coinage of Vindex and Galba, AD 68, and the Continuity of the Augustan Principate', *The Numismatic Chronicle and Journal of the Royal Numismatic Society*, Sixth Series, Vol. 9, No. 3/4 (1949), pp.129–49; Kluczek, A. A., *Vindex, Neron et...Probus. 'Concordia' et 'orbis' dans le discours politico-ideologique romain* (academia.edu, 2011), pp.1–10; Brunt, P. A., 'The Revolt of Vindex and the Fall of Nero', *Latomus*, T. 18, Fasc. 3 (July–September 1959), pp.531–55; Sutherland, C. H. V., 'The Concepts Adsertor and Salus as used by Vindex and Galba', *The Numismatic Chronicle* (1966), Vol. 144 (1984), pp.29–32; Wiedemann, T. E., Bowman, A. K. & Champlin, E., 'From Nero to Vespasian' *The Cambridge Ancient History, 10, The Augustan Empire, 43 BC–AD 69* (1996), pp.256–57; MacMullen, Ramsay, *Changes in the Roman Empire, Essays in the Ordinary* (Princeton University Press, 1990), p.200.
34. Dio 63.22.1; Suetonius, *Galba*, 9; Tacitus, *Histories*, 1.33.7, 1.51.4, 1.51, 1.65, 4.17.3, 4.79; *Annals*, 11.1.2; Pliny, *Natural History*, 4.106, 4.109; Drinkwater, J. F., 'The Rise and Fall of the Gallic Iulii', *Latomus*, T. 37, Fasc. 4 (October–December 1978), pp.817–50; Wiedemann, T. E., Bowman, A. K. & Champlin, E., 'From Nero to Vespasian', *The Cambridge Ancient History, 10, The Augustan Empire, 43 BC–AD 69*, p.273; Goudineau, C., Bowman, A. K. & Champlin, E., 'The West: Gaul', *The Cambridge Ancient History, 10, The Augustan Empire, 43 BC–AD 69*, pp.470, 492; Syme, R., 'Partisans of Galba', *Historia: Zeitschrift für Alte Geschichte*, Bd. 31, H. 4 (4th Qtr, 1982), pp.460–83, citing CIL XII. 1859ff as evidence for Fonteius as patron of Vienne. Also see Birley, Anthony R., *The Fasti of Roman Britain* (Clarendon, 1981), p.70; Levick, Barbara, *Claudius* (Routledge, 1993), p.63; MacMullen, Ramsay, *Changes in the Roman Empire, Essays in the Ordinary*, p.202.
35. Suetonius, *Galba*, 9; Plutarch, *Galba*, 4.3; Shotter, D. C. A., 'A Time-Table for the "*Bellum Neronis*"', *Historia: Zeitschrift für Alte Geschichte*, Bd. 24, H. 1 (1st Qtr, 1975), pp.59–74.
36. Drinkwater, J. F., 'The Rise and Fall of the Gallic Iulii', *Latomus*, T. 37, Fasc. 4 (October–December 1978), pp.817–50; Wellesley, Kenneth, *The Year of the Four Emperors* (Routledge, 2000), p.5.
37. Suetonius, *Nero*, 41.
38. Suetonius, *Nero*, 40.4, 41; Dio 63.23.2; Griffin, Miriam T., *Nero, The End of a Dynasty*, p.181.
39. Plutarch, *Galba*, 5; Brunt, P. A., 'The Revolt of Vindex and the Fall of Nero', *Latomus*, T. 18, Fasc. 3 (July–September 1959), pp.531–55, Syme, R., 'Partisans of Galba', *Historia: Zeitschrift für Alte Geschichte*, Bd. 31, H. 4 (4th Qtr, 1982), pp.460–83.
40. Suetonius, Galba, 9.2 & 10 states that Vindex did not acclaim Galba as emperor, which is contradicted by Plutarch, *Galba*, 22.2. However, Galba's initial coinage only refers to him as legate. Syme, R., *The Augustan Aristocracy* (Oxford, 1986), p.290; Syme, R., 'Partisans of Galba', *Historia: Zeitschrift für Alte Geschichte*, Bd. 31, H. 4 (4th Qtr, 1982), pp.460–83.
41. Tacitus, *Histories*, 2.59; Kraay, Colin M., 'The Coinage of Vindex and Galba', *The Numismatic Chronicle and Journal of the Royal Numismatic Society*, Sixth Series, Vol. 9, No. 3/4 (1949), pp.129–49.
42. Tacitus, *Annals*, 14.40; *Histories*, 1.65; Suetonius, *Galba*, 10; Plutarch, *Galba*, 5; Wellesley, Kenneth, *The Year of the Four Emperors*, p.5; Shotter, D. C. A., 'A Time-Table for the

"Bellum Neronis", *Historia: Zeitschrift für Alte Geschichte*, Bd. 24, H. 1 (1st Qtr, 1975), pp.59–74.

43. Suetonius, *Galba*, 10. The only support Galba provided was to appoint Q. Pomponius Rufus as a naval commander for the coast of Spain and Gallia Narbonensis, with the title of *Praefectus orae maritimae Hispaniae Citerioris Galliae Narbonensis*. See Shotter, D. C. A., 'A Time-Table for the "*Bellum Neronis*"', *Historia: Zeitschrift für Alte Geschichte*, Bd. 24, H. 1 (1st Qtr, 1975), pp.59–74.
44. Suetonius, *Otho*, 3.
45. Suetonius, *Nero*, 33.3; Tacitus, *Annals*, 16.6.
46. Tacitus, *Histories*, 1.37.3; Graßl, Herbert, 'War Obultronius Sabinus Proconsul der Baetica und L. Cornelius Marcellus', *Historia: Zeitschrift für Alte Geschichte*, Bd. 25, H. 4 (4th Qtr, 1976), pp.496–98; Syme, R., 'Partisans of Galba', *Historia: Zeitschrift für Alte Geschichte*, Bd. 31, H. 4 (4th Qtr, 1982), pp.460–83; Syme, R., 'The Colony of Cornelius Fuscus: An Episode in the Bellum Neronis', *The American Journal of Philology*, Vol. 58, No. 1 (1937), pp.7–18; Rickard, T. A., 'The Mining of the Romans in Spain', *The Journal of Roman Studies*, Vol. 18 (1928), pp.129–43; Wiedemann, T. E., Bowman, A. K. & Champlin, E., 'From Nero to Vespasian', *The Cambridge Ancient History, 10, The Augustan Empire, 43 BC–AD 69*, p.258.
47. Suetonius, *Galba*, 10; Campbell, J. B., *The Emperor and the Roman Army 31 BC–AD 235*, p.31.
48. Suetonius, *Galba*, 10; Vervaet, Frederik Juliaan, *Domitius Corbulo and the Senatorial Opposition to the Reign of Nero*, Vol. 32 (2002), pp.135–93. Chilver, G. E. F., 'The Army in Politics, A.D. 68–70', *The Journal of Roman Studies*, Vol. 47, No. 1/2 (1957), pp.29–35, notes that Tiberius Alexander would issue an edict in Galba's name less than a month after Nero's death. Also see Del Castillo, Arcadio, 'The Emperor Galba's Assumption of Power: Some Chronological Considerations', *Historia: Zeitschrift für Alte Geschichte*, Bd. 51, H. 4 (4th Qtr, 2002), pp.449–61; Wiedemann, T. E. J., 'From Nero to Vespasian', in Bowman, A.K., Champlin, E. & Lintott, A. (eds), *The Cambridge Ancient History* (Cambridge University Press, 1996), p.275.
49. Plutarch, *Galba*, 5; Suetonius, *Nero*, 42, 49.4.
50. Suetonius, *Nero*, 43–44, states that Nero replaced both consuls to become sole consul. However, an inscription records Nero sharing the office with Silius Italicus. See Shotter, D. C. A., 'A Time-Table for the "*Bellum Neronis*"', *Historia: Zeitschrift für Alte Geschichte*, Bd. 24, H. 1 (1st Qtr, 1975), pp.59–74, citing CIL VI. 8639. Tacitus, *Histories*, 2.11.1; Woodside, M. St. A., 'The Role of Eight Batavian Cohorts in the Events of 68–69 A.D', *Transactions and Proceedings of the American Philological Association*, Vol. 68 (1937), pp.277–83.
51. Suetonius, *Nero*, 44; Tacitus, *Annals*, 15.72.2. Shotter, D. C. A., 'A Time-Table for the '*Bellum Neronis*'', *Historia: Zeitschrift für Alte Geschichte*, Bd. 24, H. 1 (1st Qtr, 1975), pp.59–74, highlights the integrity of Rubrius Gallus, who assisted the defeated forces of Otho surrender to the victorious Vitellean army after the Battle of Bedriacum. He later acted as a middleman enabling Caecina to change his allegiance from Vitellius to Vespasian, and then remained a loyal advisor to the Flavian emperors.
52. Plutarch, *Galba*, 6.
53. Plutarch, *Galba*, 6; Tacitus, *Histories*, 1.73, 2.97.2, 4.49.4; Fields, Nic, *AD 69: Emperors, Armies and Anarchy* (Pen & Sword, 2014), p.21; Morgan, Gwyn, 'The Publica Fames of A.D. 68 (Suetonius, Nero 45.1)', *The Classical Quarterly*, Vol. 50, No. 1 (2000), pp.210–22.

54. Chilver, G. E. F., 'The Army in Politics, A.D. 68–70', *The Journal of Roman Studies*, Vol. 47, No. 1/2 (1957), pp.29–35; Wiedemann, T. E. J., 'From Nero to Vespasian', in Bowman, A. K., Champlin, E. & Lintott, A. (eds), *The Cambridge Ancient History* (Vol. 10) (Cambridge University Press, 1996), p.259.
55. Tacitus, *Histories*, 2.27; Wellesley, Kenneth, *The Year of the Four Emperors*, p.170; Siofstra, J., 'Batavians and Romans on the Lower Rhine. The Romanisation of a Frontier Area', *Archaeological Dialogues*, vol. 9, no. 1 (2002), pp.16–38.
56. Tacitus, *Histories*, 2.86; Syme, R., 'The Colony of Cornelius Fuscus: An Episode in the Bellum Neronis', *The American Journal of Philology*, Vol. 58, No. 1 (1937), pp.7–18.
57. Dio 63.27.1[a]; Tacitus, *Histories*, 1.64–65; Wellesley, Kenneth, *The Year of the Four Emperors*, p.5; Levick, Barbara, 'L. Verginius Rufus and the Four Emperors', *Rheinisches Museum für Philologie*, Neue Folge, 128. Bd., H. 3/4 (1985), pp.318–46; Wiedemann, T. E., Bowman, A. K. & Champlin, E., 'From Nero to Vespasian', *The Cambridge Ancient History, 10, The Augustan Empire, 43 BC–AD 69*, p.260; Shotter, D. C. A., 'Tacitus and Verginius Rufus', *The Classical Quarterly*, Vol. 17, No. 2 (November 1967), pp.370–81.
58. Tacitus, *Histories*, 1.7.
59. Tacitus, *Histories*, 1.7.1, 1.52–53, 1.58, 3.62; Plutarch, *Galba*, 10.3; Syme, R., 'Partisans of Galba', *Historia: Zeitschrift für Alte Geschichte*, Bd. 31, H. 4 (4th Qtr, 1982), pp.460–83.
60. Dio 64.2.3.
61. Tacitus, *Histories*, 1.7.1, 1.58, 1.66; Levick, Barbara L., 'Verginius Rufus and the Four Emperors', *Rheinisches Museum für Philologie*, Neue Folge, 128. Bd., H. 3/4 (1985), pp.318–46; Syme, R., 'Partisans of Galba', *Historia: Zeitschrift für Alte Geschichte*, Bd. 31, H. 4 (4th Qtr, 1982), pp.460–83. Although Plutarch, *Galba*, 15.2 and Suetonius, *Galba*, 11 state Galba ordered the execution of Capito, Tacitus, *Histories*, 1.7.1 writes that Galba approved of the execution only after it had taken place. Also, Rudich, Vasily, *Political Dissidence Under Nero, The Price of Dissimulation* (Routledge, 1993), p.213.
62. Tacitus, *Histories*, 1.8, 1.53, 4.17; Dio 63.241; Kraay, Colin M., 'The Coinage of Vindex and Galba', *The Numismatic Chronicle and Journal of the Royal Numismatic Society*, Sixth Series, Vol. 9, No. 3/4 (1949), pp.129–49; Królczyk, K., 'Rebellion of Caius Iulius Vindex Against Emperor Nero', *Vestnik of Saint Petersburg University, History*, vol. 63, issue 3 (2018), pp.858–71; Mattingly, Harold, 'Verginius at Lugdunum?', *The Numismatic Chronicle and Journal of the Royal Numismatic Society*, Sixth Series, Vol. 14, No. 44 (1954), pp.32–39.
63. Tacitus, *Histories*, 4.17.
64. Dio 63.24.2.
65. John of Antioch *frag.* 91 Muell. V. 10–22.
66. Dio 63.24.3; Plutarch, *Galba*, 6.2.
67. Tacitus, *Histories*, 4.17; Master, Jonathan, *Provincial Soldiers and Imperial Instability in the Histories of Tacitus* (University of Michigan Press, 2016), p.50.
68. Tacitus, *Histories*, 1.51.
69. Dio 63.24.4.
70. Tacitus, *Histories*, 1.51, 2.94.
71. Dio 63.25.1.
72. Tacitus, *Histories*, 1.8, 1.51.
73. Plutarch, *Galba*, 10; Daly, Lawrence J., 'Verginius at Vesontio: The Incongruity of the "*Bellum Neronis*"', *Historia: Zeitschrift für Alte Geschichte*, Bd. 24, H. 1 (1st Qtr, 1975), pp.75–100, suggests that Galba, Vindex and Verginius had come to a secret understanding before the battle, which was kept from the legionaries. However, the

subsequent plundering of the lands of Vindex's Gallic allies after the battle and the evident reluctance of Verginius to declare for Galba even when he knew of Nero's death would suggest otherwise.

74. Tacitus, *Histories*, 1.28, 2.37, 3.62, 3.72; Campbell, J. B., *The Emperor and the Roman Army 31 BC–AD 235*, pp.108, 369, draws attention to the dubious loyalty of officers in contrast to the soldiers who often remained loyal to their ruler.
75. Tacitus, *Histories*, 2.71; Syme, R., 'Partisans of Galba', *Historia: Zeitschrift für Alte Geschichte*, Bd. 31, H. 4 (4th Qtr, 1982), pp.460–83.
76. Plutarch, *Galba*, 6; Dio 63.25.1–3.
77. Plutarch, *Galba*, 6.
78. Tacitus, *Histories*, 1.8; Hainsworth, J. B., 'Verginius and Vindex', *Historia: Zeitschrift für Alte Geschichte*, Bd. 11, H. 1 (January 1962), pp.86–96.
79. Plutarch, *Galba*, 10; Levick, Barbara, 'L. Verginius Rufus and the Four Emperors', *Rheinisches Museum für Philologie*, Neue Folge, 128. Bd., H. 3/4 (1985), pp.318–46; Chilver, G. E. F., 'The Army in Politics, A.D. 68–70', *The Journal of Roman Studies*, Vol. 47, No. 1/2 (1957), pp.29–35.
80. Tacitus, *Histories*, 1.52; Levick, Barbara, 'L. Verginius Rufus and the Four Emperors', *Rheinisches Museum für Philologie*, Neue Folge, 128. Bd., H. 3/4 (1985), pp.318–46; Southern, Pat, *Domitian, The Tragic Tyrant* (Routledge, 2009), p.14; MacMullen, Ramsay, *Changes in the Roman Empire, Essays in the Ordinary*, p.198.
81. Tacitus, *Histories*, 1.8.
82. Tacitus, *Histories*, 1.52; Plutarch, *Galba*, 10.
83. Plutarch, *Galba*, 6.4.
84. Tacitus, *Histories*, 1.9, 4.14; Levick, Barbara, 'L. Verginius Rufus and the Four Emperors', *Rheinisches Museum für Philologie*, Neue Folge, 128. Bd., H. 3/4 (1985), pp.318–46.
85. Tacitus, *Histories*, 1.53.
86. Plutarch, *Galba*, 10.
87. Tacitus, *Histories*, 1.8–9; Connal, Robert, 'Rational Mutiny in the Year of Four Emperors', *Arctos* 46 (2012), pp.33–52.
88. Tacitus, *Histories*, 1.6.
89. Dio 63.29.5.
90. Rudich, Vasily, *Political Dissidence Under Nero*, p.216, citing ILS, 982; Levick, Barbara, 'L. Verginius Rufus and the Four Emperors', *Rheinisches Museum für Philologie*, Neue Folge, 128. Bd., H. 3/4 (1985), pp.318–46; Várhelyi, Zsuzsanna, *The Religion of Senators in the Roman Empire: Power and the Beyond* (Cambridge University Press, 2010), p.202.
91. Plutarch, *Galba*, 10.
92. Dio 63.29.5; Plutarch, *Galba*, 10.
93. Tacitus, *Histories*, 1.8; Levick, Barbara, 'L. Verginius Rufus and the Four Emperors', *Rheinisches Museum für Philologie*, Neue Folge, 128. Bd., H. 3/4 (1985), pp.318–46.
94. Pliny the Younger, *Letters*, 2.1; Levick, Barbara, 'L. Verginius Rufus and the Four Emperors', *Rheinisches Museum für Philologie*, Neue Folge, 128. Bd., H. 3/4 (1985), pp.318–46; Wiedemann, T. E., Bowman, A. K. & Champlin, E., 'From Nero to Vespasian', *The Cambridge Ancient History, 10, The Augustan Empire, 43 BC–AD 69*, p.260; Townend, G. B., 'The Reputation of Verginius Rufus', *Latomus*, T. 20, Fasc. 2 (April–June 1961), pp. 337–41.
95. Pliny the Younger, *Letters*, IX.19.5; Rudich, Vasily, *Political Dissidence Under Nero*, p.217; Townend, G. B., 'The Reputation of Verginius Rufus', *Latomus*, T. 20, Fasc. 2 (April–June 1961), pp.337–41.

96. Pliny the Younger, *Letters*, IX.19.5; Levick, Barbara, 'L. Verginius Rufus and the Four Emperors', *Rheinisches Museum für Philologie*, Neue Folge, 128. Bd., H. 3/4 (1985), pp.318–46; Rudich, Vasily, *Political Dissidence Under Nero*, p.217.
97. Tacitus, *Histories*, 1.6; Griffin, Miriam T., *Nero, The End of a Dynasty*, p.185; Syme, R., *The Praetorian Guard*, The Roman Papers VI, pp.25–34.
98. Tacitus, *Histories*, 1.89.
99. Dio 63.27.2; Plutarch, *Galba*, 2.1; Tacitus, *Histories*, 1.31; Suetonius, *Nero*, 47.1. Shotter, D. C. A., 'A Time-Table for the "*Bellum Neronis*"', *Historia: Zeitschrift für Alte Geschichte*, Bd. 24, H. 1 (1st Qtr, 1975), pp.59–74, suggests that defection of the eight Batavian cohorts is what Suetonius alludes to when mentioning 'the defection of other armies'.
100. Dio 63.27.1, 1[a].
101. Plutarch, *Galba*, 17.3; Shotter, D. C. A., 'A Time-Table for the "*Bellum Neronis*"', *Historia: Zeitschrift für Alte Geschichte*, Bd. 24, H. 1 (1st Qtr, 1975), pp.59–74.
102. Tacitus, *Histories*, 1.6; Plutarch, *Galba*, 15.2.
103. Plutarch, *Otho*, 2; *Galba*, 17; Rudich, Vasily, *Political Dissidence Under Nero*, p.232; Wiedemann, T. E., Bowman, A. K. & Champlin, E., 'From Nero to Vespasian', *The Cambridge Ancient History, 10, The Augustan Empire, 43 BC–AD 69*, p.261.
104. Tacitus, *Histories*, 1.25, 1.72.
105. Plutarch, *Galba*, 8–9, reports that in AD 69, the Guard had 'long been well disposed' to Nymphidius Sabinus. Also see Rudich, Vasily, *Political Dissidence Under Nero*, p.234.
106. Plutarch, *Galba*, 13.3.
107. Suetonius, *Nero*, 47–48; Dio 63.27.3; Weaver, Paul, 'Phaon, Freedman of Nero', *Zeitschrift für Papyrologie und Epigraphik*, Bd. 151 (2005), pp.243–52. Dio states that it was the Senate that persuaded the Guard to withdraw their support for Nero. This, however, is unlikely as they would not have listened and were hostile to the Senate throughout their history. See Hammond, Mason, 'The Transmission of the Powers of the Roman Emperor from the Death of Nero in 68 AD to That of Alexander Severus in AD 235, *Memoirs of the American Academy in Rome*, Vol. 24 (1956), pp.61–133.
108. Plutarch, *Galba*, 8–9, 17; Suetonius, *Nero*, 49; *Domitian*, 14; Gregory, A. P., 'A Study in Survival: the Case of the Freedman L. Domitius Phaon', *Athenaeum* (1 January 1995), p.401; Weaver, P. R. C., 'Epaphroditus, Josephus, and Epictetus', *The Classical Quarterly*, Vol. 44, No. 2 (1994), pp.468–79.
109. Suetonius, *Nero*, 48; Tacitus, *Histories*, 1.5; Plutarch, *Galba*, 2, 8, 14.3; Wiedemann, T. E., Bowman, A. K. & Champlin, E., 'From Nero to Vespasian', *The Cambridge Ancient History, 10, The Augustan Empire, 43 BC–AD 69*, p.261; Rudich, Vasily, *Political Dissidence Under Nero*, p.235; Bingham, Sandra, *The Praetorian Guard in the Political and Social Life of Julio-Claudian Rome* (PhD thesis, University of British Columbia, 1997), p.114; Watson, G. R., *The Roman Soldier*, p.110.
110. Tacitus, *Histories*, 1.5; Plutarch, *Galba*, 3; Suetonius, *Nero*, 48.
111. Suetonius, *Nero*, 48.
112. Suetonius, *Nero*, 48.

Chapter 5

1. Dio, 63.3.2; Plutarch, *Galba*, 3.1; Tacitus, *Histories,* 1.5–7; Macrobius, *Saturnalia*, 2.4.8; Wiedemann, T. E. J., 'From Nero to Vespasian', in Bowman, A. K., Champlin, E. & Lintott, A. (eds) *The Cambridge Ancient History* (Vol. 10) (Cambridge University Press, 1996), p.258.
2. Tacitus, *Histories*, 1.13.

3. Tacitus, *Histories*, 1.13; Syme, R., 'Partisans of Galba', *Historia: Zeitschrift für Alte Geschichte*, Bd. 31, H. 4 (4th Qtr, 1982), pp.460–83.
4. Tacitus, *Histories*, 1.14; Dio 63.5.1.
5. Tacitus, *Histories*, 1.13. Also see Suetonius, *Otho*, 5.
6. Plutarch, *Galba*, 6.2.
7. Plutarch, *Galba*, 7.1.
8. Plutarch, *Galba*, 8.4.
9. Tacitus, *Histories*, 1.6, 1.9, 1.52, 1.56; Dio 64.4.1; Syme, R., 'Partisans of Galba', *Historia: Zeitschrift für Alte Geschichte*, Bd. 31, H. 4 (4th Qtr, 1982), pp.460–83.
10. Tacitus, *Histories*, 1.7–8; Suetonius, *Galba*, 12; Rathbun, Bessie S., 'Vesontio: Crossroads of History', *The Classical Journal*, Vol. 42, No. 8 (May 1947), pp.465–70.
11. Plutarch, *Galba*, 8.1–4, 9.3.
12. Plutarch, *Galba*, 13.1–2.
13. Plutarch, *Galba*, 13.2.
14. Tacitus, *Histories*, 1.5.
15. Plutarch, *Galba*, 13.
16. Tacitus, *Annals*, 15.72.
17. Plutarch, *Galba*, 9.
18. Plutarch, *Galba*, 13.4, 14.4; Fields, Nic, *AD 69 Emperors, Armies and Anarchy*, p.174 n.74.
19. Plutarch, *Galba*, 13.4.
20. Epictetus, *Discourses and Selected Writings*, trans. by Dobbin, Robert (Penguin, 2008), 4.60.
21. Epictetus, *Discourses*, 7.1.
22. Plutarch, *Galba*, 14.1–4.
23. Plutarch, *Galba*, 14.5–6.
24. Tacitus, *Histories*, 1.6; Plutarch, *Galba*, 15.1–2.
25. Tacitus, *Histories*, 1.23; Perkins, Caroline A., 'Tacitus on Otho', *Latomus*, T. 52, Fasc. 4 (October–December 1993), pp.848–55; Chilver, G. E. F., 'The Army in Politics, A.D. 68–70', *The Journal of Roman Studies*, Vol. 47, No. 1/2 (1957), pp.29–35.
26. Tacitus, *Histories*, 1.6; Dio 63.3.2; Plutarch, *Galba,* 15.4; Phang, Sara Elise, *Roman Military Service, Ideologies of Discipline in the Late Republic and Early Principate* (Cambridge University Press, 2008), pp.112, 128–29.
27. Plutarch, *Galba*, 14.4.
28. Tacitus, *Histories*, 1.20, 1.31; Suetonius, *Galba*, 16.
29. CIL. 3.14387 = (ILS 9199) trans. Bigham, Sandra, *The Praetorian Guard*, pp. 173–74 n. 109, also pp.65–66.
30. Plutarch, *Galba*, 18.2.
31. Campbell, J. B., *The Emperor and the Roman Army 31 BC–AD 235*, pp.186–87.
32. Plutarch, *Galba*, 18.2; Suetonius, *Galba*, 16.
33. Suetonius, *Galba*, 12, 20; Tacitus, *Histories*, 1.31; Wellesley, Kenneth, *The Year of the Four Emperors*, p.60; Wiedemann, T. E. J., 'From Nero to Vespasian', in Bowman, A. K., Champlin, E. & Lintott, A. (eds), *The Cambridge Ancient History* (Vol. 10) (Cambridge University Press, 1996), p.264.
34. Tacitus, *Histories*, 1.5.
35. Plutarch, *Galba*, 21.1–2; Phang, Sara Elise, *Roman Military Service, Ideologies of Discipline in the Late Republic and Early Principate*, p.112.
36. Tacitus, *Histories*, 1.23.

37. Plutarch, *Galba*, 20.4.
38. Tacitus, *Histories*, 1.24.
39. Plutarch, *Galba*, 20.4.
40. Tacitus, *Histories*, 1.24; Suetonius, *Augustus*, 74; Claudius, 35; Epictetus, *Discourses*, 4.13.5; Dio 52.37.2, 60.3.3; Philostratus, *Life of Apollonius*, 4.43; Watson, G. R., *The Roman Soldier*, p.85; Bingham, Sandra, *The Praetorian Guard in the Political and Social Life of Julio-Claudian Rome*, University of Columbia PhD thesis, p.137, citing CIL 16.21= ILS 1993. Strechie, Mădălina, 'The Praetorian Guard, Rome's Intelligent Service', *International Conference Knowledge-Based Organization*, Vol. 27, No. 1, pp.136–43, suggests the Praetorian *speculatores* were established under Tiberius and numbered 100.
41. Tacitus, *Histories*, 1.24; Suetonius, *Otho*, 4.
42. Tacitus, *Histories*, 1.6, 1.24, 1.26; Suetonius, *Galba*, 14.
43. Tacitus, *Histories*, 1.24.
44. Dio 64.3.4; Plutarch, *Galba*, 17.2; Tacitus, *Histories*, 1.7; Suetonius, *Galba*, 20.
45. Tacitus, *Histories*, 1.52, 1.58, 1.59; Plutarch, *Galba*, 22.2; Suetonius, *Galba*, 16; Dio 63.4.1; Syme, R., 'Partisans of Galba', *Historia: Zeitschrift für Alte Geschichte*, Bd. 31, H. 4 (4th Qtr, 1982), pp.460–83; Wiedemann, T. E. J., 'From Nero to Vespasian', in Bowman, A. K., Champlin, E. & Lintott, A. (eds), *The Cambridge Ancient History* (Vol. 10), p.262.
46. Suetonius, *Vitellius*, 7.
47. Syme, R., 'Partisans of Galba', *Historia: Zeitschrift für Alte Geschichte*, Bd. 31, H. 4 (4th Qtr, 1982), pp.460–83.
48. Tacitus, *Histories*, 2.86; Campbell, J. B., *The Emperor and the Roman Army 31 BC–AD 235*, p.336.
49. Phang, Sara Elise, *Roman Military Service, Ideologies of Discipline in the Late Republic and Early Principate*, p.128; Wellesley, Kenneth, *The Year of the Four Emperors*, p.80. Watson, G. R., *The Roman Soldier*, p.120, cites three diplomas (CIL XVI 7, 8, 9) showing the recognition of the *I Aduitrix* by 22 December.
50. Plutarch, *Galba*, 22.1–4; Suetonius, *Galba*, 16.
51. Tacitus, *Histories*, 1.14; Plutarch, *Galba*, 23.1.
52. Plutarch, *Galba*, 23.3; Tacitus, *Histories*, 1.14, 1.18; Suetonius, *Galba*, 17.
53. Suetonius, *Otho*, 5; Dio 63.5.2; Plutarch, *Galba*, 23.3–4; Tacitus, *Histories*, 1.21.
54. Plutarch, *Galba*, 23.4; Tacitus, *Histories*, 1.22.
55. Suetonius, *Otho*, 6.
56. Suetonius, *Otho*, 5.
57. Tacitus, *Histories*, 1.25; Plutarch, *Galba*, 24.1.
58. Breeze, David J., 'Pay Grades and Ranks below the Centurionate', *The Journal of Roman Studies*, Vol. 61 (1971), pp.130–35; Eaton, Jonathan, 'The Political Significance of the Imperial Watchword in the Early Empire', *Greece & Rome*, Vol. 58, No. 1, pp.48–63.
59. Tacitus, *Histories*, 1.25.
60. Tacitus, *Histories*, 1.27.
61. Tacitus, *Histories*, 1.25.
62. Tacitus, *Histories*, 1.26; Plutarch, *Galba*, 25.5
63. Dio 64.5.3; Tacitus, *Histories*, 1.27; Plutarch, *Galba*, 24.2–3; Suetonius, *Otho*, 6.
64. Tacitus, *Histories*, 1.26.
65. Tacitus, *Histories*, 1.27; Plutarch, *Galba*, 24.3.
66. Tacitus, *Histories*, 1.27; Plutarch, *Galba*, 24.4.

67. Tacitus, *Histories*, 1.27; Plutarch, *Galba*, 25.1.
68. Tacitus, *Histories*, 1.27; Plutarch, *Galba*, 25.2–3; Suetonius, *Otho*, 6.
69. Tacitus, *Histories*, 1.28; Plutarch, *Galba*, 25.3.
70. Tacitus, *Histories*, 1.29; Plutarch, *Galba*, 26.4.
71. Tacitus, *Histories*, 1.29–31; Plutarch, *Galba*, 26.4.
72. Suetonius, *Galba*, 19.
73. Tacitus, *Histories*, 1.31; Plutarch, *Galba*, 25.4–5, 27.6; Suetonius, *Galba*, 20; Syme, R., 'Pliny the Procurator', *Harvard Studies in Classical Philology*, Vol. 73 (1969), pp.201–36.
74. Tacitus, *Histories*, 1.33–34; Plutarch, *Galba*, 26.1.
75. Suetonius, *Galba*, 19; Tacitus, *Histories*, 1.34.
76. Tacitus, *Histories*, 1.35; Plutarch, *Galba*, 26.2.
77. Tacitus, *Histories*, 1.35–38; Connal, Robert, 'Rational Mutiny in the Year of Four Emperors', *Arctos* 46 (2012), pp.33–52.
78. Tacitus, *Histories*, 1.39; Plutarch, *Galba*, 26.3.
79. Tacitus, *Histories*, 1.39.
80. Tacitus, *Histories*, 1.40; Plutarch, *Galba*, 26.3–4; Suetonius, *Galba*, 20.
81. Tacitus, *Histories*, 1.40; Suetonius, *Galba*, 19.
82. Tacitus, *Histories*, 1.40–41.
83. Dio 64.3.4; Plutarch, *Galba*, 26.5; Tacitus, *Histories*, 1.43.
84. Tacitus, *Histories*, 1.41; Suetonius, *Galba*, 20; Plutarch, *Galba*, 27.1–3.
85. Plutarch, *Galba*, 27.4; Tacitus, *Histories*, 42, 44.
86. Suetonius, *Galba*, 20; Plutarch, *Galba*, 28.1–3; Connal, Robert, 'Rational Mutiny in the Year of Four Emperors', *Arctos* 46 (2012), pp.33–52.
87. Tacitus, *Histories*, 1.80: Suetonius, *Otho*, 8; Wellesley, Kenneth, *The Year of the Four Emperors*, pp.58–59.
88. Tacitus, *Histories*, 1.81–82; Plutarch, *Otho*, 3.3.
89. Tacitus, *Histories*, 1.82–84; Watson, G. R., *The Roman Soldier*, p.109.
90. Tacitus, *Histories*, 1.85. Also see Plutarch, *Otho*, 3.2–3; Campbell, J. B., *The Emperor and the Roman Army 31 BC–AD 235*, p.117; MacMullen, Ramsay, 'The Legion as a Society', *Historia: Zeitschrift für Alte Geschichte*, Bd. 33, H. 4 (4th Qtr,1984), pp.440–56, who notes that the soldiers saw the tribunes and centurions as a unit too closely linked to the Senate.
91. Wellesley, Kenneth, *The Year of the Four Emperors*, p.63.
92. Tacitus, His*tories*, 2.41.
93. Wellesley, Kenneth, *The Year of the Four Emperors*, pp.80–83.
94. Dio 63.13.2, 63.14.1; Tacitus, *Histories*, 2.46–48.
95. Tacitus, *Histories*, 2.49.
96. Tacitus, *Histories*, 2.51.
97. Tacitus, *Histories*, 2.60.
98. Plutarch, *Galba*, 18.4; Kajanto, Iliro, 'Tacitus' Attitude to War and the Soldier', *Latomus*, T. 29, Fasc. 3 (July–September 1970), pp.699–718; Campbell, J. B., *The Emperor and the Roman Army 31 BC–AD 235*, p.387.
99. Connal, Robert, 'Rational Mutiny in the Year of Four Emperors', *Arctos* 46 (2012), pp.33–52.

Chapter 6

1. Tacitus, *Histories*, 1.51, 1.53; Plutarch, *Galba*, 22.1–3; Suetonius, *Galba*, 16; Chilver, G. E. F., 'The Army in Politics, A.D. 68–70', *The Journal of Roman Studies*, Vol. 47, No. 1/2 (1957), pp.29–35.

2. Dio 63.4.1; Plutarch, *Galba*, 22.1–3.
3. Tacitus, *Histories*, 1.53; Plutarch, *Galba*, 22.5; Syme, R., 'Partisans of Galba', *Historia: Zeitschrift für Alte Geschichte*, Bd. 31, H. 4 (4th Qtr, 1982), pp.460–83.
4. Tacitus, *Histories*, 1.53.
5. Tacitus, *Histories*, 1.7.1, 1.52–53, 1.58, 3.62; Plutarch, *Galba*, 10.3; Syme, R., 'Partisans of Galba', *Historia: Zeitschrift für Alte Geschichte*, Bd. 31, H. 4 (4th Qtr, 1982), pp.460–83.
6. Tacitus, *Histories*, 1.52.
7. Tacitus, *Histories*, 1.52, 1.58; Suetonius, *Vitellius*, 8; Connal, Robert, 'Rational Mutiny in the Year of Four Emperors', *Arctos* 46 (2012), pp.33–52.
8. Watson, G. R., *The Roman Soldier*, p.153; Keppie, Lawrence, 'The Changing Face of the Roman Legions (49 BC–AD 69)', *Papers of the British School at Rome*, Vol. 65 (1997), pp.89–102; Chilver, G. E. F., 'The Army in Politics, A.D. 68–70', *The Journal of Roman Studies*, Vol. 47, No. 1/2 (1957), pp. 29–35. The Treveri lost land on the Rhine between Bingen and Koblenz. See Rüger, C., 'Germany', in Bowman, A. K., Champlin, E. & Lintott, A. (eds), *The Cambridge Ancient History* (Cambridge University Press, 1996), p.529.
9. Tacitus, *Histories*, 1.54.
10. Tacitus, *Histories*, 1.54; Keppie, L., 'The Army and the Navy', in Bowman, A. K., Champlin, E. & Lintott, A. (eds), *The Cambridge Ancient History* (Cambridge University Press), p.381.
11. Tacitus, *Histories*, 1.51; Phang, Sara Elise, *Roman Military Service, Ideologies of Discipline in the Late Republic and Early Principate*, p.129.
12. Tacitus, *Histories*, 1.12, 1.58; Syme, R., 'Partisans of Galba', *Historia: Zeitschrift für Alte Geschichte*, Bd. 31, H. 4 (4th Qtr, 1982), pp.460–83.
13. Suetonius, *Vitellius*, 7.
14. Suetonius, *Vitellius*, 7; Dio 64.5.2–3.
15. Suetonius, *Vitellius*, 7.
16. Rüger, C., 'Germany', *Cambridge Ancient History*, Vol X, pp.531–34.
17. Suetonius, *Vitellius*, 7; Campbell, J. B., *The Emperor and the Roman Army 31 BC–AD 235*, pp.32, 419; Lendon, J. E., 'Contubernalis, Commanipularis, and Commilito in Roman Soldiers' Epigraphy: Drawing the Distinction', *Zeitschrift für Papyrologie und Epigraphik*, Bd. 157 (2006), pp.270–76; MacMullen, Ramsay, 'The Legion as a Society', *Historia: Zeitschrift für Alte Geschichte*, Bd. 33, H. 4 (4th Qtr, 1984), pp.440–56.
18. Suetonius, *Vitellius*, 7; Tacitus, *Histories*, 1.52.
19. Dio 64.4.1; Suetonius, *Vitellius*, 7.
20. Tacitus, *Histories*, 1.52; Suetonius, *Vitellius*, 8.
21. Tacitus, *Histories*, 1.52.
22. Tacitus, *Histories*, 1.58, 1.66; MacMullen, Ramsay, *Changes in the Roman Empire: Essays in the Ordinary* (Princeton University Press, 2019), pp.199–200.
23. Tacitus, *Histories*, 1.59.2, 4.4.3; Syme, R., 'Partisans of Galba', *Historia: Zeitschrift für Alte Geschichte*, Bd. 31, H. 4 (4th Qtr, 1982), pp.460–83.
24. Tacitus, *Histories*, 1.57; MacMullen, Ramsay, *Changes in the Roman Empire: Essays in the Ordinary*, p.200.
25. Tacitus, Histories, 1.67; Campbell, J. B., *The Emperor and the Roman Army 31 BC–AD 235*, p.107.
26. Tacitus, *Histories*, 1.55, 2.6. Chilver, G. E. F., 'The Army in Politics, A.D. 68–70', *The Journal of Roman Studies*, Vol. 47, No. 1/2 (1957), pp.29–35, believes that the revolt had been planned in detail, but Vitellius had only been in the province a month and

his actions suggest he was taken by surprise with the news of the revolt from Upper Germany. There appears to have been no coordination with the legions at Mogontiacum as they did not take an oath to Vitellius but to the Senate and the people of Rome.

27. Epictetus, *Discourses*, 1.14.15; Campbell, J. B., *The Emperor and the Roman Army 31 BC–AD 235*, pp.29–30; Phang, Sara Elise, *Roman Military Service, Ideologies of Discipline in the Late Republic and Early Principate*, p.119.
28. Philostratus, *Life of Apollonius*, 5.35.5.
29. Tacitus, *Histories*, 1.55–56; Plutarch, *Galba*, 21.3–4.
30. Connal, Robert, 'Rational Mutiny in the Year of Four Emperors', *Arctos* 46 (2012), pp.33–52; Campbell, J. B., *The Emperor and the Roman Army 31 BC–AD 235*, p.100.
31. Tacitus, *Histories*, 1.55; Plutarch, *Galba*, 21.2–3; Campbell, J. B., *The Emperor and the Roman Army 31 BC–AD 235*, pp.31, 100; Phang, Sara Elise, *Roman Military Service, Ideologies of Discipline in the Late Republic and Early Principate*, p.129.
32. Plutarch, *Galba*, 22.5.
33. Tacitus, *Histories*, 1.56; Plutarch, *Galba*, 22.6.
34. Tacitus, *Histories*, 1.56.
35. Suetonius, *Vitellius*, 8.
36. Tacitus, *Histories*, 1.57, 2.76; Suetonius, *Vitellius*, 8.
37. Plutarch, *Galba*, 22.8; Suetonius, *Vitellius*, 8; Campbell, J. B., *The Emperor and the Roman Army 31 BC–AD 235*, pp.29–30.
38. Suetonius, *Vitellius*, 8; Woodside, M. St. A., 'The Role of Eight Batavian Cohorts in the Events of 68–69 AD', *Transactions and Proceedings of the American Philological Association*, Vol. 68 (1937), pp.277–83.
39. Tacitus, *Histories*, 1.57; MacMullen, Ramsay, *Changes in the Roman Empire: Essays in the Ordinary*, p.200; Rüger, C., 'Germany', *Cambridge Ancient History*, Vol X, p.529; Chilver, G. E. F., 'The Army in Politics, A.D. 68–70', *The Journal of Roman Studies*, Vol. 47, No. 1/2 (1957), pp.29–35; Keppie, L., 'The Army and the Navy', in Bowman, A. K., Champlin, E. & Lintott, A. (eds), *The Cambridge Ancient History* (Cambridge University Press, 1996), p.391.
40. Tacitus, *Histories*, 1.65, 2.29; Chilver, G. E. F., 'The Army in Politics, A.D. 68–70', *The Journal of Roman Studies*, Vol. 47, No. 1/2 (1957), pp.29–35; Rüger, C., 'Germany', *Cambridge Ancient History*, Vol. X, p.530.
41. Tacitus, *Histories*, 1.66; MacMullen, Ramsay, *Changes in the Roman Empire: Essays in the Ordinary*, p.201.
42. Tacitus, *Annals*, 11.1.2.
43. Tacitus, *Histories*, 4.36; Campbell, J. B., *The Emperor and the Roman Army 31 BC–AD 235*, p.192; Levick, Barbara, *Vespasian*, p.58.
44. Tacitus, *Histories*, 3.13–14; Connal, Robert, 'Rational Mutiny in the Year of Four Emperors', *Arctos* 46 (2012), pp.33–52.
45. Tacitus, *Histories*, 1.57, 2.69; Suetonius, *Vitellius*, 10; Levick, Barbara, *Vespasian*, p.44.
46. Tacitus, *Histories*, 1.70; Suetonius, *Otho*, 8: Connal, Robert, 'Rational Mutiny in the Year of Four Emperors', *Arctos* 46 (2012), pp.33–52.
47. Chilver, G. E. F., 'The Army in Politics, A.D. 68–70', *The Journal of Roman Studies*, Vol. 47, No. 1/2 (1957), pp.29–35.
48. Tacitus, *Histories*, 2.88.
49. Tacitus, *Histories*, 2.67, 2.93–94; Watson, G. R., *The Roman Soldier*, p.17; Levick, Barbara, *Vespasian*, p.60.

50. Tacitus, *Histories*, 1.58–59, 2.94, 4.13; Woodside, M. St. A., 'The Role of Eight Batavian Cohorts in the Events of 68–69 AD', *Transactions and Proceedings of the American Philological Association*, Vol. 68 (1937), pp.277–83.
51. Tacitus, *Histories*, 2.60, 2.67, 3.32; Suetonius, *Vitellius*, 10.
52. Dio 63.10.3, 63.12.1; Suetonius, *Vitellius*, 10.
53. Tacitus, *Histories*, 2.70; Suetonius, *Vitellius*, 17.
54. Wellesley, Kenneth, *The Year of the Four Emperors*, pp.128–50.
55. Josephus, *Jewish War*, 4.639–641; Connal, Robert, 'Rational Mutiny in the Year of Four Emperors, *Arctos* 46 (2012), pp.33–52.
56. Tacitus, *Histories*, 2.37, 2.101, 3.72; Kajanto, Iiro, 'Tacitus' Attitude to War and the Soldier', *Latomus*, T. 29, Fasc. 3 (July–September 1970), pp.699–718; Connal, Robert, 'Rational Mutiny in the Year of Four Emperors', *Arctos* 46 (2012), pp.33–52; Campbell, J. B., *The Emperor and the Roman Army 31 BC–AD 235*, pp.367–69, 386.
57. Tacitus, *Histories*, 3.25.

Chapter 7

1. Suetonius, *Vespasian*, 4; Wallace-Hadrill, Andrew, 'The Imperial Court', in Bowman, A. K., Champlin, E. & Lintott, A. (eds), *The Cambridge Ancient History* (Cambridge University Press), p.295; Griffin, Miriam, 'The Flavians', in Barnes, T. D., *The Cambridge Ancient History (Vol. 11) The High Empire, AD 70–192* (2002), pp.2–3.
2. Tacitus, *Annals*, 12.16; Suetonius, *Nero*, 33.
3. Suetonius, *Titus*, 2.
4. Tacitus, *Histories*, 2.1; Levick, Barbara, *Vespasian*, p.44.
5. Tacitus, *Histories*, 1.46, 2.1; Dio (Zonaras) 11, 16, p.49, 1–8 D; Plutarch, *Otho*, 5.2; Griffin, Miriam, 'The Flavians', in Barnes, T. D., *The Cambridge Ancient History (Vol. 11)*, p.2.
6. Tacitus, *Histories*, 2.2–4; Suetonius, *Titus*, 5; Wiedemann, T. E., 'From Nero to Vespasian', in Bowman, A. K. & Champlin, E., *The Cambridge Ancient History (Vol. 10) The Augustan Empire, 43 BC–AD 69* (1996), p.274.
7. Dio 64. 8.3[a]; Tacitus, *Histories*, 2.6; Levick, Barbara, *Vespasian*, p.45.
8. Suetonius, *Vespasian*, 4; Chilver, G. E. F.. 'The Army in Politics AD 68–70', *The Journal of Roman Studies*, Vol. 47, No. 1/2 (1957), pp.29–35, asserts that Mucianus and Vespasian probably started their planning even before Vitellius travelled to Germany.
9. Levick, Barbara, *Vespasian*, p.54; Wiedemann, T. E., 'From Nero to Vespasian', in Bowman, A. K. & Champlin, E., *The Cambridge Ancient History (Vol. 10)*, p.275.
10. Tacitus, *Histories*, 2.5; Suetonius, *Vespasian*, 6, 13; Levick, Barbara, *Vespasian*, p.53; Fields, Nic, *AD 69: Emperors, Armies and Anarchy*, p.51.
11. Tacitus, *Histories*, 2.5.
12. Josephus, *The Jewish War*, 4.602–612; Tacitus, *Histories*, 2.6; Griffin, Miriam, 'The Flavians', in Barnes, T. D., *The Cambridge Ancient History (Vol. 11)*, p.5.
13. Philostratus, *Life of Apollonius*, 5.35.5; Suetonius, *Vespasian*, 5; Campbell, J. B., *The Emperor and the Roman Army 31 BC–AD 235*, pp.29–30.
14. Suetonius, *Vespasian*, 5; Tacitus, *Histories*, 2.78; Campbell, J. B., *The Emperor and the Roman Army 31 BC–AD 235*, p.30.
15. Josephus, *The Jewish War*, 4.592–600; Tacitus, *Histories*, 2.6, 2.78; Dio 64.89.1; Campbell, J. B., *The Emperor and the Roman Army 31 BC–AD 235*, p.419.
16. Suetonius, *Vespasian*, 4.
17. Tacitus, *Histories*, 2.5, 5.1; Dio 64.8.3[2]; Suetonius, *Titus*, 4; Campbell, J. B., *The Emperor and the Roman Army 31 BC–AD 235*, pp.34–35, 44.

18. Tacitus, *Histories*, 2.5, 2.80; Connal, Robert, 'Rational Mutiny in the Year of Four Emperors', *Arctos* 46 (2012), pp.33–52; MacMullen, Ramsay, *Changes in the Roman Empire: Essays in the Ordinary*, p.199; Keppie, l., 'The Army and Navy', in Bowman, A. K., Champlin, E. & Lintott, A. (eds), *The Cambridge Ancient History (Vol. 10)* (Cambridge University Press, (1996), p.395.
19. Tacitus, *Histories*, 3.24; Suetonius, *Vespasian*, 6; Watson, G. R., *The Roman Soldier*, pp.140–41.
20. Suetonius, *Vespasian*, 6; Tacitus, *Histories*, 2.74; Levick, Barbara, *Vespasian*, p.46.
21. Tacitus, *Histories*, 2.7.
22. Tacitus, *Histories*, 2.60; Wellesley, Kenneth, *The Year of the Four Emperors*, pp.97–98; Wiedemann, T. E ., 'From Nero to Vespasian', in Bowman, A. K. & Champlin, E., *The Cambridge Ancient History (Vol. 10)*, p.272.
23. Suetonius, *Vespasian*, 6; Tacitus, *Histories*, 2.74, 2.85.
24. Tacitus, *Histories*, 2.67, 2.82; Wiedemann, T. E., Bowman, A. K. & Champlin, E. 'From Nero to Vespasian', in *The Cambridge Ancient History (Vol. 10)*, p.273.
25. Tacitus, *Histories*, 2.82; Levick, Barbara, *Vespasian*, pp.63–64; CIL III 335.
26. Tacitus, *Histories*, 2.81; Josephus, *The Jewish War*, VII.7; Levick, Barbara, *Vespasian*, p.54.
27. Tacitus, *Histories*, 2.81.
28. Levick, Barbara, *Vespasian*, p.48; Chilver, G. E. F., 'The Army in Politics AD 68–70', *The Journal of Roman Studies*, Vol. 47, No. 1/2 (1957), pp.29–35.
29. Levick, Barbara, *Vespasian*, pp.56–57; Bingham, Sandra, *The Praetorian Guard in the Political and Social Life of Julio-Claudian Rome* (PhD Thesis, University of Columbia), pp.190–91, citing CIL 3.14387 = ILS 9199.
30. Levick, Barbara, *Vespasian*, p.47.
31. Tacitus, *Histories*, 2.79; Suetonius, *Vespasian*, 6.
32. Tacitus, *Histories*, 2.80; Suetonius, *Vespasian*, 6; Dio 64.8.4.
33. Tacitus, *Histories*, 2.80, 2.82; Chilver, G. E. F., 'The Army in Politics AD 68–70', *The Journal of Roman Studies*, Vol. 47, No. 1/2 (1957), pp.29–35; Campbell, J. B., *The Emperor and the Roman Army 31 BC–AD 235*, p.192; Hammond, Mason, 'The Transmission of the Powers of the Roman Emperor from the Death of Nero in A.D. 68 to That of Alexander Severus in A.D. 235', *Memoirs of the American Academy in Rome*, Vol. 24 (1956), pp.61–133.
34. Tacitus, *Histories*, 2.80.
35. Tacitus, *Histories*, 2.98.
36. Tacitus, *Histories*, 2.97–98, 5.26; Chilver, G. E. F., 'The Army in Politics AD 68–70', *The Journal of Roman Studies*, Vol. 47, No. 1/2 (1957), pp.29-35; Connal, Robert, 'Rational Mutiny in the Year of Four Emperors', *Arctos* 46 (2012), pp.33–52.
37. Tacitus, *Histories*, 2.81–82, 2.97.
38. Tacitus, *Histories*, 2.81.
39. Tacitus, *Histories*, 2.81; Wiedemann, T. E., 'From Nero to Vespasian', in Bowman, A. K. & Champlin, E., *The Cambridge Ancient History (Vol. 10)*, p.276.
40. Suetonius, *Vespasian*, 6; Tacitus, *Histories*, 2.82, 4.51.
41. Dio 65.8.2; Tacitus, *Histories*, 2.82; Griffin, Miriam, 'The Flavians', in Barnes, T. D., *The Cambridge Ancient History (Vol. 11): The High Empire, AD 70–192*, p.6.
42. Dio 64.9.2; Tacitus, *Histories*, 2.82–83, 2.96.
43. Tacitus, *Histories*, 2.74.
44. Tacitus, *Histories*, 2.82, 2.84; Campbell, J. B., *The Emperor and the Roman Army 31 BC–AD 235*, p.91.

45. Dio 64.9.3: Tacitus, *Histories*, 2.85, 2.96; Levick, Barbara, *Vespasian*, p.59; Wiedemann, T. E., 'From Nero to Vespasian', in Bowman, A. K. & Champlin, E., *The Cambridge Ancient History (Vol. 10)*, p.274; Brunt, P. A., 'Tacitus on the Batavian Revolt', *Latomus*, T. 19, Fasc. 3 (July–September 1960), pp.494–517.
46. Tacitus, *Histories*, 2.96.
47. Tacitus, *Histories*, 2.84, 3.2.
48. Tacitus, *Histories*, 2.86, 3.50; Wiedemann, T. E., 'From Nero to Vespasian', in Bowman, A. K. & Champlin, E., *The Cambridge Ancient History (Vol. 10)*, p.275.
49. Tacitus, *Histories*, 3.3. Also see Dio 64.9.3; Wiedemann, T. E., 'From Nero to Vespasian', in Bowman, A. K. & Champlin, E., *The Cambridge Ancient History (Vol. 10)*, p.275.
50. Tacitus, *Histories*, 2.86.
51. Tacitus, *Histories*, 4.13, 5.26; Connal, Robert, 'Rational Mutiny in the Year of Four Emperors', *Arctos* 46 (2012), pp.33–52.
52. Tacitus, *Histories*, 3.8; Wiedemann, T. E., 'From Nero to Vespasian', in Bowman, A. K. and Champlin, E., *The Cambridge Ancient History (Vol. 10)*, p.276.
53. Tacitus, *Histories*, 3.71;Wellesley, Kenneth, *The Year of the Four Emperors*, pp.192–95.
54. Tacitus, *Histories*, 3.74; Wellesley, Kenneth, *The Year of the Four Emperors*, pp.194–95.
55. Tacitus, *Histories*, 3.84.
56. Tacitus, *Histories*, 3.85.

Chapter 8

1. Tacitus, *Germania*, 14; Haynes, Holly, *The History of Make-Believe: Tacitus on Imperial Rome* (University of California Press, 2003), p.161.
2. Tacitus, *Annals*, 3.42.
3. Tacitus, *Germania*, 29; Siofstra, Jan, 'Batavians and Romans on the Lower Rhine: The Romanisation of a Frontier Area', *Archaeological Dialogues*, 9 (2002), pp.16–38; Roymans, Nico, *Ethnic Identity and Imperial Power: The Batavians in the Early Roman Empire* (Amsterdam University Press, 2004), pp.205, 246, 249; Gerrish, Jennifer, 'Sertorius, Civilis, Rome and Exile in Tacitus' Histories', *Classical Journal*, Vol. 116, No. 4 (April–May 2021), pp.473–98; Van Enckevort, Harry & Heirbaut, Elly N. A., 'Nijmegen, from Oppidum Batavorum to Ulpia Noviomagus, Civitas of the Batavi: Two Successive Civitas-Capitals', *Gallia*, Vol. 72, No. 1, La Naissance des Capitales de Cités en Gaule Chevelue (2015), pp.285–98.
4. Tacitus, *Germania*, 29; Tacitus, *Histories*, 4.12; Siofstra, Jan, 'Batavians and Romans on the Lower Rhine', *Archaeological Dialogues*, 9 (2002), p.25.
5. Dio 55.24.7; Tacitus, *Germania*, 29; Tacitus, *Histories*, 4.12; Rossum, J. A. van, *The End of the Batavian Auxiliaries as 'National' Units in Roman Rule and Civic Life: Local and Regional Perspectives* (Brill, 2004), pp.115, 124. For the funerary monument see AE 1952, 0148; Siofstra, Jan, 'Batavians and Romans on the Lower Rhine', *Archaeological Dialogues*, 9 (2002), p.25; Roymans, Nico, *Ethnic Identity and Imperial Power*, p.249; Van Enckevort, Harry & Heirbaut, Elly N. A., 'Nijmegen, from Oppidum Batavorum to Ulpia Noviomagus, Civitas of the Batavi', *Gallia*, Vol. 72, No. 1 (2015), pp.285–98.
6. Rossum, J. A. van, *The End of the Batavian Auxiliaries as 'National' Units in Roman Rule and Civic Life*, pp.125–28; Roymans, Nico, *Ethnic Identity and Imperial Power*, p.208.
7. Roymans, Nico, *Ethnic Identity and Imperial Power*, p.197; Van Enckevort, Harry & Heirbaut, Elly N. A., 'Nijmegen, from Oppidum Batavorum to Ulpia Noviomagus, Civitas of the Batavi', *Gallia*, Vol. 72, No. 1 (2015), pp.285–98.

8. Roymans, Nico, *Ethnic Identity and Imperial Power*, pp.197, 201; Siofstra, Jan, 'Batavians and Romans on the Lower Rhine', *Archaeological Dialogues*, 9 (2002), p.26.
9. Tacitus, *Histories*, 4.13, 5.26; Siofstra, Jan, 'Batavians and Romans on the Lower Rhine', *Archaeological Dialogues*, 9 (2002), p.25; Levick, Barbara, *Vespasian*, p.108; Master, Jonathan, *Provincial Soldiers and Imperial Instability in the Histories of Tacitus*, p.147.
10. Tacitus, *Histories*, 4.13, 5.26; Levick, Barbara, *Vespasian*, p.108; Master, Jonathan, *Provincial Soldiers and Imperial Instability in the Histories of Tacitus*, p.37.
11. Tacitus, *Histories*, 1.59.
12. Tacitus, *Histories*, 2.27; Siofstra, Jan, 'Batavians and Romans on the Lower Rhine', *Archaeological Dialogues*, 9 (2002), p.32.
13. Tacitus, *Histories*, 2.27, 2.64.
14. Tacitus, *Histories*, 2.28.
15. Keppie, Lawrence, 'The Army and the Navy', in Bowman, A. Champlin, E. & Lintott, A. (eds), *The Cambridge Ancient History* (Cambridge University Press, 1996), pp.378, 391; Chilver, G. E. F., 'The Army in Politics, A.D. 68–70', *The Journal of Roman Studies*, Vol. 47, No. 1/2 (1957), pp.29–35; Campbell, J. B., *The Emperor and the Roman Army 31 BC–AD 235*, pp.161–63; Watson, G. R., *The Roman Soldier*, pp.100, 109, 148.
16. Tacitus, *Agricola*, 35; Tacitus, *Histories*, 2.28–29; Master, Jonathan, *Provincial Soldiers and Imperial Instability in the Histories of Tacitus* (University of Michigan Press, 2016), pp.50, 58.
17. Tacitus, *Histories*, 2.66.
18. Tacitus, *Histories*, 2.66.
19. Tacitus, *Histories*, 2.68.
20. Tacitus, *Histories*, 2.68.
21. Tacitus, *Histories*, 2.69.
22. Tacitus, *Histories*, 2.97; Levick, Barbara, *Vespasian*, pp.44, 108.
23. Tacitus, *Histories*, 4.14; Rossum, J. A. van, *The End of the Batavian Auxiliaries as 'National' Units in Roman Rule and Civic Life*, p.120; Van Enckevort, Harry & Heirbaut, Elly N. A., 'Nijmegen, from Oppidum Batavorum to Ulpia Noviomagus, Civitas of the Batavi', *Gallia*, Vol. 72, No. 1, (2015), pp.285–98; Brunt, P. A., 'Tacitus on the Batavian Revolt', *Latomus*, T. 19, Fasc. 3 (July–September 1960), pp.494–517; Master, Jonathan, *Provincial Soldiers and Imperial Instability in the Histories of Tacitus*, p.40.
24. Tacitus, *Histories*, 4.13; Brunt, P. A., 'Tacitus on the Batavian Revolt', *Latomus*, T. 19, Fasc. 3 (July–September 1960), pp.494–517; Campbell, J. B., *The Emperor and the Roman Army 31 BC–AD 235*, p.369.
25. Tacitus, *Histories*, 4.14, 4.61; Dyson, Stephen L., 'Native Revolts in the Roman Empire', *Historia: Zeitschrift für Alte Geschichte*, Bd. 20, H. 2/3 (2nd Qtr, 1971), pp.239–74; Aldhouse-Green, Miranda, *Caesar's Druids: Story of an Ancient Priesthood* (Yale University Press, 2010), p.233.
26. Roymans, Nico, *Ethnic Identity and Imperial Power*, pp.202, 209, 242–43, 247; Rossum, J. A. van, *The End of the Batavian Auxiliaries as 'National' Units in Roman Rule and Civic Life*, p.130.
27. Tacitus, *Germania*, 3; Tacitus, *Histories*, 4.32.
28. Tacitus, *Histories*, 4.13; Gerrish, Jennifer, 'Sertorius, Civilis, Rome and Exile in Tacitus' Histories', *Classical Journal*, Vol. 116, No. 4 (April–May 2021), pp.473–98; Dyson, Stephen L., 'Native Revolts in the Roman Empire', *Historia: Zeitschrift für Alte Geschichte*, Bd. 20, H. 2/3 (2nd Qtr, 1971), pp.239–74.
29. Tacitus, *Histories*, 4.15; Levick, Barbara, *Vespasian*, p.109; Flaig, E., 'Romer werden um jeden Preis? Integrationskapazitlit und Integrationswilligkeit am Beispiel des

Bataveraufstandes', in Weinmann-Walser, M. (ed)., *Historische Interpretationen: Gerold Walser zum 75.* Geburtstag, dargebracht von Freunden, Kollegen, Schulern (Stuttgart, 1995), pp.45–60.

30. Tacitus, *Histories*, 4.15.
31. Ptolemy, *Geography*, 2.9.1; Tacitus, *Histories*, 4.15; Roymans, Nico, *Ethnic Identity and Imperial Power*, p.206; Haynes, Holly, *The History of Make-Believe: Tacitus on Imperial Rome*, pp.149–50; Venmans, L. A. W. C., 'De Incendio Castrorum Romanorum, Quae Fuerunt In Media Urbe Traiecto ad Rhenum', *Mnemosyne*, 3(1) (1935), pp.83–87.
32. Tacitus, *Histories*, 4.15.
33. Tacitus, *Histories*, 4.16.
34. Tacitus, *Histories*, 4.16; Siofstra, Jan, 'Batavians and Romans on the Lower Rhine', *Archaeological Dialogues*, 9 (2002), p.32.
35. Tacitus, *Histories*, 4.17; Rossum, J. A. van, *The End of the Batavian Auxiliaries as 'National' Units in Roman Rule and Civic Life*, p.128.
36. Tacitus, *Histories*, 4.18, 4.63; Rossum, J. A. van, *The End of the Batavian Auxiliaries as 'National' Units in Roman Rule and Civic Life*, p.115; Siofstra, Jan, 'Batavians and Romans on the Lower Rhine', *Archaeological Dialogues*, 9 (2002), p.32.
37. Tacitus, *Histories*, 4.18; Levick, Barbara, *Vespasian*, p.108.
38. Tacitus, *Histories*, 4.18.
39. Tacitus, *Histories*, 4.19; Brunt, P. A., 'Tacitus on the Batavian Revolt', *Latomus*, T. 19, Fasc. 3 (July–September 1960), pp.494–517.
40. Tacitus, *Histories*, 4.19.
41. Tacitus, *Histories*, 4.20.
42. Tacitus, *Histories*, 4.20.
43. Tacitus, *Histories*, 4.21
44. Tacitus, *Histories*, 4.61; Levick, Barbara, *Vespasian*, p.109; Dyson, Stephen L., 'Native Revolts in the Roman Empire', *Historia: Zeitschrift für Alte Geschichte*, Bd. 20, H. 2/3 (2nd Qtr, 1971), pp.239–74; Aldhouse-Green, Miranda, *Caesar's Druids: Story of an Ancient Priesthood* (Yale University Press, 2010), p.233.
45. Tacitus, *Histories*, 4.22–23; Keppie, Lawrence, 'The Changing Face of the Roman Legions (49 BC–AD 69)', *Papers of the British School at Rome*, Vol. 65 (1997), pp.89–102.
46. Tacitus, *Histories*, 4.23.
47. Tacitus, *Histories*, 4.23.
48. Tacitus, *Histories*, 4.24; Connal, Robert, 'Rational Mutiny in the Year of Four Emperors', *Arctos* 46 (2012), pp.33–52.
49. Tacitus, *Histories*, 4.25.
50. Tacitus, *Histories*, 4.25; Fulkerson, Laurel, *Staging a Mutiny: Competitive Role Playing on the Rhine (Annals 1.31–51)* (Cambridge University Press, 2014), p.183.
51. Tacitus, *Histories*, 4.27.
52. Tacitus, *Histories*, 4.25.
53. CIL VI. 1402 records his first post as a military tribune with *Legio I.* This may have been the *I Germanica* or *I Minerva*; Tacitus, *Histories*, 4.56, Syme, R., 'Partisans of Galba', *Historia: Zeitschrift für Alte Geschichte*, Bd. 31, H. 4 (4th Qtr, 1982), pp.460–83.
54. Tacitus, *Histories*, 4.26, 4.28; Carbone, Martin, E., 'The First Relief of Castra Vetera in the Revolt of Civilis (A Note on Tacitus 'Hist.' 4.26.3), *Phoenix*, Vol. 21, No. 4 (Winter, 1967), pp.296–98.
55. Tacitus, *Histories*, 4.26.
56. Tacitus, *Histories*, 4.27.

57. Tacitus, *Histories*, 4.28.
58. Tacitus, *Histories*, 4.28.
59. Tacitus, *Histories*, 4.29.
60. Tacitus, *Histories*, 4.29.
61. Tacitus, *Histories*, 4.30.
62. Tacitus, *Histories*, 4.31; Connal, Robert, 'Rational Mutiny in the Year of Four Emperors', *Arctos* 46 (2012), pp.33–52.
63. Tacitus, *Histories*, 4.32; Connal, Robert, 'Rational Mutiny in the Year of Four Emperors', *Arctos* 46 (2012), pp.33–52; Campbell, J. B., *The Emperor and the Roman Army 31 BC–AD 235*, pp.29, 369.
64. Tacitus, *Histories*, 4.32.
65. Tacitus, *Histories*, 4.32.
66. Brunt, P. A., 'Tacitus on the Batavian Revolt', *Latomus*, T. 19, Fasc. 3 (July–September 1960), pp.494–517; Wiedemann, T. E. J., 'From Nero to Vespasian', in Bowman, A., Champlin, E. & Lintott, A. (eds), *The Cambridge Ancient History* (1996), p.280.
67. Tacitus, *Histories*, 4.33–34.
68. Tacitus, *Histories*, 4.33–34.
69. Tacitus, *Histories*, 4.34.
70. Tacitus, *Histories*, 4.35.
71. Tacitus, *Histories*, 4.35.
72. Tacitus, *Histories*, 4.36.
73. Tacitus, *Histories*, 4.37.
74. Tacitus, *Histories*, 4.37–38.
75. Tacitus, *Histories*, 4.55; Siofstra, Jan, 'Batavians and Romans on the Lower Rhine', *Archaeological Dialogues*, 9 (2002), p.27; Wiedemann, T. E. J., 'From Nero to Vespasian', in Bowman, Champlin & Lintott (eds), *The Cambridge Ancient History* (1996), p.281.
76. Tacitus, *Histories*, 4.55. Also see Dio 65.3.1.
77. Tacitus, *Histories*, 4.56, 4.67; Haynes, Holly, *The History of Make-Believe: Tacitus on Imperial Rome*, p.155; Wiedemann, T. E. J., 'From Nero to Vespasian', in Bowman, Champlin & Lintott (eds), *The Cambridge Ancient History* (1996), p.281.
78. Tacitus, *Histories*, 4.54; Haynes, Holly, *The History of Make-Believe: Tacitus on Imperial Rome*, p.160; Aldhouse-Green, Miranda, *Caesar's Druids: Story of an Ancient Priesthood*, p. 232.
79. Tacitus, *Histories*, 4.56.
80. Tacitus, *Histories*, 4.57; Keppie, Lawrence, 'The Army and the Navy', in Bowman, Champlin & Lintott (eds), *The Cambridge Ancient History*, p.395.
81. Tacitus, *Histories*, 4.59; Haynes, Holly, *The History of Make-Believe: Tacitus on Imperial Rome*, p.159; Carbone, Martin, E., 'The First Relief of Castra Vetera in the Revolt of Civilis', *Phoenix*, Vol. 21, No. 4 (Winter, 1967), pp.296–98.
82. Tacitus, *Histories*, 4.59.
83. Tacitus, *Histories*, 4.60; Connal, Robert, 'Rational Mutiny in the Year of Four Emperors', *Arctos* 46 (2012), pp.33–52.
84. Tacitus, *Germania*, 31; Tacitus, *Histories*, 4.61.
85. Tacitus, *Histories*, 4.61; Parker, Philip, *The Empire Stops Here, A Journey Along the Frontiers of the Roman World* (Pimlico, 2009), p.128.
86. Tacitus, *Histories*, 4.61, 4.63–65, 4.79; Levick, Barbara, *Vespasian*, p.110.
87. Tacitus, *Histories*, 4.66.
88. Tacitus, *Histories*, 4.67.

89. Tacitus, *Histories*, 4.68, 4.76; Levick, Barbara, *Vespasian*, p.110; Brunt, P. A., 'Tacitus on the Batavian Revolt', *Latomus*, T. 19, Fasc. 3 (July–September 1960), pp.494–517.
90. Tacitus, *Histories*, 4.70.
91. Tacitus, *Histories*, 4.70–71, 5.21; Levick, Barbara, *Vespasian*, p.111; Siofstra, Jan, 'Batavians and Romans on the Lower Rhine', *Archaeological Dialogues*, 9 (2002), p.33.
92. Tacitus, *Histories*, 4.72; Connal, Robert, 'Rational Mutiny in the Year of Four Emperors', *Arctos* 46 (2012), pp.33–52.
93. Tacitus, *Histories*, 4.72; Wiedemann, T. E. J.' 'From Nero to Vespasian', in Bowman, Champlin & Lintott (eds), *The Cambridge Ancient History* (1996), p.281; Master, Jonathan, *Provincial Soldiers and Imperial Instability in the Histories of Tacitus*, p.37.
94. Phang, Sara Elise, *Roman Military Service, Ideologies of Discipline in the Late Republic and Early Principate* (Cambridge University Press, 2008), p.145.
95. Tacitus, *Histories*, 4.76–79, 5.23; Dyson, Stephen L., 'Native Revolts in the Roman Empire', *Historia: Zeitschrift für Alte Geschichte*, Bd. 20, H. 2/3 (2nd Qtr, 1971), pp.239–74.
96. Dio 65.3.3; Levick, Barbara, *Vespasian*, p.112.
97. Tacitus, *Histories*, 5.24; Statius, *Silvae*, 1.4; Siofstra, Jan, 'Batavians and Romans on the Lower Rhine', *Archaeological Dialogues*, 9 (2002), p.32; Dyson, Stephen L., 'Native Revolts in the Roman Empire', *Historia: Zeitschrift für Alte Geschichte*, Bd. 20, H. 2/3 (2nd Qtr, 1971), pp.239–74; Van Enckevort, Harry & Heirbaut, Elly N. A., 'Nijmegen, from Oppidum Batavorum to Ulpia Noviomagus, Civitas of the Batavi', *Gallia*, Vol. 72, No. 1 (2015), pp.285–98.
98. Tacitus, *Histories*, 5.26; Wiedemann, T. E. J., 'From Nero to Vespasian', in Bowman, Champlin & Lintott (eds), *The Cambridge Ancient History* (1996), p.281; Campbell, J. B., *The Emperor and the Roman Army 31 BC–AD 235*, p.369.

Chapter 9

1. Dio, 67.1.2, 67.16.1; Suetonius, *Titus*, 10; Suetonius, *Domitian*, 1–2.4, 15; Philostratus, *Life of Apollonius*, 7.24; Southern, Pat, *Domitian, Tragic Tyrant*, pp.120–22.
2. Suetonius, *Domitian*, 8; Jones, Brian W., *The Emperor Domitian*, pp.99–100.
3. Ryan, F. X., 'The Lex Scantinia and the Prosecution of Censors and Aediles', *Classical Philology*, Vol. 89, No. 2 (April 1994), pp.159–62; Charles, Michael B. & Anagnostou-Laoutides, Eva, 'The Sexual Hypocrisy of Domitian: Suet., Dom. 8, 3', *L'Antiquité Classique*, T. 79 (2010), pp.173–87; Bauman, R. A., 'The Résumé of Legislation in Suetonius', *Aus der Zeitschrift Zeitschrift der Savigny-Stiftung für Rechtsgeschichte: Romanistische Abteilung*, 99 (1982), pp.81–127; Jones, Brian W., *The Emperor Domitian*, p.171.
4. Suetonius, *Domitian*, 8; Jones, Brian W., *The Emperor Domitian*, p.147; Bauman, Richard A., *Crime and Punishment in Ancient Rome* (Taylor & Francis Group, 1996), pp.71–72.
5. Aelian fr. 112 (Hercher); Suda A 2762; PIR^2 A 874; CIL IX 5420; Syme, R., *Antonius Saturninus*, Roman Papers vol. III (Oxford University Press, 1984), pp.1070–85; Jones, Brian W., *The Emperor Domitian*, p.145.
6. Suda A 2762.
7. Aelian fr. 115b D-F (112 Hercher); Bennett, Julian, *Trajan: Optimus Princeps* (Routledge, 2001), p.29.
8. Suetonius, *Domitian*, 10.
9. Dio 67.11.4.

10. Epitome de Caesaribus 11.9.
11. Southern, Pat, *Domitian, Tragic Tyrant*, p.101; Syme, Ronald, *Domitian: The Last Years* (Chiron, 1983), pp.121–46.
12. Southern, Pat, *Domitian, Tragic Tyrant*, p.105; Syme, R., *Antonius Saturninus*, Roman Papers vol. III, pp.1070–85.
13. Dio 67.112–13.
14. Suetonius, *Domitian*, 7.
15. Southern, Pat, *Domitian, Tragic Tyrant,* p.105; Murison, C. L., 'The Revolt of Saturninus in Upper Germany, A.D. 89', *Echos du monde classique: Classical views*, Vol. XXIX, n.s. 4, No. 1 (1985), pp.31–49; Syme, Ronald, *Domitian: The Last Years*, pp.121–46.
16. Martial, *Epigrams*, IV.XI.
17. Jones, Brian W., *The Emperor Domitian*, p.147.
18. *Acta Fratrum Arvalium* of AD 88–89; Southern, Pat, *Domitian, Tragic Tyrant*, p.101.
19. Dio 67.3.5; Suetonius, *Domitian*, 7.3, 23; Philostratus, *Lives of the Sophists*, 1.7.1; Murison, C. L., 'The Revolt of Saturninus in Upper Germany, A.D. 89', *Echos du monde classique: Classical views*, Vol. XXIX, n.s. 4, No. 1 (1985), pp.31–49; Watson, G. R., *The Roman Soldier*, p.91; Jones, Brian W., *The Emperor Domitian*, p.142; Berriman, Andrew & Todd, Malcolm, 'A Very Roman Coup: The Hidden War of Imperial Succession, AD 96–8', *Historia: Zeitschrift für Alte Geschichte*, Bd. 50, H. 3 (3rd Qtr, 2001), pp.312–31; Waters, K. H., 'The Character of Domitian', *Phoenix*, Vol. 18, No. 1 (Spring, 1964), pp.49–77; Campbell, J. B., *The Emperor and the Roman Army 31 BC–AD 235*, pp.44–45.
20. Jones, Brian W., *The Emperor Domitian*, pp.126–31; Southern, Pat, *Domitian, Tragic Tyrant,* pp.79–85.
21. Suetonius, *Domitian*, 6.
22. Pliny, *Panegyric*, 14.5; Jones, Brian W., *The Emperor Domitian*, p.145; Bennett, Julian, *Trajan: Optimus Princeps*, p.30.
23. Dio 67.11.1; Southern, Pat, *Domitian, Tragic Tyrant*, p.102; Murison, C. L., 'The Revolt of Saturninus in Upper Germany, A.D. 89', *Echos du monde classique: Classical views*, Vol. XXIX, n.s. 4, No. 1 (1985), pp.31–49; Starr, Chester G., *The Roman Imperial Navy, 31 BC–AD 324* (Cornell University Press, 1975), pp.146–47; Syme, Ronald, *Domitian: The Last Years*, pp.121–46; Bennett, Julian, *Trajan: Optimus Princeps*, p.30.
24. Martial, *Epigrams*, IX.84.
25. Dio 67.15.2.
26. Suetonius, *Domitian*, 6; ILS 1006; Statius, *Silvae*, 3.3.168; Southern, Pat, *Domitian, Tragic Tyrant*, p.102; Jones, Brian W., *The Emperor Domitian*, pp.148, 150; Bennett, Julian, *Trajan: Optimus Princeps*, p.30.
27. Southern, Pat, *Domitian, Tragic Tyrant,* pp.106, 110; Jones, Brain W., *The Emperor Domitian*, p.151; Berriman, Andrew & Todd, Malcolm, 'A Very Roman Coup: The Hidden War of Imperial Succession, AD 96–8', *Historia: Zeitschrift für Alte Geschichte*, Bd. 50, H. 3 (3rd Qtr, 2001), pp.312–31; Bennett, Julian, *Trajan: Optimus Princeps*, p.243 n.19.
28. Dio 67.12.2–4; Tacitus, *Agricola*, 42; Rutledge, Steven H., *Imperial Inquisitions, Prosecutors and Informers from Tiberius to Domitian* (Routledge, 2001), loc. 3127 & 4191, believes the prosecution of Cerealis to be linked to the revolt of Saturninus rather than the 'False Nero'. Jones, Brian W., 'Senatorial Influence in the Revolt of Saturninus', *Latomus*, T. 33, Fasc. 3 (July–September 1974), pp.529–35; Roche, P. A., 'The Execution of L. Salvius Otho Cocceianus', *The Classical Quarterly*, New Series, Vol. 53, No. 1 (May 2003), pp.319–22.

29. Dio 67.11.5; ZPE-165-219 & ZPE-165-227; Southern, Pat, *Domitian, Tragic Tyrant*, p.103.
30. Plutarch, *Aemilius Paulus*, 25.4.
31. Suetonius, *Tiberius*, 25.
32. Jones, Brian W., *The Emperor Domitian*, pp.151–52.
33. Suetonius, *Domitian*, 7; Southern, Pat, *Domitian, Tragic Tyrant*, pp.105–08; Jones, Brian W., 'Senatorial Influence in the Revolt of Saturninus, *Latomus*, T. 33, Fasc. 3 (July–September 1974), pp.529–35; Watson, G. R., *The Roman Soldier*, p.49.
34. Southern, Pat, *Domitian, Tragic Tyrant*, p.104.
35. Dio 67.9.1–3, 67.9.6; Paterson, J., 'Friends in High Places: the Creation of the Court of the Roman Emperor', in Spawforth, A. J. S. (ed.), *The Court and Court Society in Ancient Monarchies* (Cambridge University Press, 2007), p.150; Waters, K. H., 'The Character of Domitian', *Phoenix*, Vol. 18, No. 1 (Spring, 1964), pp.49–77; Southern, Pat, *Domitian, Tragic Tyrant*, p.120, notes that Dio places the banquet in AD 89, and contextually it fits with Domitian's increased insecurity after the revolt.
36. Dio 67.9.4.
37. Dio 67.9.5; Jones, Brian W., 'Domitian and the Court', *Pallas*, No. 40 (1994), pp.329–35.
38. Dio 68.3.3; Epitome De Caesaribus 12, 7–8 Rutledge, Steven H., *Imperial Inquisitions, Prosecutors and Informers from Tiberius to Domitian*, loc. 164, 3127–37, 4191; Jones, Brian W., 'Senatorial Influence in the Revolt of Saturninus', *Latomus*, T. 33, Fasc. 3 (July–September 1974), pp.529–35.

Conclusion

1. Phang, Sara Elise, *Roman Military Service, Ideologies of Discipline in the Late Republic and Early Principate*, pp.15–16; MacMullen, Ramsay, 'The Legion as Society', *Historia: Zeitschrift für Alte Geschichte*, Bd. 33, H. 4 (4th Qtr, 1984), pp.440–56.
2. Kajanto, Iiro, 'Tacitus' Attitude to War and the Soldier', *Latomus* , T. 29, Fasc. 3 (July–September 1970), pp.699–718; Phang, Sara Elise, *Roman Military Service*, p.18.
3. Phang, Sara Elise, *Roman Military Service*, p.111; Hammond, Mason, 'The Transmission of the Powers of the Roman Emperor from the Death of Nero in A.D. 68 to That of Alexander Severus in A.D. 235', *Memoirs of the American Academy in Rome*, Vol. 24 (1956), pp.63–133.
4. Phang, Sara Elise, *Roman Military Service*, pp.112, 129–30; Lammers, Cornelis J., 'Strikes and Mutinies: A Comparative Study of Organizational Conflicts between Rulers and Ruled', *Administrative Science Quarterly*, Vol. 14, No. 4, 'Conflict within and between Organizations' (December 1969), pp.558–72; Campbell, J. B., *The Emperor and the Roman Army 31 BC–AD 235*, p.311.
5. Tacitus, *Annals*, 1.1–8; Tacitus, *Histories*, 2.2; Keppie, L., 'The Army and the Navy', in Bowman, A. K., Champlin, E. & Lintott, A. (eds), *The Cambridge Ancient History* (Cambridge University Press, 1996), p.391; Phang, Sara Elise, *Roman Military Service*, p.144; MacMullen, Ramsay, 'The Legion as Society', *Historia: Zeitschrift für Alte Geschichte*, Bd. 33, H. 4 (4th Qtr, 1984), pp.440–56; Watson, G. R., *The Roman Soldier*, p.37.
6. Campbell, J. B., *The Emperor and the Roman Army 31 BC–AD 235*, p.178; Watson, G. R., *The Roman Soldier*, pp.103–04, 178.
7. Tacitus, *Annals*, 1.17–18, 1.37, 1.39, 1.44; Keppie, L., 'The Army and the Navy', in Bowman, Champlin & Lintott (eds), *The Cambridge Ancient History*, pp.377–78.

8. Tacitus, *Annals*, 1.20–23, 1.34; Woodman, A. J., 'Mutiny and Madness: Tacitus "Annals" 1.16–49', *Arethusa*, Vol. 39, No. 2, 'Ingens Eloquentiae Materia: Rhetoric and Empire in Tacitus' (Spring 2006), pp.303–29.
9. Suetonius, *Nero*, 48; Tacitus, *Histories*, 1.5; Tacitus, *Annals*, 2.76; Plutarch, *Galba*, 2, 8, 14.3; Campbell, J. B., *The Emperor and the Roman Army 31 BC–AD 235*, p.31.
10. Tacitus, *Histories*, 3.72; Suetonius, *Otho*, 1.4.
11. Tacitus, *Histories*, 2.76; Saller, R. P., *Personal Patronage Under the Early Empire* (Cambridge University Press, 1982), pp.21, 29, 41, 69; Wellesley, Kenneth, *The Year of the Four Emperors*, p.117.
12. Seneca, *De Beneficia*, 7.31.1; Saller, R. P., *Personal Patronage Under the Early Empire*, pp.13–15.
13. Tacitus, *Annals*, 1.65, 14.40; Tacitus, *Histories*, 1.37.3, 1.65; Suetonius, *Vitellius*, 7; Suetonius, *Galba*, 10; Dio 64.5.2–3; Plutarch, *Galba*, 5, 20.4.
14. Lammers, Cornelis J., 'Strikes and Mutinies', *Administrative Science Quarterly*, Vol. 14, No. 4 (December 1969), pp.558–72; Messer, William Stuart, 'Mutiny in the Roman Army. The Republic', *Classical Philology*, Vol. 15, No. 2 (April 1920), pp.158–75.
15. Tacitus, *Annals*, 1.38; Phang, Sara Elise, *Roman Military Service*, p.123.
16. Tacitus, *Histories*, 1.36, 1.82, 2.60; Connal, Robert, 'Rational Mutiny in the Year of Four Emperors', *Arctos* 46 (2012), pp.33–52.
17. Tacitus, *Annals*, 1.28; Campbell, J. B., *The Emperor and the Roman Army 31 BC–AD 235*, pp.25, 27, 100.
18. Tacitus, *Annals*, 1.43; Connal, Robert, 'Rational Mutiny in the Year of Four Emperors, *Arctos* 46 (2012), pp.33–52; Campbell, J. B., *The Emperor and the Roman Army 31 BC–AD 235*, pp. 31, 187.
19. Tacitus, *Annals*, 1.30.
20. Tacitus, *Annals*, 1.44, 1.48–49.
21. Plutarch, Galba, 26.4; Connal, Robert, 'Rational Mutiny in the Year of Four Emperors', *Arctos* 46 (2012), pp.33–52; Campbell, J. B., *The Emperor and the Roman Army 31 BC–AD 235*, p.29.
22. Suetonius, *Claudius*, 13; Suetonius, *Titus*, 5; Suetonius, *Vespasian*, 5; Tacitus, *Histories*, 2.2–4, 2.78.
23. Tacitus, *Histories*, 2.98; MacMullen, Ramsay, *Changes in the Roman Empire, Essays in the Ordinary*, p.199.
24. Campbell, J. B., *The Emperor and the Roman Army 31 BC–AD 235*, p.198.
25. Tacitus, *Histories*, 3.36.
26. Tacitus, *Histories*, 2.82.
27. Tacitus, *Annals*, 11.1.2; Tacitus, *Histories*, 2.6, 2.82–84, 2.92; Breeze, David J., 'Pay Grades and Ranks below the Centurionate', *The Journal of Roman Studies*, Vol. 61 (1971), pp.130–35; Phang, Sara Elise, *Roman Military Service*, p.16; Campbell, J. B., *The Emperor and the Roman Army 31 BC–AD 235*, pp.102–06; MacMullen, Ramsay, *Changes in the Roman Empire, Essays in the Ordinary*, p.200.
28. Tacitus, *Histories*, 2.5; Campbell, J. B., *The Emperor and the Roman Army 31 BC–AD 235*, p.149.
29. Tacitus, *Histories*, 2.5; Suetonius, *Gaius*, 9; Suetonius, *Vitellius*, 7; Phang, Sara Elise, *Roman Military Service*, p.33.
30. Lendon, J. E., 'Contubernalis, Commanipularis, and Commilito in Roman Soldiers' Epigraphy: Drawing the Distinction', *Zeitschrift für Papyrologie und Epigraphik*, Bd. 157 (2006), pp.270–76.

31. Tacitus, *Annals*, 4.30; Suetonius, *Vitellius*, 8.
32. Suetonius, *Vespasian*, 6.
33. Tacitus, *Histories*, 2.74.
34. Tacitus, *Histories*, 2.80.
35. Tacitus, *Histories*, 2.80.

Bibliography

Abbreviations

AE *L'Annee Epigraphique* (Paris, 1888)
CIL *Corpus Inscriptionum Latinarum* (Berlin, 1867)
ILS Dessau, H., *Inscriptiones Latinae Selectae* (Berlin, 1892–1916)
PIR *Prosopographia Imperii Romani* (Berlin and Leipzig, 1933)

Ancient Sources

Aurelius Victor, *De Caesaribus*, trans. Bird, H. W. (Liverpool University Press, 1994)
Cassius Dio, *Roman History* (Loeb Classical Library, 1989, trans. Cary, E.)
Epictetus, *Discourses*, trans. Oldfather, W. A. (Loeb, 1989)
Epitome de Caesaribus, https://web.archive.org/web/20220311020340/http://www.roman-emperors.org/epitome.htm
Josephus, *Jewish Antiquities* (Wordsworth Classics of World Literature, 2006)
Josephus, *The Jewish Wars*, trans. Hammond, Martin (Oxford University Press, 2017)
Justinian, *Digest of Justinian* (University of Pennsylvania Press, 2008)
Juvenal, *Satires*, in Juvenal and Persius, trans. Braund, Susanna Morton (Loeb, 2004)
Macrobius, *Saturnalia*, trans. Kaster, Robert A. (Loeb, 2010)
Martial, *Epigrams*, trans. Nisbet, Gideon (Oxford University Press, 2015)
Perseus, *Satires*, in Juvenal and Perseus, trans. Braund, Susanna Morton (Loeb, 2004)
Philostratus, *Life of Apollonius of Tyana* (Legare Street Press, 2022)
Philostratus, *Lives of the Sophists*, in Philostratus, Lives of the Sophists, and Eunapius, Lives of the Philosophers (Loeb, 1813)
Pliny the Elder, *Natural History*, trans. Bostock, John (independently published, 2021)
Pliny the Younger, *Letters* (Loeb Classical Library, 1989, Vol. 1, trans. Radice, Betty)
Pliny the Younger, *Panegyricus*, (Loeb Classical Library, 1989, Vol. 1, trans. Radice, Betty)
Plutarch, *Life of Aemilius Paulus,* trans. Perrin, Bernadotte (Loeb Classical Library, 1989)
Plutarch, *Life of Caesar*, in Fall of the Roman Republic (Penguin, 1982)
Plutarch, *Life of Galba*, in Lives, Vol. XI (Loeb, 1989)
Plutarch, *Life of Otho*, Volu. XI (Loeb, 1989)
Seneca, *Moral and Political Essays*, trans. Cooper, John M. (Cambridge University Press, 1995)
Seneca, *The Apocolocyntosis of the Divine Claudius* (Penguin Classics,1986, trans. Sullivan, J. P.)
Statius, *Silvae*, trans. Shackleton Bailey, D. R. (Loeb Classical Library, 2003)
Suetonius, *The Twelve Caesars* (Penguin Classics,1986)
Tacitus, *Agricola*, in Agricola and Germania, trans. Mattingly, H. (Penguin, 2010)
Tacitus, *Annals*, trans. Jackson, John (Loeb Classical Library, 1989)
Tacitus, *Germania*, in Agricola and Germania, trans. Mattingly, H. (Penguin, 2010)
Tacitus, *Histories*, trans. Moore, Clifford H. (Loeb, 1989)
Velleius Paterculus, *The Roman History*, trans. Yardley J. C. & Barrett, Anthony A. (Hackett Publishing Company, 2011)

Modern Sources

Aldhouse-Green, Miranda, *Caesar's Druids: Story of an Ancient Priesthood* (Yale University Press, 2010)

Bauman, Richard A., *Crime and Punishment in Ancient Rome* (Taylor & Francis Group, 1996)

Bauman, Richard A., 'The Resumé of Legislation in Suetonius', *Zeitschrift der Savigny-Stiftung für Rechtsgeschichte: Romanistische Abteilung*, 99(1) IV (1982)

Bellemore, Jane, 'Cassius Dio and the Chronology of A.D. 21', *The Classical Quarterly*, New Series, Vol. 53, No. 1 (May 2003)

Bennett, Julian, *Trajan: Optimus Princeps* (Routledge, 2001)

Berriman, Andrew, Todd, Malcolm & Todd, Malcolm, 'A Very Roman Coup: The Hidden War of Imperial Succession, AD 96–8', *Historia: Zeitschrift für Alte Geschichte*, Bd. 50, H. 3 (3rd Qtr, 2001)

Bingham, Sandra, *The Praetorian Guard, A History Of Rome's Special Forces* (Bloomsbury, 2013)

Bingham, Sandra, *The Praetorian Guard in the Political and Social Life of Julio-Claudian Rome* (University of British Columbia, PhD Thesis, 1997)

Birley, Anthony R., *The Fasti of Roman Britain* (Clarendon, 1981)

Breeze, David J., 'Pay Grades and Ranks below the Centurionate', *The Journal of Roman Studies*, Vol. 61 (1971)

Brice, Lee L., 'Indiscipline in the Roman Army of the Late Republic and Principate', in *New Approaches to Greek and Roman Warfare* (John Wiley & Sons, 2020), pp.113–26

Brunt, P. A., 'Pay and Superannuation in the Roman Army', *Papers of the British School at Rome*, Vol. 18 (1950)

Brunt, P. A., 'The Revolt of Vindex and the Fall of Nero', *Latomus*, T. 18, Fasc. 3 (July—September 1959)

Campbell, Brian, 'Who Were the "Viri Militares"?', *The Journal of Roman Studies*, Vol. 65 (1975)

Campbell, J. B., *The Emperor and the Roman Army 31 BC–AD 235* (Clarendon Press, 1984)

Carbone, Martin E., 'The First Relief of Castra Vetera in the Revolt of Civilis (A Note on Tacitus "Hist." 4.26.3)', *Phoenix*, Vol. 21, No. 4 (Winter, 1967)

Charles, Michael B. & Anagnostou-Laoutides, Eva, 'The Sexual Hypocrisy of Domitian: Suet., Dom. 8, 3', *L'Antiquité Classique* T. 79 (2010)

Chilver, G. E. F., 'The Army in Politics, A.D. 68–70', *The Journal of Roman Studies*, Vol. 47, No. 1/2 (1957)

Christopherson, A. J., 'The Provincial Assembly of the Three Gauls in the Julio-Claudian Period', *Historia: Zeitschrift für Alte Geschichte*, Bd. 17, H. 3 (July 1968)

Connal, Robert, 'Rational Mutiny in the Year of Four Emperors', *Arctos* 46 (2012)

Daly, Lawrence J., 'Verginius at Vesontio: The Incongruity of the "Bellum Neronis"', *Historia: Zeitschrift für Alte Geschichte*, Bd. 24, H. 1 (1st Qtr, 1975)

Dando-Collins, Stephen, *Legions of Rome, The Definitive History of Every Imperial Roman Legion* (Quercus, 2010)

Del Castillo, Arcadio, 'The Emperor Galba's Assumption of Power: Some Chronological Considerations', *Historia: Zeitschrift für Alte Geschichte*, Bd. 51, H. 4 (4th Qtr, 2002)

Dornberg, John, 'Battle of the Teutoburg Forest', *Archaeology*, Vol. 45, No. 5 (September/October 1992)

Drinkwater, J. F., 'The Rise and Fall of the Gallic Iulii: Aspects of the Development of the Aristocracy of the Three Gauls under the Early Empire', *Latomus*, T. 37, Fasc. 4 (October–December 1978)

Dyson, Stephen L., 'Native Revolts in the Roman Empire', *Historia: Zeitschrift für Alte Geschichte*, Bd. 20, H. 2/3 (2nd Qtr, 1971)

Eaton, Jonathan, 'The Political Significance of the Imperial Watchword in the Early Empire', *Greece & Rome* 58, no. 1 (2011)

Fields, Nic, *AD 69: Emperors, Armies and Anarchy* (Pen & Sword, 2014)

Fulkerson, Laurel, 'Staging a Mutiny: Competitive Roleplaying on the Rhine (Annals 1.31–51)', *Ramus* 35 (2)

Garzetti, Albino, *From Tiberius to the Antonines, A History of the Roman Empire AD 14–192* (Methuen and Co Ltd, 1974)

Gerrish, Jennifer, 'Sertorius, Civilis, Rome and Exile in Tacitus' Histories', *Classical Journal*, Vol. 116, No. 4 (April–May 2021)

Goudineau C., 'Gaul', in *The Augustan Empire, 43 BC–69 AD*, Cambridge Ancient History, Vol. 10, ed. Alan K. Bowman, Edward Champlin & Andrew Lintott (Cambridge University Press, 1996)

Graßl, Herbert, 'War Obultronius Sabinus Proconsul der Baetica und L. Cornelius Marcellus', *Historia: Zeitschrift für Alte Geschichte*, Bd. 25, H. 4 (4th Qtr, 1976)

Gregory, A. P., 'A Study in Survival: the Case of the Freedman L. Domitius Phaon', *Athenaeum* (1 January 1995)

Griffin, Miriam T., *Nero, The End of a Dynasty* (Routledge, 1984)

Griffin, Miriam T., 'The Flavians', in *The High Empire, AD 70–192*, Cambridge Ancient History, Vol. 11, ed. A.K. Bowman, P. Garnsey & D. Rathbone (Cambridge University Press, 2000)

Hainsworth, J. B., 'Verginius and Vindex', *Historia: Zeitschrift für Alte Geschichte*, Bd. 11, H. 1 (January 1962)

Hammond, Mason, 'The Transmission of the Powers of the Roman Emperor from the Death of Nero in 68 AD to That of Alexander Severus in AD 235', *Memoirs of the American Academy in Rome*, Vol. 24 (1956)

Haynes, Holly, *The History of Make-Believe: Tacitus on Imperial Rome* (University of California Press, 2003)

Henige, David, 'He Came, He Saw, He Counted: The Historiography and Demography of Caesar's Gallic Numbers', *Annales de Démographie Historique*, No. 1 (1998)

Holland, Richard, *Nero: the Man Behind the Myth* (Sutton Publishing, 2000)

Hirt, Alfred M., 'Gold and Silver Mining in the Roman Empire', https://livrepository.liverpool.ac.uk/3066254/

Jones, Brian W., 'Senatorial Influence in the Revolt of Saturninus', *Latomus*, T. 33, Fasc. 3 (July–September 1974)

Jones, Brian W., *The Emperor Domitian* (Routledge, 1992)

Kajanto, Iiro, 'Tacitus' Attitude to War and the Soldier', *Latomus*, T. 29, Fasc. 3 (July–September 1970)

Keppie, Lawrence, 'The Army and the Navy', in *The Augustan Empire, 43 BC–69 AD*, Cambridge Ancient History, Vol. 10, ed. Alan K. Bowman, Edward Champlin & Andrew Lintott (Cambridge University Press, 1996)

Keppie, Lawrence, 'The Changing Face of the Roman Legions (49 BC–AD 69)', *Papers of the British School at Rome*, Vol. 65 (1997)

Keppie, Lawrence, *The Making of the Roman Army, From Republic to Empire* (Batsford, 1991)

Kluczek, A. A., 'Vindex, Neron et…Probus. "Concordia" et "orbis" dans le discours politico-ideologique romain', *academia.edu* (2011)

Kos, M. Šašel, 'The 15th Legion at Emona, Some Thoughts', *Zeitschrift für Papyrologie und Epigraphik*, Bd. 109 (1995), https://www.academia.edu/11150509

Kraay, Colin M., 'The Coinage of Vindex and Galba, AD 68, and the Continuity of the Augustan Principate', *The Numismatic Chronicle and Journal of the Royal Numismatic Society*, Sixth Series, Vol. 9, No. 3/4 (1949)
Królczyk, K., 'Rebellion of Caius Iulius Vindex Against Emperor Nero, Vestnik of Saint Petersburg University', *History*, Vol. 63, issue 3 (2018)
Lammers, Cornelis J., 'Strikes and Mutinies: A Comparative Study of Organizational Conflicts between Rulers and Ruled', *Administrative Science Quarterly*, Vol. 14, No. 4, Conflict within and between Organizations (December 1969)
Last, Hugh, 'Rome and the Druids: A Note', *The Journal of Roman Studies*, Vol. 39, Parts 1 and 2 (1949)
Lendon, J. E., 'Contubernalis, Commanipularis, and Commilito in Roman Soldiers' Epigraphy: Drawing the Distinction', *Zeitschrift für Papyrologie und Epigraphik*, Bd. 157 (2006)
Levick, Barbara, *Claudius* (Routledge, 1993)
Levick, Barbara, 'L. Verginius Rufus and the Four Emperors', *Rheinisches Museum für Philologie*, Neue Folge, 128. Bd., H. 3/4 (1985)
Levick, Barbara, *Tiberius the Politician* (Routledge, 1999)
MacMullen, Ramsay, *Changes in the Roman Empire, Essays in the Ordinary* (Princeton University Press, 2019)
MacMullen, Ramsay, *Enemies of the Roman Order* (Routledge, 1992)
MacMullen, Ramsay, 'The Legion As Society', *Historia: Zeitschrift für Alte Geschichte*, Bd. 33, H. 4 (4th Qtr, 1984)
Malloch, S. J. V., 'The End of the Rhine Mutiny in Tacitus, Suetonius, and Dio', *The Classical Quarterly* 2, Vol. 54, No. 1 (May 2004)
Master, Jonathan, *Provincial Soldiers and Imperial Instability in the Histories of Tacitus* (University of Michigan Press, 2016)
Mattingly, Harold, 'Verginius at Lugdunum?', *The Numismatic Chronicle and Journal of the Royal Numismatic Society*, Sixth Series, Vol. 14, No. 44 (1954)
McHugh, J. S., *Sejanus, Regent of Rome* (Pen & Sword, 2020)
Messer, William Stuart, 'Mutiny in the Roman Army. The Republic', *Classical Philology*, Vol. 15, No. 2 (April 1920)
Morgan, Gwyn, 'The Publica Fames of A.D. 68 (Suetonius, Nero 45.1)', *The Classical Quarterly*, Vol. 50, No. 1 (2000)
Murison, C. L., 'The Revolt of Saturninus in Upper Germany, A.D. 89', *Echos du monde classique: Classical views*, Volume XXIX, n.s. 4, No. 1 (1985)
Pagán, Victoria E., 'Beyond Teutoburg: Transgression and Transformation in Tacitus Annales 1.61–62', *Classical Philology*, Vol. 94, No. 3 (July 1999)
Parker, Philip, *The Empire Stops Here, A Journey Along the Frontiers of the Roman World* (Pimlico, 2009)
Paterson, J., 'Friends in High Places: the Creation of the Court of the Roman Emperor', in A. J. S. Spawforth (ed.), *The Court and Court Society in Ancient Monarchies* (Cambridge University Press, 2007)
Perkins, Caroline A., 'Tacitus on Otho', *Latomus*, T. 52, Fasc. 4 (October–December 1993)
Phang, Sara Elise, *Roman Military Service: Ideologies of Discipline in the Late Republic and Early Principate* (Cambridge University Press, 2008)
Powell, Lindsay, *Eager For Glory, The Untold Story of Drusus The Elder, Conqueror of Germania* (Pen & Sword, 2011)
Raaflaub, Kurt A., 'Caesar and Genocide, Confronting the Dark Side of Caesar's Gallic Wars', *New England Classical Journal*, Vol. 48, Iss. 1

Radman-Livaja, Ivan & Dizdar, Marko, *Archaeological Traces of the Pannonian Revolt 6 –9 AD: Evidence and Conjectures*, Imperium Varus und seine Zeit Beiträge zum internationalen Kolloquium des LWL-Römermuseums am 28. und 29. April 2008

Rathbun, Bessie S., 'Vesontio: Crossroads of History', *The Classical Journal,* Vol. 42, No. 8 (May 1947)

Rickard, T. A., 'The Mining of the Romans in Spain', *The Journal of Roman Studies*, Vol. 18 (1928)

Rogers, Robert Samuel, 'Notes on the Gallic Revolt, A.D. 21', *The Classical Weekly*, Vol. 36, No. 7 (30 November 1942)

Rogers, Robert Samuel, *Studies in the Reign of Tiberius* (The Johns Hopkins Press, 1943)

Roche, P. A., 'The Execution of L. Salvius Otho Cocceianus', *The Classical Quarterly*, New Series, Vol. 53, No. 1 (May 2003)

Rossum, J. A. van, *The End of the Batavian Auxiliaries as 'National' Units in Roman Rule and Civic Life: Local and Regional Perspectives* (Brill, January 2004)

Rothenhöfer, Peter, 'Emperor Tiberius and His praecipua legionum cura in a New Bronze Tablet from AD 14', *Gephyra*, 19 (2020)

Royen, R. V., 'Slavery and Conquest', *Actes du Groupe de Recherches sur l'Esclavage depuis l'Antiquité*, 29(1) (2007)

Rudich, Vasily, *Political Dissidence Under Nero, The Price of Dissimulation* (Routledge, 1993)

Rüger, C., 'Roman Germany', in *The Augustan Empire, 43 BC–69 AD*, Cambridge Ancient History, Vol. 10, ed. Alan K. Bowman, Edward Champlin & Andrew Lintott (Cambridge University Press, 1996)

Rutland, Linda W., 'The Tacitean Germanicus: Suggestions for a Re-Evaluation', *Rheinisches Museum für Philologie*, Neue Folge, 130. Bd., H. 2 (1987)

Rutledge, Steven H., *Imperial Inquisitions: Prosecutors and Informants from Tiberius to Domitian* (Routledge, 2001)

Ryan, F. X., 'The Lex Scantinia and the Prosecution of Censors and Aediles', *Classical Philology*, Vol. 89, No. 2 (April 1994)

Saller, R. P., *Personal Patronage Under the Early Empire* (Cambridge University Press, 1982)

Šašel Kos, M., Kaj se je leta 14/15 dogajalo v *Emoni–cesarski napis in upor panonskih legij/ What Was Happening in Emona in AD 14/15? An Imperial Inscription and the Mutiny of the Pannonian Legions V*: M. Ferle (ed./ur.), Emona. Mesto v imperiju/Emona. A City of the Empire. (Ljubljana, 2014)

Seager, Robin, *Tiberius* (Blackwell, 2005)

Shotter, David, 'A Time-Table for the "Bellum Neronis"', *Historia: Zeitschrift für Alte Geschichte*, Bd. 24, H. 1 (1st Qtr, 1975)

Shotter, David, 'Tacitus and Verginius Rufus', *The Classical Quarterly*, Vol. 17, No. 2 (November 1967)

Shotter, David, 'Tacitus, Tiberius and Germanicus', *Historia: Zeitschrift für Alte Geschichte*, Bd. 17, H. 2 (April 1968)

Shotter, David, 'The Trial of Gaius Silius (A.D. 24)', *Latomus*, T. 26, Fasc. 3 (July–September 1967)

Shotter, David, *Tiberius Caesar* (Routledge, 1992)

Siofstra, J., 'Batavians and Romans on the Lower Rhine. The Romanisation of a Frontier Area', *Archaeological Dialogues*, Vol. 9, No. 1 (2002)

Southern, Pat, *Domitian, The Tragic Tyrant* (Routledge, 2009)

Sparavigna, Amelia Carolina, *The Orientation of the Plan of Novaesium, a Roman Fort on the Rhine* (6 July 2021). SSRN: https://ssrn.com/abstract=3392789 or http://dx.doi.org/10.2139/ssrn.3392789

Starr, Chester G., *The Roman Imperial Navy, 31 BC–AD 324* (Cornell University Press, 1975)
Strechie, Mădălina, 'The Praetorian Guard, Rome's Intelligent Service', *International Conference Knowledge-Based Organization*, Vol. 27, No. 1
Sumner, G. V., 'Germanicus and Drusus Caesar', *Latomus*, T. 26, Fasc. 2 (April–June 1967)
Sutherland, C. H. V., 'The Concepts Adsertor and Salus as used by Vindex and Galba', *The Numismatic Chronicle* (1966-), Vol. 144 (1984)
Syme, R., 'Antonius Saturninus', *Roman Papers Vol. III* (Oxford University Press, 1984)
Syme, R., 'Domitian: The Last Years', *Chiron* (1983)
Syme, R., 'Partisans of Galba', *Historia: Zeitschrift für Alte Geschichte*, Bd. 31, H. 4 (4th Qtr, 1982)
Syme, R., 'Pliny the Procurator', *Harvard Studies in Classical Philology*, Vol. 73 (1969)
Syme, R., *The Augustan Aristocracy* (Oxford University Press, 1986)
Syme, R., 'The Colony of Cornelius Fuscus: An Episode in the Bellum Neronis', *The American Journal of Philology*, Vol. 58, No. 1 (1937)
Syme, R., 'The Praetorian Guard', *The Roman Papers Vol. VI* (ed. Birley, Anthony R.) (Clarendon Press, 1991)
Syme, R., *The Roman Revolution* (Oxford University Press, 1979)
Toit, Lois Du, 'The Senatorial Debate on 17th September AD 14 and Drusus' journey to Pannonia', *Acta Classica*, Vol. 23 (1980)
Townend, G. B., 'The Reputation of Verginius Rufus', *Latomus*, T. 20, Fasc. 2 (April–June 1961)
Van Enckevort, Harry & Heirbaut, Elly N. A., 'Nijmegen, from Oppidum Batavorum to Ulpia Noviomagus, Civitas of the Batavi: Two Successive Civitas-Capitals', *Gallia*, Vol. 72, No. 1, La Naissance des Capitales de Cités en Gaule Chevelue (2015)
Várhelyi, Zsuzsanna, *The Religion of Senators in the Roman Empire: Power and the Beyond* (Cambridge University Press, 2010)
Venmans, L. A. W. C., 'De Incendio Castrorum Romanorum, Quae Fuerunt In Media Urbe Traiecto ad Rhenum', *Mnemosyne*, 3(1) (1935)
Vervaet, Frederik Juliaan, 'Domitius Corbulo and the Senatorial Opposition to the Reign of Nero', *Ancient Society*, Vol. 32 (2002)
Wallace-Hadrill, Andrew, 'Civilis Princeps: Between Citizen and King', *The Journal of Roman Studies*, Vol. 72 (1982)
Waters, K. H., 'The Character of Domitian', *Phoenix*, Vol. 18, No. 1 (Spring, 1964)
Watson, G. R., *The Roman Soldier* (Thames and Hudson, 1981)
Weaver, P. R. C., 'Epaphroditus, Josephus, and Epictetus', *The Classical Quarterly*, Vol. 44, No. 2 (1994)
Weaver, P. R. C., 'Phaon, Freedman of Nero', *Zeitschrift für Papyrologie und Epigraphik*, Bd. 151 (2005)
Wellesley, Kenneth, *The Year of the Four Emperors* (Routledge, 2000)
Wiedemann, T. E. J., 'From Nero to Vespasian', in A. Bowman, E. Champlin & A. Lintott (eds), *The Cambridge Ancient History* (1996)
Wiedemann, T. E. J., 'Tiberius to Nero', in *The Augustan Empire, 43 BC–69 AD*, Cambridge Ancient History, Vol. 10, ed. Alan K. Bowman, Edward Champlin & Andrew Lintott (Cambridge University Press, 1996)
Wilkes, J. J., 'The Danubian and Balkan Provinces', in *The Augustan Empire, 43 BC–69 AD*, Cambridge Ancient History, Vol. 10, ed. Alan K. Bowman, Edward Champlin & Andrew Lintott (Cambridge University Press, 1996)
Wilkes, J. J., 'A Note on the Mutiny of the Pannonian Legions in A. D. 14', *The Classical Quarterly*, Vol. 13, No. 2 (November 1963)

Williams, Mary Frances, 'Four Mutinies: Tacitus "Annals" 1.16–30; 1.31–49 and Ammianus Marcellinus "Res Gestae" 20.4.9–20.5.7; 24.3.1–8', *Phoenix*, Vol. 51, No. 1 (Spring, 1997)

Woodside, M. St. A., 'The Role of Eight Batavian Cohorts in the Events of 68–69 A.D.', *Transactions and Proceedings of the American Philological Association*, Vol. 68 (1937)

Woodman, A. J., 'Mutiny and Madness: Tacitus "Annals" 1.16–49', *Arethusa*, Vol. 39, No. 2 (Spring, 2006)

Woolf, Greg, 'Generations of Aristocracy, Continuities and Discontinuities in the Societies of Interior Gaul', *Archaeological Dialogues* 9(1) (July 2002)

Index